Merry Christmas 2017-

Ana Bulinavuwai.

Love You Always

Senidamanu Adilagilagi

PRESENTED TO

_____

FROM

_____

DATE

_____

MyDaily™ SCRIPTURE DEVOTIONAL

GOD'S WISDOM®
for TODAY

A Division of Thomas Nelson Publishers

THOMAS NELSON
Since 1798

God's Wisdom® for Today: MyDaily™ Scripture Devotional

© 2013 by Thomas Nelson

Published in Nashville, Tennessee, by Thomas Nelson. Thomas Nelson is a registered trademark of HarperCollins Christian Publishing.

Thomas Nelson titles may be purchased in bulk for educational, business, fund-raising, or sales promotional use. For information, please email SpecialMarkets@ThomasNelson.com.

ISBN 978-0-7180-1112-3
ISBN 978-1-4003-7928-6 (custom)

Printed in China

16 17 18 19 20 DSC 12 11 10 9

www.thomasnelson.com

Introduction

The Bible is rich with God's wisdom, especially in Psalms, Proverbs, and Ecclesiastes. This devotional will guide you on a journey with a one-year study of the wisdom passages from Scripture and devotional insights from fifty pastors who have devoted their lives to God's Word.

Each week you will have the opportunity to journal your thoughts on the scripture and devotions you have read. God's vast wisdom will be revealed to bless your life and help you cope with everyday circumstances.

"Trust in the LORD with all your heart, and lean not on your own understanding; in all your ways acknowledge Him, and He shall direct your paths" (Proverbs 3:5–6). May God's wisdom fill you with His presence as you enjoy these devotions throughout the coming year.

Johnny M. Hunt

Dr. Johnny M. Hunt
Senior Pastor, First Baptist Church of Woodstock
Woodstock, Georgia

MyDaily™ SCRIPTURE DEVOTIONAL

GOD'S WISDOM®
for TODAY

Contents

MyDaily™ SCRIPTURE DEVOTIONAL

GOD'S WISDOM®
for TODAY

JANUARY 1

The Way of the Righteous

Psalm 1:1–6

B LESSED *is* the man
Who walks not in the counsel of the
    ungodly,
    Nor stands in the path of sinners,
    Nor sits in the seat of the scornful;
2 But his delight *is* in the law of the Lord,
    And in His law he meditates day and
    night.
3 He shall be like a tree
    Planted by the rivers of water,
    That brings forth its fruit in its season,
    Whose leaf also shall not wither;
And whatever he does shall prosper.

4 The ungodly *are* not so,
But *are* like the chaff which the wind drives
    away.
5 Therefore the ungodly shall not stand in the
    judgment,
Nor sinners in the congregation of the
    righteous.

6 For the Lord knows the way of the righteous,
But the way of the ungodly shall perish.

DEVOTIONAL

P salm 1 has been used throughout time to point the way to a blessed life and to warn of impending dangers of divine judgment to the wayward. *Blessed* speaks of the blissful, happy, joyful life that is controlled not by circumstances but by the inner strength of our Creator.

This psalm stands as a faithful doorkeeper confronting those who would be in "the congregation of the righteous" (v. 5). Wisdom literature will unfold the seven characteristics of James 3:17: "But the wisdom that is from above is first pure, then peaceable, gentle, willing to yield, full of mercy and good fruits, without partiality and without hypocrisy."

If you enjoy this Psalm 1 passage, you should take the time to read the closest parable from the prophet Jeremiah 17:5–8. God wants to bless His people and direct them into a life of faithfulness and fruitfulness. Then we can be not only recipients but channels of God's blessings. God blesses us in order to make us a blessing to others.

Psalm 1 reminds us that there is a narrow road and a broad road. Take note at the triplets in verse 1: "walks," "stands," "sits"; "counsel," "path," "seat'" and then "ungodly," "sinners," "scornful." Remember there are no blow-outs in the Christian life, only slow leaks.

Taking heed of these truths will lead you into right principles, right practices, and right partnerships. Follow these truths and be blessed.

Dr. Johnny Hunt, First Baptist Church Woodstock
Woodstock, GA

JANUARY 2

The Messiah's Triumph

Psalm 2:1–12

WHY do the nations rage,
And the people plot a vain thing?
2 The kings of the earth set themselves,
And the rulers take counsel together,
Against the LORD and against His Anointed,
saying,
3 "Let us break Their bonds in pieces
And cast away Their cords from us."

4 He who sits in the heavens shall laugh;
The LORD shall hold them in derision.
5 Then He shall speak to them in His wrath,
And distress them in His deep displeasure:
6 "Yet I have set My King
On My holy hill of Zion."

7 "I will declare the decree:
The LORD has said to Me,
'You *are* My Son,
Today I have begotten You.
8 Ask of Me, and I will give *You*
The nations *for* Your inheritance,
And the ends of the earth *for* Your possession.
9 You shall break them with a rod of iron;
You shall dash them to pieces like a potter's
vessel.'"

10 Now therefore, be wise, O kings;
Be instructed, you judges of the earth.
11 Serve the LORD with fear,
And rejoice with trembling.
12 Kiss the Son, lest He be angry,
And you perish *in* the way,

When His wrath is kindled but a little.
Blessed *are* all those who put their trust in
Him.

DEVOTIONAL

You don't have to read far into this chapter in order to see the sinfulness of man's heart. If we do not keep our hearts in check with our heavenly Father, it won't be long until we attempt to occupy His place on the throne. Rebellion is an ever-present reality in the heart of unbelievers and believers as we reflect an attitude of entitlement rather than a spirit of humility.

Solomon had it right when he wrote Proverbs 4:23: "Keep your heart with all diligence, for out of it spring the issues of life." If you wish to benefit most from your time in the Word, reflect more on personalizing God's truths in light of your own heart as you seek to understand the depth of His truth. The warning is accurate; we can attempt to set ourselves against the Lord (Ps. 2:2).

As we humble ourselves and seek His rule in our lives, we must be careful and sensitive to our hearts' wickedness that seeks to rule and reign in our lives. As the Lord gives us glimpses of the King He has sent to rule (v. 6), our hearts can be turned to realize that He indeed is our only hope. In this context, He becomes the hope of the nations that has full control of the earth (v. 8). Therefore, "Be wise . . . serve the LORD with fear" (vv. 10–11).

You will be blessed as you put your trust in Him (v. 12).

Dr. Johnny Hunt, First Baptist Church Woodstock
Woodstock, GA

JANUARY 3
The Lord Helps His Troubled People

Psalm 3:1–8

L ORD, how they have increased who trouble me!
  Many *are* they who rise up against me.

2 Many *are* they who say of me,
  "*There is* no help for him in God."   Selah

3 But You, O LORD, *are* a shield for me,
  My glory and the One who lifts up my head.

4 I cried to the LORD with my voice,
  And He heard me from His holy hill.   Selah

5 I lay down and slept;
  I awoke, for the LORD sustained me.

6 I will not be afraid of ten thousands of people
  Who have set *themselves* against me all
          around.

7 Arise, O LORD;
  Save me, O my God!
  For You have struck all my enemies on the
          cheekbone;
  You have broken the teeth of the ungodly.

8 Salvation *belongs* to the LORD.
  Your blessing *is* upon Your people.   Selah

DEVOTIONAL

E ver sense that you are surrounded by trouble as well as enemies? The psalmist often reminds us of his despair; it is in these times that he also reminds us that his help does not come from the north, south, east, or west. His help comes from the Lord!

The Lord is "the One who lifts up my head" (v. 3). Sin and bad choices can cause us to drag our heads in disappointment, shame, guilt, and fear. We are like the person on the nightly news who's been exposed for a particular crime and does all he can to cover his face from the camera's view. However, to God be the glory, He can lift our heads!

In the country of Kenya, in East Africa, the children always approach their elders with lowered heads. It is not until the elder recognizes the child by the touch of his hand on the young one's head that the child looks up. God's Son, the Lord Jesus Christ, has the power to touch us and lift our heads in order that we may once again walk with a humble heart before Him as a result of His abounding mercy and glorious grace.

If your decisions have you looking more at the dirt from which He brought you than at the Savior with whom He bought you, ask for His touch of mercy and grace, and experience the sunlight of His love with a lifted head.

Dr. Johnny Hunt, First Baptist Church Woodstock
Woodstock, GA

JANUARY 4

The Safety of the Faithful

Psalm 4:1–8

Hear me when I call, O God of my
righteousness!
You have relieved me in *my* distress;
Have mercy on me, and hear my prayer.

2 How long, O you sons of men,
Will you turn my glory to shame?
How long will you love worthlessness
And seek falsehood?   Selah

3 But know that the Lord has set apart for
Himself him who is godly;
The Lord will hear when I call to Him.

4 Be angry, and do not sin.
Meditate within your heart on your bed, and
be still.   Selah

5 Offer the sacrifices of righteousness,
And put your trust in the Lord.

6 *There are* many who say,
"Who will show us *any* good?"
Lord, lift up the light of Your countenance
upon us.

7 You have put gladness in my heart,
More than in the season that their grain and
wine increased.

8 I will both lie down in peace, and sleep;
For You alone, O Lord, make me dwell in
safety.

DEVOTIONAL

Ever feel as though you are entering a day you
are not sure you will exit? In other words,
you're not sure you can make it through this day.

It is in these times in particular that we should
rejoice in our Savior for His Word and His wisdom to encourage us and direct our thoughts and
actions.

It can begin with the fact that the only reason
we have a worthy standing (position) before the
Lord is His imputed righteousness. Indeed, we are
no different from any of the 7.5 billion inhabitants on this planet, other than we are recipients of
His righteousness. Our sins have been redeemed
(paid in full) by the Lord Jesus Christ in that He
has taken our sins away, having nailed them to the
cross. Therefore, our perseverance is pre-directed
on His faithfulness. It is in the context of His
mercy that we can rest assured He hears us when
we call on Him.

He directs our thoughts to our ever-present
need of Him. In these moments He becomes as
real as the sunrise and we can catch glimpses of
who He is. This awareness can serve as a "game
changer" in setting us out on a day that becomes
a new adventure. What a way to live and to experience a day of joy that leads to an evening of
real rest.

Dr. Johnny Hunt, First Baptist Church Woodstock
Woodstock, GA

JANUARY 5

A Prayer for Guidance

Psalm 5:1–12

G IVE ear to my words, O LORD,
Consider my meditation.
2   Give heed to the voice of my cry,
My King and my God,
For to You I will pray.
3   My voice You shall hear in the morning, O LORD;
In the morning I will direct *it* to You,
And I will look up.

4   For You *are* not a God who takes pleasure in
wickedness,
Nor shall evil dwell with You.
5   The boastful shall not stand in Your sight;
You hate all workers of iniquity.
6   You shall destroy those who speak falsehood;
The LORD abhors the bloodthirsty and
deceitful man.

7   But as for me, I will come into Your house in
the multitude of Your mercy;
In fear of You I will worship toward Your holy
temple.
8   Lead me, O LORD, in Your righteousness
because of my enemies;
Make Your way straight before my face.

9   For *there is* no faithfulness in their mouth;
Their inward part *is* destruction;
Their throat *is* an open tomb;
They flatter with their tongue.
10   Pronounce them guilty, O God!
Let them fall by their own counsels;
Cast them out in the multitude of their
transgressions,
For they have rebelled against You.

11   But let all those rejoice who put their trust in
You;
Let them ever shout for joy, because You
defend them;
Let those also who love Your name
Be joyful in You.
12   For You, O LORD, will bless the righteous;
With favor You will surround him as *with* a
shield.

DEVOTIONAL

W hen you are going through difficulty, do
you find yourself slowing your pace, speaking words that are heavy, and listening intensely?

There are times we feel as though we have everything under control; however, at other times we sense an overwhelming need for the Lord to take His rightful place as King and God. When this happens, there seems to be an awakened depth to our sinfulness before a righteous Judge. If it were not for our Lord's mercy endued here, we would be overcome by our own wickedness and shortcomings.

This chapter contrasts the wicked and the righteous. One cannot stand in His presence without His righteousness and mercy. Those who can stand before Him are ever aware that it's because of His mercy they are not consumed. This will lead us to rejoice and shout for joy in His defense of us, and we will bless His righteousness.

Dr. Johnny Hunt, First Baptist Church Woodstock
Woodstock, GA

JANUARY 6

A Prayer of Faith in Time of Distress

Psalm 6:1–10

O LORD, do not rebuke me in Your anger,
Nor chasten me in Your hot displeasure.

2 Have mercy on me, O LORD, for I *am* weak;
O LORD, heal me, for my bones are troubled.

3 My soul also is greatly troubled;
But You, O LORD—how long?

4 Return, O LORD, deliver me!
Oh, save me for Your mercies' sake!

5 For in death *there is* no remembrance of You;
In the grave who will give You thanks?

6 I am weary with my groaning;
All night I make my bed swim;
I drench my couch with my tears.

7 My eye wastes away because of grief;
It grows old because of all my enemies.

8 Depart from me, all you workers of iniquity;
For the LORD has heard the voice of my
weeping.

9 The LORD has heard my supplication;
The LORD will receive my prayer.

10 Let all my enemies be ashamed and greatly
troubled;
Let them turn back *and* be ashamed suddenly.

DEVOTIONAL

It seems that it's when I find myself in the context of disobedience that I realize and acknowledge my sinfulness to the Lord. This is not the time to attempt to remind myself of my goodness but to acknowledge His forbearance and long-suffering.

The psalmist is definitely in a time of distress and uncertainty as he cries out from deep within for the Lord to stay His wrath and displeasure. This passage serves as the first of "penitential psalms," which speaks of seeing our need for repentance. In this moment the psalmist is mindful of sleepless nights. He is being troubled each day and night, and now in his distress he calls on the Lord to deliver him from his helplessness and hopelessness. What a terrible predicament to be in.

I've heard it said that we can live forty days without food, four days without water, four minutes without air, but only four seconds without hope. The greatest truth gleaned from this text is, "The Lord is my hope!" I am not sure what has led you into distress today; however, get quiet, listen, seek the Lord, and place your hopelessness in His care. You will be amazed at His capacity to care for your deepest need. Remember, no one ever cared for you like Jesus. He is our hope!

Dr. Johnny Hunt, First Baptist Church Woodstock
Woodstock, GA

JANUARY 7

Do you have a burden you cannot carry? Take a moment and tell it to Jesus. Write it out and trust Him!

_____

_____

_____

_____

_____

_____

_____

_____

_____

_____

_____

Have you meditated on who He is to you? Think about His mercy, righteousness, and forbearance. Write what you are sensing.

_____

_____

_____

_____

_____

_____

_____

_____

_____

_____

JANUARY 8

Prayer and Praise for Deliverance

Psalm 7:1–8

O LORD my God, in You I put my trust;
Save me from all those who persecute me;
And deliver me,

2 Lest they tear me like a lion,
Rending *me* in pieces, while *there is* none to
deliver.

3 O LORD my God, if I have done this:
If there is iniquity in my hands,

4 If I have repaid evil to him who was at peace
with me,
Or have plundered my enemy without cause,

5 Let the enemy pursue me and overtake *me;*
Yes, let him trample my life to the earth,
And lay my honor in the dust.   Selah

6 Arise, O LORD, in Your anger;
Lift Yourself up because of the rage of my
enemies;
Rise up for me *to* the judgment You have
commanded!

7 So the congregation of the peoples shall
surround You;
For their sakes, therefore, return on high.

8 The LORD shall judge the peoples;
Judge me, O LORD, according to my
righteousness,
And according to my integrity within me.

DEVOTIONAL

Help! This is exactly what David was praying for in Psalm 7. It was a loud cry for help. The superscription of this psalm in the biblical text reads, "A Meditation of David, which he sang to the LORD concerning the words of Cush, a Benjamite." The word *meditation* is translated from the Hebrew word *Shiggaion*, which comes from a word meaning "to roar," as in a loud cry when experiencing trouble. We all can understand trouble in life, trouble caused by others and trouble we have brought on ourselves. This psalm shows us what to do when we are facing "roaring" troubles: "O LORD my God, in You I put my trust" (v. 1).

David had an unwavering confidence in God while experiencing trouble. Remember the days when he was fleeing King Saul? Cush the Benjamite may have been a member of Saul's court. Some believe he was an evil man who slandered and harmed David. David compares his deep hurt to being torn to pieces by a lion in verse 2.

Is there an application for us? Our first focus must be on the Lord. He is our defender, and we must trust His judicial sovereignty (vv. 6–8). We can have confidence that God will do His job. As we focus on God, we must also look within. The roaring cry may be from pain that is self-inflicted (v. 3). It is important that we are honest with our Lord and with ourselves. We may need to be delivered from ourselves, and repentance is the needed response. In all situations, we can trust God for deliverance. He is able to save us from the roaring lions, from our self-inflicted wounds, and from our personal sin. He is always faithful!

Jeff Crook, Blackshear Place Baptist Church
Flowery Branch, GA

JANUARY 9

God Tests the Righteous

Psalm 7:9–17

9　Oh, let the wickedness of the wicked come to
　　　an end,
　　But establish the just;
　　For the righteous God tests the hearts and minds.
10　My defense *is* of God,
　　Who saves the upright in heart.

11　God *is* a just judge,
　　And God is angry *with the wicked* every day.
12　If he does not turn back,
　　He will sharpen His sword;
　　He bends His bow and makes it ready.
13　He also prepares for Himself instruments of
　　　death;
　　He makes His arrows into fiery shafts.

14　Behold, *the wicked* brings forth iniquity;
　　Yes, he conceives trouble and brings forth
　　　falsehood.
15　He made a pit and dug it out,
　　And has fallen into the ditch *which* he made.
16　His trouble shall return upon his own head,
　　And his violent dealing shall come down on
　　　his own crown.

17　I will praise the LORD according to His
　　　righteousness,
　　And will sing praise to the name of the LORD
　　　Most High.

DEVOTIONAL

David concludes Psalm 7 with one of the revealed names of our great and awesome God. He writes, "I will praise the LORD according to His righteousness, and will sing praise to the name of the LORD Most High" (v. 17). The Most High God is *El Elyon* in the Hebrew. This name for God is found twenty-three times in the book of Psalms and is also used throughout the Old Testament. The name emphasizes God's supremacy above all others and all circumstances. It reveals His power to deliver us from all trouble and to use our trouble for His divine purpose and plans.

In the midst of pain and trouble, David worships the Most High God. He acknowledges that the Most High God sees all things, is in control of all things, and brings His justice to all things. In the book of Romans, we are reminded that the Most High God can use all things for our good and for His glory with the purpose of conforming us to His righteous Son (Rom. 8:28–29).

The question before us is whether we can trust the Most High God. When we are in the pit, we have the best view of our Lord. Today, you may feel helpless, but you are never hopeless. Our steadfast hope is in the Most High God, who will never vacate His throne. It's so assuring to know that we have a Friend in high places. We echo the words of David, who wrote, "For the righteous God tests the hearts and minds. My defense is of God, who saves the upright in heart" (vv. 9–10). The Most High God knows the righteous and sees them from His high throne. He will not forsake His own.

Jeff Crook, Blackshear Place Baptist Church
Flowery Branch, GA

JANUARY 10

The Glory of the Lord in Creation

Psalm 8:1–9

O LORD, our Lord,
How excellent is Your name in all the earth,
Who have set Your glory above the heavens!

2 Out of the mouth of babes and nursing infants
You have ordained strength,
Because of Your enemies,
That You may silence the enemy and the avenger.

3 When I consider Your heavens, the work of
Your fingers,
The moon and the stars, which You have ordained,

4 What is man that You are mindful of him,
And the son of man that You visit him?

5 For You have made him a little lower than the
angels,
And You have crowned him with glory and honor.

6 You have made him to have dominion over the
works of Your hands;
You have put all *things* under his feet,

7 All sheep and oxen—
Even the beasts of the field,

8 The birds of the air,
And the fish of the sea
That pass through the paths of the seas.

9 O LORD, our Lord,
How excellent *is* Your name in all the earth!

DEVOTIONAL

How tragic it is when we do not recognize the glory of God. The psalmist declared, "How excellent is Your name in all the earth . . . Your glory above the heavens!" (v. 1). Caution! It's easy to lose the wonder and amazement of how big God is and how very small we are. Consider the question in this psalm: "What is man that You are mindful of him?" (v. 4). How does the infinite God of the universe take interest in finite humanity? When we lose our wonder of God, we no longer ponder thoughts like this.

Think for a moment about a child. Children haven't lost the wonder. They still have the capacity to be amazed, to believe, and to see. They have not been distracted yet by the cheap illusions of this present world. In verse 2, there is a reference to children and their ability to recognize God's glory: "Out of the mouth of babes and nursing infants You have ordained strength." Jesus mentioned this verse after healing the blind and lame in the temple. The children began shouting, "Hosanna to the Son of David," and the religious leaders sharply criticized the children. Jesus then quoted Psalm 8:2, defending the pure praise of these little ones (Matt. 21:15–16). They saw what the others tragically did not see; that is, the glory of God.

We must never lose the wonder of the name and fame of God and His glory, the wonder of Him being mindful of us and desiring a relationship with us. Let this cause you to wonder: God is so big that the earth is unable to contain His glory and greatness, yet He is small enough to take residence in our hearts. This is amazing! God, how excellent is Your name in all the earth!

Jeff Crook, Blackshear Place Baptist Church
Flowery Branch, GA

JANUARY II

Prayer and Thanksgiving

Psalm 9:1–10

I WILL praise You, O LORD, with my whole heart;
I will tell of all Your marvelous works.

2 I will be glad and rejoice in You;
I will sing praise to Your name, O Most High.

3 When my enemies turn back,
They shall fall and perish at Your presence.

4 For You have maintained my right and my
cause;
You sat on the throne judging in righteousness.

5 You have rebuked the nations,
You have destroyed the wicked;
You have blotted out their name forever and ever.

6 O enemy, destructions are finished forever!
And you have destroyed cities;
Even their memory has perished.

7 But the LORD shall endure forever;
He has prepared His throne for judgment.

8 He shall judge the world in righteousness,
And He shall administer judgment for the
peoples in uprightness.

9 The LORD also will be a refuge for the oppressed,
A refuge in times of trouble.

10 And those who know Your name will put their
trust in You;
For You, LORD, have not forsaken those who
seek You.

DEVOTIONAL

P salms 9 and 10 go together. In some ancient
versions, they appear as one single psalm, yet
they have different forms. Psalm 9 is a hymn of
praise, and Psalm 10 is a lament over evil. Both
psalms call us to a renewed focus on Jehovah God.
In today's psalm, David begins with strong praise
to our mighty God.

How often do you praise God? We never can
praise God enough. We can eat and sleep too
much. We can stay on our computers and smart
phones too much. But we can't praise God too
much. There aren't enough lifetimes we could live
to adequately give God the praise He deserves.

Praise reminds us of who God is and gives us
a proper view of God. David said that God's works
are marvelous (v. 1). He speaks of enemies falling
and perishing in God's presence, of His throne
that is high above the earth, and of His own experience of never being forsaken by Him.

Praise also provides a correct view of ourselves.
"The LORD also [is] a refuge for the oppressed, a
refuge in times of trouble" (v. 9). We are so needy,
and we need Him to be with us in the trouble
that is impossible to avoid in this life. Praising
God reminds us of our frailty, our feet of clay, and
our utter dependence upon Him. Did you notice
in verse 2 how David did not steal God's praise?
David, the great warrior, recognized the One who
gave the victory. We are not deserving of the praise
that is rightly due to Him. He is the One with the
great name, and to know the name is to offer Him
praise. "And those who know Your name will put
their trust in You" (v. 10). Let's spend the rest of
our days giving Him praise!

Jeff Crook, Blackshear Place Baptist Church
Flowery Branch, GA

JANUARY 12

The Remembrance of God

Psalm 9:11–20

¹¹ Sing praises to the Lord, who dwells in Zion!
Declare His deeds among the people.

¹² When He avenges blood, He remembers them;
He does not forget the cry of the humble.

¹³ Have mercy on me, O Lord!
Consider my trouble from those who hate me,
You who lift me up from the gates of death,

¹⁴ That I may tell of all Your praise
In the gates of the daughter of Zion.
I will rejoice in Your salvation.

¹⁵ The nations have sunk down in the pit *which*
they made;
In the net which they hid, their own foot is
caught.

¹⁶ The Lord is known *by* the judgment He executes;
The wicked is snared in the work of his own
hands.
Meditation.   Selah

¹⁷ The wicked shall be turned into hell,
And all the nations that forget God.

¹⁸ For the needy shall not always be forgotten;
The expectation of the poor shall *not* perish
forever.

¹⁹ Arise, O Lord,
Do not let man prevail;
Let the nations be judged in Your sight.

²⁰ Put them in fear, O Lord,
That the nations may know themselves *to be
but* men.   Selah

A preacher tells the story of two older men talking on a front porch. The man said to his friend, "Bill, was it you or your brother who was killed in the war?"

Senility and forgetfulness are realities in life. However, they're not realities with God. The process of aging does not affect God. He never gets old or becomes tired. The Lord never says confusing things that are contradictory or senseless. And most important, God never has memory problems. We all become forgetful at times, but not God. "He remembers them; He does not forget the cry of the humble" (v. 12). God will never forget His own. He assured us of this through the prophet's pen: "Can a mother forget her nursing child, and not have compassion on the son of her womb? Surely they may forget, yet I will not forget you" (Isa. 49:15).

God *sees* you today. He sees exactly where you are in real time. God *hears* when you speak, and you can speak to Him anywhere and anytime. God *knows* what you are feeling and experiencing this very moment. Feeling pain or discouragement? He knows and cares! Experiencing mistreatment or injustice? This is exactly what the psalmist is referring to in verse 13.

Always remember that God remembers. He is a just God. Absolutely nothing gets by God, nor does anyone get away with ignoring Him. Verse 17 says, "The wicked shall be turned into hell, and all the nations that forget God." Don't forget the warning that to forget Him is to be forsaken. Don't forget the promise that God will never forget or forsake His own. Let us always remember!

Jeff Crook, Blackshear Place Baptist Church
Flowery Branch, GA

JANUARY 13

God's Triumph over Evil

Psalm 10:1–7

W HY do You stand afar off, O Lord?
   Why do You hide in times of trouble?
2 The wicked in *his* pride persecutes the poor;
   Let them be caught in the plots which they
      have devised.

3 For the wicked boasts of his heart's desire;
   He blesses the greedy *and* renounces the Lord.
4 The wicked in his proud countenance does
      not seek *God;*
   God *is* in none of his thoughts.

5 His ways are always prospering;
   Your judgments *are* far above, out of his sight;
   As for all his enemies, he sneers at them.
6 He has said in his heart, "I shall not be moved;
   I shall never be in adversity."
7 His mouth is full of cursing and deceit and
      oppression;
   Under his tongue *is* trouble and iniquity.

DEVOTIONAL

I t's a deep question. It's a question about an
   age-old problem millions have wrestled with.
It's also a heart-wrenching question. It's phrased
many ways when asked, but always inquires about
the same issue. Here is the question: Why doesn't
the Lord do something about the prosperity of the
evil and the suffering of the righteous?

In this psalm, we see the heart of the problem
as the psalmist pours out his heart. "Why do You
stand afar off, O Lord?" (v. 1). We also see the heart
of the wicked up close, and it's ugly. The psalm
concludes with a view into the heart of God, where
we will find justice and mercy.

The heart of the evil doer will be exposed.
There are no cosmetics that can cover up the vileness found within the heart of the wicked. Their
hearts are full of deception and pride with their
evil boasting, "There is no God!" The psalmist says they do not seek God, nor is He in their
thoughts (v. 4). In their audacity and arrogance,
they disregard God's laws, saying, "I shall not be
moved" (v. 6). In other words, they believe there
is no future judgment. They laugh as they mock
God and relish in their false sense of security.
Their arrogance is ignorance. They may use their
mouths momentarily to blaspheme and deceive.
However, there is a day coming when all mouths
will be shut, and the only voice that will be heard
is that of the righteous Judge. To the guilty He will
say, "Depart from Me, all you workers of iniquity"
(Luke 13:27). To the formerly guilty now cleansed
by the blood of His Son, He will say, "Enter into
the joy of your lord" (Matt. 25:21). We have many
questions in this life. However, the sovereignty of
God is unquestionable. God will triumph.

Jeff Crook, Blackshear Place Baptist Church
Flowery Branch, GA

JANUARY 14

"I will praise the LORD according to His righteousness, and will sing praise to the name of the LORD Most High" (Ps. 7:17). In looking back over your week, what can you write down that would give praise to El Elyon, the Most High God? Get specific as you write detailed things you can praise God for.

"He remembers them; He does not forget the cry of the humble" (Ps. 9:12). Our God remembers us. Do you remember Him and His promises? We have many promises of God to claim in the four psalms we have read this week. Take a moment and write out a few of them. Writing out His promises will help us not to forget Him and His faithfulness.

JANUARY 15

The Lord Is Our Helper

Psalm 10:8–18

8 He sits in the lurking places of the villages;
In the secret places he murders the innocent;
His eyes are secretly fixed on the helpless.

9 He lies in wait secretly, as a lion in his den;
He lies in wait to catch the poor;
He catches the poor when he draws him into his net.

10 So he crouches, he lies low,
That the helpless may fall by his strength.

11 He has said in his heart,
"God has forgotten;
He hides His face;
He will never see."

12 Arise, O Lord!
O God, lift up Your hand!
Do not forget the humble.

13 Why do the wicked renounce God?
He has said in his heart,
"You will not require *an account*."

14 But You have seen, for You observe trouble and grief,
To repay *it* by Your hand.
The helpless commits himself to You;
You are the helper of the fatherless.

15 Break the arm of the wicked and the evil *man;*
Seek out his wickedness *until* You find none.

16 The Lord *is* King forever and ever;
The nations have perished out of His land.

17 Lord, You have heard the desire of the humble;
You will prepare their heart;
You will cause Your ear to hear,

18 To do justice to the fatherless and the oppressed,
That the man of the earth may oppress no more.

DEVOTIONAL

Trouble. Life on earth is full of it: cursing, deceit, oppression, mischief, iniquity, and murder (vv. 7–8). All you have to do is watch the evening news to see just how widespread the trouble is. The psalmist asked why. He is singing, "Nobody knows the trouble I've seen." We all have days when we feel this way.

The wicked live as if there is no God, no accountability, and no judgment. If God does exist, they believe He does not see (v. 11). It is true that there are enemies on the inside and on the outside. As 1 Peter 5:8 tells us, our adversary, the Devil, is like a roaring lion (Ps. 10:9).

Hebrews 4:13 says, "And there is no creature hidden from His sight, but all things are naked and open to the eyes of Him to whom we must give account." He will defend the defenseless (Ps. 10:14). He is a Helper to the helpless and a Father to the fatherless. It may look like the wicked one is winning, but we have read the last book in the Bible. The Lord is King forever and ever! Now that is something to sing about! Today He will hear your prayer. He will strengthen your heart.

Have faith in God. He is on His throne! Have faith in God. He watches over His own. He cannot fail. He must prevail. Have faith in God. Have faith in God.

Dr. Grant Ethridge, Liberty Baptist Church
Hampton, VA

JANUARY 16

Faith in the Lord's Righteousness

Psalm 11:1–7

I N the Lord I put my trust;
How can you say to my soul,
"Flee *as* a bird to your mountain"?

2　For look! The wicked bend *their* bow,
They make ready their arrow on the string,
That they may shoot secretly at the upright in
heart.

3　If the foundations are destroyed,
What can the righteous do?

4　The Lord *is* in His holy temple,
The Lord's throne *is* in heaven;
His eyes behold,
His eyelids test the sons of men.

5　The Lord tests the righteous,
But the wicked and the one who loves violence
His soul hates.

6　Upon the wicked He will rain coals;
Fire and brimstone and a burning wind
Shall be the portion of their cup.

7　For the Lord *is* righteous,
He loves righteousness;
His countenance beholds the upright.

DEVOTIONAL

C risis. It happens when you least expect it. One doctor's appointment or phone call can change your life forever. How do you handle and react to global and personal crisis?

Some people run from life. Running never works because you take the problem with you. It follows you wherever you go. We look at the problem on the outside and fail to see that the bigger problem is on the inside.

The foundation of law and order, truth and justice, morality and decency is being destroyed in society (v. 3). Vance Havner said, "Nowadays a liar is just an extrovert with a lively imagination. A murderer is just a victim of a traumatic experience; his mother wouldn't let him push his oatmeal dish off the tray when he was little, so now he pushes his wife off the Brooklyn Bridge." Havner went on to say, "Father would let me sit up late on Saturday night before the open fire, while he and the minister talked long and late about the things of God. They built a wall around my soul that the world, the flesh, and the devil could not breach, and deposited a sediment of conviction in my soul that has stood the test of the years."[1]

Don't run from your problems or regret what you cannot change. Take your problems to Jesus and rest in the throne of God (v. 4). Second Timothy 2:19 says, "The solid foundation of God stands, having this seal: 'The Lord knows those who are His,' and, 'Let everyone who names the name of Christ depart from iniquity.'" Pray that God would make you righteous and help you love what He loves (Ps. 11:7).

Dr. Grant Ethridge, Liberty Baptist Church
Hampton, VA

JANUARY 17

God's Constancy

Psalm 12:1–8

HELP, LORD, for the godly man ceases!
For the faithful disappear from among the
sons of men.

2 They speak idly everyone with his neighbor;
With flattering lips *and* a double heart they
speak.

3 May the LORD cut off all flattering lips,
And the tongue that speaks proud things,

4 Who have said,
"With our tongue we will prevail;
Our lips are our own;
Who is lord over us?"

5 "For the oppression of the poor, for the sighing of the needy,
Now I will arise," says the LORD;
"I will set *him* in the safety for which he
yearns."

6 The words of the Lord *are* pure words,
Like silver tried in a furnace of earth,
Purified seven times.

7 You shall keep them, O LORD,
You shall preserve them from this generation
forever.

8 The wicked prowl on every side,
When vileness is exalted among the sons of
men.

DEVOTIONAL

Help! Some days our prayers are short and
simple. "Help!" is the universal cry.

In Psalm 11, David was upset that the foundation was being destroyed. In today's psalm, the
faithful were disappearing. The moral minority
was getting smaller.

David was upset with those who said one thing
and did another, who made promises they did not
keep, who told one lie after another when it would
have been easier to tell the truth. What would he
say about the information age in which we live?

God will arise. He answers prayer. He knows
what we yearn for. We wring our hands over the
little things and forget that our God can do anything. Nothing is too difficult for Him.

Stand on God's Word. Romans 3:4 says, "Let
God be true but every man a liar." Matthew 24:35
says, "Heaven and earth will pass away, but My
words will by no means pass away."

Man's word can be deceptive. God keeps His
promises. Talk is cheap. God's Word is priceless.
Man's word is momentary. God's Word is eternal.

May our words today be seasoned with salt
and may we communicate His Word to a hurting
world.

Dr. Grant Ethridge, Liberty Baptist Church
Hampton, VA

JANUARY 18

Trust in the Salvation of the Lord

Psalm 13:1–6

H OW long, O LORD? Will You forget me
      forever?
   How long will You hide Your face from me?
² How long shall I take counsel in my soul,
   Having sorrow in my heart daily?
   How long will my enemy be exalted over me?

³ Consider *and* hear me, O Lord my God;
   Enlighten my eyes,
   Lest I sleep the *sleep of* death;
⁴ Lest my enemy say,
   "I have prevailed against him";
   Lest those who trouble me rejoice when I am
      moved.

⁵ But I have trusted in Your mercy;
   My heart shall rejoice in Your salvation.
⁶ I will sing to the LORD,
   Because He has dealt bountifully with me.

DEVOTIONAL

I mpatience. If you have ever been on a long trip
   with small children then you know they inevitably ask the question, "How much longer?"

That is the question David asked four times
in Psalm 13. In verses 1–2, we read about David's
protest. David was tired and exhausted. He felt forgotten and forsaken, as if he could not take it anymore. When you are feeling weak or impatient, be
honest about how you feel. God is not offended by
your humble inquiry, especially when He is what
you are wanting.

We can express our concerns to God. In verses
3–4, we read about David's prayer. Even when you
are upset with God, you need to confess it. He
knows what is in your heart. God is big enough to
handle your questions.

He will not change our circumstances until He
first changes us. In verses 5–6, David praised God
despite the fact that his situation had not changed.
David trusted in God's mercy and salvation,
knowing that God had not changed. Hebrews 13:8
says, "Jesus Christ is the same yesterday, today,
and forever."

Rejoice in who God is and what He has done.
Be faithful to do what God wants you to do, and
wherever you are right now, His mercy is enough
for you today (Ps. 13:5).

Dr. Grant Ethridge, Liberty Baptist Church
Hampton, VA

JANUARY 19

God's Final Triumph

Psalm 14:1–7

T HE fool has said in his heart,
"*There is* no God."
They are corrupt,
They have done abominable works,
There is none who does good.

2 The LORD looks down from heaven upon the
children of men,
To see if there are any who understand, who
seek God.

3 They have all turned aside,
They have together become corrupt;
There is none who does good,
No, not one.

4 Have all the workers of iniquity no
knowledge,
Who eat up my people *as* they eat bread,
And do not call on the LORD?

5 There they are in great fear,
For God *is* with the generation of the
righteous.

6 You shame the counsel of the poor,
But the LORD *is* his refuge.

7 Oh, that the salvation of Israel *would come* out
of Zion!
When the LORD brings back the captivity of
His people,
Let Jacob rejoice *and* Israel be glad.

DEVOTIONAL

D epravity. Without God, men are fools (v. 1),
never doing good (vv. 1–2), straying, corrupt,

and ignorant (vv. 3–4). We live in a depraved world. Jeremiah 17:9 says, "The heart is deceitful above all things, and desperately wicked; who can know it?" Genesis 6:5 says, "The LORD saw that the wickedness of man was great in the earth, and that every intent of the thoughts of his heart was only evil continually."

So many people live foolishly. They live as if there is no God or standard of right and wrong. They think like fools, having all the right answers when they don't even know the right questions. Ultimately, they die like fools fearing death, knowing deep down that there is a God and a judgment.

Billy Graham said, "When my decision for Christ was made I walked slowly down and knelt in prayer. I opened my heart and knew for the first time the sweetness and joy of God, of truly being born again. If some newspaperman had asked me the next day what happened, I couldn't have told him. I didn't know, but I knew in my heart that I was somehow different and changed."[2]

Salvation is a matter of the heart. John 3:18 says, "He who believes in Him is not condemned; but he who does not believe is condemned already, because he has not believed in the name of the only begotten Son of God." All are lost and our only hope is Jesus. Salvation has come out of Zion (Ps. 14:7). His name is Jesus!

Dr. Grant Ethridge, Liberty Baptist Church
Hampton, VA

JANUARY 20

The Character of Those Who May Dwell with the Lord

Psalm 15:1–5

L ORD, who may abide in Your tabernacle?
Who may dwell in Your holy hill?

2 He who walks uprightly,
And works righteousness,
And speaks the truth in his heart;

3 He *who* does not backbite with his tongue,
Nor does evil to his neighbor,
Nor does he take up a reproach against his
friend;

4 In whose eyes a vile person is despised,
But he honors those who fear the LORD;
He *who* swears to his own hurt and does not
change;

5 He *who* does not put out his money at usury,
Nor does he take a bribe against the
innocent.

He who does these *things* shall never be
moved.

DEVOTIONAL

H eaven. You can spend eternity with God in
a place called heaven. David loved God's
house because he longed to be in God's presence.
A tabernacle is temporary. A hill is permanent.
God wants us to dwell in His presence on earth
and in eternity.

People are always asking, "What is church?
Is it people, buildings, singing, preaching, small
groups, or a big group?" It is all of the above!
Christians are a group of people who are exiles on
earth and citizens of heaven. Why would someone
want to spend forever in heaven, yet they don't
want to spend one hour in church?

I cannot look at my wife and say, "I love you,"
and then not give her my time, energy, income,
and life. Do you love God's presence like David did?
You can love the church and not love Jesus, but you
cannot love Jesus without loving His church.

Don't just attend church. Be the church!
Worship should be a way of life. We are called to
live upright. It does not mean perfect but blameless (v. 2). We are to love our neighbor (v. 3). We are
to carefully choose our friends and keep our word
(v. 4). God's people are generous with what God
has given to them (v. 5).

Today, take inventory of your walk with the
Lord, your words, and your ways. Psalm 15 does
not tell us the way to go to heaven but rather the
way people should live who are going to heaven.

Dr. Grant Ethridge, Liberty Baptist Church
Hampton, VA

JANUARY 21

Read Psalm 15 and the Sermon on the Mount in Matthew 5–7. Both focus on practical Christian living: your walk, heart, neighbors, words, and money. Are you building your house upon the rock? Those who do these things shall never be shaken.

_____

_____

_____

_____

_____

_____

_____

_____

_____

Each devotion this week started with one word. Which one word best describes what is going on in your life right now and why?

_____

_____

_____

_____

_____

_____

_____

_____

_____

_____

_____

JANUARY 22

The Hope of the Faithful

Psalm 16:1–11

P RESERVE me, O God, for in You I put my trust.

2   *O my soul*, you have said to the LORD,
"You *are* my Lord,
My goodness is nothing apart from You."

3   As for the saints who *are* on the earth,
"They are the excellent ones, in whom is all my delight."

4   Their sorrows shall be multiplied who hasten *after* another *god*;
Their drink offerings of blood I will not offer,
Nor take up their names on my lips.

5   O LORD, *You are* the portion of my inheritance and my cup;
You maintain my lot.

6   The lines have fallen to me in pleasant *places*;
Yes, I have a good inheritance.

7   I will bless the LORD who has given me counsel;
My heart also instructs me in the night seasons.

8   I have set the LORD always before me;
Because *He is* at my right hand I shall not be moved.

9   Therefore my heart is glad, and my glory rejoices;
My flesh also will rest in hope.

10   For You will not leave my soul in Sheol,
Nor will You allow Your Holy One to see corruption.

11   You will show me the path of life;
In Your presence *is* fullness of joy;
At Your right hand *are* pleasures forevermore.

DEVOTIONAL

U ncertainty abounds in our generation. The challenges we face politically, financially, morally, militarily, and spiritually seem at times to be insurmountable.

We need the kind of wisdom David modeled in Psalm 16 daily. He cried out to God in prayer, pleading with the Lord to protect him, believing He would. This is why he declared, "In You I put my trust" (v. 1).

The Lord was David's refuge. It was not the people he led, the places he lived, or the pleasures he enjoyed that comforted his heart when he faced uncertainty in his life. He proclaimed clearly and boldly that only in the Lord did he place his complete trust and hope.

The story of God's activity in his life is what created and affirmed his complete trust in God. He testified in this psalm that only God is good. He had been faithful to bless him and walk beside him continually, even through the threat of death. With confidence, David knew God would show him where to go in the future and would never leave his side.

Whatever uncertainty or fear you face today, it is God alone who can see you through it. Call upon Him! Review your life and see the work of the divine Artist, God Himself, who has been working in your life masterfully. Whatever your future holds for you, know God will show you where to go and will empower you to go there when you are refreshed in His presence daily.

Dr. Ronnie Floyd, Cross Church
Springdale, AR

JANUARY 23
Prayer with Confidence

Psalm 17:1–15

H EAR a just cause, O LORD,
Attend to my cry;
Give ear to my prayer *which is* not from
    deceitful lips.

2 Let my vindication come from Your presence;
Let our eyes look on the things that are upright.

3 You have tested my heart;
You have visited *me* in the night;
You have tried me and have found nothing;
I have purposed that my mouth shall not
    transgress.

4 Concerning the works of men,
By the word of Your lips,
I have kept away from the paths of the
    destroyer.

5 Uphold my steps in Your paths,
That my footsteps may not slip.

6 I have called upon You, for You will hear me,
    O God;
Incline Your ear to me, *and* hear my speech.

7 Show Your marvelous lovingkindness by Your
    right hand,
O You who save those who trust *in You*
From those who rise up *against them.*

8 Keep me as the apple of Your eye;
Hide me under the shadow of Your wings,

9 From the wicked who oppress me,
From my deadly enemies who surround me.

10 They have closed up their fat *hearts*;
With their mouths they speak proudly.

11 They have now surrounded us in our steps;
They have set their eyes, crouching down to
    the earth,

12 As a lion is eager to tear his prey,
And like a young lion lurking in secret places.

13 Arise, O LORD,
Confront him, cast him down;
Deliver my life from the wicked with Your sword,

14 With Your hand from men, O LORD,
From men of the world *who have* their portion
    in *this* life,
And whose belly You fill with Your hidden
    treasure.
They are satisfied with children,
And leave the rest of their *possession* for their
    babes.

15 As for me, I will see Your face in righteousness;
I shall be satisfied when I awake in Your likeness.

DEVOTIONAL

W hen we pray, we are depending on the Lord. When we do not pray, we are depending on ourselves.

In Psalm 16, David declared that his trust was in God alone. In Psalm 17, David was facing tests and trials, and so he employed his trust in God and called upon the Lord continually. David wanted God to guard him and protect him from the assaults of life.

Choose to pray today. Choose to pray this week. Choose to pray every day. When you pray, and perhaps don't know what to say, pray God's Word. Pray Psalm 17.

Dr. Ronnie Floyd, Cross Church
Springdale, AR

JANUARY 24

God, the Sovereign Savior

Psalm 18:1–12

I WILL love You, O LORD, my strength.
² The LORD is my rock and my fortress and my
    deliverer;
My God, my strength, in whom I will trust;
My shield and the horn of my salvation, my
    stronghold.
³ I will call upon the LORD, *who is worthy* to be
    praised;
So shall I be saved from my enemies.

⁴ The pangs of death surrounded me,
And the floods of ungodliness made me afraid.
⁵ The sorrows of Sheol surrounded me;
The snares of death confronted me.
⁶ In my distress I called upon the LORD,
And cried out to my God;
He heard my voice from His temple,
And my cry came before Him, *even* to His ears.

⁷ Then the earth shook and trembled;
The foundations of the hills also quaked and
    were shaken,
Because He was angry.
⁸ Smoke went up from His nostrils,
And devouring fire from His mouth;
Coals were kindled by it.
⁹ He bowed the heavens also, and came down
With darkness under His feet.
¹⁰ And He rode upon a cherub, and flew;
He flew upon the wings of the wind.
¹¹ He made darkness His secret place;
His canopy around Him *was* dark waters
And thick clouds of the skies.

¹² From the brightness before Him,
His thick clouds passed with hailstones and
    coals of fire.

DEVOTIONAL

When we are victorious over the battles of
life, we are relieved. As we recall God's
faithfulness, there is a spiritual bond between us
and God. An intimacy is established and deep-
ened that only victory can create.

David felt this way as well. God had protected
him from his enemies, and he was relieved.
Nothing gives relief like victory. David had seen
the hand of God guide, protect, and sustain him.
Because God's activity was so strong within him,
through him, and around him, David became
more devoted to God than ever before.

God Himself became his divine Warrior! Using
many military metaphors about God, David testified of God's strength and power. He shared that
God was his Fortress, his Rock, his Mighty One,
his Protector, his Refuge, and his Security. When
we walk through the battles of life, God teaches us
about Himself. We discover who He is. We learn
as David learned of His sovereign power and protection in our lives. When deliverance comes, not
only is relief felt, but praise to God alone comes
from the depths of our hearts.

Has God delivered you? If so, tell God you love
Him. Fill heaven with your gratitude. Lift up all
that God has been to you during the battles in
your life. Bless the Lord today.

Dr. Ronnie Floyd, Cross Church
Springdale, AR

JANUARY 25

God Still Speaks

Psalm 18:13–27

13 The LORD thundered from heaven,
And the Most High uttered His voice,
Hailstones and coals of fire.

14 He sent out His arrows and scattered the foe,
Lightnings in abundance, and He vanquished
them.

15 Then the channels of the sea were seen,
The foundations of the world were uncovered
At Your rebuke, O LORD,
At the blast of the breath of Your nostrils.

16 He sent from above, He took me;
He drew me out of many waters.

17 He delivered me from my strong enemy,
From those who hated me,
For they were too strong for me.

18 They confronted me in the day of my calamity,
But the LORD was my support.

19 He also brought me out into a broad place;
He delivered me because He delighted in me.

20 The LORD rewarded me according to my
righteousness;
According to the cleanness of my hands
He has recompensed me.

21 For I have kept the ways of the LORD,
And have not wickedly departed from
my God.

22 For all His judgments *were* before me,
And I did not put away His statutes from me.

23 I was also blameless before Him,
And I kept myself from my iniquity.

24 Therefore the LORD has recompensed me
according to my righteousness,
According to the cleanness of my hands in His
sight.

25 With the merciful You will show Yourself
merciful;
With a blameless man You will show Yourself
blameless;

26 With the pure You will show Yourself pure;
And with the devious You will show Yourself
shrewd.

27 For You will save the humble people,
But will bring down haughty looks.

DEVOTIONAL

I want God to speak to me daily. I sit before Him every morning with an open Bible and pray for a clean heart. I am ready to hear Him. Whether He speaks to me through His Word, through godly people, or through His still, small voice, it is like thunder in my spiritual ears.

David wanted the same, and just as God did on Sinai, He spoke to David loudly and demonstratively. With His thunderous voice heard from His creation, God answered David and delivered him when he seemed to be drowning in the depths of the ocean of death.

God's thunderous voice is heard today through His Word. Open the Bible and let Him speak to you. God's dynamic deliverance is yours through the battles of life. Yield your life to the Holy Spirit daily. You will never be the same.

Dr. Ronnie Floyd, Cross Church
Springdale, AR

JANUARY 26

Look for the Light

Psalm 18:28–36

28 For You will light my lamp;
    The LORD my God will enlighten my darkness.

29 For by You I can run against a troop,
    By my God I can leap over a wall.

30 *As for* God, His way *is* perfect;
    The word of the LORD is proven;
    He *is* a shield to all who trust in Him.

31 For who *is* God, except the LORD?
    And who *is* a rock, except our God?

32 *It is* God who arms me with strength,
    And makes my way perfect.

33 He makes my feet like the *feet of* deer,
    And sets me on my high places.

34 He teaches my hands to make war,
    So that my arms can bend a bow of bronze.

35 You have also given me the shield of Your
        salvation;
    Your right hand has held me up,
    Your gentleness has made me great.

36 You enlarged my path under me,
    So my feet did not slip.

DEVOTIONAL

Even when the sun shines brightly outside, darkness can seems to prevail when circumstances become grim.

I have been there personally. I experienced that darkness when my wife was diagnosed with cancer when she was only thirty-five years old. I experienced that darkness when my dad died suddenly. I stood overwhelmed by that darkness when my mom's body became wrecked and frail due to leukemia, which led to her death. I have watched that darkness come upon others as they sit and await the death of a loved one. I have walked through darkness with people who have lost their marriages, experienced financial ruin, or buried their children.

When the blackness of the night seemingly prevails, the Light of the world, Jesus, the Son of God, shows up. While David gave prophecies about this coming Messiah, the Lord appeared to him many times, lighting up his personal darkness. He experienced God's mighty salvation in such a way that David was filled with confidence that God Himself would empower him to do the impossible!

God was the foundation of David's life and personal strength. He believed God would empower him to run as fast as a deer, granting him the skill and swiftness to go places that only God could take him. As David walked by faith and in humility, God seemed to open doors for his future that were only explainable by God Himself.

Have you ever been so overcome with darkness that you were gripped with fear and hope seemed to depart? If not yet, one day you will. When it happens, look for the Light! Jesus is there! Lift up your hands and choose to believe again. God is the foundation of your life, so you are unshakable! His Spirit is in you to empower you every moment of every day. He is so powerful He is able to provide places for you to go, opening doors of opportunity that are only explainable by God Himself. Walk in personal humility before the Lord, and He will enlarge your life and influence.

Dr. Ronnie Floyd, Cross Church
Springdale, AR

JANUARY 27

God's Mercy to His Anointed

Psalm 18:37–50

37 I have pursued my enemies and overtaken them;
Neither did I turn back again till they were destroyed.

38 I have wounded them,
So that they could not rise;
They have fallen under my feet.

39 For You have armed me with strength for the battle;
You have subdued under me those who rose up against me.

40 You have also given me the necks of my enemies,
So that I destroyed those who hated me.

41 They cried out, but *there was* none to save;
Even to the LORD, but He did not answer them.

42 Then I beat them as fine as the dust before the wind;
I cast them out like dirt in the streets.

43 You have delivered me from the strivings of the people;
You have made me the head of the nations;
A people I have not known shall serve me.

44 As soon as they hear of me they obey me;
The foreigners submit to me.

45 The foreigners fade away,
And come frightened from their hideouts.

46 The LORD lives!
Blessed *be* my Rock!
Let the God of my salvation be exalted.

47 *It is* God who avenges me,
And subdues the peoples under me;

48 He delivers me from my enemies.
You also lift me up above those who rise against me;
You have delivered me from the violent man.

49 Therefore I will give thanks to You, O LORD, among the Gentiles,
And sing praises to Your name.

50 Great deliverance He gives to His king,
And shows mercy to His anointed,
To David and his descendants forevermore.

DEVOTIONAL

When Jesus talked about building His church, He said the church was going to be so powerful that the gates of hell would not overpower it. Some think this means the church should stand still, awaiting the challenges and playing defense, and then respond. This idea is the complete opposite of Jesus' words. Jesus expects His church to play offense aggressively, knowing His power will prevail even over the gates of hell.

David understood the kind of confidence Jesus was speaking about in Matthew 16. David had experienced the deliverance of God, giving him such confidence in the Lord that he pursued his enemies, ending once and for all their threats against him. This is why he declared, "Let the God of my salvation be exalted" (v. 46). The Lord was active, real, and personal in his life; therefore, he exalted Him!

Friend, if Jesus is in your life, you do not fight *for* victory, but *from* victory. You are His church and you will prevail. You will win because Jesus wins in the end!

Dr. Ronnie Floyd, Cross Church
Springdale, AR

JANUARY 28

Take time to reflect on what you have learned this week. Write down at least three lessons God has taught you about Himself.

_____

_____

_____

_____

_____

_____

_____

_____

_____

_____

How will these lessons affect your life? Write down at least three steps of action you are going to take in your life based on all you have learned this week.

_____

_____

_____

_____

_____

_____

_____

_____

JANUARY 29

The Perfect Revelation of the Lord

Psalm 19:1–14

T HE heavens declare the glory of God;
And the firmament shows His handiwork.
2   Day unto day utters speech,
And night unto night reveals knowledge.
3   *There is* no speech nor language
Where their voice is not heard.
4   Their line has gone out through all the earth,
And their words to the end of the world.

In them He has set a tabernacle for the sun,
5   Which *is* like a bridegroom coming out of his
chamber,
And rejoices like a strong man to run its race.
6   Its rising *is* from one end of heaven,
And its circuit to the other end;
And there is nothing hidden from its heat.

7   The law of the LORD *is* perfect, converting the
soul;
The testimony of the LORD *is* sure, making
wise the simple;
8   The statutes of the LORD *are* right, rejoicing the
heart;
The commandment of the LORD *is* pure,
enlightening the eyes;
9   The fear of the LORD *is* clean, enduring forever;
The judgments of the LORD *are* true *and*
righteous altogether.
10   More to be desired *are they* than gold,
Yea, than much fine gold;
Sweeter also than honey and the honeycomb.
11   Moreover by them Your servant is warned,
And in keeping them *there is* great reward.

12   Who can understand *his* errors?
Cleanse me from secret *faults.*
13   Keep back Your servant also from
presumptuous *sins;*
Let them not have dominion over me.
Then I shall be blameless,
And I shall be innocent of great transgression.

14   Let the words of my mouth and the
meditation of my heart
Be acceptable in Your sight,
O LORD, my strength and my Redeemer.

DEVOTIONAL

W hen it comes to learning how to know
God, many consider Psalm 19 to be the
greatest of all the psalms. With remarkable clarity,
the writer gives us three specific ways in which we
may be assured of His existence.

First, we may know Him by what we *see.* "The
heavens declare the glory of God" (v. 1)—and they
do it with astounding beauty and grace. How could
anyone see His handiwork and deny that He exists?

Second, we may know Him by what we *read.*
His law is perfect and His testimony is sure, "converting the soul . . . making wise the simple . . .
rejoicing the heart . . . and . . . enlightening the
eyes" (vv. 7–8).

Third, we may know Him by what we *feel.* When
we read His law, it is like a mirror clearly reflecting our guilt by showing us our "errors," our "secret
faults," and our "presumptuous sins" (vv. 12–13).

Those who are willing to see, read, and feel
eventually come to believe that He is indeed God
and is worthy to be praised.

Junior Hill, Junior Hill Ministries
Hartselle, AL

JANUARY 30

The Assurance of God's Saving Work

Psalm 20:1–9

M AY the LORD answer you in the day of
trouble;
May the name of the God of Jacob defend you;

2 May He send you help from the sanctuary,
And strengthen you out of Zion;

3 May He remember all your offerings,
And accept your burnt sacrifice.   Selah

4 May He grant you according to your heart's
desire,
And fulfill all your purpose.

5 We will rejoice in your salvation,
And in the name of our God we will set up *our*
banners!
May the LORD fulfill all your petitions.

6 Now I know that the LORD saves His anointed;
He will answer him from His holy heaven
With the saving strength of His right hand.

7 Some *trust* in chariots, and some in horses;
But we will remember the name of the LORD
our God.

8 They have bowed down and fallen;
But we have risen and stand upright.

9 Save, LORD!
May the King answer us when we call.

DEVOTIONAL

M any commentators suggest that Psalm 20 is a
plea for God's protection in a time of approach-
ing trouble and that Psalm 21 is a *praise for God's provision* in overcoming that trouble. A careful reading of
those two psalms seems to indicate that to be true.

In today's reading, the psalmist is pleading
with God's people to call out to Him so that He will
"answer you in the day of trouble . . . defend you . . .
send you help from the sanctuary . . . strengthen
you . . . remember all your offerings . . . accept your
burnt sacrifice . . . grant you according to your
heart's desire . . . and fulfill all your purpose" (vv.
1–4). How refreshing it is to hear the heart cries
of desperate people—those who are wise enough
to know from whence cometh their help and bold
enough to earnestly cry out for it.

The psalmist knew that the first step to receiving what *God could do* was renouncing what *he
himself could do*! No one will ever experience the
"saving strength of His right hand" (v. 6) as long as
he is trusting in chariots and horses. As someone
has wisely said, "In the midst of troubles, some
buy crutches, while others sprout wings."

Unfortunately, many in our day are far too fond
of crutches, and those who insist on using them
will eventually be "bowed down and fallen" (v. 8).
While crutches may help you stand *right up* when
you have fallen, trusting in the name of the Lord
will help you stand *upright* before you have fallen!

Junior Hill, Junior Hill Ministries
Hartselle, AL

JANUARY 31

Joy in the Salvation of the Lord

Psalm 21:1–13

THE king shall have joy in Your strength,
O LORD;
And in Your salvation how greatly shall he
rejoice!

2 You have given him his heart's desire,
And have not withheld the request of
his lips.   Selah

3 For You meet him with the blessings of
goodness;
You set a crown of pure gold upon his head.

4 He asked life from You, *and* You gave *it* to him—
Length of days forever and ever.

5 His glory *is* great in Your salvation;
Honor and majesty You have placed upon him.

6 For You have made him most blessed forever;
You have made him exceedingly glad with
Your presence.

7 For the king trusts in the LORD,
And through the mercy of the Most High he
shall not be moved.

8 Your hand will find all Your enemies;
Your right hand will find those who hate You.

9 You shall make them as a fiery oven in the
time of Your anger;
The LORD shall swallow them up in His wrath,
And the fire shall devour them.

10 Their offspring You shall destroy from the
earth,
And their descendants from among the sons
of men.

11 For they intended evil against You;
They devised a plot *which* they are not able *to*
perform.

12 Therefore You will make them turn their back;
You will make ready *Your arrows* on Your
string toward their faces.

13 Be exalted, O LORD, in Your own strength!
We will sing and praise Your power.

DEVOTIONAL

If you consider Psalm 20 to be a *prayer before the battle*, then Psalm 21 would be the *praise after the battle*. Few things are as encouraging to the child of God as answered prayers, and this particular psalm is heavily laden with a plurality of them. Almost every verse makes mention of some act of God's grace that has been lovingly bestowed upon the one who trusts in the Lord.

Not only does the psalmist stress what God has done for those who love Him, but he also reminds the reader of what God has done to those who hate and despise Him. While God's mercy is always extended to those who are willing to receive it, His wrath awaits those who spurn and reject it. No wonder the writer of Hebrews would so solemnly declare, "It is a fearful thing to fall into the hands of the living God" (10:31).

Junior Hill, Junior Hill Ministries
Hartselle, AL

FEBRUARY I

*The Suffering, Praise,
and Posterity of the Messiah*

Psalm 22:1–15

MY God, My God, why have You forsaken Me?
Why are You so far from helping Me,
And from the words of My groaning?

2 O My God, I cry in the daytime, but You do not hear;
And in the night season, and am not silent.

3 But You *are* holy,
Enthroned in the praises of Israel.

4 Our fathers trusted in You;
They trusted, and You delivered them.

5 They cried to You, and were delivered;
They trusted in You, and were not ashamed.

6 But I *am* a worm, and no man;
A reproach of men, and despised by the people.

7 All those who see Me ridicule Me;
They shoot out the lip, they shake the head, *saying,*

8 "He trusted in the LORD, let Him rescue Him;
Let Him deliver Him, since He delights in Him!"

9 But You *are* He who took Me out of the womb;
You made Me trust *while* on My mother's breasts.

10 I was cast upon You from birth.
From My mother's womb
You *have been* My God.

11 Be not far from Me,
For trouble *is* near;
For *there is* none to help.

12 Many bulls have surrounded Me;
Strong *bulls* of Bashan have encircled Me.

13 They gape at Me *with* their mouths,
Like a raging and roaring lion.

14 I am poured out like water,
And all My bones are out of joint;
My heart is like wax;
It has melted within Me.

15 My strength is dried up like a potsherd,
And My tongue clings to My jaws;
You have brought Me to the dust of death.

DEVOTIONAL

Psalm 22 is what theologians call a "Messianic psalm." Although written by David and descriptive of the personal struggles and sorrows he faced in his own life, this psalm has a far wider and more precious application.

Warren Wiersbe put it well when he said, "The intense suffering described here isn't that of a sick man in bed or a soldier in battle. It is the description of a criminal being executed."[1]

Since death by crucifixion was uncommon in David's day and may not have even been known to him as a way to die, his words become even more remarkable and astounding.

Although penned over a thousand years before Jesus was even born, David's words contain thirty-three specific prophecies that came to pass when Jesus died on Calvary's cross. David might not have understood all he said—but God did!

Junior Hill, Junior Hill Ministries
Hartselle, AL

FEBRUARY 2

The Lord Is My Strength

Psalm 22:16–31

16 For dogs have surrounded Me;
The congregation of the wicked has enclosed Me.
They pierced My hands and My feet;

17 I can count all My bones.
They look *and* stare at Me.

18 They divide My garments among them,
And for My clothing they cast lots.

19 But You, O LORD, do not be far from Me;
O My Strength, hasten to help Me!

20 Deliver Me from the sword,
My precious *life* from the power of the dog.

21 Save Me from the lion's mouth
And from the horns of the wild oxen!

You have answered Me.

22 I will declare Your name to My brethren;
In the midst of the assembly I will praise You.

23 You who fear the LORD, praise Him!
All you descendants of Jacob, glorify Him,
And fear Him, all you offspring of Israel!

24 For He has not despised nor abhorred the
affliction of the afflicted;
Nor has He hidden His face from Him;
But when He cried to Him, He heard.

25 My praise *shall be* of You in the great assembly;
I will pay My vows before those who fear Him.

26 The poor shall eat and be satisfied;
Those who seek Him will praise the LORD.
Let your heart live forever!

27 All the ends of the world
Shall remember and turn to the LORD,
And all the families of the nations
Shall worship before You.

28 For the kingdom *is* the LORD's,
And He rules over the nations.

29 All the prosperous of the earth
Shall eat and worship;
All those who go down to the dust
Shall bow before Him,
Even he who cannot keep himself alive.

30 A posterity shall serve Him.
It will be recounted of the Lord to the *next*
generation,

31 They will come and declare His righteousness
to a people who will be born,
That He has done *this*.

DEVOTIONAL

Those who would suggest that the Old Testament saints knew nothing about a coming Savior would do well to carefully read Psalm 22—especially verses 16–18. With astounding clarity and precision, the writer describes the horrific death of Jesus on the cross—even down to the minute details of the thieves casting lots for His garments. How could someone living hundreds of years before that event happened possibly know those facts? Because God revealed them to him! That's why those of us who believe the Bible love it so much. To men and women of faith, the words of Scripture are far more than mere suppositions cleverly woven together by ancient opportunists. They are, in fact, the very words of God, divinely imparted to the writers. Thank God for the Bible that is true and accurate!

Junior Hill, Junior Hill Ministries
Hartselle, AL

FEBRUARY 3

The Lord the Shepherd of His People

Psalm 23:1–6

T HE LORD *is* my shepherd;
   I shall not want.

2   He makes me to lie down in green pastures;
    He leads me beside the still waters.

3   He restores my soul;
    He leads me in the paths of righteousness
    For His name's sake.

4   Yea, though I walk through the valley of the
         shadow of death,
    I will fear no evil;
    For You *are* with me;
    Your rod and Your staff, they comfort me.

5   You prepare a table before me in the presence
         of my enemies;
    You anoint my head with oil;
    My cup runs over.

6   Surely goodness and mercy shall follow me
    All the days of my life;
    And I will dwell in the house of the LORD
    Forever.

DEVOTIONAL

O f all the 150 psalms recorded in the canon of Scripture, the twenty-third is by far the best known—and for many, the most beloved. One would be hard-pressed to find a large number of God's children who have not at some time taken solace from those majestic words.

They have given us comfort when we have stood at the open graves of cherished loved ones, quieted our fears when we were surrounded by evil, and calmed us when we were assaulted by the harsh and caustic accusations of our enemies.

In his insightful book *Exploring Psalms*, Dr. John Phillips so beautifully summarized this psalm when he wrote, "In the first part of the psalm he introduces us to One who can take care of *our frailty*; then to One who can take care of our *foes*; and finally to One who can take care of *our future*. But of all the ways we can divide this psalm, I like best the one I found in my mother's open Bible, there beside her bed, the day after she died. Alongside this psalm she had written: 'secret of *a happy life*, *a happy death*, and *a happy eternity*.'"[2]

That pretty well spans the whole spectrum of all our worries and anxieties, does it not? No wonder those six small verses stand like an indestructible fortress of comfort and hope into which the hurting, the troubled, and the fearful may retreat.

Those treasured words offer no shallow and unrealistic platitudes of a life without valleys—but they do majestically promise that there is One who will be by our side as we walk through them. He will comfort us with His rod and His staff, feed us at His table, and anoint our heads with His oil. And with promises like that, no wonder our cups run over!

Junior Hill, Junior Hill Ministries
Hartselle, AL

FEBRUARY 4

As you examine the psalms you have read this week, make a list of the specific promises you have observed and how they can help you be more victorious in the weeks to come.

_____

_____

_____

_____

_____

_____

_____

_____

_____

_____

Since the psalmist speaks of the Lord as the Great Shepherd, what specific things can you list that He promises to do for His sheep?

_____

_____

_____

_____

_____

_____

_____

_____

_____

_____

FEBRUARY 5

The King of Glory and His Kingdom

Psalm 24:1–10

T HE earth *is* the LORD's, and all its fullness,
The world and those who dwell therein.

2 For He has founded it upon the seas,
And established it upon the waters.

3 Who may ascend into the hill of the LORD?
Or who may stand in His holy place?

4 He who has clean hands and a pure heart,
Who has not lifted up his soul to an idol,
Nor sworn deceitfully.

5 He shall receive blessing from the LORD,
And righteousness from the God of his
salvation.

6 This *is* Jacob, the generation of those who seek
Him,
Who seek Your face.   Selah

7 Lift up your heads, O you gates!
And be lifted up, you everlasting doors!
And the King of glory shall come in.

8 Who *is* this King of glory?
The LORD strong and mighty,
The LORD mighty in battle.

9 Lift up your heads, O you gates!
Lift up, you everlasting doors!
And the King of glory shall come in.

10 Who is this King of glory?
The LORD of hosts,
He *is* the King of glory.   Selah

DEVOTIONAL

I n today's text we find five huge God statements. The first is that God is the only Ruler over the entire world. The entire universe is God's (vv. 1–2). Mount Everest? God's! The Grand Canyon? God's! David says that God owns it all! The second big statement is that we struggle with accepting God as the ruler of our world (v. 3). There is a canyon separating sinful people and a holy God. We are separated from our Creator. But the third big statement is that God made a way to bridge the gap (v. 4). The only way to stand in the presence of a holy God is to have a pure heart and clean hands. The "heart" represents our entire being, and clean "hands" are living in grace, mercy, and love day by day.

The fourth big statement is that Jesus was sent into this world to make that heart and those hands available to us (vv. 5–6). We stand in the presence of God, not because of our own goodness, but because there is none righteous, not even one. The fifth big statement is that Jesus wins, and we get to enjoy the blessings of victory (vv. 7–10)! How do we know that? Because He is the Lord of hosts and the King of glory! No one else but the coming King Jesus can deliver new hearts and hands to us.

Today, the risen King of glory longs for you to lift up your head and allow Him to direct your every thought and action. You can chose to live in the righteousness and blessing of the holy God who creates, sustains, and owns all things. He loves you!

Chuck Allen, Sugar Hill Church
Duluth, GA

FEBRUARY 6

A Plea for Deliverance

Psalm 25:1–11

T O You, O Lord, I lift up my soul.
² O my God, I trust in You;
Let me not be ashamed;
Let not my enemies triumph over me.
³ Indeed, let no one who waits on You be
ashamed;
Let those be ashamed who deal treacherously
without cause.

⁴ Show me Your ways, O Lord;
Teach me Your paths.
⁵ Lead me in Your truth and teach me,
For You *are* the God of my salvation;
On You I wait all the day.

⁶ Remember, O Lord, Your tender mercies and
Your lovingkindnesses,
For they *are* from of old.
⁷ Do not remember the sins of my youth, nor
my transgressions;
According to Your mercy remember me,
For Your goodness' sake, O Lord.

⁸ Good and upright *is* the Lord;
Therefore He teaches sinners in the way.
⁹ The humble He guides in justice,
And the humble He teaches His way.
¹⁰ All the paths of the Lord *are* mercy and truth,
To such as keep His covenant and His
testimonies.
¹¹ For Your name's sake, O Lord,
Pardon my iniquity, for it *is* great.

DEVOTIONAL

D avid struggled with great fear because his life was in danger. There was no peace in his life. He also struggled with being alone. If that were not enough to cause a few sleepless nights, he also struggled with his guilt as a result of his poor choices. Put all of those raw emotions together and you've got a confused young man. A person who might sound and feel like the one you saw in the mirror this morning. We've all been there, or we are there right now.

And the counsel you hear from the distressed David, a man after God's own heart is . . .

Jesus came to walk through fear, loneliness, guilt, and hopelessness with you, and He isn't caught off guard by those emotions. Rather, He calls you to bring them all to Him. David also teaches us that when we bring it all to Him we shouldn't hide anything. Unload your burdens and leave them all on the table. He has the cure for all that is weighing on you. And then David teaches us that when we bring all our frustrations, fears, and faults in humility and in the fear of the Lord, He is faithful to give us a clear path of correction, restoration, healing, and peace.

Today, try this amazing teaching in your life. Start by admitting your sins, then humble yourself before the Lord. Choose to obey His commands and claim His promises for you. Then trust His wisdom, mercy, and path for your day. In other words, pray, "Show me Your ways, O Lord."

Chuck Allen, Sugar Hill Church
Duluth, GA

FEBRUARY 7

A Fear of the Lord

Psalm 25:12–22

12 Who *is* the man that fears the LORD?
   Him shall He teach in the way He chooses.

13 He himself shall dwell in prosperity,
   And his descendants shall inherit the earth.

14 The secret of the LORD *is* with those who fear Him,
   And He will show them His covenant.

15 My eyes *are* ever toward the LORD,
   For He shall pluck my feet out of the net.

16 Turn Yourself to me, and have mercy on me,
   For I *am* desolate and afflicted.

17 The troubles of my heart have enlarged;
   Bring me out of my distresses!

18 Look on my affliction and my pain,
   And forgive all my sins.

19 Consider my enemies, for they are many;
   And they hate me with cruel hatred.

20 Keep my soul, and deliver me;
   Let me not be ashamed, for I put my trust in You.

21 Let integrity and uprightness preserve me,
   For I wait for You.

22 Redeem Israel, O God,
   Out of all their troubles!

DEVOTIONAL

I was watching *Good Morning America* the other day when a story captured my attention. A young brother and sister were fishing off the coast of a Caribbean Island when their charted fishing boat sank. They survived more than seventeen hours in the water before swimming in an unknown direction and finally washing up on a desolate shoreline. The young siblings spoke of their ordeal and referenced their fears on *GMA*. They talked about how the initial fear of drowning was overwhelming. Then they spoke of the fear of shark bite. Then the fear that they were isolated as the crew was missing. Those fears drove them to start swimming. They had to move. One fear rose to the top of their collective and mounting fears and drove them to swim, even though the captain had told them to remain and the SOS would eventually be answered.

Fear—the driving force that causes some of us to freeze and some of us to move. The psalmist referred to a fear of the Lord that is best described as a state of awe, reverence, attention, adoration, and respect. Fear of the Lord should drive us to action. To rise above the clutter in our hectic days. That fear should cause us to live, love, and lead more like the God we adore, are in awe of, and fear.

Today, are you in awe? Are you fearing the God of all creation and are drawn to Him with a passion that calls you to action—action that leads to your rescue in times of great need?

Chuck Allen, Sugar Hill Church
Duluth, GA

FEBRUARY 8

To Walk with Integrity

Psalm 26:1–12

V INDICATE me, O LORD,
   For I have walked in my integrity.
I have also trusted in the LORD;
I shall not slip.

2 Examine me, O LORD, and prove me;
   Try my mind and my heart.

3 For Your lovingkindness *is* before my eyes,
   And I have walked in Your truth.

4 I have not sat with idolatrous mortals,
   Nor will I go in with hypocrites.

5 I have hated the assembly of evildoers,
   And will not sit with the wicked.

6 I will wash my hands in innocence;
   So I will go about Your altar, O LORD,

7 That I may proclaim with the voice of
      thanksgiving,
   And tell of all Your wondrous works.

8 LORD, I have loved the habitation of Your
      house,
   And the place where Your glory dwells.

9 Do not gather my soul with sinners,
   Nor my life with bloodthirsty men,

10 In whose hands *is* a sinister scheme,
   And whose right hand is full of bribes.

11 But as for me, I will walk in my integrity;
   Redeem me and be merciful to me.

12 My foot stands in an even place;
   In the congregations I will bless the LORD.

DEVOTIONAL

A famous old football announcer would start every game with these words, "Let me set the picture for you." In that same manner, let me set this picture from today's scripture reading.

David was in exile and being pursued by King Saul. Even though David knew that he was to be the next king of Israel, he would not lift his hand against Saul. David had integrity, which meant he would be as steady as a rock in his obedience to God regardless of his circumstances.

David most certainly was not perfect. He had more than his own share of sin and failures. Yet, even in all of his sin, David was still a man of integrity! Integrity means that our ultimate goal and our final decisions always lead us back to being obedient in following the Lord. David, running from Saul, wrote this psalm, pleading with God to put his heart to the test. Stop! What? He wanted God to test him? If I were to design my own test, it would definitely be a multiple choice test. With God, however, it's either right or wrong, and it's never multiple choice or fill in the blanks!

If you asked God to test your heart today, what would He find in that essential organ of life? Would He find Him or you? Would He find His righteousness or your self-centeredness? My old math teacher would say to us with great regularity, "If you prepare for tomorrow today, tomorrow will prepare you for life." Lord, test us today so that we will be ready for tomorrow.

Chuck Allen, Sugar Hill Church
Duluth, GA

FEBRUARY 9

Wait on the Lord

Psalm 27:1–14

THE LORD *is* my light and my salvation;
 Whom shall I fear?
The LORD *is* the strength of my life;
Of whom shall I be afraid?

2 When the wicked came against me
To eat up my flesh,
My enemies and foes,
They stumbled and fell.

3 Though an army may encamp against me,
My heart shall not fear;
Though war may rise against me,
In this I *will be* confident.

4 One *thing* I have desired of the LORD,
That will I seek:
That I may dwell in the house of the LORD
All the days of my life,
To behold the beauty of the LORD,
And to inquire in His temple.

5 For in the time of trouble
He shall hide me in His pavilion;
In the secret place of His tabernacle
He shall hide me;
He shall set me high upon a rock.

6 And now my head shall be lifted up above my
 enemies all around me;
Therefore I will offer sacrifices of joy in His
 tabernacle;
I will sing, yes, I will sing praises to the LORD.

7 Hear, O LORD, *when* I cry with my voice!
Have mercy also upon me, and answer me.

8 *When You said,* "Seek My face,"
My heart said to You, "Your face, LORD, I will seek."

9 Do not hide Your face from me;
Do not turn Your servant away in anger;
You have been my help;
Do not leave me nor forsake me,
O God of my salvation.

10 When my father and my mother forsake me,
Then the LORD will take care of me.

11 Teach me Your way, O LORD,
And lead me in a smooth path, because of my
 enemies.

12 Do not deliver me to the will of my adversaries;
For false witnesses have risen against me,
And such as breathe out violence.

13 *I would have lost heart,* unless I had believed
That I would see the goodness of the LORD
In the land of the living.

14 Wait on the LORD;
Be of good courage,
And He shall strengthen your heart;
Wait, I say, on the LORD!

DEVOTIONAL

We all need light to see clearly. When life is beating the life out of us, He is our salvation. He is light. He is Hope. He is our Rock. He always wants to rescue you. Allow God to go before you today and make a way for you. Allow Him to go within you and bring you peace, joy, and contentment. Allow Him to come along behind you and carry you through life's darkest days. Today, wait on the Lord to do these things. Wait, be full of courage, and He will strengthen you. Wait on Him!

Chuck Allen, Sugar Hill Church
Duluth, GA

FEBRUARY 10

Rejoicing in Answered Prayer

Psalm 28:1–9

TO You I will cry, O Lord my Rock:
  Do not be silent to me,
Lest, if You *are* silent to me,
I become like those who go down to the pit.

2 Hear the voice of my supplications
When I cry to You,
When I lift up my hands toward Your holy
        sanctuary.

3 Do not take me away with the wicked
And with the workers of iniquity,
Who speak peace to their neighbors,
But evil *is* in their hearts.

4 Give them according to their deeds,
And according to the wickedness of their
        endeavors;
Give them according to the work of their
        hands;
Render to them what they deserve.

5 Because they do not regard the works of the
        Lord,
Nor the operation of His hands,
He shall destroy them
And not build them up.

6 Blessed *be* the Lord,
Because He has heard the voice of my
        supplications!

7 The Lord *is* my strength and my shield;
My heart trusted in Him, and I am helped;
Therefore my heart greatly rejoices,
And with my song I will praise Him.

8 The Lord *is* their strength,
And He *is* the saving refuge of His anointed.

9 Save Your people,
And bless Your inheritance;
Shepherd them also,
And bear them up forever.

DEVOTIONAL

The psalmist came to worship one day needing a little help. A lot was going on in his life, and he was desperate. He felt isolated and alone, and he needed to know that God was there listening to him. He saw himself surrounded by all sorts of difficult folks. The psalmist came to worship a little out of sorts with his neighbors, and he needed a little help. And he got it.

First, he speaks about that feeling of being alone and unheard (vv. 1–2). Then he talks about those folks he's stuck with and brings that concern to the Lord (vv. 3–5). Then, a turning point. He gets his help, he feels different, and something happens for him (vv. 6–9).

He brought his whole self to worship, not just a part. Maybe you need a little help today? God is waiting on you to let Him be your strength, to be your shield, to be your refuge. He will be your strong tower, if you allow Him to be!

On this day, February 10, simply ask God to be your strength, your shield, your strong tower. He is faithful to hear you and answer your prayer. Go ahead, call on God. He's waiting.

Chuck Allen, Sugar Hill Church
Duluth, GA

FEBRUARY 11

Are you in desperate need of seeing God do a life-changing work in certain areas of your life? Make a list and be very specific. Beside each item, rank (from 1 to 10) your willingness to surrender it to God to allow Him to take over. Don't fake it; it's just you and God. Then begin to ask God to make every number a 10. Step back, and take a flying leap of faith into the arms of the One who can change it all. He will catch you.

_____

_____

_____

_____

_____

_____

_____

_____

_____

Now make a new list of all the things you are afraid of. Rank them from 1 to 10 in the degree to which you are fearful of them. God tells us to fear Him, but He also tells us not to live fearfully. Ask God to remove your fear and replace it with faith. Ask Him to help you see Him with awe and wonder and a healthy fear of the Lord . . . every day. Are you willing to fear Him so that you don't have to live in fear?

_____

_____

_____

_____

_____

_____

_____

FEBRUARY 12

Praise to God in His Majesty

Psalm 29:1–11

G IVE unto the LORD, O you mighty ones,
Give unto the LORD glory and strength.
2 Give unto the LORD the glory due to His name;
Worship the LORD in the beauty of holiness.

3 The voice of the LORD *is* over the waters;
The God of glory thunders;
The LORD *is* over many waters.
4 The voice of the LORD *is* powerful;
The voice of the LORD *is* full of majesty.

5 The voice of the LORD breaks the cedars,
Yes, the LORD splinters the cedars of Lebanon.
6 He makes them also skip like a calf,
Lebanon and Sirion like a young wild ox.
7 The voice of the LORD divides the flames
     of fire.

8 The voice of the LORD shakes the wilderness;
The LORD shakes the Wilderness of Kadesh.
9 The voice of the LORD makes the deer give
     birth,
And strips the forests bare;
And in His temple everyone says, "Glory!"

10 The LORD sat *enthroned* at the Flood,
And the LORD sits as King forever.
11 The LORD will give strength to His people;
The LORD will bless His people with peace.

DEVOTIONAL

W hat comes to mind when you think of worship? For some, singing is worship; others may think of prayer or other religious exercises.

In other words, most individuals tend to think of worship as an activity.

Worship, in reality, isn't that complicated. Simply stated, worship takes place when we rightly respond to God. The author of this psalm is contemplating the enormity, majesty, and power of God, and as he does so, he is inspired to worship.

A massive thunderstorm is most likely the backdrop of this particular psalm. Each aspect of the storm allows the psalmist to envision God. He hears the thunder and remembers the God of glory. When the storm front moves across the water, the God who created the seas comes to mind. In the palpable concussion of the thunder, he imagines the voice of God. The storm on land moving into and leveling those vast stalwart cedar forests of Lebanon demonstrates clearly the power of the psalmist's God.

Just as Isaiah was moved to worship when he saw God sitting upon His throne, the writer of this psalm saw in nature a reminder of the greatness of God and was moved to worship. This psalm encourages us to consider God; for when we do, we will be compelled to worship as well.

Trevor Barton, Hawk Creek Church
London, KY

FEBRUARY 13

The Blessedness of Answered Prayer

Psalm 30:1–12

I WILL extol You, O LORD, for You have lifted
me up,
And have not let my foes rejoice over me.

2 O LORD my God, I cried out to You,
And You healed me.

3 O LORD, You brought my soul up from the
grave;
You have kept me alive, that I should not go
down to the pit.

4 Sing praise to the LORD, you saints of His,
And give thanks at the remembrance of His
holy name.

5 For His anger *is but for* a moment,
His favor *is for* life;
Weeping may endure for a night,
But joy *comes* in the morning.

6 Now in my prosperity I said,
"I shall never be moved."

7 LORD, by Your favor You have made my mountain stand strong;
You hid Your face, *and* I was troubled.

8 I cried out to You, O LORD;
And to the LORD I made supplication:

9 "What profit *is there* in my blood,
When I go down to the pit?
Will the dust praise You?
Will it declare Your truth?

10 Hear, O LORD, and have mercy on me;
LORD, be my helper!"

11 You have turned for me my mourning into
dancing;
You have put off my sackcloth and clothed me
with gladness,

12 To the end that *my* glory may sing praise to
You and not be silent.
O LORD my God, I will give thanks to You
forever.

DEVOTIONAL

Quite frequently, gratitude is something we
feel rather than something we express. For
various reasons, we are content to just feel grateful
and never take the next step of actually expressing
gratitude. In truth, gratitude that isn't expressed
doesn't exist.

In today's passage, the psalmist makes a decision to feel grateful and, more importantly, to
express that gratitude. He is grateful that God
heard and answered his prayers and preserved
his life. Throughout these verses, the psalmist
recounts the highs and lows of his life. In addition
to weeping, mourning, and death, there has been
joy, celebration, and life.

This psalm reminds us that if we are aware of
the goodness we have received, then no matter
the current circumstances of our lives, we should
choose to be grateful—and then express it!

Gratitude changes everything.

Trevor Barton, Hawk Creek Church
London, KY

FEBRUARY 14

The Lord a Fortress in Adversity

Psalm 31:1–13

I N You, O LORD, I put my trust;
Let me never be ashamed;
Deliver me in Your righteousness.

2 Bow down Your ear to me,
Deliver me speedily;
Be my rock of refuge,
A fortress of defense to save me.

3 For You *are* my rock and my fortress;
Therefore, for Your name's sake,
Lead me and guide me.

4 Pull me out of the net which they have secretly
laid for me,
For You *are* my strength.

5 Into Your hand I commit my spirit;
You have redeemed me, O LORD God of truth.

6 I have hated those who regard useless idols;
But I trust in the LORD.

7 I will be glad and rejoice in Your mercy,
For You have considered my trouble;
You have known my soul in adversities,

8 And have not shut me up into the hand of
the enemy;
You have set my feet in a wide place.

9 Have mercy on me, O LORD, for I am in trouble;
My eye wastes away with grief,
Yes, my soul and my body!

10 For my life is spent with grief,
And my years with sighing;
My strength fails because of my iniquity,
And my bones waste away.

11 I am a reproach among all my enemies,
But especially among my neighbors,
And *am* repulsive to my acquaintances;
Those who see me outside flee from me.

12 I am forgotten like a dead man, out of mind;
I am like a broken vessel.

13 For I hear the slander of many;
Fear *is* on every side;
While they take counsel together against me,
They scheme to take away my life.

DEVOTIONAL

T his particular passage emphatically tells us
that trouble in life requires trust in God. The
psalm evokes a low point in the author's life when
he was hated and pursued by his enemies, gripped
by grief, suffering from failing health, and living
life waiting for the next bad thing to happen.

Have you ever been there? Have you been hated
without cause and had your enemies conspire
against you? Has the stress from relationships and
the trouble of life left you emotionally distraught
and physically drained? Have the circumstances
of your life robbed you not only of your joy but
also your appetite? If so, you know how the psalmist felt. These aren't just words on a page; this is life
with all the pain that often accompanies it.

When this is our reality, we can't fix it or undo
it. In that moment the only thing to do is trust that
God has a plan and purpose for the pain; we must
believe that He will work out all the bad for our
good. As David did, cry out for mercy (v. 9) and
lean in closer to the Lord.

Trevor Barton, Hawk Creek Church
London, KY

FEBRUARY 15

David's Dependence on God

Psalm 31:14–24

14 But as for me, I trust in You, O LORD;
    I say, "You *are* my God."
15 My times *are* in Your hand;
    Deliver me from the hand of my enemies,
    And from those who persecute me.
16 Make Your face shine upon Your servant;
    Save me for Your mercies' sake.
17 Do not let me be ashamed, O LORD, for I have
         called upon You;
    Let the wicked be ashamed;
    Let them be silent in the grave.
18 Let the lying lips be put to silence,
    Which speak insolent things proudly and con-
        temptuously against the righteous.
19 Oh, how great *is* Your goodness,
    Which You have laid up for those who fear You,
    Which You have prepared for those who trust
        in You
    In the presence of the sons of men!
20 You shall hide them in the secret place of
        Your presence
    From the plots of man;
    You shall keep them secretly in a pavilion
    From the strife of tongues.
21 Blessed *be* the LORD,
    For He has shown me His marvelous kindness
        in a strong city!
22 For I said in my haste,
    "I am cut off from before Your eyes";
    Nevertheless You heard the voice of my
        supplications
When I cried out to You.
23 Oh, love the LORD, all you His saints!
    For the LORD preserves the faithful,
    And fully repays the proud person.
24 Be of good courage,
    And He shall strengthen your heart,
    All you who hope in the LORD.

DEVOTIONAL

When life turns its ugly head, the phrase "trust God" can become a cheap cliché, a vague platitude, or just another inspirational coffee mug. When you lose your job, face the sting of betrayal, or experience the death of a loved one, trusting God is easier said than done.

The words of this psalm weren't penned by a man who lived life in a bubble of God's favor. David was a chronic failure as a father and an innocent man forced into hiding from a king who wanted to kill him despite his loyal service. David's sons were murderers, incestuous rapists, and traitors. Later in life he was guilty of murder and adultery. However, in the midst of these trials and failures, he had the audacity to say, "I trust in You, O LORD" (v. 14). His trust in God was the result of a life that frequently proved the truth Paul penned in his letter to the Romans: "And we know that all things work together for good to those who love God, to those who are called according to His purpose" (8:28).

Remember all God has done in your life and in the lives of those around you. Remember He is working in the midst of your circumstances for your good. Even when it doesn't make sense, let those facts fuel your dependence on Him.

Trevor Barton, Hawk Creek Church
London, KY

FEBRUARY 16

The Joy of Forgiveness

Psalm 32:1–11

BLESSED *is he whose* transgression *is* forgiven,
Whose sin *is* covered.

2 Blessed *is* the man to whom the LORD does not
impute iniquity,
And in whose spirit *there is* no deceit.

3 When I kept silent, my bones grew old
Through my groaning all the day long.

4 For day and night Your hand was heavy upon
me;
My vitality was turned into the drought of
summer.   Selah

5 I acknowledged my sin to You,
And my iniquity I have not hidden.
I said, "I will confess my transgressions to the
LORD,"
And You forgave the iniquity of my sin.   Selah

6 For this cause everyone who is godly shall
pray to You
In a time when You may be found;
Surely in a flood of great waters
They shall not come near him.

7 You *are* my hiding place;
You shall preserve me from trouble;
You shall surround me with songs of
deliverance.   Selah

8 I will instruct you and teach you in the way
you should go;
I will guide you with My eye.

9 Do not be like the horse *or* like the mule,
Which have no understanding,
Which must be harnessed with bit and bridle,
Else they will not come near you.

10 Many sorrows *shall be* to the wicked;
But he who trusts in the LORD, mercy shall
surround him.

11 Be glad in the LORD and rejoice, you righteous;
And shout for joy, all *you* upright in heart!

DEVOTIONAL

All debts paid! No, seriously … your mortgage,
car loan, student loans, credit cards—all of
it gone. At first you think there must be a clerical
error or a glitch. You call your creditors, the bank,
and your college, and they all confirm what at first
you wouldn't allow yourself to believe: you owe
them nothing.

What do you do next? What does the next hour
of your debt-free life look like? The rest of your
day? Week? Year? Life?

In a single moment, everything changed; you
would be experiencing some massive levels of joy.

Odds are good that in the past week, day, or
even hour, "joy" wasn't the theme of your existence. But if you are a believer, it should be. You
have been forgiven a debt you could never repay,
pardoned of treason and treachery against the
sovereign King of the universe, and then adopted
into the King's family. You are now a son or daughter of the most high King, an heir of heaven. It's
really a big, big deal. That act of forgiveness from
our God, King, and Father changes our every
moment, every day.

Trevor Barton, Hawk Creek Church
London, KY

FEBRUARY 17

The Sovereignty of the Lord

Psalm 33:1–12

REJOICE in the LORD, O you righteous!
For praise from the upright is beautiful.

2 Praise the LORD with the harp;
Make melody to Him with an instrument of
ten strings.

3 Sing to Him a new song;
Play skillfully with a shout of joy.

4 For the word of the LORD *is* right,
And all His work *is done* in truth.

5 He loves righteousness and justice;
The earth is full of the goodness of the LORD.

6 By the word of the LORD the heavens were made,
And all the host of them by the breath of His
mouth.

7 He gathers the waters of the sea together as a
heap;
He lays up the deep in storehouses.

8 Let all the earth fear the LORD;
Let all the inhabitants of the world stand in
awe of Him.

9 For He spoke, and it was *done;*
He commanded, and it stood fast.

10 The LORD brings the counsel of the nations to
nothing;
He makes the plans of the peoples of no effect.

11 The counsel of the LORD stands forever,
The plans of His heart to all generations.

12 Blessed *is* the nation whose God *is* the LORD,
The people He has chosen as His own
inheritance.

DEVOTIONAL

If you listened to and watched the day-to-day happenings around the world, it would be quite easy to conclude that the world is spinning out of control. It certainly feels out of our control, doesn't it? Because if we could control the world, things would be different, wouldn't they? But since we are not in control, we often find ourselves pining over world events to such a degree that we appear to have forgotten a central idea presented in Scripture: God is in control.

Paul, in his letter to the Romans, taught that we are to be subject to our governments. He wrote that all in authority (even those with whom we disagree) are in power because God placed them there (Rom. 13). The book of Proverbs teaches that men make plans, but God will ultimately direct their steps (Prov. 16:9). One chapter even goes so far as to say that you can roll the dice, but God Himself will determine the numbers that land (Prov. 16:33).

It gives me a sense of confidence to know God is in control of the details of the world and, more specifically, my life. Paul said it best: God is working *all* things according to His own will and purpose. So do not be shaken by events and circumstances! God is in control of it all and has promised to work it all for our good.

Trevor Barton, Hawk Creek Church
London, KY

FEBRUARY 18

What are some ways you can express your gratitude toward God for His many blessings today?

_____

_____

_____

_____

_____

_____

_____

_____

_____

_____

_____

Do you ever worry about things over which you have no control? Make a list and then pray and release those things into God's hands.

_____

_____

_____

_____

_____

_____

_____

_____

_____

_____

FEBRUARY 19

God Cares for Those Who Wait

Psalm 33:13–22

13 The LORD looks from heaven;
He sees all the sons of men.

14 From the place of His dwelling He looks
On all the inhabitants of the earth;

15 He fashions their hearts individually;
He considers all their works.

16 No king *is* saved by the multitude of an army;
A mighty man is not delivered by great
strength.

17 A horse *is* a vain hope for safety;
Neither shall it deliver *any* by its great
strength.

18 Behold, the eye of the LORD *is* on those who
fear Him,
On those who hope in His mercy,

19 To deliver their soul from death,
And to keep them alive in famine.

20 Our soul waits for the LORD;
He *is* our help and our shield.

21 For our heart shall rejoice in Him,
Because we have trusted in His holy name.

22 Let Your mercy, O LORD, be upon us,
Just as we hope in You.

DEVOTIONAL

*T*he Lord knows! Isn't it comforting to know that God is constantly aware of what is going on in our lives? Not only does He know us, but He cares for us. God wants us to give Him all our burdens and concerns rather than carry them ourselves. We are encouraged to do this by Peter, who challenges us to cast "all your care upon Him, for He cares for you" (1 Pet. 5:7).

The Lord also sees! Never forget that God sees His children. He is the all-knowing, all-powerful, and all-seeing God. God is much more concerned with what He sees in your heart than with all the circumstances that surround your life. Only a heart fashioned by God can endure the hardships, trials, and tribulations this world has to offer.

Do you fear God or do you fear men? Have you placed your hope in God alone or in something or someone else? You must decide! In those times of drought and famine in your life, draw strength and breath from the source of life and the breath of life, God Himself.

I have learned that the greater my personal worship of God is, the better I am able to wait on Him. We should be encouraged by the words of Isaiah the prophet, "Have you not known? Have you not heard? The everlasting God, the LORD, the Creator of the ends of the earth, neither faints nor is weary. His understanding is unsearchable. He gives power to the weak, and to those who have no might He increases strength. Even the youths shall faint and be weary, and the young men shall utterly fall, but those who wait on the LORD shall renew their strength; they shall mount up with wings like eagles, they shall run and not be weary, they shall walk and not faint" (Isa. 40:28–31).

So, while you wait, be encouraged by the truth that God knows. He is not unaware. He has His eye on you. As you wait, He will become your strength. Wait on the Lord, and let God care for you as His child.

Scott Cannon, Pump Springs Baptist Church
Harrogate, TN

FEBRUARY 20

Happiness for Those Who Trust

Psalm 34:1–10

I WILL bless the LORD at all times;
His praise *shall* continually *be* in my mouth.

2   My soul shall make its boast in the LORD;
The humble shall hear *of it* and be glad.

3   Oh, magnify the LORD with me,
And let us exalt His name together.

4   I sought the LORD, and He heard me,
And delivered me from all my fears.

5   They looked to Him and were radiant,
And their faces were not ashamed.

6   This poor man cried out, and the LORD
heard *him,*
And saved him out of all his troubles.

7   The angel of the LORD encamps all around
those who fear Him,
And delivers them.

8   Oh, taste and see that the Lord *is* good;
Blessed *is* the man *who* trusts in Him!

9   Oh, fear the LORD, you His saints!
There is no want to those who fear Him.

10 The young lions lack and suffer hunger;
But those who seek the LORD shall not lack any
good *thing.*

DEVOTIONAL

The Bible is full of promises by God. These promises can be trusted because God is a faithful God. He is consistent and never changes. And because God never changes, we can take Him at His Word, which is Truth. God promises joy and happiness to those who trust in Him.

Joy is obtained by trusting God, not ourselves. In his letter to the Romans, Paul reminds us that joy is found by having faith in God: "Now may the God of hope fill you with all joy and peace in believing, that you may abound in hope by the power of the Holy Spirit" (15:13).

The good news is that if we seek God, we will find Him (Matt. 7:7). When the psalmist sought the Lord, God heard him. And when God heard him, He delivered him. So, are you actively seeking the Lord right now with your heart and life? God could be ready to deliver you, but He might be waiting on you to come to Him. God is more concerned with you seeking Him than He is with delivering you. God wants you to love Him, not just His help!

Remember God's great commandment to us, His children, that is recorded in Matthew 22:37: "Jesus said to him, 'You shall love the LORD your God with all of your heart, with all of your soul, and with all of your mind.'" If we love God with all that we are, we will always have all that we need. He is truly all we need!

Is God all you need today? He knows our physical needs, but He knows our greatest need is Him! God is concerned about our relationship with Him. He loves it when we finally get a glimpse of Him and see that He is all that really matters. If you feel like you are doing without something you think you need, maybe, just maybe, God is allowing you to go without because He wants you to see how much you need Him.

What is your greatest desire? This world? Or God? Get to know God and learn to trust Him. When you do this, you will begin to understand true joy and happiness.

Scott Cannon, Pump Springs Baptist Church
Harrogate, TN

FEBRUARY 21

The Lord Is Near and Cares

Psalm 34:11–22

11 Come, you children, listen to me;
   I will teach you the fear of the LORD.
12 Who *is* the man *who* desires life,
   And loves *many* days, that he may see good?
13 Keep your tongue from evil,
   And your lips from speaking deceit.
14 Depart from evil and do good;
   Seek peace and pursue it.
15 The eyes of the LORD *are* on the righteous,
   And His ears *are open* to their cry.
16 The face of the LORD *is* against those who do evil,
   To cut off the remembrance of them from the earth.
17 *The righteous* cry out, and the LORD hears,
   And delivers them out of all their troubles.
18 The LORD *is* near to those who have a broken heart,
   And saves such as have a contrite spirit.
19 Many *are* the afflictions of the righteous,
   But the LORD delivers him out of them all.
20 He guards all his bones;
   Not one of them is broken.
21 Evil shall slay the wicked,
   And those who hate the righteous shall be condemned.
22 The LORD redeems the soul of His servants,
   And none of those who trust in Him shall be condemned.

DEVOTIONAL

God wants us, His children, to honor and respect Him. When you honor and respect the Lord, you are more likely to listen to His voice. But God encourages us to do more than just listen to His voice. He calls us to obedience and to action! Remember the words of James, "But be doers of the word, and not hearers only" (1:22).

Will you draw near to the Lord and hear His voice? Are there sins that you need to depart from, confess, and forsake? The Lord despises evil and can't look at your sin. However, He is in tune to the cries of a broken heart.

David knew this truth well. Here is a glimpse from the heart of David: "Create in me a clean heart, O God, and renew a steadfast spirit within me. . . . Restore to me the joy of Your salvation, and uphold me by Your generous Spirit. . . . The sacrifices of God are a broken spirit, a broken and a contrite heart—these, O God, You will not despise" (Ps. 51:10, 12, 17).

The question is, does your heart break over the things that break the very heart of God? As our heart breaks, God promises to be close to us, bringing us His peace and protection.

Do you need God today? You should, and you always will. Admit it. Tell God you need Him and thank Him for being there. You will need to remember this truth throughout your life. The Bible does not promise a Christian a life free from struggle. But it does promise that God will always be with you. He will be present in the easy times as well as the difficult times.

Scott Cannon, Pump Springs Baptist Church
Harrogate, TN

FEBRUARY 22

The Lord the Avenger of His People

Psalm 35:1–14

PLEAD *my cause*, O LORD, with those who
strive with me;
Fight against those who fight against me.

2 Take hold of shield and buckler,
And stand up for my help.

3 Also draw out the spear,
And stop those who pursue me.
Say to my soul,
"I *am* your salvation."

4 Let those be put to shame and brought to
dishonor
Who seek after my life;
Let those be turned back and brought to
confusion
Who plot my hurt.

5 Let them be like chaff before the wind,
And let the angel of the LORD chase *them*.

6 Let their way be dark and slippery,
And let the angel of the LORD pursue them.

7 For without cause they have hidden their net
for me *in* a pit,
Which they have dug without cause for my life.

8 Let destruction come upon him unexpectedly,
And let his net that he has hidden catch
himself;
Into that very destruction let him fall.

9 And my soul shall be joyful in the LORD;
It shall rejoice in His salvation.

10 All my bones shall say,
"LORD, who *is* like You,

Delivering the poor from him who is too
strong for him,
Yes, the poor and the needy from him who
plunders him?"

11 Fierce witnesses rise up;
They ask me *things* that I do not know.

12 They reward me evil for good,
To the sorrow of my soul.

13 But as for me, when they were sick,
My clothing *was* sackcloth;
I humbled myself with fasting;
And my prayer would return to my own heart.

14 I paced about as though *he were* my friend *or*
brother;
I bowed down heavily, as one who mourns *for*
his mother.

DEVOTIONAL

Friends, you must take a stand against sin and evil. We are at war! When you are truly about the things of God, there is always attack. But we have help! His name is Jesus. Jesus said, "I do not pray that You should take them out of the world, but that You should keep them from the evil one" (John 17:15). The devil hates you and seeks to destroy you, but Jesus promises life. "The thief does not come except to steal, and to kill, and to destroy. I [Jesus] have come that they might have life, and that they may have it more abundantly" (John 10:10).

So, pray for protection from the Enemy. God will prevail! "He [Jesus] who is in you is greater than he [the devil] who is in the world" (1 John 4:4). The good news is that God has already won the battle. Take a moment to remind the devil.

Scott Cannon, Pump Springs Baptist Church
Harrogate, TN

FEBRUARY 23

David's Plea for the Lord's Help

Psalm 35:15–28

15 But in my adversity they rejoiced
And gathered together;
Attackers gathered against me,
And I did not know *it;*
They tore *at me* and did not cease;
16 With ungodly mockers at feasts
They gnashed at me with their teeth.

17 Lord, how long will You look on?
Rescue me from their destructions,
My precious *life* from the lions.
18 I will give You thanks in the great assembly;
I will praise You among many people.

19 Let them not rejoice over me who are
wrongfully my enemies;
Nor let them wink with the eye who hate me
without a cause.
20 For they do not speak peace,
But they devise deceitful matters
Against *the* quiet ones in the land.
21 They also opened their mouth wide against me,
And said, "Aha, aha!
Our eyes have seen *it.*"

22 *This* You have seen, O Lord;
Do not keep silence.
O Lord, do not be far from me.
23 Stir up Yourself, and awake to my vindication,
To my cause, my God and my Lord.
24 Vindicate me, O Lord my God, according to
Your righteousness;
And let them not rejoice over me.

25 Let them not say in their hearts, "Ah, so we
would have it!"
Let them not say, "We have swallowed him up."
26 Let them be ashamed and brought to mutual
confusion
Who rejoice at my hurt;
Let them be clothed with shame and dishonor
Who exalt themselves against me.
27 Let them shout for joy and be glad,
Who favor my righteous cause;
And let them say continually,
"Let the Lord be magnified,
Who has pleasure in the prosperity of His
servant."
28 And my tongue shall speak of Your
righteousness
And of Your praise all the day long.

DEVOTIONAL

There is a fact that you can count on. If you are on God's side, the Enemy will rise up against you with lies, attacks, and accusations. However, his only motive is to discredit and dishonor you and the Lord you serve.

We, like David, need to cry out to the Lord during these attacks. Don't act unjustly on your own. Don't lash out. God is waiting for you to turn to Him, and He is always willing to help you.

Let God fight for you. Remember that God is for you, because He loves you. Remember Paul's words, "If God is for us, who can be against us?" (Rom. 8:31). The Lord stands ready with His army to fight for His bride. So let God fight for you. Only then can you truly stand up in victory.

Scott Cannon, Pump Springs Baptist Church
Harrogate, TN

FEBRUARY 24

God's Perfection

Psalm 36:1–12

AN oracle within my heart concerning the transgression of the wicked:
There is no fear of God before his eyes.

2 For he flatters himself in his own eyes,
When he finds out his iniquity *and* when he hates.

3 The words of his mouth *are* wickedness and deceit;
He has ceased to be wise *and* to do good.

4 He devises wickedness on his bed;
He sets himself in a way *that is* not good;
He does not abhor evil.

5 Your mercy, O Lord, *is* in the heavens;
Your faithfulness *reaches* to the clouds.

6 Your righteousness *is* like the great mountains;
Your judgments *are* a great deep;
O LORD, You preserve man and beast.

7 How precious *is* Your lovingkindness, O God!
Therefore the children of men put their trust under the shadow of Your wings.

8 They are abundantly satisfied with the fullness of Your house,
And You give them drink from the river of Your pleasures.

9 For with You *is* the fountain of life;
In Your light we see light.

10 Oh, continue Your lovingkindness to those who know You,
And Your righteousness to the upright in heart.

11 Let not the foot of pride come against me,
And let not the hand of the wicked drive me away.

12 There the workers of iniquity have fallen;
They have been cast down and are not able to rise.

DEVOTIONAL

Don't be discouraged by what you see. Often it seems that people living for themselves are happy. And they may be, but their happiness will not last.

Today there appears to be no real fear of God, both within and outside the church. People keep on living in their self-indulgence and sin; however, sin will be dealt with and judged.

Romans 3:23 says, "For all have sinned and fall short of the glory of God." Romans 6:23 says, "For the wages of sin is death, but the gift of God is eternal life in Christ Jesus our Lord."

Romans 10:9–10 says, "If you confess with your mouth the Lord Jesus and believe in your heart that God has raised Him from the dead, you will be saved. For with the heart one believes unto righteousness, and with the mouth confession is made unto salvation."

Do you need to place your trust in Jesus today?

God also tells us in His Word that He is ready to deal with our sin as a believer. "If we say that we have no sin, we deceive ourselves, and the truth is not in us. If we confess our sins, He is faithful and just to forgive us our sins and to cleanse us from all unrighteousness" (1 John 1:8–9). God offers forgiveness and cleansing to those who repent.

Scott Cannon, Pump Springs Baptist Church
Harrogate, TN

FEBRUARY 25

In what area of your life do you feel God has you waiting? Why do you think God wants your to wait? Is your hope is God alone? Do you trust God?

_____

_____

_____

_____

In what way do you need God to be real in your life today?

_____

_____

_____

_____

Is God enough? Why or why not?

_____

_____

_____

_____

Are you presently seeking God? If so, how? In what ways has God revealed Himself to you recently?

_____

_____

_____

_____

_____

FEBRUARY 26

The Heritage of the Righteous

Psalm 37:1–11

D O not fret because of evildoers,
Nor be envious of the workers of iniquity.

2 For they shall soon be cut down like the grass,
And wither as the green herb.

3 Trust in the LORD, and do good;
Dwell in the land, and feed on His faithfulness.

4 Delight yourself also in the LORD,
And He shall give you the desires of your
heart.

5 Commit your way to the LORD,
Trust also in Him,
And He shall bring *it* to pass.

6 He shall bring forth your righteousness as the
light,
And your justice as the noonday.

7 Rest in the LORD, and wait patiently for Him;
Do not fret because of him who prospers in
his way,
Because of the man who brings wicked
schemes to pass.

8 Cease from anger, and forsake wrath;
Do not fret—*it* only *causes* harm.

9 For evildoers shall be cut off;
But those who wait on the LORD,
They shall inherit the earth.

10 For yet a little while and the wicked *shall be*
no *more;*
Indeed, you will look carefully for his place,
But it *shall be* no *more.*

11 But the meek shall inherit the earth,
And shall delight themselves in the abundance of peace.

DEVOTIONAL

T he greatest struggles in life are the struggles we have with God. Often, we yield to temptation and feel anger because we do not understand the ways of God. We may look at the wicked prospering and question why. We see ourselves as faithful and wonder why God seems silent.

This passage begins with an exhortation to not fret or become discouraged and is sprinkled with commands against becoming angry. The answer to how we can do this is found in verse 11, "But the meek . . ." We received Christ by humbling ourselves at the cross without any sense of entitlement or selfish ambition. Colossians 2:6 says, "As you therefore have received Christ Jesus the Lord, so walk in Him."

Once we have received Christ, we are to walk in that same humble manner. We are to have no sense of entitlement, no demand for our way, no ego that must be stroked. This humble, cross-centered life is reflected in the psalmist's commands. "Trust in the LORD" (v. 3). As you trusted Him with your soul at salvation, trust Him with daily living. "Delight" or enjoy the Lord (v. 4). "Commit your way" (v. 5). Have God's ambition, not your own. Desire His will. Then "rest in the LORD" (v. 7). When we want what He wants, it follows that we can rest from our stress—trusting Him with the outcome.

Dr. Dwayne Mercer, First Baptist Oviedo
Oviedo, FL

FEBRUARY 27

The Calamity of the Wicked

Psalm 37:12–24

12 The wicked plots against the just,
   And gnashes at him with his teeth.
13 The Lord laughs at him,
   For He sees that his day is coming.
14 The wicked have drawn the sword
   And have bent their bow,
   To cast down the poor and needy,
   To slay those who are of upright conduct.
15 Their sword shall enter their own heart,
   And their bows shall be broken.

16 A little that a righteous man has
   Is better than the riches of many wicked.
17 For the arms of the wicked shall be broken,
   But the Lord upholds the righteous.

18 The Lord knows the days of the upright,
   And their inheritance shall be forever.
19 They shall not be ashamed in the evil time,
   And in the days of famine they shall be satisfied.
20 But the wicked shall perish;
   And the enemies of the Lord,
   Like the splendor of the meadows, shall vanish.
   Into smoke they shall vanish away.

21 The wicked borrows and does not repay,
   But the righteous shows mercy and gives.
22 For *those* blessed by Him shall inherit the
      earth,
   But *those* cursed by Him shall be cut off.

23 The steps of a *good* man are ordered by the Lord,
   And He delights in his way.

24 Though he fall, he shall not be utterly cast
      down;
   For the Lord upholds *him with* His hand.

DEVOTIONAL

A young boy was sitting in an elementary school classroom in Romania. Romania in the 1970s was under the dictatorship of Ceausescu and persecution of Christians was intense. The military came that morning and demanded every child line up outside. Standing in the snow, an officer threw a Bible on the ground. One by one he demanded that the children spit on it. The boy stood, so nervous he could barely move. Could he, as a believer in Christ, do such a thing? The girl who stood next to him, his friend, was also a believer. When confronted by the officer, she stooped down and, with her knees in the snow, picked up the Bible and kissed it. Without warning, the officer pulled his revolver and shot her in the head—then the officers left. The boy's life was spared, but his friend was gone.

We do not understand why God does not protect us all in the same way. Some are rescued and proclaim that "God is good." Is He not also good to others to whom calamity and trials befall? The psalmist is clear: life may seem unfair, but one day, justice will prevail.

This passage concludes with a promise that God will support us through all our trials. Remember, "all things work together for good to those who love God" (Rom. 8:28).

Dr. Dwayne Mercer, First Baptist Oviedo
Oviedo, FL

FEBRUARY 28

The Lord Loves Justice

Psalm 37:25–40

25 I have been young, and *now* am old;
Yet I have not seen the righteous forsaken,
Nor his descendants begging bread.

26 *He is* ever merciful, and lends;
And his descendants *are* blessed.

27 Depart from evil, and do good;
And dwell forevermore.

28 For the LORD loves justice,
And does not forsake His saints;
They are preserved forever,
But the descendants of the wicked shall be cut off.

29 The righteous shall inherit the land,
And dwell in it forever.

30 The mouth of the righteous speaks wisdom,
And his tongue talks of justice.

31 The law of his God *is* in his heart;
None of his steps shall slide.

32 The wicked watches the righteous,
And seeks to slay him.

33 The LORD will not leave him in his hand,
Nor condemn him when he is judged.

34 Wait on the LORD,
And keep His way,
And He shall exalt you to inherit the land;
When the wicked are cut off, you shall see *it.*

35 I have seen the wicked in great power,
And spreading himself like a native green tree.

36 Yet he passed away, and behold, he *was* no *more;*
Indeed I sought him, but he could not be found.

37 Mark the blameless *man,* and observe the upright;
For the future of *that* man *is* peace.

38 But the transgressors shall be destroyed together;
The future of the wicked shall be cut off.

39 But the salvation of the righteous *is* from the LORD;
He is their strength in the time of trouble.

40 And the LORD shall help them and deliver them;
He shall deliver them from the wicked,
And save them,
Because they trust in Him.

DEVOTIONAL

When we think of justice today, we think of worthy ministries such as feeding the poor and helping the homeless. But there is another kind of justice in Scripture: the judgment of the wicked and the reward of the believer. We often wonder why the wicked seem to prosper and the righteous sometimes suffer. There is a day when accounts will be balanced. The Bible says, "Be sure your sin will find you out" (Num. 32:23). Galatians 6:7 says, "Do not be deceived, God is not mocked; for whatever a man sows, this he will also reap."

Though we should never rejoice in the demise of the wicked, we can be comforted that an all-powerful, just God is in control. We are exhorted to "wait on the LORD" (Ps. 37:9) and trust in Him. He will deliver us.

Dr. Dwayne Mercer, First Baptist Oviedo
Oviedo, FL

MARCH 1

Prayer in Time of Chastening

Psalm 38:1–10

O LORD, do not rebuke me in Your wrath,
Nor chasten me in Your hot displeasure!

2 For Your arrows pierce me deeply,
And Your hand presses me down.

3 *There is* no soundness in my flesh
Because of Your anger,
Nor *any* health in my bones
Because of my sin.

4 For my iniquities have gone over my head;
Like a heavy burden they are too heavy for me.

5 My wounds are foul *and* festering
Because of my foolishness.

6 I am troubled, I am bowed down greatly;
I go mourning all the day long.

7 For my loins are full of inflammation,
And *there is* no soundness in my flesh.

8 I am feeble and severely broken;
I groan because of the turmoil of my heart.

9 Lord, all my desire *is* before You;
And my sighing is not hidden from You.

10 My heart pants, my strength fails me;
As for the light of my eyes, it also has gone
from me.

DEVOTIONAL

There are many reasons for suffering. We live in a sinful world, and often we are affected by that sin. Because death comes to us all, we suffer the ways of trials, disease, and death. We also suffer for the sins of others. We are heartbroken over the sins of our children, and we are affected by crime, theft, and greed. Sometimes, however, suffering comes from our own sin. For the believer, this kind of malady is called chastening or the disciplining hand of God.

In this psalm, the psalmist is experiencing pain (vv. 7–8) and personal guilt (v. 4) that is overwhelming. The psalmist never blames God but confesses his sin (v. 3) and feels the weight of his guilt. He cries out for forgiveness and reconciliation with God. God's discipline is often painful. We tend to feel that God is nowhere to be found—that His discipline is more than we can endure.

However, know that when God chastens you, it proves two things: (1) You are His child, and a parent disciplines his children. The person who commits sin and experiences no discipline is one who should be concerned with his spiritual state. (2) He loves you. Hebrews 12:6 states, "For those whom the Lord loves He disciplines." Just as wise parents discipline their child because they want their child to avoid a destructive lifestyle, so your heavenly Father disciplines you. It's times like these when we need to cry out to God for forgiveness. It is then that our relationship will be restored and our lives set on the right path.

Dr. Dwayne Mercer, First Baptist Oviedo
Oviedo, FL

MARCH 2

David's Plea for Help

Psalm 38:11–22

11 My loved ones and my friends stand aloof
  from my plague,
And my relatives stand afar off.

12 Those also who seek my life lay snares *for me;*
Those who seek my hurt speak of destruction,
And plan deception all the day long.

13 But I, like a deaf *man,* do not hear;
And *I am* like a mute *who* does not open his
  mouth.

14 Thus I am like a man who does not hear,
And in whose mouth *is* no response.

15 For in You, O LORD, I hope;
You will hear, O Lord my God.

16 For I said, *"Hear me,* lest they rejoice over me,
Lest, when my foot slips, they exalt *themselves*
  against me."

17 For I *am* ready to fall,
And my sorrow *is* continually before me.

18 For I will declare my iniquity;
I will be in anguish over my sin.

19 But my enemies *are* vigorous, *and* they are
  strong;
And those who hate me wrongfully have
  multiplied.

20 Those also who render evil for good,
They are my adversaries, because I follow
  what is good.

21 Do not forsake me, O LORD;
O my God, be not far from me!

22 Make haste to help me,
  O Lord, my salvation!

DEVOTIONAL

Our sin will eventually affect every part of our lives. Sin isolates us and keeps us from fellowship with God. This affects our disposition and personality and, therefore, our relationships with others. David was, in every aspect of life, affected because of his sin. Rather than suffer like Job, who requested answers from God, David isolated himself (v. 13). He stated that his friends had abandoned him and his enemies sought to destroy him. Although he had done no wrong to the people, they were attacking him (v. 20). Those around him were repaying evil for good.

As we walk away from God and remain in sinful ways, He often uses others for correction. Sin has a way of isolating us, whether it is pride, lack of faith, lust, greed, or anger at God. We often live so long in sin, we are hardened by it. We do not want to hear rebuke (v. 13). Perhaps we do not want to socialize with others for fear they will see through us. Depression sets in and relationships are adversely affected. Usually, others will not know what is in our hearts. However, God will use those around us to bring us to our knees at the cross, even if it is people who have evil intentions. The Bible teaches that those who return evil for good will themselves be punished. However, God can use them to gain our attention and convict us in our problem areas.

Come to the cross today. Repent and enjoy your salvation again.

Dr. Dwayne Mercer, First Baptist Oviedo
Oviedo, FL

MARCH 3

Prayer for Wisdom and Forgiveness

Psalm 39:1–13

I SAID, "I will guard my ways,
Lest I sin with my tongue;
I will restrain my mouth with a muzzle,
While the wicked are before me."

2 I was mute with silence,
I held my peace *even* from good;
And my sorrow was stirred up.

3 My heart was hot within me;
While I was musing, the fire burned.
Then I spoke with my tongue:

4 "LORD, make me to know my end,
And what *is* the measure of my days,
That I may know how frail I *am*.

5 Indeed, You have made my days *as*
handbreadths,
And my age *is* as nothing before You;
Certainly every man at his best state *is* but
vapor. Selah

6 Surely every man walks about like a shadow;
Surely they busy themselves in vain;
He heaps up *riches,*
And does not know who will gather them.

7 "And now, Lord, what do I wait for?
My hope *is* in You.

8 Deliver me from all my transgressions;
Do not make me the reproach of the foolish.

9 I was mute, I did not open my mouth,
Because it was You who did *it*.

10 Remove Your plague from me;
I am consumed by the blow of Your hand.

11 When with rebukes You correct man for iniquity,
You make his beauty melt away like a moth;
Surely every man *is* vapor. Selah

12 "Hear my prayer, O LORD,
And give ear to my cry;
Do not be silent at my tears;
For I *am* a stranger with You,
A sojourner, as all my fathers *were*.

13 Remove Your gaze from me, that I may regain
strength,
Before I go away and am no more."

DEVOTIONAL

In this psalm, the psalmist is dealing with the purpose of life. These verses remind us that our days are "handbreadths" (v. 5), or a couple of inches in the grander scheme of life. As the writer cries out for wisdom, he realizes that meaning is found in God (v. 7). He then prays for forgiveness and reconciliation with God.

His prayer in verse 13, "Remove Your gaze from me," indicates to us that although he is in a covenant relationship with God, he has not *received* forgiveness from the sin that controls him. Forgiveness is three-dimensional: downward to you from God, inward to yourself, and then outward to others. They are all interconnected.

What are we saying to God when He forgives us but we cannot forgive ourselves? Are we saying that we have a higher standard of righteousness than a holy God? "God, You can forgive me, but I'm a little too righteous to do the same." As we cry out to God, He will forgive us based on the cross. We need to be humble enough to forgive ourselves.

Dr. Dwayne Mercer, First Baptist Church
Oviedo, FL

MARCH 4

What is your priority in life? How is this goal reflected in your everyday living?

_____

_____

_____

_____

_____

_____

_____

_____

_____

_____

_____

_____

Can you remember a time when God disciplined you? What benefits did you receive from this correction?

_____

_____

_____

_____

_____

_____

_____

_____

_____

_____

_____

MARCH 5

Faith Persevering in Trial

Psalm 40:1–8

I WAITED patiently for the LORD;
   And He inclined to me,
   And heard my cry.
2 He also brought me up out of a horrible pit,
   Out of the miry clay,
   And set my feet upon a rock,
   And established my steps.
3 He has put a new song in my mouth—
   Praise to our God;
   Many will see *it* and fear,
   And will trust in the LORD.

4 Blessed *is* that man who makes the LORD his
     trust,
   And does not respect the proud, nor such as
     turn aside to lies.
5 Many, O LORD my God, *are* Your wonderful
     works
   Which You have done;
   And Your thoughts toward us
   Cannot be recounted to You in order;
   If I would declare and speak *of them,*
   They are more than can be numbered.

6 Sacrifice and offering You did not desire;
   My ears You have opened.
   Burnt offering and sin offering You did not
     require.
7 Then I said, "Behold, I come;
   In the scroll of the book *it is* written of me.
8 I delight to do Your will, O my God,
   And Your law *is* within my heart."

DEVOTIONAL

Did you wake up today and find yourself in a pit, just as Joseph did many centuries ago (Gen. 37)? Erma Bombeck wrote a book titled *If Life Is a Bowl of Cherries, What Am I Doing in the Pits?*[1] We do not know what pit David was in (v. 2); perhaps it was sickness, slander, or sin. But we do know that he cried out to the Lord and the Lord replaced his sighing with singing (v. 3). He will do that for you too.

Why would a child of God sing even when the circumstances of life are the pits? David sang because the Lord had listened to his cry. Saying a quick prayer about something and then moving on is not the same as crying out to the Lord. Every loving father is moved by the cry of his child, and our heavenly Father pays special attention and inclines His ear when one of His children cry out in desperation to Him.

That kind of praying requires humility and patience. Because of his patience and passion, God listened to his cry and lifted him out of the miry clay. Have you ever tried to climb up a hill after a long rain? Your feet probably kept slipping out from under you, and with every two steps forward you slipped back one. Good news! The same God who hears you will also help you get on solid ground!

Today, take your eyes off your difficult situation and focus on Jesus. Determine to do His work, declare to others His Word, and delight to do His will. If you do, the Lord will place music in your heart and a song in your mouth. Just as God rescued Joseph from his pit, He will bring you out of yours.

Dr. Michael Cloer, Englewood Baptist Church
Rocky Mount, NC

MARCH 6

The Lord Be Magnified

Psalm 40:9–17

9 I have proclaimed the good news of righteousness
In the great assembly;
Indeed, I do not restrain my lips,
O Lord, You Yourself know.

10 I have not hidden Your righteousness within my heart;
I have declared Your faithfulness and Your salvation;
I have not concealed Your lovingkindness and Your truth
From the great assembly.

11 Do not withhold Your tender mercies from me, O Lord;
Let Your lovingkindness and Your truth continually preserve me.

12 For innumerable evils have surrounded me;
My iniquities have overtaken me, so that I am not able to look up;
They are more than the hairs of my head;
Therefore my heart fails me.

13 Be pleased, O Lord, to deliver me;
O Lord, make haste to help me!

14 Let them be ashamed and brought to mutual confusion
Who seek to destroy my life;
Let them be driven backward and brought to dishonor
Who wish me evil.

15 Let them be confounded because of their shame,
Who say to me, "Aha, aha!"

16 Let all those who seek You rejoice and be glad in You;
Let such as love Your salvation say continually,
"The Lord be magnified!"

17 But I *am* poor and needy;
Yet the Lord thinks upon me.
You *are* my help and my deliverer;
Do not delay, O my God.

DEVOTIONAL

Problems are nothing new to the child of God; all of us have them. David certainly faced his share. Through it all, his only concern was that the Lord be magnified. What does that mean?

When something is magnified it appears closer, becomes more recognizable, and the details of its nature that were once hidden become clearly seen. David wanted God to be magnified to others through his public and personal declaration of Him. Today you will have opportunities to either declare His righteousness, His love, and His salvation to someone else, or to conceal those truths from them. Please tell them!

David also desired for the Lord to be magnified through his deliverance from the enemy. What is your response to those who seek to harm you? Today, why not respond with these same words David prayed, which is probably similar to what our Lord Jesus prayed that night in Gethsemane?

Allow Him to be magnified through you.

Dr. Michael Cloer, Englewood Baptist Church
Rocky Mount, NC

MARCH 7

The Blessing of the Godly

Psalm 41:1–13

B LESSED *is* he who considers the poor;
The LORD will deliver him in time of trouble.

2 The LORD will preserve him and keep him
alive,
And he will be blessed on the earth;
You will not deliver him to the will of his
enemies.

3 The LORD will strengthen him on his bed of
illness;
You will sustain him on his sickbed.

4 I said, "LORD, be merciful to me;
Heal my soul, for I have sinned against You."

5 My enemies speak evil of me:
"When will he die, and his name perish?"

6 And if he comes to see *me*, he speaks lies;
His heart gathers iniquity to itself;
When he goes out, he tells *it*.

7 All who hate me whisper together against me;
Against me they devise my hurt.

8 "An evil disease," *they say*, "clings to him.
And *now* that he lies down, he will rise up no
more."

9 Even my own familiar friend in whom I
trusted,
Who ate my bread,
Has lifted up *his* heel against me.

10 But You, O LORD, be merciful to me, and raise
me up,
That I may repay them.

11 By this I know that You are well pleased
with me,
Because my enemy does not triumph over me.

12 As for me, You uphold me in my integrity,
And set me before Your face forever.

13 Blessed *be* the LORD God of Israel
From everlasting to everlasting!
Amen and Amen.

DEVOTIONAL

B rother John, will you lead us in the benediction
as we leave?" In the church where I grew up,
this was how our worship services ended. This
psalm begins with a benediction, one of three
psalms to do so. Would you like the blessing of
God pronounced upon your life today? Then begin
by putting others before yourself. When you know
of someone who is poor, weak, helpless, powerless,
or in trouble and you allow the Lord to use you to
minister to that person, the Lord will meet you in
return at the point of your greatest need.

The weak and the destitute are mostly avoided,
and the world deserts them. Those of us who have
been partakers of God's divine grace have His
tender nature. We don't just write a check and go
our way, but we inquire into their sorrows, share
the good news of deliverance, and come to their
relief.

God promises us He will also come to our aid
in our times of trouble. He delivers help for us in
the time of scorn and health for us in the time of
sickness. Do you need His help? Do you need His
healing? Then get personally involved in relieving
others, and He will lead you in a benediction.

Dr. Michael Cloer, Englewood Baptist Church
Rocky Mount, NC

MARCH 8

Yearning for God

Psalm 42:1–11

AS the deer pants for the water brooks,
So pants my soul for You, O God.

2 My soul thirsts for God, for the living God.
When shall I come and appear before God?

3 My tears have been my food day and night,
While they continually say to me,
"Where *is* your God?"

4 When I remember these *things,*
I pour out my soul within me.
For I used to go with the multitude;
I went with them to the house of God,
With the voice of joy and praise,
With a multitude that kept a pilgrim feast.

5 Why are you cast down, O my soul?
And *why* are you disquieted within me?
Hope in God, for I shall yet praise Him
For the help of His countenance.

6 O my God, my soul is cast down within me;
Therefore I will remember You from the land
of the Jordan,
And from the heights of Hermon,
From the Hill Mizar.

7 Deep calls unto deep at the noise of Your
waterfalls;
All Your waves and billows have gone
over me.

8 The LORD will command His lovingkindness
in the daytime,
And in the night His song *shall be* with me—
A prayer to the God of my life.

9 I will say to God my Rock,
"Why have You forgotten me?
Why do I go mourning because of the
oppression of the enemy?"

10 *As* with a breaking of my bones,
My enemies reproach me,
While they say to me all day long,
"Where *is* your God?"

11 Why are you cast down, O my soul?
And why are you disquieted within me?
Hope in God;
For I shall yet praise Him,
The help of my countenance and my God.

DEVOTIONAL

Old-timers talk about depression in this way: "I feel lower than a snake's belly in a wagon rut." That is mighty low. Ever felt this way? You are in good company. In this psalm, David talks about his despair, his depression, and his discouragement when he was separated from worshiping with the assembly of God's people.

The answer for his despair, and ours, is a passionate desire for intimacy with the Lord and with His people. In times of dryness, a child of God should be as intentional about finding fellowship with Jesus and with other Christians as a thirsty deer is focused on finding water. If you hunger and thirst for Him, daily feeding on His Word and drinking from the fountain of living water, He will fill you to overflowing.

When the outlook is depressing, try the uplook. Like the psalmist, put all your hope in God. "Hope in God; for I shall yet praise Him" (v. 11).

Dr. Michael Cloer, Englewood Baptist Church
Rocky Mount, NC

MARCH 9

Prayer to God in Time of Trouble

Psalm 43:1–5

V INDICATE me, O God,
And plead my cause against an ungodly
nation;
Oh, deliver me from the deceitful and unjust
man!

2 For You *are* the God of my strength;
Why do You cast me off?
Why do I go mourning because of the oppres-
sion of the enemy?

3 Oh, send out Your light and Your truth!
Let them lead me;
Let them bring me to Your holy hill
And to Your tabernacle.

4 Then I will go to the altar of God,
To God my exceeding joy;
And on the harp I will praise You,
O God, my God.

5 Why are you cast down, O my soul?
And why are you disquieted within me?
Hope in God;
For I shall yet praise Him,
The help of my countenance and my God.

DEVOTIONAL

T he land of Israel is a good description of the
Christian life: "a land of hills and valleys"
(Deut. 11:11). As we read these psalms, we hear
someone experiencing the hills of delight and the
valleys of depression. Up and down, up and down;
the psalmist's emotions were like a spiritual roller
coaster. Have you ever been like that?

Hills and valleys—and sometimes both in
the same day! "You are the God of my strength,"
immediately followed by, "Why do You cast me
off?" (v. 2).

In some people, there are physical reasons
for their manic behavior: a chemical imbalance
or a brain tumor. But often discontentment and
despair are self-induced. The fact is, today you can
choose to praise or choose to pout.

Why do we get so down, so disquieted? The
first clue is the author's use of personal pronouns
in this psalm. In five verses, he used the pronouns
I, *me*, and *my* seventeen times. One reason we can
be depressed is having an unhealthy fixation on
ourselves: *my* problems, *my* feelings, *my* needs, *me*,
me, *me* . . .

If you look closely you will discover not only
the cause of depression but the cure. The psalmist
began with a plea in the valley, but five verses later
he was praising God on the hills. He came to realize
a healthy attitude can change a disposition—it's
not about us; it's about God!

It's not about your weaknesses; God is your
strength. Like this psalmist, cry out to God. Focus
on His deliverance, His defense, and His absolute
dependability. You can trust Him. Remember, it's
not about you.

Then instead of following feelings or friends,
trust Him to direct you in the way you should go.
He will lead and guide you with His Word because
His Word is truth. Before you know it, you have
traveled from praying to pondering, and now you
are praising Him in unrestrained joyful worship.
What started with *me* ended with *God*!

Dr. Michael Cloer, Englewood Baptist Church
Rocky Mount, NC

MARCH 10

Redemption Remembered

Psalm 44:1–12

WE have heard with our ears, O God,
Our fathers have told us,
The deeds You did in their days,
In days of old:

2 You drove out the nations with Your hand,
But them You planted;
You afflicted the peoples, and cast them out.
For they did not gain possession of the land
by their own sword,
Nor did their own arm save them;
But it was Your right hand, Your arm, and the
light of Your countenance,
Because You favored them.

4 You are my King, O God;
Command victories for Jacob.

5 Through You we will push down our enemies;
Through Your name we will trample those
who rise up against us.

6 For I will not trust in my bow,
Nor shall my sword save me.

7 But You have saved us from our enemies,
And have put to shame those who hated us.

8 In God we boast all day long,
And praise Your name forever.   Selah

9 But You have cast *us* off and put us to shame,
And You do not go out with our armies.

10 You make us turn back from the enemy,
And those who hate us have taken spoil for
themselves.

11 You have given us up like sheep *intended* for food,
And have scattered us among the nations.

12 You sell Your people for *next to* nothing,
And are not enriched by selling them.

DEVOTIONAL

Most Americans remember where they were and what they were doing on the morning of September 11, 2001. Do you remember where you were and what you were doing the evening of September 12, 2001? Church buildings, auditoriums, and house churches across America were filled with people praying and mourning.

While we do not know exactly when this psalm was written or know the name of its human writer, we do know it was given by inspiration of the Holy Spirit at a time of national disaster and humiliation. The nation was in great peril. The enemy had delivered a devastating defeat, but in his country's desperate time of need, this psalmist prayed. This is what God wants us to do for our nation today.

The history of Israel parallels that of the United States. This patriot reminded God, and himself, of how that nation began. It was not the result of an act of rebellion, but Israel had been divinely planted by God (v. 2). Israel, like America, was also divinely protected by God (vv. 5–7). He praised the Lord because he knew that his nation, like ours, had been prospered by God (v. 8). All that this nation had was given to them by God.

Because they had turned their backs on God, the psalmist mourned because he knew his nation was being divinely punished by God, crippling their economy. Today, on behalf of our nation, let us pray, remember, and repent.

Dr. Michael Cloer, Englewood Baptist Church
Rocky Mount, NC

MARCH 11

Psalm 40:5 reminds us that God's deeds, His wonders, and His blessings toward us are too numerous to even list. In the remaining space, try to list as many as you can and before each one say, "Thank You, Lord, for . . ."

_____

_____

_____

_____

_____

_____

_____

_____

_____

_____

Psalm 42 and Psalm 43 ask the question "Why?" ten different times. Evidently the Lord is not bothered by our questions. Write out the top seven questions you have for the Lord today.

_____

_____

_____

_____

_____

_____

_____

_____

_____

_____

_____

MARCH 12

A Plea to the Shepherd

Psalm 44:13–26

¹³ You make us a reproach to our neighbors,
   A scorn and a derision to those all around us.
¹⁴ You make us a byword among the nations,
   A shaking of the head among the peoples.
¹⁵ My dishonor *is* continually before me,
   And the shame of my face has covered me,
¹⁶ Because of the voice of him who reproaches
      and reviles,
   Because of the enemy and the avenger.

¹⁷ All this has come upon us;
   But we have not forgotten You,
   Nor have we dealt falsely with Your covenant.
¹⁸ Our heart has not turned back,
   Nor have our steps departed from Your way;
¹⁹ But You have severely broken us in the place of
      jackals,
   And covered us with the shadow of death.

²⁰ If we had forgotten the name of our God,
   Or stretched out our hands to a foreign god,
²¹ Would not God search this out?
   For He knows the secrets of the heart.
²² Yet for Your sake we are killed all day long;
   We are accounted as sheep for the slaughter.

²³ Awake! Why do You sleep, O Lord?
   Arise! Do not cast *us* off forever.
²⁴ Why do You hide Your face,
   And forget our affliction and our oppression?
²⁵ For our soul is bowed down to the dust;
   Our body clings to the ground.

²⁶ Arise for our help,
   And redeem us for Your mercies' sake.

DEVOTIONAL

How do you respond when you are doing your best to live for the Lord, yet it seems everything is going against you? How do you handle it when your classmates or coworkers are ridiculing you? You have examined your life, your heart, and your motives and see nothing that would cause this to happen—but it is! Like the psalmist, do you call out to God and tell Him that you haven't sinned against His commands and that you haven't been acting deceitfully but have been walking in obedience? Do you remind God and yourself that you are aware He would know if you were focused on something besides serving Him?

In the midst of his questioning, the psalmist in verse 22 acknowledges that suffering is a part of serving God! But why? Sometimes people say, "We will never know until we get to heaven." I'm not sure we will care in heaven! But back to the "now."

As I am writing this devotional, I am thinking about a grieving friend, the grandfather of a precious six-year-old girl who was killed in a tragic accident last Sunday. I am praying for other friends who have spouses or children battling cancer. "Why?" we cry. I don't know. But the Word of God is clear. Paul reminds us in Romans 8:36 that God still loves us and there is nothing that can separate us from His love!

Dennis Nunn, Every Believer a Witness Ministries
Dallas, GA

MARCH 13

The Messiah and His Bride

Psalm 45:1–9

MY heart is overflowing with a good theme;
I recite my composition concerning the
King;
My tongue *is* the pen of a ready writer.

2 You are fairer than the sons of men;
Grace is poured upon Your lips;
Therefore God has blessed You forever.

3 Gird Your sword upon *Your* thigh, O Mighty One,
With Your glory and Your majesty.

4 And in Your majesty ride prosperously because
of truth, humility, *and* righteousness;
And Your right hand shall teach You awesome
things.

5 Your arrows *are* sharp in the heart of the
King's enemies;
The peoples fall under You.

6 Your throne, O God, *is* forever and ever;
A scepter of righteousness *is* the scepter of
Your kingdom.

7 You love righteousness and hate wickedness;
Therefore God, Your God, has anointed You
With the oil of gladness more than Your
companions.

8 All Your garments are scented with myrrh and
aloes *and* cassia,
Out of the ivory palaces, by which they have
made You glad.

9 Kings' daughters *are* among Your honorable
women;
At Your right hand stands the queen in gold
from Ophir.

DEVOTIONAL

One of the most intriguing things about Old Testament scriptures is that while they were written about an actual occurrence during the time of the writer, they also often have a prophetical aspect pointing to the Lord Jesus Christ. Psalm 45 is one such passage and is one of the "messianic psalms."

When it was written, it was a song to the Davidic king of Israel. However, when the writer of Hebrews was pointing out the superiority of Jesus to the angels in Hebrews 1:9, he quotes verses 6 and 7 from this psalm to show that Jesus is *the* eternal and righteous King, the One who would fulfill all that was promised to David.

While there are several applications for us here, such as the power of the King in verses 4–6 and His eternal rule and righteousness in verses 7–8, I want to point out that the writer begins in verse 1 by telling about his personal response to these attributes of the King, saying, "My heart is overflowing . . ."

Is that description true of your heart today? When you read the Bible, is it an objective, informational, learning exercise—or is your heart stirred by the greatness of the King and His graciousness to you? Do you talk to God, praising Him from your heart? Will you do that right now? Will you make it your theme for today?

Think about the great power of the King. He can handle anything that comes your way today. Think about the fact that He is eternal and constant. We can depend on Him. May this stir our hearts to overflow!

Dennis Nunn, Every Believer a Witness Ministries
Dallas, GA

MARCH 14

Homage to the King

Psalm 45:10–17

¹⁰ Listen, O daughter,
Consider and incline your ear;
Forget your own people also, and your father's
house;

¹¹ So the King will greatly desire your beauty;
Because He *is* your Lord, worship Him.

¹² And the daughter of Tȳre *will come* with a
gift;
The rich among the people will seek your
favor.

¹³ The royal daughter *is* all glorious within *the
palace;*
Her clothing *is* woven with gold.

¹⁴ She shall be brought to the King in robes of
many colors;
The virgins, her companions who follow her,
shall be brought to You.

¹⁵ With gladness and rejoicing they shall be
brought;
They shall enter the King's palace.

¹⁶ Instead of Your fathers shall be Your sons,
Whom You shall make princes in all the earth.

¹⁷ I will make Your name to be remembered in
all generations;
Therefore the people shall praise You forever
and ever.

DEVOTIONAL

While the readers of Psalms were very familiar with the customs and practices of a
Jewish wedding, they are unfamiliar to us, so their
significance is often lost on us. But there is one
aspect of a wedding in this psalm that is clearly
applicable to every follower of Jesus Christ. In
verse 10, the writer says to the bride, "Forget your
own people also, and your [earthly] father's house."
Becoming totally focused on Jesus as preeminent
in our lives is a recurring truth throughout the New
Testament. When Jesus called His first disciples,
Peter and Andrew, "they immediately left their nets
and followed him" (Matt. 4:20). Then when Jesus
called James and John, "they left the boat and their
father, and followed Him" (v. 22).

Jesus Himself said, "He who loves father or
mother more than Me is not worthy of Me" (Matt.
10:37). Is that how much you love Him? Sometimes
I think I do, and sometimes I don't. But as I write
this on a Wednesday afternoon, the Lord has spoken to me through this devotional, telling me that
as much as I love my wife, my children, and (especially) my grandchildren, He wants me to love
Him more than all these.

Does loving Jesus more than your family mean
you need to prioritize spending time with Him?
Does it mean you are going to have to accept not
being as close to some of them as you could if you
weren't unashamedly a devoted follower of Jesus?
Does it mean that some of your family may even
reject you? Thirty-five years after the funeral of
my grandfather, some of my family won't have any
contact with me because I shared that although he
was a good man, just being good would not get
him to heaven—only Jesus could do that. What
does loving Him more look like to you?

Dennis Nunn, Every Believer a Witness Ministries
Dallas, GA

MARCH 15

God, the Refuge of His People

Psalm 46:1–11

G OD *is* our refuge and strength,
A very present help in trouble.
2   Therefore we will not fear,
Even though the earth be removed,
And though the mountains be carried into the
midst of the sea;
3   *Though* its waters roar *and* be troubled,
Though the mountains shake with its swelling.
Selah

4   *There is* a river whose streams shall make glad
the city of God,
The holy *place* of the tabernacle of the Most
High.
5   God *is* in the midst of her, she shall not be
moved;
God shall help her, just at the break of dawn.
6   The nations raged, the kingdoms were moved;
He uttered His voice, the earth melted.

7   The LORD of hosts *is* with us;
The God of Jacob *is* our refuge.   Selah

8   Come, behold the works of the LORD,
Who has made desolations in the earth.
9   He makes wars cease to the end of the earth;
He breaks the bow and cuts the spear in two;
He burns the chariot in the fire.

10   Be still, and know that I *am* God;
I will be exalted among the nations,
I will be exalted in the earth!

11   The LORD of hosts *is* with us;
The God of Jacob *is* our refuge.   Selah

DEVOTIONAL

A s a pastor for twenty years prior to becoming an evangelist, I made a countless number of visits to hospitals to pray with friends and their families who were facing serious illness, surgery, or even death. I think I read Psalm 46:1 more than any other single verse or passage in the Bible.

While we are not told the specific challenge the psalmist was facing, it is possible it was an earthquake. Despite his situation, the psalmist said his response would not be one of fear. In fact, the psalmist stated his confident assurance in the ever-present, powerful God as his refuge and strength.

Before Jesus came to earth, God's presence dwelled in the innermost part of the tabernacle, then in the temple in the city of Jerusalem. Jews confidently spoke of how His presence made them secure. But the writer was looking beyond just the current time when he spoke of a river flowing in the city. There was no river in ancient or modern-day Jerusalem (v. 4). And wars certainly hadn't ceased (v. 9). The picture is of a heavenly Jerusalem, where the river of life is flowing (Rev. 22:1). The eternality of God means He was, is, and will be a refuge for His people.

What great problems are you facing today? Have the attitude and confidence of the psalmist. Be still, and sense God's presence. Exalt Him and praise Him! God is your ever-present Helper!

Dennis Nunn, Every Believer a Witness Ministries
Dallas, GA

MARCH 16

Praise to God, the Ruler of the Earth

Psalm 47:1–9

OH, clap your hands, all you peoples!
Shout to God with the voice of triumph!

2 For the LORD Most High *is* awesome;
He is a great King over all the earth.

3 He will subdue the peoples under us,
And the nations under our feet.

4 He will choose our inheritance for us,
The excellence of Jacob whom He loves.   Selah

5 God has gone up with a shout,
The LORD with the sound of a trumpet.

6 Sing praises to God, sing praises!
Sing praises to our King, sing praises!

7 For God *is* the King of all the earth;
Sing praises with understanding.

8 God reigns over the nations;
God sits on His holy throne.

9 The princes of the people have gathered
together,
The people of the God of Abraham.
For the shields of the earth *belong* to God;
He is greatly exalted.

DEVOTIONAL

One of the great challenges believers face is the battle over what will guide us in religious matters—the Bible or tradition.

The most important battle is over the path to salvation. Proverbs 14:12 says, "There is a way that seems right to a man, but its end is the way of death." To many, being a good person is the way to please God and earn heaven. But the Bible is clear that salvation is a free gift and that we cannot earn our way to heaven. Ephesians 2:8–9 says, "For by grace you have been saved through faith … not of works."

Probably the next greatest area of controversy is worship style. Worship style has been, and still is, a source of disagreement among Christians. Should worship be quiet, reflective, and reverent? Or should it be loud and celebratory? Someone has called Psalms the hymn book of the Israelites. And in Psalms, we see *both* types of worship! Psalms speaks repeatedly of singing a "new song," of responding aloud, of lifting hands, and in Psalm 47, all the people (that would include us) are instructed to clap our hands and shout. The church I grew up in didn't do either of these!

However, I don't want us to focus on style as much as on the fact that the psalmist repeatedly tells us the *reasons* for worshiping God. The psalmist says that God is awesome, that He is over all the earth, and that He gives victory in battle; therefore, we should sing praises to Him. In fact, five times he says we should sing praises to God!

Are you facing some spiritual battles today? Satan is not happy that you have become a follower of the Lord Jesus Christ. Peter tells us that the devil is our adversary and that he is trying to devour us. But your God not only gives His people victory over human foes but also over our greatest foe! You are more than a conqueror through Christ who gives you strength—and you have a song to sing!

My pastor says that to praise God you don't have to have a good voice; you only have to have a song! Sing praises to God!

Dennis Nunn, Every Believer a Witness Ministries
Dallas, GA

MARCH 17

The Glory of God in Zion

Psalm 48:1–14

GREAT *is* the LORD, and greatly to be praised
In the city of our God,
In His holy mountain.

2 Beautiful in elevation,
The joy of the whole earth,
Is Mount Zion *on* the sides of the north,
The city of the great King.

3 God *is* in her palaces;
He is known as her refuge.

4 For behold, the kings assembled,
They passed by together.

5 They saw *it, and* so they marveled;
They were troubled, they hastened away.

6 Fear took hold of them there,
And pain, as of a woman in birth pangs,

7 *As when* You break the ships of Tarshish
With an east wind.

8 As we have heard,
So we have seen
In the city of the LORD of hosts,
In the city of our God:
God will establish it forever.   Selah

9 We have thought, O God, on Your lovingkindness,
In the midst of Your temple.

10 According to Your name, O God,
So *is* Your praise to the ends of the earth;
Your right hand is full of righteousness.

11 Let Mount Zion rejoice,
Let the daughters of Judah be glad,
Because of Your judgments.

12 Walk about Zion,
And go all around her.
Count her towers;

13 Mark well her bulwarks;
Consider her palaces;
That you may tell *it* to the generation following.

14 For this *is* God,
Our God forever and ever;
He will be our guide
Even to death.

DEVOTIONAL

This psalm is much like Psalm 46, which we read two days ago. At the time the psalmist was writing, the presence of God dwelled in the temple, which was located in Jerusalem, and thus Jerusalem was called the "holy city." The Israelites believed that God's presence made the city absolutely secure, and even struck fear into the hearts of their enemies. The psalmist exhorted the readers to walk around and check out the security of the city, then tell the next generation about it.

Here are two main applications for us: First, today the Spirit of God does not dwell in a building, but within His people. The temple of God is in the church collectively (1 Cor. 3:16) and in us individually (1 Cor. 6:19). That makes you both holy and secure!

Second, as the readers of Psalms were instructed, we have a responsibility to tell our children and our grandchildren of the things of God (Deut. 4:9). In a world that is growing more insecure each day, reassure your children about the faithfulness and goodness of our Lord. No matter what is going on in the world around us, we can walk in security, all the days of our lives (v. 14).

Dennis Nunn, Every Believer a Witness Ministries
Dallas, GA

 # MARCH 18

As we reflect back on this week's readings, one of the themes has been that God's children face adversity and enemies. What is the greatest challenge or problem you are facing today? As you look back over Psalms 44–48, how much confidence can you have in God being there for you and His ability to help you?

This week's readings exhort us to tell following generations about our Lord. Do you find yourself telling others, especially your children, about God's faithfulness to you? Write about a couple of times when you have done that recently.

MARCH 19

The Confidence of the Foolish

Psalm 49:1–9

H EAR this, all peoples;
    Give ear, all inhabitants of the world,
2 Both low and high,
    Rich and poor together.
3 My mouth shall speak wisdom,
    And the meditation of my heart *shall give*
      understanding.
4 I will incline my ear to a proverb;
    I will disclose my dark saying on the harp.

5 Why should I fear in the days of evil,
    When the iniquity at my heels surrounds me?
6 Those who trust in their wealth
    And boast in the multitude of their riches,
7 None *of them* can by any means redeem *his*
      brother,
    Nor give to God a ransom for him—
8 For the redemption of their souls *is* costly,
    And it shall cease forever—
9 That he should continue to live eternally,
    And not see the Pit.

DEVOTIONAL

S omewhere between the foolishness of youth and the wisdom of age we cross over to the land of the listening. Many of life's issues may be solved less painfully if we listen to the experienced and wise. The psalmist would have us heed the lessons he has learned.

He learned that the trouble nipping at his heels was actually all around him. It is like the little girl on the Morton's salt box who reminds us, "When it rains, it pours!" One falling domino leads to another and another until our whole world is in a state of collapse. When we have times like this, we need someone to turn to, who will lead us out of the valley.

When in trouble, some will look for a bailout, a person of means with the power needed to drive them out of the ditch. However, the psalmist learned that no amount of money or power can liberate the soul held captive. Jesus once asked what someone could give in exchange for his own soul. The answer: there is no amount large enough to redeem ourselves. So it goes without saying that the price to redeem another is out of the question too.

What, then, is the answer for the troubled heart? It is the power of God's love! The source of redemption is the power in the blood, not our balance in the bank. Wealth is a tool, not a savior. This bit of wisdom comes to us from one who had it all—wealth, power, and money—yet to find life eternal and joy, he turned to God alone.

Our challenge today is to cross over to the land of the listening. Let us be humble enough to seek the wisdom in God's Word and mature enough to heed the lessons given. The God of our salvation is the God of all joy!

Randy Ray, North Florida Baptist Church
Tallahassee, FL

MARCH 20

Beauty and Riches Also Die

Psalm 49:10–20

10 For he sees wise men die;
Likewise the fool and the senseless person
      perish,
And leave their wealth to others.

11 Their inner thought *is that* their houses *will
      last* forever,
Their dwelling places to all generations;
They call *their* lands after their own names.

12 Nevertheless man, *though* in honor, does not
      remain;
He is like the beasts *that* perish.

13 This is the way of those who *are* foolish,
And of their posterity who approve their
      sayings.   Selah

14 Like sheep they are laid in the grave;
Death shall feed on them;
The upright shall have dominion over them in
      the morning;
And their beauty shall be consumed in the
      grave, far from their dwelling.

15 But God will redeem my soul from the power
      of the grave,
For He shall receive me.   Selah

16 Do not be afraid when one becomes rich,
When the glory of his house is increased;

17 For when he dies he shall carry nothing away;
His glory shall not descend after him.

18 Though while he lives he blesses himself
(For *men* will praise you when you do well for
      yourself),

19 He shall go to the generation of his fathers;
They shall never see light.

20 A man *who is* in honor, yet does not
      understand,
Is like the beasts *that* perish.

DEVOTIONAL

Perspective has an impact on outcome. Sometimes I will hit a golf shot that lands on the green, and from where I stand it looks as though it has stopped only a foot or two from the cup. "Now, that's a golf shot!" someone will say. Then we arrive at the green only to discover that it ran not two but twelve feet past the hole. A sure one putt becomes two and, heaven forbid, three!

There have been a lot of people who treasured a part of life that looked much different from another perspective. Beauty is not so important when word comes of illness or loss. The joy of riches tends to fade as our remaining years grow fewer in number.

How do we ensure that life gets better and not bitter as our days advance? The key to a better life is in our perspective. When we treasure the things of earth, we see them slipping away as life moves on. The bitter miser once had an outlook of promise as treasure accumulated. When the reality of leaving this earth came into view, that optimism changed and life grew bitter.

To become better instead of bitter, our treasure must be above. When our treasure is laid up in heaven, we go to our reward. We are not leaving it! Keep life and its treasure in perspective. It will make a difference both now and forever.

Randy Ray, North Florida Baptist Church
Tallahassee, FL

MARCH 21

God, the Righteous Judge

Psalm 50:1–11

T HE Mighty One, God the LORD,
Has spoken and called the earth
From the rising of the sun to its going down.

2 Out of Zion, the perfection of beauty,
God will shine forth.

3 Our God shall come, and shall not keep silent;
A fire shall devour before Him,
And it shall be very tempestuous all around
Him.

4 He shall call to the heavens from above,
And to the earth, that He may judge His people:

5 "Gather My saints together to Me,
Those who have made a covenant with Me by
sacrifice."

6 Let the heavens declare His righteousness,
For God Himself *is* Judge.   Selah

7 "Hear, O My people, and I will speak,
O Israel, and I will testify against you;
I *am* God, your God!

8 I will not rebuke you for your sacrifices
Or your burnt offerings,
Which are continually before Me.

9 I will not take a bull from your house,
Nor goats out of your folds.

10 For every beast of the forest *is* Mine,
And the cattle on a thousand hills.

11 I know all the birds of the mountains,
And the wild beasts of the field *are* Mine.

T he Declaration of Independence was written to King George III of England. However, those poignant words are for the benefit of every American and have served others around the world. It was not written to us, but it is for us! This chapter in Psalms is a great example of how the Bible benefits the reader. These words were written to Israel, but they have value for you and me.

Here is a psalm written not by David but by Asaph, a leading musician in Israel. In this psalm, God is pictured as an ominous, decisive, and able judge. Standing before someone with the power to decide our fate is unnerving. When that judge is "the Mighty One, God the LORD" (v. 1), it is awesome, in the truest sense of the word.

Verses 4 through 6 tell us of a viewing gallery but speak nothing of a jury. The Mighty One has no need of the opinions of man but does allow all the universe to observe in His courtroom. We know this from Hebrews 12:1, which speaks of a cloud of witnesses. Just as Israel was and is always on display, so are we who are called by His name.

Once the position of God is established, His possessions are emphasized (vv. 10–11). He clarifies that we have nothing to offer Him that He has not given to us. Our gifts, even our sacrifices, are a returning to Him. However, like the parent who gives the children Christmas money to do some shopping, the gifts are accepted with joy. God has given to you all talent, treasure, and time. Today, give Him back the gift of your best and your highest praise for all of His goodness!

Randy Ray, North Florida Baptist Church
Tallahassee, FL

MARCH 22

A Request for Deliverance

Psalm 50:12–23

¹² "If I were hungry, I would not tell you;
For the world *is* Mine, and all its fullness.
¹³ Will I eat the flesh of bulls,
Or drink the blood of goats?
¹⁴ Offer to God thanksgiving,
And pay your vows to the Most High.
¹⁵ Call upon Me in the day of trouble;
I will deliver you, and you shall glorify Me."

¹⁶ But to the wicked God says:
"What *right* have you to declare My statutes,
Or take My covenant in your mouth,
¹⁷ Seeing you hate instruction
And cast My words behind you?
¹⁸ When you saw a thief, you consented with
him,
And have been a partaker with adulterers.
¹⁹ You give your mouth to evil,
And your tongue frames deceit.
²⁰ You sit *and* speak against your brother;
You slander your own mother's son.
²¹ These *things* you have done, and I kept silent;
You thought that I was altogether like you;
But I will rebuke you,
And set *them* in order before your eyes.

²² "Now consider this, you who forget God,
Lest I tear *you* in pieces,
And *there be* none to deliver:
²³ Whoever offers praise glorifies Me;
And to him who orders *his* conduct *aright*
I will show the salvation of God."

DEVOTIONAL

When we talk about something written *for* us though not necessarily *to* us, this passage is a perfect example. God gave Asaph an understanding that transcends the ages.

First, we must comprehend the source of our strength. Does God need us or do we need God? God needs us only because He has chosen to include us in His plan. God doesn't need our tithe, but He receives it as an act of obedience and worship to Him. God does not need our thanksgiving, praise, and worship. But we praise the Lord because He is the author of praise and we believe He is the giver of all good things (Jas. 1:17).

God has something much different to say to the wicked. His warning is contemporary and relevant today. Powerful people quote portions of Scripture they do not even believe or understand to strengthen their point and make their argument. We see it as something of a current phenomenon, but it is as old as time. God's opinion is clear: they are hypocritical and speak foolishly.

There are consequences for hypocrisy. When we find ourselves manipulating rather than responding to God's Word, the warnings in this psalm are for us. But when we live our lives in harmony with the will and way of God, we find favor. Remember, your walk talks and your talk talks, but your walk talks louder than your talk talks!

Randy Ray, North Florida Baptist Church
Tallahassee, FL

MARCH 23

A Prayer of Repentance

Psalm 51:1–9

HAVE mercy upon me, O God,
According to Your lovingkindness;
According to the multitude of Your tender
mercies,
Blot out my transgressions.

2 Wash me thoroughly from my iniquity,
And cleanse me from my sin.

3 For I acknowledge my transgressions,
And my sin *is* always before me.

4 Against You, You only, have I sinned,
And done *this* evil in Your sight—
That You may be found just when You speak,
And blameless when You judge.

5 Behold, I was brought forth in iniquity,
And in sin my mother conceived me.

6 Behold, You desire truth in the inward parts,
And in the hidden *part* You will make me to
know wisdom.

7 Purge me with hyssop, and I shall be clean;
Wash me, and I shall be whiter than snow.

8 Make me hear joy and gladness,
That the bones You have broken may rejoice.

9 Hide Your face from my sins,
And blot out all my iniquities.

DEVOTIONAL

I have three grown sons, all of whom are good guys, a blessing to their mother and me. My youngest son has always been an avid follower of Apple products. He worked on me for so long that I finally broke down and got an iPhone and an iPad. My expectations were very high. I thought they were immune from typical computer problems and then I read the warning. Apple products are computers, and all computers need to be rebooted now and then. So when all else fails, you hold down the home and sleep buttons and that fixes almost everything!

David found the reset button for a life gone wrong. It is built on God's unique operating system called "Mercy." As we saw earlier this week, all the good things that come our way are gifts from God, including His mercy.

The psalmist shows us that the reset button for God's mercy is confession of sin—old-fashioned repentance. Remember 1 John 1:9: "If we confess our sins, He is faithful and just to forgive us our sins and to cleanse us from all unrighteousness." We were born in sin and have continued to sin since our birth. That sin is called depravity, and we have Adam to thank for it. No wonder our lives get so hung up!

The desire for the psalmist was restoration, to be purged from the filth he felt in his sinfulness. We have all been in this spot, probably more times than we care to admit. The answer is to remember His mercy, and to push the reset button of confession and repentance!

Randy Ray, North Florida Baptist Church
Tallahassee, FL

MARCH 24

A Request for Renewal

Psalm 51:10–19

10 Create in me a clean heart, O God,
And renew a steadfast spirit within me.
11 Do not cast me away from Your presence,
And do not take Your Holy Spirit from me.

12 Restore to me the joy of Your salvation,
And uphold me *by Your* generous Spirit.
13 *Then* I will teach transgressors Your ways,
And sinners shall be converted to You.

14 Deliver me from the guilt of bloodshed, O
God,
The God of my salvation,
And my tongue shall sing aloud of Your
righteousness.
15 O Lord, open my lips,
And my mouth shall show forth Your praise.
16 For You do not desire sacrifice, or else I would
give *it;*
You do not delight in burnt offering.
17 The sacrifices of God *are* a broken spirit,
A broken and a contrite heart—
These, O God, You will not despise.

18 Do good in Your good pleasure to Zion;
Build the walls of Jerusalem.
19 Then You shall be pleased with the sacrifices
of righteousness,
With burnt offering and whole burnt offering;
Then they shall offer bulls on Your altar.

DEVOTIONAL

Do you know someone who cannot get to the point? I'm sure that my impatience plays a part in this, but the need to get to the bottom line is important to me. Maybe this is what I like about the psalmist, the ability to make things clear! In the first part of the psalm, there is repentance, and now there are the requests.

David's desire was to get back to God's work. The condition of his soul had kept him from teaching transgressors the way of God. We can surmise that he felt so guilty about his own sin that he didn't feel qualified to speak of God's righteousness. At issue was his sin with Bathsheba and the subsequent murder of her husband, Uriah. What a horrible chapter in David's life! But now he is repenting and wants to rediscover the joy of salvation.

You may be waiting for the right time to invite Jesus Christ to be your Lord and Savior. Now is the best time to do so! Confess your sin to God and ask for His forgiveness based on the sacrifice of Jesus Christ.

Maybe for others salvation has lost some of its joy. This usually occurs when we have blocked our spiritual path to God's blessing. David knew what was blocking the path for him, and I suspect we do too. No sacrifice is as good as simple honesty with God. Let's make it a point to get to the point with God. Spiritual happiness is found in the honest life!

Randy Ray, North Florida Baptist Church
Tallahassee, FL

MARCH 25

What if you lived in a third-world country? How would your life be different from the way it is now? How did you come to be born to such privilege? Did you do something to deserve these blessings? God is the giver of all good things. How has God blessed your life? How are you serving Him with all that He has given you?

_____

_____

_____

_____

_____

_____

_____

_____

_____

We know that God's forgiveness is complete and forever. Even so, we do not want to ignore the importance of keeping a clear conscience before Him. Can you come up with a plan for keeping the path clear between your conscience and God's will for your life? How can daily confession of sin make your service for God more effective and joyful?

_____

_____

_____

_____

_____

_____

MARCH 26

The End of the Wicked

Psalm 52:1–9

WHY do you boast in evil, O mighty man?
The goodness of God *endures* continually.
2 Your tongue devises destruction,
Like a sharp razor, working deceitfully.
3 You love evil more than good,
Lying rather than speaking righteousness.

Selah

4 You love all devouring words,
You deceitful tongue.

5 God shall likewise destroy you forever;
He shall take you away, and pluck you out of
your dwelling place,
And uproot you from the land of the living.

Selah

6 The righteous also shall see and fear,
And shall laugh at him, *saying,*
7 "Here is the man *who* did not make God his
strength,
But trusted in the abundance of his riches,
And strengthened himself in his wickedness."

8 But I *am* like a green olive tree in the house of
God;
I trust in the mercy of God forever and ever.
9 I will praise You forever,
Because You have done *it;*
And in the presence of Your saints
I will wait on Your name, for *it is* good.

We find the background to this psalm in 1 Samuel 21–22. When David was fleeing from Saul, he went to Nob and the priest Ahimelech. The priest ministered to David, giving him bread and Goliath's sword. One of Saul's chief shepherds, Doeg, was present. He observed the connection between David and Ahimelech and told Saul of the activity. For helping his enemy, Saul had Doeg kill Ahimelech and the other priests.

Doeg used his tongue for evil and to bring harm to a man of God. God takes our words seriously, and we should too. Verse 5 contains three strong warnings regarding God's response to a deceitful tongue. He will "destroy you forever," "pluck you out of your dwelling place," and "uproot you from the land of the living."

Ask God today to make you like a green olive tree in the house of God (v. 8). While the wicked are destroyed, plucked out, and uprooted, the righteous dwell in the house of the Lord. The promises of Him for those who use their words for righteousness are fruitfulness and longevity. Give thanks to the Lord and dedicate your words to the Lord this day.

Do not have a deceitful tongue!

Dr. Ted Traylor, Olive Baptist Church
Pensacola, FL

MARCH 27

The Restoration of Israel

Psalm 53:1–6

THE fool has said in his heart,
"*There is* no God."
They are corrupt, and have done abominable
iniquity;
There is none who does good.

2   God looks down from heaven upon the children of men,
To see if there are *any* who understand, who
seek God.

3   Every one of them has turned aside;
They have together become corrupt;
There is none who does good,
No, not one.

4   Have the workers of iniquity no knowledge,
Who eat up my people *as* they eat bread,
And do not call upon God?

5   There they are in great fear
Where no fear was,
For God has scattered the bones of him who
encamps against you;
You have put *them* to shame,
Because God has despised them.

6   Oh, that the salvation of Israel would come out
of Zion!
When God brings back the captivity of His
people,
Let Jacob rejoice *and* Israel be glad.

DEVOTIONAL

Today's psalm and its almost identical companion, Psalm 14, open with a bold statement: when there is no acknowledgment of God,
corruption and injustice spread. As a result, there
is less and less good in the land (v. 3), and wicked
people eat up others like bread (v. 4).

The Bible does not set out to prove God
exists. He is simply announced, "In the beginning God . . ." in the first chapter of Genesis. And
thus the Bible begins. Yet today a growing number claim atheism. This is an arrogant ideology.
For a person to disclaim God's existence implies
he would know everything, and thus he is god. I
am reminded of a little boy approached by a man
carrying a big red apple. "I will give you this if you
tell me where God is," said the man. "I will give
you a basketful if you show me where He ain't,"
replied the wise young boy.

Psalm 19:1 tells us the heavens declare the
glory of God. It is in the creation we find the
fingerprint of the Creator. Werner von Braun,
the father of space science, said, "The vast mysteries of the universe should only confirm our
belief in the certainty of its Creator. I find it as
difficult to understand a scientist who does not
acknowledge the presence of a superior rational-
ity behind the existence of the universe as it is
to comprehend a theologian who would deny the
advances of science."[1]

Friend, do not be foolish!

Dr. Ted Traylor, Olive Baptist Church
Pensacola, FL

MARCH 28

Answered Prayer for Deliverance

Psalm 54:1–7

S AVE me, O God, by Your name,
And vindicate me by Your strength.

2 Hear my prayer, O God;
Give ear to the words of my mouth.

3 For strangers have risen up against me,
And oppressors have sought after my life;
They have not set God before them.   Selah

4 Behold, God *is* my helper;
The Lord *is* with those who uphold my life.

5 He will repay my enemies for their evil.
Cut them off in Your truth.

6 I will freely sacrifice to You;
I will praise Your name, O LORD, for *it is* good.

7 For He has delivered me out of all trouble;
And my eye has seen *its desire* upon my
enemies.

DEVOTIONAL

L et's refer to 1 Samuel 23 for a moment. King
Saul was hunting for David to kill him. The
next king was hiding in the wilderness of Ziph,
and the Ziphites came to Saul, offering their help
with the search. Yet God provided shelter for David
at the Rock of Escape. Out of this event David gave
us today's psalm, the song regarding prayer and
God's protection.

How do we respond when enemies come
against us? Let us consider all the times David
was hunted for or attacked by enemies. He was
certainly familiar with relying on God for protection. David gives us a pattern to follow:

1. **Call out to the Lord** (vv. 1–3). David asked
God to save him and hear his prayer. He identified
the enemy as strangers and violent men who did
not follow God. Wicked people will come against
you. Pray for them like Jesus prayed for His killers
on the Cross (Luke 23:34).

2. **Rest in the Lord** (vv. 4–7). David stated
that God was his helper. He did not say, "God *will*
be my helper." He said, "God *is* my helper." David
acknowledged God as his sustainer, gave thanks
unto the Lord, and called Him good. David was
walking by faith. Proverbs 3:5, 6 is a favorite text
for many. Read it and rest in Jesus.

Dr. Ted Traylor, Olive Baptist Church
Pensacola, FL

MARCH 29

Trust in God

Psalm 55:1–11

GIVE ear to my prayer, O God,
And do not hide Yourself from my
supplication.

2 Attend to me, and hear me;
I am restless in my complaint, and moan
noisily,

3 Because of the voice of the enemy,
Because of the oppression of the wicked;
For they bring down trouble upon me,
And in wrath they hate me.

4 My heart is severely pained within me,
And the terrors of death have fallen upon me.

5 Fearfulness and trembling have come upon
me,
And horror has overwhelmed me.

6 So I said, "Oh, that I had wings like a dove!
I would fly away and be at rest.

7 Indeed, I would wander far off,
And remain in the wilderness.   Selah

8 I would hasten my escape
From the windy storm *and* tempest."

9 Destroy, O Lord, *and* divide their tongues,
For I have seen violence and strife in the city.

10 Day and night they go around it on its walls;
Iniquity and trouble *are* also in the midst of it.

11 Destruction *is* in its midst;
Oppression and deceit do not depart from its
streets.

DEVOTIONAL

The psalmist was facing trouble. He was restless because of the voice of the enemy and the pressure of the wicked. Someone bore a grudge of hate against him. Anyone who has been faithful about seriously living for God has known trouble from others. What do we do?

David was in such anguish he longed to give in and flee the situation. He longed to have wings like a dove so he could fly away and live in the wilderness to escape trouble. If you have known heat in the kitchen of faithfulness, you have at some time just wanted out.

However, the Lord does not call us to flee but to live faithfully. We are not to run but to stand. Do not take the coward's road, but find courage in God.

Andy Andrews is a *New York Times* best-selling author. His book, *The Traveler's Gift*, is wonderful. In it, the main character, David Ponder, goes on a great journey. Along the way, when he is in a tough situation and doesn't know what to do, he meets the angel Gabriel. "Circumstances are rulers of the weak," says Gabriel, "but they are weapons of the wise."[2] David Ponder learns his emotions and resolve are not controlled by circumstances. To persist without exception becomes his battle cry.

Do not long for the wings of a dove today. Persist!

Dr. Ted Traylor, Olive Baptist Church
Pensacola, FL

MARCH 30

Cast Your Burdens on the Lord

Psalm 55:12–23

12 For *it is* not an enemy *who* reproaches me;
Then I could bear *it*.
Nor *is it* one *who* hates me who has exalted
himself against me;
Then I could hide from him.

13 But *it was* you, a man my equal,
My companion and my acquaintance.

14 We took sweet counsel together,
And walked to the house of God in the throng.

15 Let death seize them;
Let them go down alive into hell,
For wickedness *is* in their dwellings *and*
among them.

16 As for me, I will call upon God,
And the LORD shall save me.

17 Evening and morning and at noon
I will pray, and cry aloud,
And He shall hear my voice.

18 He has redeemed my soul in peace from the
battle *that was* against me,
For there were many against me.

19 God will hear, and afflict them,
Even He who abides from of old.   Selah
Because they do not change,
Therefore they do not fear God.

20 He has put forth his hands against those who
were at peace with him;
He has broken his covenant.

21 *The words* of his mouth were smoother than
butter,
But war *was* in his heart;
His words were softer than oil,
Yet they *were* drawn swords.

22 Cast your burden on the LORD,
And He shall sustain you;
He shall never permit the righteous to be moved.

23 But You, O God, shall bring them down to the
pit of destruction;
Bloodthirsty and deceitful men shall not live
out half their days;
But I will trust in You.

DEVOTIONAL

Betrayal by a close friend is one of the deepest hurts of life. David was dealing with it in Psalm 55. He seems to be speaking of the situation with his son Absalom's rebellion and David's advisor Ahithophel's treacherous actions.

David gives a formula for response when we are betrayed by those close to us.

1. Let God be the God of judgment (v. 16). This is not our role.
2. Be a prayerful person (v. 17). David prayed in the evening, in the morning, and at noon.
3. Learn from the deception (v. 21). The unfaithful one had smooth speech but a heart of war. Watch actions more than words.
4. Cast your burden on the Lord (v. 22). He promises to sustain and steady us.

No matter what man may do to us, we have a Friend who sticks closer to a brother (Prov. 18:24). Draw near to Him and seek to be a faithful friend to others.

Dr. Ted Traylor, Olive Baptist Church
Pensacola, FL

MARCH 31

Prayer for Relief from Tormentors

Psalm 56:1–13

B E merciful to me, O God, for man would
      swallow me up;
  Fighting all day he oppresses me.
2 My enemies would hound *me* all day,
  For *there are* many who fight against me, O
    Most High.

3 Whenever I am afraid,
  I will trust in You.
4 In God (I will praise His word),
  In God I have put my trust;
  I will not fear.
  What can flesh do to me?

5 All day they twist my words;
  All their thoughts *are* against me for evil.
6 They gather together,
  They hide, they mark my steps,
  When they lie in wait for my life.
7 Shall they escape by iniquity?
  In anger cast down the peoples, O God!

8 You number my wanderings;
  Put my tears into Your bottle;
  Are they not in Your book?
9 When I cry out *to You,*
  Then my enemies will turn back;
  This I know, because God *is* for me.
10 In God (I will praise *His* word),
  In the LORD (I will praise *His* word),
11 In God I have put my trust;
  I will not be afraid.
  What can man do to me?

12 Vows *made* to You *are binding* upon me, O
    God;
  I will render praises to You,
13 For You have delivered my soul from death.
  Have You not *kept* my feet from falling,
  That I may walk before God
  In the light of the living?

DEVOTIONAL

I n this psalm, we see a man honest before the
Lord. David had some big enemies, men who
constantly oppressed, hounded, and fought him
(v. 2). They turned his words, thought about ways
to harm him, and watched his every move (vv.
5–6). What misery!

But do you notice what David chose to do?
Instead of complaining, retreating, or returning
evil for evil, he lifted praises to God, in whom he
had put his trust (vv. 4, 10, 12).

Several years ago I faced a specific spiritual
attack. Fear and what-ifs threatened to grip my
heart. Calling out praises for who God is became
a powerful weapon against the Enemy. Although
I did not know how the situation would resolve,
speaking aloud of God's love, faithfulness, truth,
power, and many other attributes brought peace
that He was in control.

Are you facing a situation that threatens to
swallow you up? I encourage you to read this
psalm aloud in prayer to God. David put his confidence in His Word. You can, too. We are in the
hands of the Mighty One. We have nothing to fear.

Dr. Ted Traylor, Olive Baptist Church
Pensacola, FL

APRIL I

Read James 1:1–12. What are some ways God has blessed you during times of trial?

_____

_____

_____

_____

_____

_____

_____

_____

_____

_____

The Ziphites helped Saul in his search to find David so that he could harm him. Who are the Ziphites in your life? Call their names before the Lord. Ask God to work in their hearts and for strength for the journey. And ask God to help you not be one of their rank in the life of another.

_____

_____

_____

_____

_____

_____

_____

_____

APRIL 2

Prayer for Safety from Enemies

Psalm 57:1–11

B E merciful to me, O God, be merciful to me!
For my soul trusts in You;
And in the shadow of Your wings I will make
my refuge,
Until *these* calamities have passed by.

2 I will cry out to God Most High,
To God who performs *all things* for me.

3 He shall send from heaven and save me;
He reproaches the one who would swallow
me up. Selah
God shall send forth His mercy and His truth.

4 My soul *is* among lions;
I lie *among* the sons of men
Who are set on fire,
Whose teeth *are* spears and arrows,
And their tongue a sharp sword.

5 Be exalted, O God, above the heavens;
Let Your glory *be* above all the earth.

6 They have prepared a net for my steps;
My soul is bowed down;
They have dug a pit before me;
Into the midst of it they *themselves* have fallen.
Selah

7 My heart is steadfast, O God, my heart is
steadfast;
I will sing and give praise.

8 Awake, my glory!
Awake, lute and harp!
I will awaken the dawn.

9 I will praise You, O Lord, among the peoples;
I will sing to You among the nations.

10 For Your mercy reaches unto the heavens,
And Your truth unto the clouds.

11 Be exalted, O God, above the heavens;
Let Your glory *be* above all the earth.

DEVOTIONAL

W here do you go when it seems like the whole
world is coming down on your head? When
it seems as though everyone is out to get you?

Most of us were picked on or bullied as kids.
When I was a little boy, I would run to my mother
and hide behind her, and she would protect me.
But as I grew up, I learned the safest place to be is
in the arms of the Lord.

In today's psalm, David was running from King
Saul. God had just delivered him from Gath (Ps. 56),
and he fled first to the cave of Adullam, and later to
a cave in Engedi (1 Sam. 22:1; 24). But as we read
Psalm 57, we note that whether at home, with the
sheep, in the palace, or in a cave, David's routine
never seemed to change: he would pray to the Lord
(vv. 1–6), sing praises to the Lord (vv. 7–11), and
exalt the Lord (vv. 5–11). While his circumstances
may have determined what he prayed, they did not
stop him from praying.

If we are faithfully praying, praising, and exalting the Lord, then we should have little trouble
trusting the Lord in all we do, say, or even suffer.
Remember His promise, "I will not leave you nor
forsake you" (Josh. 1:5). God is with you always, no
matter your circumstances.

Dr. Rob Zinn, Immanuel Baptist Church
Highland, CA

APRIL 3

The Just Judgment of the Wicked

Psalm 58:1–11

DO you indeed speak righteousness, you
silent ones?
Do you judge uprightly, you sons of men?

2 No, in heart you work wickedness;
You weigh out the violence of your hands in
the earth.

3 The wicked are estranged from the womb;
They go astray as soon as they are born,
speaking lies.

4 Their poison *is* like the poison of a serpent;
They are like the deaf cobra *that* stops its ear,

5 Which will not heed the voice of charmers,
Charming ever so skillfully.

6 Break their teeth in their mouth, O God!
Break out the fangs of the young lions, O LORD!

7 Let them flow away as waters *which* run
continually;
When he bends *his bow,*
Let his arrows be as if cut in pieces.

8 *Let them be* like a snail which melts away as it
goes,
Like a stillborn child of a woman, that they
may not see the sun.

9 Before your pots can feel *the burning* thorns,
He shall take them away as with a whirlwind,
As in His living and burning wrath.

10 The righteous shall rejoice when he sees the
vengeance;
He shall wash his feet in the blood of the
wicked,

11 So that men will say,
"Surely *there is* a reward for the righteous;
Surely He is God who judges in the earth."

DEVOTIONAL

This is a psalm of righteous anger written by
David. Most likely he penned this during his
exile as he watched Saul lead the nation of Israel
down a path of spiritual and political ruin by dis-
obeying God's law. Saul had gone astray and so
had his leaders. The result was innocent people
suffering because of unwise, unjust, and ungodly
leadership.

Similar warnings can be found in Proverbs
16:12, which reminds us, "It is an abomination
for kings to commit wickedness, for a throne is
established by righteousness," and Proverbs 29:2,
which says, "When the righteous are in authority,
the people rejoice; but when a wicked man rules,
the people groan."

However, in Psalm 58:11, David seems to find
comfort and reminds us there is a God who judges
the earth. Sometimes we suffer and many injustices will take place, but always remember God
knows and there is a day of judgment coming.
As someone said, "The sands of God's judgment
move slowly, but they move surely."

Dr. Rob Zinn, Immanuel Baptist Church
Highland, CA

APRIL 4

The Assured Judgment of the Wicked

Psalm 59:1–7

DELIVER me from my enemies, O my God;
Defend me from those who rise up against
me.

2 Deliver me from the workers of iniquity,
And save me from bloodthirsty men.

3 For look, they lie in wait for my life;
The mighty gather against me,
Not *for* my transgression nor *for* my sin, O LORD.

4 They run and prepare themselves through no
fault *of mine.*
Awake to help me, and behold!

5 You therefore, O LORD God of hosts, the God of
Israel,

Awake to punish all the nations;
Do not be merciful to any wicked
transgressors.   Selah

6 At evening they return,
They growl like a dog,
And go all around the city.

7 Indeed, they belch with their mouth;
Swords *are* in their lips;
For *they say,* "Who hears?"

DEVOTIONAL

The setting for this psalm is found in 1 Samuel
16:14 and 1 Samuel 19. The Spirit of the Lord
had departed from Saul, and Samuel had already
anointed David to be king. An evil spirit continued to move Saul to rage. Twice he had tried to pin
David to the wall with his spear, and now he sent
messengers to David's house to watch for him in
order to put him to death in the morning. Because
of Saul's fear and hatred of David, he was willing
to kill an innocent man. But the Lord used David's
wife to help him escape by letting him out the
window so he could run to Samuel.

This psalm can be divided into two parts:
God the Deliverer (vv. 1–9) and God the Judge
(vv. 10–17). As we look at these first seven verses
today, we find the assurance that no matter what
the circumstances, we have a God to whom we can
turn. In fact, our text is a great reminder of the
providence of God, who knows all the thoughts,
plans, and intentions of the heart and overrules
them for His glory and our good. Saul knew David
was innocent and didn't care. God knew David
was innocent and delivered him from Saul.

Note from 1 Samuel 19 that David didn't just sit
there in his house. He put his life in God's hands,
yes, but did what he needed to do to escape. James
reminds us that faith without works is dead
(2:17). We are to be doers of the Word, and David
acted on what he knew and could do.

As you read his descriptions of Saul's men in
verses 2–7, you not only see David's disdain but
also their character. However, David was on watch,
and God delivered him. If you're going to live,
walk, and witness for the Lord, you too will have
your enemies. Be on the alert and trust God to
take care of you.

Dr. Rob Zinn, Immanuel Baptist Church
Highland, CA

APRIL 5

God's Mercy

Psalm 59:8–17

8 But You, O Lord, shall laugh at them;
   You shall have all the nations in derision.

9 I will wait for You, O You his Strength;
   For God *is* my defense.

10 My God of mercy shall come to meet me;
   God shall let me see *my desire* on my enemies.

11 Do not slay them, lest my people forget;
   Scatter them by Your power,
   And bring them down,
   O Lord our shield.

12 *For* the sin of their mouth *and* the words of
        their lips,
   Let them even be taken in their pride,
   And for the cursing and lying *which* they speak.

13 Consume *them* in wrath, consume *them,*
   That they *may* not *be;*
   And let them know that God rules in Jacob
   To the ends of the earth.   Selah

14 And at evening they return,
   They growl like a dog,
   And go all around the city.

15 They wander up and down for food,
   And howl if they are not satisfied.

16 But I will sing of Your power;
   Yes, I will sing aloud of Your mercy in the morning;
   For You have been my defense
   And refuge in the day of my trouble.

17 To You, O my Strength, I will sing praises;
   For God *is* my defense,
   My God of mercy.

Yesterday we looked at God who is our Deliverer (Ps. 59:1–7). Today we see God who is the Judge. I have always taught the congregation I pastor that the principles of the Christian life are found in the New Testament, while many times the pictures of these principles are found in the Old Testament.

In James 5:7–12, you will find a passage where James is instructing believers how to face life's trials. What do you do when you are mistreated, hurt, abused, or attacked? Our natural tendencies are to retaliate, to return evil for evil, to get back at the person or persons who are causing the pain. James says that is not the way to respond. Rather, we are to (1) be patient, (2) strengthen our hearts, and (3) not complain. Well, how do we do that? By keeping our eyes focused on God and knowing He has: a plan, a purpose, and a reason.

Our hope is not in circumstances but in Him. And God will judge! Romans 12:17–19 says, "Repay none evil for evil. Have regard for good things in the sight of all men. If it is possible, as much as depends on you, live peaceably with all men. Beloved, do not avenge yourselves, but rather give place to wrath; for it is written, 'Vengeance is Mine, I will repay,' says the Lord." Is this not what David was doing in our text? He was patient, he strengthened his heart in the Lord (v. 17), and he asked God to judge. Twice he had the chance to kill Saul, but he would not. Instead, he waited on God. And, my beloved, so should we. You face your life trials best when you do it His way.

Dr. Rob Zinn, Immanuel Baptist Church
Highland, CA

APRIL 6

Urgent Prayer to Restore God's Favor

Psalm 60:1–12

O GOD, You have cast us off;
　You have broken us down;
You have been displeased;
Oh, restore us again!

2　You have made the earth tremble;
　You have broken it;
　Heal its breaches, for it is shaking.

3　You have shown Your people hard things;
　You have made us drink the wine of confusion.

4　You have given a banner to those who fear You,
　That it may be displayed because of the truth.
　　　　　　　　　　　　　　　　　Selah

5　That Your beloved may be delivered,
　Save *with* Your right hand, and hear me.

6　God has spoken in His holiness:
　"I will rejoice;
　I will divide Shechem
　And measure out the Valley of Succoth.

7　Gilead *is* Mine, and Manasseh *is* Mine;
　Ephraim also *is* the helmet for My head;
　Judah *is* My lawgiver.

8　Moab *is* My washpot;
　Over Edom I will cast My shoe;
　Philistia, shout in triumph because of Me."

9　Who will bring me *to* the strong city?
　Who will lead me to Edom?

10　*Is it* not You, O God, *who* cast us off?
　And You, O God, *who* did not go out with our
　　　　armies?

11　Give us help from trouble,

For the help of man *is* useless.

12　Through God we will do valiantly,
　For *it is* He *who* shall tread down our enemies.

DEVOTIONAL

Have you ever noticed that when something takes you by surprise, your first reaction is usually the wrong one? As spiritual as we think we are, we do not seem to be wired for the unexpected. Now, that does not mean we stay that way, or that our minds and spirits don't get in gear, and we do the right thing. It's just that when life throws us a curve ball, it takes us time to make an attitude adjustment.

This seems to be where we find King David and Israel in Psalm 60. If we put scripture together from 2 Samuel 8, 10, and 1 Chronicles 18, David was winning battles and making a name for himself. While he was in the north fighting the Arameans (Syrians), the Edomites attacked Israel from the south and did a great deal of damage. As you read Psalm 60, in verses 1–5, you see the people's reaction to the news. They felt that God was angry with them and had rejected them; they were stunned and dismayed. However, in verses 6–8, David got a word from God that their enemies would be defeated and he was quick to believe it. He sent Joab and his brother Abishai and the army south, standing on God's promise and trusting the Lord for victory (vv. 9–12). And that's exactly what happened.

David trusted in the Lord, and the Lord honored his faith. The storms will come, but remember, God is faithful. He didn't save you to spoil your life, but to bless you and be glorified through you. When the surprises come, stand on the promises of God.

Dr. Rob Zinn, Immanuel Baptist Church
Highland, CA

APRIL 7

Assurance of God's Eternal Protection

Psalm 61:1–8

H EAR my cry, O God;
Attend to my prayer.
2 From the end of the earth I will cry to You,
When my heart is overwhelmed;
Lead me to the rock that is higher than I.

3 For You have been a shelter for me,
A strong tower from the enemy.
4 I will abide in Your tabernacle forever;
I will trust in the shelter of Your wings. Selah

5 For You, O God, have heard my vows;
You have given *me* the heritage of those who
fear Your name.
6 You will prolong the king's life,
His years as many generations.
7 He shall abide before God forever.
Oh, prepare mercy and truth, *which* may
preserve him!

8 So I will sing praise to Your name forever,
That I may daily perform my vows.

DEVOTIONAL

T oday's psalm is one David could have written
on many different occasions when he was
in danger. However, based on the context, it was
most likely written during the rebellion of his son
Absalom recorded in 2 Samuel 15–18.

You will note that David prayed about God
sheltering him from the enemy (v. 3), prolong-
ing his life (v. 6), and securing his throne (v. 7; the
word *abide* means "enthroned"). Throughout his
life, David had faced many trials and dangerous

situations, and yet he never wavered in his faith
and trust in God. We could well ask why God
allowed His servant, "a man," 1 Samuel 13:14 says,
"after His own heart," to go through all he did. But
the same could be asked about Noah, Abraham,
Job, Joseph, the disciples, and others.

Could it be that God allows trials to grow us up
and teach us to trust Him? Let's be really honest.
When have your greatest times of spiritual growth
been—in the good times, or in the trials of life?
Listen, if we never had problems, then we would
never know that God could solve them.

David knew who his source of strength was. He
knew the promise God had made to him, and he
knew the love that God had for him. We can see
his cry for help and his confidence that God would
answer. He stood on the promises of God, and he
decided to sing praises to His name forever. The
more you know Him, the more you will trust Him.

Dr. Rob Zinn, Immanuel Baptist Church
Highland, CA

APRIL 8

What is the Lord doing in your life right now that is teaching you to trust Him?

_____

_____

_____

_____

_____

_____

_____

_____

_____

_____

_____

What promises in Scripture are you standing on right now?

_____

_____

_____

_____

_____

_____

_____

_____

_____

APRIL 9

Wait for the Salvation of God

Psalm 62:1–12

TRULY my soul silently *waits* for God;
From Him *comes* my salvation.

2 He only *is* my rock and my salvation;
He is my defense;
I shall not be greatly moved.

3 How long will you attack a man?
You shall be slain, all of you,
Like a leaning wall and a tottering fence.

4 They only consult to cast *him* down from his
high position;
They delight in lies;
They bless with their mouth,
But they curse inwardly. Selah

5 My soul, wait silently for God alone,
For my expectation *is* from Him.

6 He only *is* my rock and my salvation;
He is my defense;
I shall not be moved.

7 In God *is* my salvation and my glory;
The rock of my strength,
And my refuge, *is* in God.

8 Trust in Him at all times, you people;
Pour out your heart before Him;
God *is* a refuge for us. Selah

9 Surely men of low degree *are* a vapor,
Men of high degree *are* a lie;
If they are weighed on the scales,
They *are* altogether *lighter* than vapor.

10 Do not trust in oppression,
Nor vainly hope in robbery;
If riches increase,
Do not set *your* heart *on them.*

11 God has spoken once,
Twice I have heard this:
That power *belongs* to God.

12 Also to You, O Lord, *belongs* mercy;
For You render to each one according to his work.

DEVOTIONAL

Look closely at the repetitions in this wonderful psalm of David's. It's as if he can't praise his God long enough or loudly enough. David says God is his rock and that He is his salvation, defense, glory, strength, refuge, and the Owner of both power and mercy. He is a great God!

David wrote this psalm during one of the darkest periods of his life. He had all but lost his kingdom. It has been said that when God is all you have, that's when you find out He is all you need. I believe David would agree.

In light of his distress, how could David write and no doubt sing such a confident hymn? Because he had experienced the fulfilled promises of his God! He was the beneficiary of God's power demonstrated in the death of Goliath. He had felt God's restoring mercies in the incident of Uriah and Bathsheba. David knew he could trust God completely even in the face of powerful and ruthless men.

How about you, dear friend? Are you confident in God's promises? Do you know them? Are they yours, personal and precious? If they are, rejoice, for our God never changes. He will deliver on every promise He has ever made, and He has made many. Praise His name!

Dr. Johnny Hunt, First Baptist Church Woodstock
Woodstock, GA

APRIL 10

Joy in the Fellowship of God

Psalm 63:1–11

O GOD, You *are* my God;
Early will I seek You;
My soul thirsts for You;
My flesh longs for You
In a dry and thirsty land
Where there is no water.

2 So I have looked for You in the sanctuary,
To see Your power and Your glory.

3 Because Your lovingkindness *is* better than
life,
My lips shall praise You.

4 Thus I will bless You while I live;
I will lift up my hands in Your name.

5 My soul shall be satisfied as with marrow and
fatness,
And my mouth shall praise You with joyful
lips.

6 When I remember You on my bed,
I meditate on You in the *night* watches.

7 Because You have been my help,
Therefore in the shadow of Your wings I will
rejoice.

8 My soul follows close behind You;
Your right hand upholds me.

9 But those *who* seek my life, to destroy *it,*
Shall go into the lower parts of the earth.

10 They shall fall by the sword;
They shall be a portion for jackals.

11 But the king shall rejoice in God;
Everyone who swears by Him shall glory;

But the mouth of those who speak lies shall be
stopped.

DEVOTIONAL

This has been one of the most popular psalms in Christian history. David's inspired words have motivated several songwriters and musicians.

Of all the things I have done in life, nothing outweighs the importance of time spent alone reading, meditating on, and praying God's Word. The greatest return on investment I have ever known is from my morning quiet time with my heavenly Father.

David wrote this psalm while he was hiding from King Saul in caves near the Dead Sea, which is one of the most arid places on earth. I've been there, and it's the last place I would want to hide. Yet notice David's words. He is not complaining about a lack of water or even the heat. David states that his need, his thirst, is for the presence of his God. That's what he asked for and that is what he got. David identified God's presence as loving-kindness. He says it is better than life; in essence, more important than the water his body desperately needed.

We think we need so many things today, but we primarily need God's presence. He has promised to be with us always, so, like David, let's spend time with Him daily!

Dr. Johnny Hunt, First Baptist Church Woodstock
Woodstock, GA

APRIL II

Oppressed by the Wicked

Psalm 64:1–10

HEAR my voice, O God, in my meditation;
Preserve my life from fear of the enemy.

2 Hide me from the secret plots of the wicked,
From the rebellion of the workers of iniquity,

3 Who sharpen their tongue like a sword,
And bend *their bows to shoot* their arrows—
bitter words,

4 That they may shoot in secret at the blameless;
Suddenly they shoot at him and do not fear.

5 They encourage themselves *in an* evil matter;
They talk of laying snares secretly;
They say, "Who will see them?"

6 They devise iniquities:
"We have perfected a shrewd scheme."
Both the inward thought and the heart of man
are deep.

7 But God shall shoot at them *with* an arrow;
Suddenly they shall be wounded.

8 So He will make them stumble over their own
tongue;
All who see them shall flee away.

9 All men shall fear,
And shall declare the work of God;
For they shall wisely consider His doing.

10 The righteous shall be glad in the LORD, and
trust in Him.
And all the upright in heart shall glory.

DEVOTIONAL

While King David certainly had the lion's share of enemies and conflicts, many scholars believe this psalm is prophetic in nature referring to the end times when Israel will experience a Great Tribulation. As believers in Jesus Christ, we will be spared this time of Jacob's Trouble, but what Christian alive today doesn't believe those days can't be far off?

If you read the paper or catch the news on television or online, it's pretty easy to conclude that our world is growing more and more corrupt each day. The words of David in this psalm could just as easily be today's headlines; regularly we hear of "secret plots," "rebellion," "bitter words," and "shrewd scheme[s]" (vv. 2–3, 6). Today, as in David's day, the offenders believe they are hidden and invulnerable, but we know that judgment is certain. God's delay is not His approval. His timing is perfect, and a day is coming when God will deal with all "workers of iniquity" (v. 2).

The key phrase in this psalm is found in verse 9: "All men shall fear, and shall declare the work of God." We know the day is coming when every knee will bow before God and confess His Majesty (Phil. 2:9–11). Some will confess Him with jubilation and adoration, while others with consternation and condemnation. I know which camp I'm choosing!

Even though I can't wait for that day, I've started the celebration already by bowing my knee daily and worshiping Him with a heart of gratitude and expectancy. I'm going to be "glad in the LORD, and trust in Him" (Ps. 64:10). That's glory!

Won't you join me?

Dr. Johnny Hunt, First Baptist Church Woodstock
Woodstock, GA

APRIL 12

Praise to God for His Salvation

Psalm 65:1–13

P RAISE is awaiting You, O God, in Zion;
And to You the vow shall be performed.

² O You who hear prayer,
To You all flesh will come.

³ Iniquities prevail against me;
As for our transgressions,
You will provide atonement for them.

⁴ Blessed *is the man* You choose,
And cause to approach *You,*
That he may dwell in Your courts.
We shall be satisfied with the goodness of
Your house,
Of Your holy temple.

⁵ *By* awesome deeds in righteousness You will
answer us,
O God of our salvation,
You who are the confidence of all the ends of
the earth,
And of the far-off seas;

⁶ Who established the mountains by His strength,
Being clothed with power;

⁷ You who still the noise of the seas,
The noise of their waves,
And the tumult of the peoples.

⁸ They also who dwell in the farthest parts are
afraid of Your signs;
You make the outgoings of the morning and
evening rejoice.

⁹ You visit the earth and water it,
You greatly enrich it;

The river of God is full of water;
You provide their grain,
For so You have prepared it.

¹⁰ You water its ridges abundantly,
You settle its furrows;
You make it soft with showers,
You bless its growth.

¹¹ You crown the year with Your goodness,
And Your paths drip *with* abundance.

¹² They drop *on* the pastures of the wilderness,
And the little hills rejoice on every side.

¹³ The pastures are clothed with flocks;
The valleys also are covered with grain;
They shout for joy, they also sing.

DEVOTIONAL

W hen I admire the beauty of God's creation, I can only wonder what life will be like in the new heaven and new earth. It saddens me that so many are missing the universe's grandeur, each speck of it shouting out the glory of God.

Why do some see it while others can't? Because of the hardness of their hearts, where no praise for their Creator can be found! They are consumed with greed, which is idolatry; they serve themselves and a false god, mammon.

But a day is coming when everyone will praise our King and He will rule in righteousness. His reign will satisfy everyone, and His awesome deeds will bring confidence to His people.

That will be a day of rejoicing indeed, and by faith we can experience its peace right now as we worship our Creator. Let's praise the Lord for the wonderful future He has promised us!

Dr. Johnny Hunt, First Baptist Church Woodstock
Woodstock, GA

APRIL 13

Praise to God for His Awesome Works

Psalm 66:1–7

MAKE a joyful shout to God, all the earth!
² Sing out the honor of His name;
Make His praise glorious.

³ Say to God,
"How awesome are Your works!
Through the greatness of Your power
Your enemies shall submit themselves to You.

⁴ All the earth shall worship You
And sing praises to You;
They shall sing praises *to* Your name."   Selah

⁵ Come and see the works of God;
He is awesome *in His* doing toward the sons
of men.

⁶ He turned the sea into dry *land;*
They went through the river on foot.
There we will rejoice in Him.

⁷ He rules by His power forever;
His eyes observe the nations;
Do not let the rebellious exalt themselves.

Selah

DEVOTIONAL

The Bible is full of marvelous and miraculous things our Lord has done throughout the course of human history. He revealed His power through the nation of Israel, and He revealed His grace through His Son, Jesus Christ. He has slain nations and wept over them. He defeated the mighty armies of Egypt and emboldened the cowardly Gideon. Jesus took a ragtag band of commoners and turned the world upside down.

In spite of all God has shown us, many still refuse to acknowledge Him; not just His sovereignty, but even His very existence. But a day is coming when all the earth will recognize Him. David foresaw that day through the Holy Spirit and wrote this hymn of praise. It is a hymn you and I can sing today. David's reign was a foreshadowing of Christ's great reign yet to come, and as we sing of that day, our hearts should long for it because it will be incredible!

Still, we don't have to wait for that day to experience the reign of Christ. Jesus told Pilate that His kingdom was "not of this world" (John 18:36). Jesus has a far greater throne room than earth. Though "heaven and earth will pass away" (Matt. 24:35), our immortal spirits were created to live forever, and that's where Jesus desires to reign most. Yes, "the heavens declare the glory of God" (Ps. 19:1), and the wonders of the universe are mind boggling, but the greatest work God ever does is when He changes human hearts, when He redeems souls from slavery to sin and grants them adoption in His celestial family.

Have you experienced the life-changing power of God in your own heart? I remember the day He changed my life, and nothing would thrill me more than for you to let Him change yours as well. By faith you can call on Jesus to forgive you and save you (Rom. 10:9–13). He is anxiously waiting!

If you are already a believer, then recall the day He changed your life and revisit that experience. Praise the Lord for this great work He has done—it is a story that will never grow old. Tell it to everyone you can!

Dr. Johnny Hunt, First Baptist Church Woodstock
Woodstock, GA

APRIL 14

God's Continuing Goodness

Psalm 66:8–20

8 Oh, bless our God, you peoples!
And make the voice of His praise to be heard,

9 Who keeps our soul among the living,
And does not allow our feet to be moved.

10 For You, O God, have tested us;
You have refined us as silver is refined.

11 You brought us into the net;
You laid affliction on our backs.

12 You have caused men to ride over our heads;
We went through fire and through water;
But You brought us out to rich *fulfillment*.

13 I will go into Your house with burnt offerings;
I will pay You my vows,

14 Which my lips have uttered
And my mouth has spoken when I was in
trouble.

15 I will offer You burnt sacrifices of fat animals,
With the sweet aroma of rams;
I will offer bulls with goats.   Selah

16 Come *and* hear, all you who fear God,
And I will declare what He has done for my soul.

17 I cried to Him with my mouth,
And He was extolled with my tongue.

18 If I regard iniquity in my heart,
The Lord will not hear.

19 *But* certainly God has heard *me;*
He has attended to the voice of my prayer.

20 Blessed *be* God,
Who has not turned away my prayer,
Nor His mercy from me!

DEVOTIONAL

How many times have you heard or read, "God bless America," and what a great request it is. God certainly has blessed America; in fact, God has blessed every nation. Sometimes we think financial blessings are the highest form of blessing, but riches can be a burden. How many times has prosperity led a person and even a nation away from true God-worship?

In this psalm, David entreats us to bless God! Yes, it is about time we put the shoe on the other foot, about time we paused from always asking and start being a blessing to the only One worthy of being blessed. I love David's transparency in verse 14; haven't we all made promises to God in times of distress, and haven't we forgotten to fulfill those vows once the trouble was past? While we may not be able to repay our vows with burnt offerings (and thank God He doesn't want them), we have a far better payment in the sacrifice of our own lives. We are to present our bodies as living sacrifices, according to the apostle Paul (Rom. 12:1). How? By not forgetting God like the unredeemed do! By telling others about His good and perfect will!

Telling others about God's goodness was the natural outflow of David's heart (vv. 16–17), and it should be ours as well. Maybe that's why I shout so much from the pulpit. Maybe I just can't help it, and maybe I don't want to help it!

Dr. Johnny Hunt, First Baptist Church Woodstock
Woodstock, GA

 # APRIL 15

Take a moment to admire God's creative genius. What aspects of this universe do you admire the most? Make a list and praise Him for these things.

_____

_____

_____

_____

_____

_____

_____

_____

_____

_____

Think about a time God rescued you from distress or trouble. How did He minister to you through it? Briefly record the incident below, then thank God for His intervention.

_____

_____

_____

_____

_____

_____

_____

_____

_____

APRIL 16

An Invocation and a Doxology

Psalm 67:1–7

G OD be merciful to us and bless us,
And cause His face to shine upon us,   Selah
2 That Your way may be known on earth,
Your salvation among all nations.

3 Let the peoples praise You, O God;
Let all the peoples praise You.

4 Oh, let the nations be glad and sing for joy!
For You shall judge the people righteously,
And govern the nations on earth.   Selah

5 Let the peoples praise You, O God;
Let all the peoples praise You.

6 *Then* the earth shall yield her increase;
God, our own God, shall bless us.

7 God shall bless us,
And all the ends of the earth shall fear Him.

DEVOTIONAL

A merica is a divided nation. It does not take a close presidential election to recognize the increasing gap of ideas. Watch any cable news show on any cable news channel, and it does not matter whether you would put a D or an R or an I next to your name, someone will say something that will get under your skin. Politics or not, it is a part of our nature to draw conclusions and create perceptions about those different from us. It only takes the slightest contrast to trigger the sometimes ever-so-slight involuntary response of reservation and judgment. And yet God, the ultimate Judge of us and them, objectively and righteously judges the whole of creation on the same playing field.

When I read "all nations" or "the nations on earth" (vv. 2, 4), I think about the political and religious divide that affected the globe during the time this psalm was authored. For a people group so wrapped up in the nationalistic idea that God would save only Israel, these statements about salvation for the rest of the world are radical ideas. However, if you really grasp the concept of God's grace and blessing, if you truly understand what it takes to "be glad and sing with joy" (v. 4), then you know you cannot let differences get in the way of making known the glory of God to absolutely everyone.

We know what is coming. We know God "shall judge the people righteously" and "the ends of the earth shall fear Him" (vv. 4, 7). We know the only formula that stands a chance of bringing peace on earth, let alone in our personal lives, is the light of the gospel of Jesus Christ.

I guarantee you have someone in your life you think will never become a believer. You could probably name some people right now who force a giant eye roll or make your head shake just thinking about them. Do they deserve to miss out on the grace of God? Are the frustrations and discomforts so great to justify not sharing with them God's mercy and blessing . . . again and always? That co-worker, relative, friend, or foe who has given every indication they will say no needs you to finally let go and continually reveal the God you know.

If we agree with the author that it is a better goal to aim for all peoples to praise God instead of a mediocre "some," how much pride are you willing to set aside to do your part in helping the earth "yield her increase" (v. 6)?

Will Goodwin, Oak Leaf Church
Canton, GA

APRIL 17

The Glory of God in His Goodness

Psalm 68:1–10

L ET God arise,
  Let His enemies be scattered;
  Let those also who hate Him flee before Him.

2 As smoke is driven away,
   So drive *them* away;
   As wax melts before the fire,
   So let the wicked perish at the presence of God.

3 But let the righteous be glad;
   Let them rejoice before God;
   Yes, let them rejoice exceedingly.

4 Sing to God, sing praises to His name;
   Extol Him who rides on the clouds,
   By His name YAH,
   And rejoice before Him.

5 A father of the fatherless, a defender of widows,
   Is God in His holy habitation.

6 God sets the solitary in families;
   He brings out those who are bound into prosperity;
   But the rebellious dwell in a dry *land*.

7 O God, when You went out before Your people,
   When You marched through the wilderness,
                                      Selah

8 The earth shook;
   The heavens also dropped *rain* at the presence
     of God;
   Sinai itself *was moved* at the presence of God,
     the God of Israel.

9 You, O God, sent a plentiful rain,
   Whereby You confirmed Your inheritance,
   When it was weary.

10 Your congregation dwelt in it;
    You, O God, provided from Your goodness for
      the poor.

DEVOTIONAL

T he radio station was playing 80s music, and my wife, Jamie, was transported back to middle school dances and big hair. I probably would have been as well had I not mostly listened to Allies, Wayne Watson, and The Imperials during the same time period. Eventually, a song came on we both recognized and we belted it out. That is until we started paying attention to the words. We were in shock. It is amazing how much context is wrought with just a little bit of maturity.

Can you imagine the revival that would occur if that same scene took place in churches across America every Sunday? The first chord is struck and people stand with a little prompt from the music leader. The song is one of their favorites so they don't need to know the stanza or have to follow along with the potentially out-of-sync and misspelled words on the screen. Then, as if hearing the song for the first time, the God they are singing about becomes far more than a singable line in a catchy tune. He becomes the One who has gone before us to protect us and guide us. He becomes the One who scatters our problems. He becomes the One who provides for our every need. He becomes the One who deserves praise to His name!

When you sing to God, do you think about Him or the song you are singing? If we are to really exalt "Him who rides on the clouds" (v. 4), we must never forget why we sing and to whom we are singing.

Will Goodwin, Oak Leaf Church
Canton, GA

APRIL 18

The God of Our Salvation

Psalm 68:11–23

11 The Lord gave the word;
Great *was* the company of those who
proclaimed *it:*
12 "Kings of armies flee, they flee,
And she who remains at home divides the
spoil.
13 Though you lie down among the sheepfolds,
You will be like the wings of a dove covered
with silver,
And her feathers with yellow gold."
14 When the Almighty scattered kings in it,
It was *white* as snow in Zalmon.
15 A mountain of God *is* the mountain of
Bashan;
A mountain *of many* peaks *is* the mountain
of Bashan.
16 Why do you fume with envy, you mountains of
many peaks?
This is the mountain *which* God desires to
dwell in;
Yes, the LORD will dwell *in it* forever.
17 The chariots of God *are* twenty thousand,
Even thousands of thousands;
The Lord is among them *as in* Sinai, in the
Holy *Place.*
18 You have ascended on high,
You have led captivity captive;
You have received gifts among men,
Even *from* the rebellious,
That the LORD God might dwell *there.*

19 Blessed *be* the Lord,
Who daily loads us *with benefits,*
The God of our salvation! Selah
20 Our God *is* the God of salvation;
And to GOD the Lord *belong* escapes from death.
21 But God will wound the head of His enemies,
The hairy scalp of the one who still goes on in
his trespasses.
22 The Lord said, "I will bring back from Bashan,
I will bring *them* back from the depths of the sea,
23 That your foot may crush *them* in blood,
And the tongues of your dogs *may have* their
portion from *your* enemies."

DEVOTIONAL

Ever have one of those days when everything seems to go wrong? You wake up late. The dog got into the trash during the night. There is no more orange juice. Everyone else in the house woke up with an attitude. You forgot to set the garbage can by the curb. You dropped the iron on your toe. It's raining a monsoon outside. The kids missed the bus. And all of that before you leave for work. In my life, I have found not only do life's curve balls come constantly in every direction, but they come when I most need to stop and remember "the God of our salvation" (v. 19).

If God promises to "daily [load] us with benefits" (v. 19), we owe it to ourselves to begin each day with the proper focus and recognition. We have a new day because of God. We have the breath we breathe because of God. We have another chance to thank God for life now and life everlasting. Have you done that today?

Will Goodwin, Oak Leaf Church
Canton, GA

APRIL 19

Nothing Compares to God

Psalm 68:24–35

24 They have seen Your procession, O God,
The procession of my God, my King, into the
sanctuary.

25 The singers went before, the players on instruments *followed* after;
Among *them were* the maidens playing timbrels.

26 Bless God in the congregations,
The Lord, from the fountain of Israel.

27 There *is* little Benjamin, their leader,
The princes of Judah *and* their company,
The princes of Zebulun *and* the princes of
Naphtali.

28 Your God has commanded your strength;
Strengthen, O God, what You have done for us.

29 Because of Your temple at Jerusalem,
Kings will bring presents to You.

30 Rebuke the beasts of the reeds,
The herd of bulls with the calves of the peoples,
Till everyone submits himself with pieces
of silver.
Scatter the peoples *who* delight in war.

31 Envoys will come out of Egypt;
Ethiopia will quickly stretch out her hands
to God.

32 Sing to God, you kingdoms of the earth;
Oh, sing praises to the Lord,   Selah

33 To Him who rides on the heaven of heavens,
which were of old!
Indeed, He sends out His voice, a mighty voice.

34 Ascribe strength to God;

His excellence *is* over Israel,
And His strength *is* in the clouds.

35 O God, *You are* more awesome than Your holy
places.
The God of Israel *is* He who gives strength and
power to *His* people.
Blessed *be* God!

DEVOTIONAL

A few months after we were married, Jamie and I were driving around and ended up in a cul-de-sac by a creek in the very back of a brand-new neighborhood development. "Maybe one day," I said, dreaming about our family's future.

Several years later we were in the market for a larger home. Ironically, after searching for the right fit for months, we found ourselves back at that same neighborhood putting an offer on a resale not too far from that cul-de-sac. The offer fell through. It was frustrating until we realized we had planned a lot but prayed very little. So we changed strategies. We put it in God's hands and asked Him to demonstrate His strength and provision. A few days later we found out that a buyer had backed out of one of the last new houses in that same neighborhood. The builder was desperate to sell it and threw in a free fridge, washer and dryer, and several other upgrades throughout the house. Not only that, it was thousands of dollars less than the other house. Oh yeah, and it was in that cul-de-sac by the creek.

If you are relying on your own strength to solve your problems, you may very well miss out on the blessing God has planned for you. His way is always best.

Will Goodwin, Oak Leaf Church
Canton, GA

APRIL 20

An Urgent Plea for Help in Trouble

Psalm 69:1–12

SAVE me, O God!
For the waters have come up to *my* neck.

2 I sink in deep mire,
Where *there is* no standing;
I have come into deep waters,
Where the floods overflow me.

3 I am weary with my crying;
My throat is dry;
My eyes fail while I wait for my God.

4 Those who hate me without a cause
Are more than the hairs of my head;
They are mighty who would destroy me,
Being my enemies wrongfully;
Though I have stolen nothing,
I *still* must restore *it*.

5 O God, You know my foolishness;
And my sins are not hidden from You.

6 Let not those who wait for You, O Lord GOD of
hosts, be ashamed because of me;
Let not those who seek You be confounded
because of me, O God of Israel.

7 Because for Your sake I have borne reproach;
Shame has covered my face.

8 I have become a stranger to my brothers,
And an alien to my mother's children;

9 Because zeal for Your house has eaten me up,
And the reproaches of those who reproach You
have fallen on me.

10 When I wept *and chastened* my soul with fasting,
That became my reproach.

11 I also made sackcloth my garment;
I became a byword to them.

12 Those who sit in the gate speak against me,
And I *am* the song of the drunkards.

DEVOTIONAL

Several years ago I was hanging out with a group of friends when a buddy of mine said, and I quote, "Man, Will, you're not a conceited jerk at all." Was that a compliment? My friend went on to tell me that before he was my friend, he had made some incredible assumptions about me from across the room. Turns out, he was not the only one. Apparently, I was giving off a "conceited jerk" vibe while I thought I was just minding my own business. Since I was a Christian and people knew me as a Christian, being perceived as something some might consider to be the polar opposite of Christ was obviously something I needed to work on.

We do not get to carry the label "Christian" just because we believe in a god but are not Jewish or Muslim. It is not enough to wear a "Do the Jew" T-shirt or have a fish emblem on your car. We represent the brand that has cornered the market on hope and life everlasting. So when one who truly wants to represent Jesus in everything he does finds out people are making rash judgments about his character "without a cause" (v. 4), it is no wonder he loses his voice crying out to God, "Let not those who seek You be confounded because of me" (v. 6).

How do you respond when you know someone thinks less of you than they should? Do you create a list of reasons why it is their fault and not yours, or do you appeal to God to restore the example you committed to live by when you decided to follow Christ?

Will Goodwin, Oak Leaf Church
Canton, GA

APRIL 21

A Plea for God's Mercy

Psalm 69:13–21

13 But as for me, my prayer *is* to You,
O Lord, *in* the acceptable time;
O God, in the multitude of Your mercy,
Hear me in the truth of Your salvation.

14 Deliver me out of the mire,
And let me not sink;
Let me be delivered from those who hate me,
And out of the deep waters.

15 Let not the floodwater overflow me,
Nor let the deep swallow me up;
And let not the pit shut its mouth on me.

16 Hear me, O Lord, for Your lovingkindness *is*
good;
Turn to me according to the multitude of Your
tender mercies.

17 And do not hide Your face from Your servant,
For I am in trouble;
Hear me speedily.

18 Draw near to my soul, *and* redeem it;
Deliver me because of my enemies.

19 You know my reproach, my shame, and my
dishonor;
My adversaries *are* all before You.

20 Reproach has broken my heart,
And I am full of heaviness;
I looked *for someone* to take pity, but *there
was* none;
And for comforters, but I found none.

21 They also gave me gall for my food,
And for my thirst they gave me vinegar to drink.

DEVOTIONAL

I used to be a thief. Stealing things was my hobby in elementary school. I was pretty good at it too—never once got caught. After I stopped stealing and "rededicated my life" a few summers later, I never thought what I stole amounted to much and therefore never lost a night's sleep over it. With "I was a minor" and some other lame excuses, I swept that part of my life under a rug, believing it to be a forgotten smudge on a relatively squeaky-clean childhood.

Not until college, when I started to get a deeper understanding of the glory of God and forgiveness, did I begin to better comprehend conviction and holiness. Regardless of what caused the author to pen this poem, the words are as fitting a plea to God for help in the most desperate of circumstances as they are a cry of remorse over the smallest infraction that contradicts the character of God.

The more I see God for who He is, the more "deliver me out of the mire" is the burden I feel when I let my wife down (v. 14). The more I recognize my place in creation, the more "reproach has broken my heart" is the conviction that follows losing patience with my children (v. 20). The more I move to where God wants me to be, the more "I am full of heaviness" becomes an honest look at areas in my life I still have not completely surrendered (v. 20).

How do you address sin in your life? Do you ignore it and sweep it under the rug or do you confront it and lay it at the Father's feet? Take heart in knowing God has a multitude of mercies to pour over our shame, big or small, if we come to Him with our troubles.

*Will Goodwin, Oak Leaf Church
Canton, GA*

APRIL 22

The passages we read this week remind us how much God values and loves His creation. What are some ways you can prove how much God is worth to you?

_____

_____

_____

_____

_____

_____

_____

_____

_____

_____

_____

What are some areas in your life you can confess right now that could use some spiritual rejuvenation?

_____

_____

_____

_____

_____

_____

_____

_____

_____

APRIL 23

Seek God and Live

Psalm 69:22–36

22 Let their table become a snare before them,
And their well-being a trap.

23 Let their eyes be darkened, so that they do
not see;
And make their loins shake continually.

24 Pour out Your indignation upon them,
And let Your wrathful anger take hold of them.

25 Let their dwelling place be desolate;
Let no one live in their tents.

26 For they persecute the *ones* You have struck,
And talk of the grief of those You have
wounded.

27 Add iniquity to their iniquity,
And let them not come into Your righteousness.

28 Let them be blotted out of the book of the
living,
And not be written with the righteous.

29 But I *am* poor and sorrowful;
Let Your salvation, O God, set me up on high.

30 I will praise the name of God with a song,
And will magnify Him with thanksgiving.

31 *This* also shall please the LORD better than an
ox *or* bull,
Which has horns and hooves.

32 The humble shall see *this and* be glad;
And you who seek God, your hearts shall live.

33 For the LORD hears the poor,
And does not despise His prisoners.

34 Let heaven and earth praise Him,
The seas and everything that moves in them.

35 For God will save Zion
And build the cities of Judah,
That they may dwell there and possess it.

36 Also, the descendants of His servants shall
inherit it,
And those who love His name shall dwell in it.

DEVOTIONAL

One of the benefits of our salvation is the union we have with Christ. When we trust Jesus alone to save us, His life, death, and resurrection become our life, death, and resurrection.

David foreshadowed this union in Psalm 69. He showed that oneness with Christ means more than the "easy life." If we truly unite with Christ in salvation, we will also join with Him in the persecution and suffering He endured (1 Pet. 2:20–24).

You may be thinking, *How in the world can union with Christ be beneficial if it means I must endure persecution and suffering?* That is a great question, and one that David answered: "And you who seek God, your hearts shall live" (v. 32). Those who truly seek God will live forever because "in Christ" they are already victorious over the persecution and suffering that will come their way. Though evildoers may crowd around you, in Christ you have already overcome! For this reason, "Let heaven and earth praise Him, the seas and everything that moves in them" (v. 34).

Those who do evil against you may never be brought to justice on this earth, but justice will come when the King returns. Regardless of the timing of His coming, in Christ you can persevere now. Praise God for your union with Jesus, and rest in the victory He won at the cross on your behalf.

Peyton Hill, Highland Baptist Church
Grove City, OH

APRIL 24

Prayer for Relief from Adversaries

Psalm 70:1–5

MAKE *haste*, O God, to deliver me!
Make haste to help me, O LORD!

2 Let them be ashamed and confounded
Who seek my life;
Let them be turned back and confused
Who desire my hurt.

3 Let them be turned back because of their shame,
Who say, "Aha, aha!"

4 Let all those who seek You rejoice and be glad
in You;
And let those who love Your salvation say
continually,
"Let God be magnified!"

5 But I *am* poor and needy;
Make haste to me, O God!
You *are* my help and my deliverer;
O LORD, do not delay.

DEVOTIONAL

There are two types of people in Scripture: those who run from God and those who run to God. These two groups of individuals are the focus of our psalm. On one hand we have those rebelling against God by seeking the demise of His people. On the other hand we have the people whom God has redeemed. These call out to Him for deliverance. They realize that they are spiritually bankrupt and in need of salvation. Their cry is, "Make haste, O God, to deliver me!" (v. 1).

The question we must all consider is this: Have I come to understand my need for Jesus? Each of us must answer as we make our way through this life. When you see that you need Him, you can then cry out to Him to deliver you.

The psalmist cried out for the quick salvation of the Lord, and in his cry we find the desperation of a sinner for the graceful touch of the Almighty. In this hour, amidst the craziness of life, people need the Lord. O God, deliver us!

Those who are rescued by God and seek His glory can say in the face of hard times that they "rejoice . . . in [Him]" (v. 4). True gladness of heart is found in the Lord alone. When temptations come and tribulation is all around, there will be little room to rejoice in our situation. When the culture becomes more and more godless, there will be little room to be glad in our environment. But in spite of our situation and environment, we still serve a God who has delivered us from sin, death, and Satan. Because of this, we rejoice and are glad. He alone brings us joy!

Sometimes it seems as if the world mocks us at every turn. This is the life of a disciple. Yet we are encouraged to seek the face of God even when the world mocks us. We are to seek God's glory despite the fact that our adversaries seek our demise. Our cry must be, "Let God be magnified!" (v. 4). We need to ask ourselves: Is He being magnified in my life? Is He being magnified in my family? Is He being magnified among my neighbors? Is He being magnified among my co-workers?

There are adversaries all around, but let us seek the glory of the Lord and the exaltation of His name above all else. He has rescued us so that we can go about our day magnifying His precious name.

Peyton Hill, Highland Baptist Church
Grove City, OH

APRIL 25

God, the Rock of Salvation

Psalm 71:1–13

IN You, O Lord, I put my trust;
Let me never be put to shame.

2 Deliver me in Your righteousness, and cause
me to escape;
Incline Your ear to me, and save me.

3 Be my strong refuge,
To which I may resort continually;
You have given the commandment to
save me,
For You *are* my rock and my fortress.

4 Deliver me, O my God, out of the hand of the
wicked,
Out of the hand of the unrighteous and
cruel man.

5 For You are my hope, O Lord God;
You are my trust from my youth.

6 By You I have been upheld from birth;
You are He who took me out of my mother's
womb.
My praise *shall be* continually of You.

7 I have become as a wonder to many,
But You *are* my strong refuge.

8 Let my mouth be filled *with* Your praise
And with Your glory all the day.

9 Do not cast me off in the time of old age;
Do not forsake me when my strength fails.

10 For my enemies speak against me;
And those who lie in wait for my life take
counsel together,

11 Saying, "God has forsaken him;

Pursue and take him, for *there is* none to
deliver *him.*"

12 O God, do not be far from me;
O my God, make haste to help me!

13 Let them be confounded *and* consumed
Who are adversaries of my life;
Let them be covered *with* reproach and
dishonor
Who seek my hurt.

DEVOTIONAL

WHAT a joy it is for the believer to cry out to
God for help when times of trouble draw
near! There is nowhere safer than the arms of the
loving Savior who made us and redeemed us for
His glory.

In today's society we are plagued with an
individualistic mind-set. Rather than resting in
the dependence we were created to have, we rest
instead in our own wants and passions. This began
in the garden with the first man and woman, and
it continues today. The first rebellion against God
is no different from the rebellion we experience
today. Just as Eve chose her own way over her
Creator's, we choose autonomy over submission to
a holy God. Yet the psalmist reminds us that God
is our rock, fortress, and hope. We were created to
trust Him and seek Him above our own desires.

When trouble comes, to whom do you cling?
When your enemies are all around mocking you,
to whom do you run? Let us be a people who trade
our independence for a relationship with the
Creator who made us. Let us find our strength in
the Redeemer who rescued us from ourselves.

Peyton Hill, Highland Baptist Church
Grove City, OH

APRIL 26

Missions Begins with Praise

Psalm 71:14–24

14 But I will hope continually,
And will praise You yet more and more.
15 My mouth shall tell of Your righteousness
And Your salvation all the day,
For I do not know *their* limits.
16 I will go in the strength of the Lord God;
I will make mention of Your righteousness, of
Yours only.

17 O God, You have taught me from my youth;
And to this *day* I declare Your wondrous works.
18 Now also when *I am* old and grayheaded,
O God, do not forsake me,
Until I declare Your strength to *this* generation,
Your power to everyone *who* is to come.

19 Also Your righteousness, O God, *is* very high,
You who have done great things;
O God, who *is* like You?
20 *You,* who have shown me great and severe
troubles,
Shall revive me again,
And bring me up again from the depths of the
earth.
21 You shall increase my greatness,
And comfort me on every side.

22 Also with the lute I will praise You—
And Your faithfulness, O my God!
To You I will sing with the harp,
O Holy One of Israel.
23 My lips shall greatly rejoice when I sing to You,
And my soul, which You have redeemed.

24 My tongue also shall talk of Your
righteousness all the day long;
For they are confounded,
For they are brought to shame
Who seek my hurt.

DEVOTIONAL

When we think of missions, it is almost impossible to avoid the Great Commission in Matthew 28:18–20. We also quote Acts 1:8 as a reminder that it is God's Spirit who empowers us for the task of missions. But the missionary call was not birthed in the New Testament. God has been a missionary God from the beginning. He called Abram with the promise than he and his people would be a blessing to the rest of the world by declaring the greatness of their God to the nations of the world (Gen. 12:1–3). We find this in Exodus too. God delivered His people in order for them to be a missionary nation. In the New Testament, Peter told believers that we have been called out of darkness and into marvelous light in order to "proclaim the praises of [God]" (1 Pet. 2:9).

There is a call to missions in the psalmist's cry of praise to the Lord. He declared that he would tell of the works of God and declare the strength of the Lord. In essence, this is missions. To be on a mission, we must tell the world who God is and what He has done in forgiving us of our sins through the life, death, and resurrection of Jesus Christ. When we make disciples, we simply tell of the works of the Lord and call people to respond in faith. Let us continue to praise God for His salvation, but let our praise go forth beyond our church walls and into the far corners of the earth!

Peyton Hill, Highland Baptist Church
Grove City, OH

APRIL 27

Glory of the Messiah's Reign

Psalm 72:1–11

G IVE the king Your judgments, O God,
And Your righteousness to the king's Son.

2 He will judge Your people with righteousness,
And Your poor with justice.

3 The mountains will bring peace to the people,
And the little hills, by righteousness.

4 He will bring justice to the poor of the people;
He will save the children of the needy,
And will break in pieces the oppressor.

5 They shall fear You
As long as the sun and moon endure,
Throughout all generations.

6 He shall come down like rain upon the grass
before mowing,
Like showers *that* water the earth.

7 In His days the righteous shall flourish,
And abundance of peace,
Until the moon is no more.

8 He shall have dominion also from sea to sea,
And from the River to the ends of the earth.

9 Those who dwell in the wilderness will bow
before Him,
And His enemies will lick the dust.

10 The kings of Tarshish and of the isles
Will bring presents;
The kings of Sheba and Seba
Will offer gifts.

11 Yes, all kings shall fall down before Him;
All nations shall serve Him.

DEVOTIONAL

A lthough the psalm at hand is usually attributed to Solomon, the king who came to reign after his father David's rule, we find as we read that there is a greater King in view. Solomon sought wisdom from God, and there was a King coming who would be called Wisdom. Solomon sought justice from God, and there was a King coming who would be called Just. Solomon sought righteousness from God, and there was a King coming who would be called Righteous. That King has come, and His name is Jesus!

The rulers of the world have been placed in positions of power to keep order in creation, and believers are instructed to submit to these authorities (1 Pet. 2:13). However, the purpose for which these kings and rulers have been given their positions is not merely for the upkeep of the cosmos. The purpose of all kings is to point to the true King who has come once and will come again in all of His glory. This King, Jesus, will execute perfect justice. He will be feared and worshiped. All other kings will bow at His feet, and He will have dominion over all. King Jesus will cause His enemies to fall, and all praise and honor and glory will be due His mighty name.

Jesus is the fulfillment of all current kingships. Our rulers point to Christ in that they have been placed in positions of authority over us. Yet as sinners they fail in their attempts to rule with justice and righteousness. Jesus is the only King who is right in all His ways. Trust that the justice and righteousness that is lacking today will be found in King Jesus at His coming.

Peyton Hill, Highland Baptist Church
Grove City, OH

APRIL 28

The Promise of God

Psalm 72:12–20

¹² For He will deliver the needy when he cries,
The poor also, and *him* who has no helper.

¹³ He will spare the poor and needy,
And will save the souls of the needy.

¹⁴ He will redeem their life from oppression and
violence;
And precious shall be their blood in His sight.

¹⁵ And He shall live;
And the gold of Sheba will be given to Him;
Prayer also will be made for Him continually,
And daily He shall be praised.

¹⁶ There will be an abundance of grain in the
earth,
On the top of the mountains;
Its fruit shall wave like Lebanon;
And *those* of the city shall flourish like grass
of the earth.

¹⁷ His name shall endure forever;
His name shall continue as long as the sun.
And *men* shall be blessed in Him;
All nations shall call Him blessed.

¹⁸ Blessed *be* the LORD God, the God of Israel,
Who only does wondrous things!

¹⁸ And blessed *be* His glorious name forever!
And let the whole earth be filled *with* His
glory.
Amen and Amen.

²⁰ The prayers of David the son of Jesse are
ended.

DEVOTIONAL

The cry of our hearts is to be, "Blessed be the LORD God, the God of Israel, who only does wondrous things! And blessed be His glorious name forever! And let the whole earth be filled with His glory" (vv. 18–19). Our Lord has indeed done wondrous things, and He is to be praised for them. When the needy have cried out to Him, He has come to their aid. When the poor have begged for mercy, they have found it in Him. He has done great things!

It is essential to understand the object of God's goodness. If we simply praise God for what He has done for others, we will lose the personal touch of Scripture. It is not merely the needy over there or the poor over here who have been helped. You are the needy one! You are the poor one! Yet in Him you will find help!

Upon realizing that we are the ones in need of God's touch, we must respond in praise. God has been good to us, and for that we must praise His name. Let the whole earth praise Him! Although many will lose their lives in proclaiming the excellencies of Christ, God will be glorified, and they will find eternal rest with Him in the new heavens and the new earth.

May we never forget that it is for us that God has come. He has come for the sick, the needy, the poor, and the restless. Who are these? The answer is a poor sinner such as you and me. Christ came for us, and we need to praise His name because He did.

Peyton Hill, Highland Baptist Church
Grove City, OH

 # APRIL 29

In the book of Psalms, you have seen Jesus Christ put forth as the great King who has come to reign over His creation. In what ways have you rebelled against His kingdom by being the king of your own life?

_____

_____

_____

_____

_____

_____

_____

_____

_____

The mission of God is to make disciples, and we do that by proclaiming His excellencies to our family, friends, co-workers, neighbors, and all nations. What has God radically changed in you through the blood of His Son that you can proclaim to those around you today?

_____

_____

_____

_____

_____

_____

_____

_____

APRIL 30

The Tragedy of the Wicked

Psalm 73:1–14

TRULY God *is* good to Israel,
To such as are pure in heart.

2 But as for me, my feet had almost stumbled;
My steps had nearly slipped.

3 For I *was* envious of the boastful,
When I saw the prosperity of the wicked.

4 For *there are* no pangs in their death,
But their strength *is* firm.

5 They *are* not in trouble *as other* men,
Nor are they plagued like *other* men.

6 Therefore pride serves as their necklace;
Violence covers them *like* a garment.

7 Their eyes bulge with abundance;
They have more than heart could wish.

8 They scoff and speak wickedly *concerning*
oppression;
They speak loftily.

9 They set their mouth against the heavens,
And their tongue walks through the earth.

10 Therefore his people return here,
And waters of a full *cup* are drained by them.

11 And they say, "How does God know?
And is there knowledge in the Most High?"

12 Behold, these *are* the ungodly,
Who are always at ease;
They increase *in* riches.

13 Surely I have cleansed my heart *in* vain,
And washed my hands in innocence.

14 For all day long I have been plagued,
And chastened every morning.

DEVOTIONAL

A great temptation threatens to overtake us at times. The temptation is to doubt God's goodness toward us and envy the lives of the wicked. Those who reject God and are consumed by the desires of their humanity often appear to have more success than the people of God. We watch them enjoy possessions we dream of having and practices we know are wrong but appear to be pleasurable.

Satan places within the crevice of contemplation the thought, *That looks like fun. I am missing out on life.* Don't believe that lie! Sure, the wicked appear at times to prosper while the redeemed suffer, but that is not the whole story

My mother has Alzheimer's. She is a godly woman. Mom does not even know her children and grandchildren anymore. It is easy to think, *Why is this happening? Others who have not served Jesus like my mom has are doing great. They are enjoying their families and loving life.*

The fact is, God is good to us. Even as the psalmist contemplated this dilemma, he knew the goodness of God toward Israel. The word *good* in verse 1 encompasses all the blessings God had given to Israel. As Christians, we are blessed with the grace of redemption. The wicked, who at times prosper on earth, will one day experience the horrors of hell. We have it great, brothers and sisters. We belong to the one true God and have an inheritance reserved for us. Do not be consumed by the smoke screens of Satan. Count your blessings today!

Mike Orr, First Baptist Church
Chipley, FL

MAY 1

The Blessedness of Trust in God

Psalm 73:15–28

15 If I had said, "I will speak thus,"
  Behold, I would have been untrue to the
    generation of Your children.

16 When I thought *how* to understand this,
  It *was* too painful for me—

17 Until I went into the sanctuary of God;
  Then I understood their end.

18 Surely You set them in slippery places;
  You cast them down to destruction.

19 Oh, how they are *brought* to desolation, as in a
    moment!
  They are utterly consumed with terrors.

20 As a dream when *one* awakes,
  So, Lord, when You awake,
  You shall despise their image.

21 Thus my heart was grieved,
  And I was vexed in my mind.

22 I *was* so foolish and ignorant;
  I was *like* a beast before You.

23 Nevertheless I *am* continually with You;
  You hold *me* by my right hand.

24 You will guide me with Your counsel,
  And afterward receive me *to* glory.

25 Whom have I in heaven *but You?*
  And *there is* none upon earth *that* I desire
    besides You.

26 My flesh and my heart fail;
  But God *is* the strength of my heart and my
    portion forever.

27 For indeed, those who are far from You shall
    perish;
  You have destroyed all those who desert You
    for harlotry.

28 But *it is* good for me to draw near to God;
  I have put my trust in the Lord GOD,
  That I may declare all Your works.

DEVOTIONAL

Things are not always as they appear. Such is the case with the wicked. If the psalmist had relied merely on emperical evidence, he would have concluded that it is best to be wicked and that we will enjoy life better when pursuing the pleasures founded by human desire. He would have been wrong.

In the context of worship and fellowship with God, a revelation came to him. Wickedness leads to misery, suffering, and eternal destruction. Our perspective always becomes clearer in the presence of God. He speaks through His Word to give us true understanding.

God's people are blessed. They are strengthened and protected by Him (vv. 23–26). They are guided by the counsel of God to live lives that are effective. His people experience eternal life, and heaven awaits the redeemed of God.

I wrote yesterday of my mom's affliction. My mom may suffer now, but one day she will experience healing when she arrives in heaven. My mom's mind will be sharper than ever before. She will know her children and her grandchildren. I praise Him as I write! We are blessed! Trust in the Lord.

Mike Orr, First Baptist Church
Chipley, FL

MAY 2

A Plea for Relief from Oppressors

Psalm 74:1–8

O GOD, why have You cast *us* off forever?
Why does Your anger smoke against the
sheep of Your pasture?

2 Remember Your congregation, *which* You have
purchased of old,
The tribe of Your inheritance, *which* You have
redeemed—
This Mount Zion where You have dwelt.

3 Lift up Your feet to the perpetual desolations.
The enemy has damaged everything in the
sanctuary.

4 Your enemies roar in the midst of Your
meeting place;
They set up their banners *for* signs.

5 They seem like men who lift up
Axes among the thick trees.

6 And now they break down its carved work, all
at once,
With axes and hammers.

7 They have set fire to Your sanctuary;
They have defiled the dwelling place of Your
name to the ground.

8 They said in their hearts,
"Let us destroy them altogether."
They have burned up all the meeting places of
God in the land.

DEVOTIONAL

This psalm was written in the midst of great
suffering. Jerusalem had experienced devastation and the temple had been destroyed. This
could be a reference to the destruction unleashed
by Nebuchadnezzar. The chaos had caused the
psalmist to cry out to God with the question,
"Why have You cast us off forever?" (v. 1). As the
psalm progresses, it becomes clear that he actually possessed hope of a recovery.

Two very sobering truths come from these
verses. First, God chastens His people. The reality of God punishing His people is often ignored
and despised by Christians today. God is longsuffering and slow to anger, but He does discipline
His people. We get angry with God and complain
about our circumstances; however, often our own
disobedience is the cause. God chastens because
He loves us and desires us to return to fellowship
with Him. Our response to discipline must be
repentance and surrender to His will.

Second, to be out of fellowship with God and
under His discipline is terrifying. The writer
of Hebrews calls it painful (12:11). The truth
revealed in the psalm is a reminder to be obedient
and have a healthy, reverential fear of God.

This is certainly not popular teaching in our
day, but it is true and beneficial. The best place to
live is dead center of our Lord's will.

Mike Orr, First Baptist Church
Chipley, FL

MAY 3

The Benefits of Discipline

Psalm 74:9–23

9 We do not see our signs;
   There is no longer any prophet;
   Nor *is there* any among us who knows how
        long.
10 O God, how long will the adversary reproach?
   Will the enemy blaspheme Your name forever?
11 Why do You withdraw Your hand, even Your
        right hand?
   Take it out of Your bosom and destroy *them.*
12 For God *is* my King from of old,
   Working salvation in the midst of the earth.
13 You divided the sea by Your strength;
   You broke the heads of the sea serpents in the
        waters.
14 You broke the heads of Leviathan in pieces,
   And gave him *as* food to the people inhabiting
        the wilderness.
15 You broke open the fountain and the flood;
   You dried up mighty rivers.
16 The day *is* Yours, the night also *is* Yours;
   You have prepared the light and the sun.
17 You have set all the borders of the earth;
   You have made summer and winter.

18 Remember this, *that* the enemy has
        reproached, O Lord,
   And *that* a foolish people has blasphemed
        Your name.
19 Oh, do not deliver the life of Your turtledove to
        the wild beast!
   Do not forget the life of Your poor forever.

20 Have respect to the covenant;
   For the dark places of the earth are full of the
        haunts of cruelty.
21 Oh, do not let the oppressed return ashamed!
   Let the poor and needy praise Your name.
22 Arise, O God, plead Your own cause;
   Remember how the foolish man reproaches
        You daily.
23 Do not forget the voice of Your enemies;
   The tumult of those who rise up against You
        increases continually.

DEVOTIONAL

The experience of suffering under God's discipline benefits us in many ways. Two occur in these verses. First, we recall the power, knowledge, and greatness of God (vv. 12–17). Second, we are driven to pray (vv. 18–23). This attitude and action must be continual elements of our lives.

While experiencing God's judgment, the psalmist recalled the greatness of God: "You divided the sea by Your strength" (v. 13). He remembered that He is the Creator of the universe: "You have set all the borders of the earth" (vv. 16–17). The psalmist prayed for deliverance, knowing God was his only hope. When we remember God's greatness and cry out to Him in prayer, it is evidence of a return to Him. Our loving Father, in His omniscience, will allow us to stay in the suffering until we are completely surrendered to Him and He has accomplished His purpose in us. Rest assured He will not forget you!

Mike Orr, First Baptist Church
Chipley, FL

MAY 4

God's Righteous Judgment

Psalm 75:1–10

WE give thanks to You, O God, we give thanks!
For Your wondrous works declare *that* Your name is near.

2 "When I choose the proper time,
I will judge uprightly.

3 The earth and all its inhabitants are dissolved;
I set up its pillars firmly.   Selah

4 "I said to the boastful, 'Do not deal boastfully,'
And to the wicked, 'Do not lift up the horn.

5 Do not lift up your horn on high;
Do *not* speak with a stiff neck.'"

6 For exaltation *comes* neither from the east
Nor from the west nor from the south.

7 But God *is* the Judge:
He puts down one,
And exalts another.

8 For in the hand of the LORD *there is* a cup,
And the wine is red;
It is fully mixed, and He pours it out;
Surely its dregs shall all the wicked of the earth
Drain *and* drink down.

9 But I will declare forever,
I will sing praises to the God of Jacob.

10 "All the horns of the wicked I will also cut off,
But the horns of the righteous shall be exalted."

When we watch the news it can be very depressing. Horrific acts of evil are committed daily. Uncertainty looms with the economy, and one tragedy after another occurs. As a result, we are often tempted with anxiety. Believers are not to be anxious but to pray about everything (Phil. 4:6). But we battle to keep anxiety at bay. In addition, the skeptics ponder the problem of evil in the world and scoffingly demand to know why God does not do something about all the suffering.

The psalmist praised God even in dismal circumstances because he knew God would ultimately judge the wicked. The curse of sin will end, and evil will be eradicated. All this will happen in God's timing (v. 2).

The Lord rules even when all appears out of control. Remember, He is on His throne.

Mike Orr, First Baptist Church
Chipley, FL

MAY 5

The Majesty of God in Judgment

Psalm 76:1–12

I N Judah God *is* known;
His name *is* great in Israel.

2 In Salem also is His tabernacle,
And His dwelling place in Zion.

3 There He broke the arrows of the bow,
The shield and sword of battle.   Selah

4 You *are* more glorious and excellent
Than the mountains of prey.

5 The stouthearted were plundered;
They have sunk into their sleep;
And none of the mighty men have found the
use of their hands.

6 At Your rebuke, O God of Jacob,
Both the chariot and horse were cast into a
dead sleep.

7 You, Yourself, *are* to be feared;
And who may stand in Your presence
When once You are angry?

8 You caused judgment to be heard from
heaven;
The earth feared and was still,

9 When God arose to judgment,
To deliver all the oppressed of the earth. Selah

10 Surely the wrath of man shall praise You;
With the remainder of wrath You shall gird
Yourself.

11 Make vows to the LORD your God, and pay
them;
Let all who are around Him bring presents to
Him who ought to be feared.

12 He shall cut off the spirit of princes;
He is awesome to the kings of the earth.

DEVOTIONAL

T he psalm for today communicates that God is fully capable of rescuing His people and judging the wicked. There is no force in existence that can stand against His power (v. 7). God has delivered His people in the past, He does so in the present, and He will bring our ultimate deliverance in the future.

Our Lord delivers us from the prince of darkness, our ultimate Enemy. He delivers us from human oppressors who are inspired by the devil. He delivers us from and through tribulation in this life. One day all who oppress the people of God will be judged, and our deliverance will be complete.

The loving Lord who saved you is able to handle your circumstances. Trust Him to be your deliverer and avenger (Rom. 12:19).

Mike Orr, First Baptist Church
Chipley, FL

 MAY 6

What promises from the readings this week act as weapons against the temptation to envy the wicked?

_____

_____

_____

_____

_____

_____

_____

_____

_____

_____

_____

_____

Do you sense that you are currently under any form of God's chastening? How will you respond?

_____

_____

_____

_____

_____

_____

_____

_____

_____

MAY 7
God's Redemptive Works

Psalm 77:1–9

I CRIED out to God with my voice—
To God with my voice;
And He gave ear to me.

2 In the day of my trouble I sought the Lord;
My hand was stretched out in the night without
ceasing;
My soul refused to be comforted.

3 I remembered God, and was troubled;
I complained, and my spirit was overwhelmed.
Selah

4 You hold my eyelids *open;*
I am so troubled that I cannot speak.

5 I have considered the days of old,
The years of ancient times.

6 I call to remembrance my song in the night;
I meditate within my heart,
And my spirit makes diligent search.

7 Will the Lord cast off forever?
And will He be favorable no more?

8 Has His mercy ceased forever?
Has *His* promise failed forevermore?

9 Has God forgotten to be gracious?
Has He in anger shut up His tender mercies?
Selah

DEVOTIONAL

Years ago I had a professor who notoriously disliked it when students asked questions. Students who raised their hands during his lectures were usually either ignored or met with an icy gaze. One day he allowed a student to ask a question and then responded, "That's essentially the same question you asked two weeks ago. It was a rotten question then, and I'm not going to answer it now!" So, is God like a grumpy professor who hates to be bothered with our questions? Thankfully, God's Word shows us otherwise.

In today's passage, Asaph was experiencing a time of spiritual pain. He asked God six tough questions in verses 7–9: (1) Will the Lord always reject us? (2) Will He never again show favor? (3) Has He stopped being merciful? (4) Has His promise failed? (5) Does He no longer remember grace? (6) Has His compassion disappeared?

We already know the answer to each one: No. God's grace, mercy, compassion, and forgiveness never go away. But even though Asaph surely already knew the right answer in his heart and mind, his experience was telling him a different story. He cried out to God in the night, but found no comfort. He was overwhelmed and tortured by memories of the past when God's presence had been so close that Asaph had sung praises to Him from his bed at night. Now, the Lord was keeping Asaph's eyelids open all night long, and the tough questions swirled in his mind. So instead of holding the questions inside, he simply asked God.

Asaph sets a great example for us when the pain of life causes us to have hard questions for God. Today, if the problems and pain in your life are causing doubts in your heart, be honest with God about them. Verbalizing your questions to God will bring you back to His goodness, grace, and mercy once more. You'll be reminded that His compassion never ceases and His promise never fails.

Dr. Stephen Rummage, Bell Shoals Baptist Church
Brandon, FL

MAY 8

Remember the Works of the Lord

Psalm 77:10–20

10 And I said, "This *is* my anguish;
But I *will remember* the years of the right hand
of the Most High."

11 I will remember the works of the LORD;
Surely I will remember Your wonders of old.

12 I will also meditate on all Your work,
And talk of Your deeds.

13 Your way, O God, *is* in the sanctuary;
Who *is* so great a God as *our* God?

14 You *are* the God who does wonders;
You have declared Your strength among the
peoples.

15 You have with *Your* arm redeemed Your
people,
The sons of Jacob and Joseph.   Selah

16 The waters saw You, O God;
The waters saw You, they were afraid;
The depths also trembled.

17 The clouds poured out water;
The skies sent out a sound;
Your arrows also flashed about.

18 The voice of Your thunder *was* in the
whirlwind;
The lightnings lit up the world;
The earth trembled and shook.

19 Your way *was* in the sea,
Your path in the great waters,
And Your footsteps were not known.

20 You led Your people like a flock
By the hand of Moses and Aaron.

I live in constant pain," a friend said to me over lunch. He smiled as he spoke, and I could tell the smile was genuine. He told me, "God has given me two gifts: blessings to keep me joyful, and pain to keep me humble."

Asaph the psalmist said something similar in Psalm 77:10–20. His pain was real. He called it "anguish" in verse 10, a term that in the Hebrew language can mean a wound or even a disease. In the middle of his pain, Asaph remembered the Lord, and that made all the difference.

Though his pain caused him great suffering, Asaph made three decisions: First, he considered what God had done in the past (v. 11). Next, he meditated on the great works of God, even going so far as to speak them aloud for others to hear (v. 12). Finally, he entered God's presence and worshiped (v. 13).

Because he knew God, Asaph understood He was working through the pain to show His glory. Even when we cannot see God's footprints (v. 19), we can still depend on His character, power, and care. When your pain is great or your pathway is darkened, instead of asking the Lord, "Why are You putting me through this?" consider asking Him, "What are You showing me through this?"

Though you may find yourself in pain, God has not forsaken you. He has not changed in His goodness, His love, or His mercy. The same God with the power to make the skies flash and the earth tremble also has the compassion to lead you in tenderness and love through the pain you are facing.

Dr. Stephen Rummage, Bell Shoals Baptist Church
Brandon, FL

MAY 9

God's Kindness to Rebellious Israel

Psalm 78:1–16

G IVE ear, O my people, *to* my law;
Incline your ears to the words of my mouth.

2 I will open my mouth in a parable;
I will utter dark sayings of old,

3 Which we have heard and known,
And our fathers have told us.

4 We will not hide *them* from their children,
Telling to the generation to come the praises
of the LORD,
And His strength and His wonderful works
that He has done.

5 For He established a testimony in Jacob,
And appointed a law in Israel,
Which He commanded our fathers,
That they should make them known to their
children;

6 That the generation to come might know *them*,
The children *who* would be born,
That they may arise and declare *them* to their
children,

7 That they may set their hope in God,
And not forget the works of God,
But keep His commandments;

8 And may not be like their fathers,
A stubborn and rebellious generation,
A generation *that* did not set its heart aright,
And whose spirit was not faithful to God.

9 The children of Ephraim, *being* armed *and*
carrying bows,
Turned back in the day of battle.

10 They did not keep the covenant of God;
They refused to walk in His law,

11 And forgot His works
And His wonders that He had shown them.

12 Marvelous things He did in the sight of their
fathers,
In the land of Egypt, *in* the field of Zoan.

13 He divided the sea and caused them to pass
through;
And He made the waters stand up like a heap.

14 In the daytime also He led them with the cloud,
And all the night with a light of fire.

15 He split the rocks in the wilderness,
And gave *them* drink in abundance like the
depths.

16 He also brought streams out of the rock,
And caused waters to run down like rivers.

DEVOTIONAL

L isten." It's a simple instruction parents give
their kids and a life-changing word God
extends to His children. Psalm 78:1 uses two
expressions to call God's people to listen: "give
ear" and "incline your ears." As the Lord spoke
to Israel in this historical psalm, He graciously
warned them about the cost of rebellion against
Him. When we listen to God, He shows us things
we would not otherwise see and alerts us to haz-
ards we would never detect on our own. There are
so many voices competing for our attention that
it's easy to forget to listen to God. When we stop
paying attention to His voice and His commands,
we will find ourselves in danger. Today, listen carefully to God as you read His Word and pray.

Dr. Stephen Rummage, Bell Shoals Baptist Church
Brandon, FL

MAY 10

The Compassion of God

Psalm 78:17–33

17 But they sinned even more against Him
By rebelling against the Most High in the
wilderness.
18 And they tested God in their heart
By asking for the food of their fancy.
19 Yes, they spoke against God:
They said, "Can God prepare a table in the
wilderness?
20 Behold, He struck the rock,
So that the waters gushed out,
And the streams overflowed.
Can He give bread also?
Can He provide meat for His people?"
21 Therefore the LORD heard *this* and was furious;
So a fire was kindled against Jacob,
And anger also came up against Israel,
22 Because they did not believe in God,
And did not trust in His salvation.
23 Yet He had commanded the clouds above,
And opened the doors of heaven,
24 Had rained down manna on them to eat,
And given them of the bread of heaven.
25 Men ate angels' food;
He sent them food to the full.
26 He caused an east wind to blow in the heavens;
And by His power He brought in the south wind.
27 He also rained meat on them like the dust,
Feathered fowl like the sand of the seas;
28 And He let *them* fall in the midst of their camp,
All around their dwellings.

29 So they ate and were well filled,
For He gave them their own desire.
30 They were not deprived of their craving;
But while their food *was* still in their mouths,
31 The wrath of God came against them,
And slew the stoutest of them,
And struck down the choice *men* of Israel.
32 In spite of this they still sinned,
And did not believe in His wondrous works.
33 Therefore their days He consumed in futility,
And their years in fear.

DEVOTIONAL

I once watched a bodybuilder demonstrate his incredible strength. He hefted heavy weights, bent steel bars with his bare hands, and even pulled a loaded bus with his teeth. Afterwards, dozens of small children ran up to the strong man, many asking the same question: "Can you pick me up?" Their question seemed silly. After all those demonstrations of strength, of course he could pick them up!

Israel asked the Lord a similarly childish question. God had brought them out of Egypt with a mighty hand, yet they wondered, "Can God prepare a table in the wilderness?" (v. 19). Though He had cared for them in the past, they worried God would let them starve. Their unbelief angered God, but He compassionately provided for His people. Still, they did not trust in Him, and fear consumed their lives (vv. 32–33).

God is more than able to carry you and provide for your needs. Are you filled with God's peace and provision, or are you worried about today?

Dr. Stephen Rummage, Bell Shoals Baptist Church
Brandon, FL

MAY 11

Grace and Forgiveness

Psalm 78:34–55

34 When He slew them, then they sought Him;
And they returned and sought earnestly for God.

35 Then they remembered that God *was* their rock,
And the Most High God their Redeemer.

36 Nevertheless they flattered Him with their mouth,
And they lied to Him with their tongue;

37 For their heart was not steadfast with Him,
Nor were they faithful in His covenant.

38 But He, *being* full of compassion, forgave *their* iniquity,
And did not destroy *them*.
Yes, many a time He turned His anger away,
And did not stir up all His wrath;

39 For He remembered that they *were but* flesh,
A breath that passes away and does not come again.

40 How often they provoked Him in the wilderness,
And grieved Him in the desert!

41 Yes, again and again they tempted God,
And limited the Holy One of Israel.

42 They did not remember His power:
The day when He redeemed them from the enemy,

43 When He worked His signs in Egypt,
And His wonders in the field of Zoan;

44 Turned their rivers into blood,
And their streams, that they could not drink.

45 He sent swarms of flies among them, which devoured them,
And frogs, which destroyed them.

46 He also gave their crops to the caterpillar,
And their labor to the locust.

47 He destroyed their vines with hail,
And their sycamore trees with frost.

48 He also gave up their cattle to the hail,
And their flocks to fiery lightning.

49 He cast on them the fierceness of His anger,
Wrath, indignation, and trouble,
By sending angels of destruction *among them*.

50 He made a path for His anger;
He did not spare their soul from death,
But gave their life over to the plague,

51 And destroyed all the firstborn in Egypt,
The first of *their* strength in the tents of Ham.

52 But He made His own people go forth like sheep,
And guided them in the wilderness like a flock;

53 And He led them on safely, so that they did not fear;
But the sea overwhelmed their enemies.

54 And He brought them to His holy border,
This mountain *which* His right hand had acquired.

55 He also drove out the nations before them,
Allotted them an inheritance by survey,
And made the tribes of Israel dwell in their tents.

DEVOTIONAL

Psalm 78 continues telling the story of Israel's rebellion and God's faithfulness. Though God's people kept sinning, "He remembered that they were but flesh" (v. 39). In His righteousness and holiness, God cannot ignore our sin. But in His grace, He chooses to forgive—even at the cost of Jesus' shed blood. Today, thank God that no sin is beyond the scope of His grace.

Dr. Stephen Rummage, Bell Shoals Baptist Church
Brandon, FL

MAY 12

Ending the Sin Cycle

Psalm 78:56–72

56 Yet they tested and provoked the Most High God,
And did not keep His testimonies,

57 But turned back and acted unfaithfully like their fathers;
They were turned aside like a deceitful bow.

58 For they provoked Him to anger with their high places,
And moved Him to jealousy with their carved images.

59 When God heard *this*, He was furious,
And greatly abhorred Israel,

60 So that He forsook the tabernacle of Shiloh,
The tent He had placed among men,

61 And delivered His strength into captivity,
And His glory into the enemy's hand.

62 He also gave His people over to the sword,
And was furious with His inheritance.

63 The fire consumed their young men,
And their maidens were not given in marriage.

64 Their priests fell by the sword,
And their widows made no lamentation.

65 Then the Lord awoke as *from* sleep,
Like a mighty man who shouts because of wine.

66 And He beat back His enemies;
He put them to a perpetual reproach.

67 Moreover He rejected the tent of Joseph,
And did not choose the tribe of Ephraim,

68 But chose the tribe of Judah,
Mount Zion which He loved.

69 And He built His sanctuary like the heights,
Like the earth which He has established forever.

70 He also chose David His servant,
And took him from the sheepfolds;

71 From following the ewes that had young He brought him,
To shepherd Jacob His people,
And Israel His inheritance.

72 So he shepherded them according to the integrity of his heart,
And guided them by the skillfulness of his hands.

DEVOTIONAL

A philosopher has said that the one thing we learn from history is that we don't learn anything from history. Instead, we keep repeating our mistakes. Considering the story of Israel (and our own lives), it does seem that sin takes us through the same cycles: God provides, but we fail to trust. God judges, and we turn back to Him. God forgives, but we rebel once again.

This psalm ends with good news, though. Despite Israel's rebellion, God chose for them a godly king, David, to be their shepherd (v. 72). We know that through David's lineage, the ultimate Shepherd and King has come to lead and redeem God's people.

Praise the Lord that God is not bound by the chains of human history! Jesus is able to redeem the failures of our past and transform our future. Today, don't put God to the test through continued disobedience and faithlessness. Make a decision to obey and trust Him with the details of your life. He longs to shepherd and guide you!

Dr. Stephen Rummage, Bell Shoals Baptist Church
Brandon, FL

MAY 13

In Psalm 77, Asaph came to God in a time of great pain with tough questions. As a result, God reminded Asaph of His unfailing grace. What are some of the hardest questions you have for God? Don't be afraid to write them down. Now, reflect on His compassion and His promises. How is God revealing His character and love in light of your questions?

_____

_____

_____

_____

_____

_____

_____

In Psalm 78, God showed faithfulness and grace to Israel even when they continued to rebel against Him. In your own life, when have you been rebellious to God or failed to trust Him? How has God shown His mercy and forgiveness to you? How is He calling you to obey and trust Him right now?

_____

_____

_____

_____

_____

_____

_____

_____

MAY 14

A Prayer for Israel

Psalm 79:1–13

O GOD, the nations have come into Your
    inheritance;
  Your holy temple they have defiled;
  They have laid Jerusalem in heaps.
2 The dead bodies of Your servants
  They have given *as* food for the birds of the
    heavens,
  The flesh of Your saints to the beasts of the
    earth.
3 Their blood they have shed like water all
    around Jerusalem,
  And *there was* no one to bury *them*.
4 We have become a reproach to our neighbors,
  A scorn and derision to those who are
    around us.

5 How long, LORD?
  Will You be angry forever?
  Will Your jealousy burn like fire?
6 Pour out Your wrath on the nations that do not
    know You,
  And on the kingdoms that do not call on
    Your name.
7 For they have devoured Jacob,
  And laid waste his dwelling place.

8 Oh, do not remember former iniquities
    against us!
  Let Your tender mercies come speedily to
    meet us,
  For we have been brought very low.
9 Help us, O God of our salvation,

For the glory of Your name;
  And deliver us, and provide atonement for
    our sins,
  For Your name's sake!
10 Why should the nations say,
  "Where *is* their God?"
  Let there be known among the nations in
    our sight
  The avenging of the blood of Your servants
    which has been shed.

11 Let the groaning of the prisoner come
    before You;
  According to the greatness of Your power
  Preserve those who are appointed to die;
12 And return to our neighbors sevenfold into
    their bosom
  Their reproach with which they have
    reproached You, O Lord.

13 So we, Your people and sheep of Your pasture,
  Will give You thanks forever;
  We will show forth Your praise to all
    generations.

DEVOTIONAL

The words of verse 8 seem to sum up the psalmist's pain: "We have been brought very low." Sooner or later, life will bring us all very low. It may be due to our own choices or those of others, or for no apparent reason. But verse 8 also gives us good news, regardless of what brings us low—we can call out for God's "tender mercies [to] come speedily to meet us." When life brings us *low*, it also brings us *near* to God. Psalm 34:18 reminds us, "The LORD is near to those who have a broken heart."

Mark Hoover, NewSpring Church
Wichita, KS

MAY 15

Prayer for Israel's Restoration

Psalm 80:1–11

G IVE ear, O Shepherd of Israel,
You who lead Joseph like a flock;
  You who dwell *between* the cherubim, shine
    forth!

2 Before Ephraim, Benjamin, and Manasseh,
  Stir up Your strength,
  And come *and* save us!

3 Restore us, O God;
  Cause Your face to shine,
  And we shall be saved!

4 O Lord God of hosts,
  How long will You be angry
  Against the prayer of Your people?

5 You have fed them with the bread of tears,
  And given them tears to drink in great
    measure.

6 You have made us a strife to our neighbors,
  And our enemies laugh among themselves.

7 Restore us, O God of hosts;
  Cause Your face to shine,
  And we shall be saved!

8 You have brought a vine out of Egypt;
  You have cast out the nations, and planted it.

9 You prepared *room* for it,
  And caused it to take deep root,
  And it filled the land.

10 The hills were covered with its shadow,
  And the mighty cedars with its boughs.

11 She sent out her boughs to the Sea,
  And her branches to the River.

DEVOTIONAL

C an you remember a time when you offended someone close to you so deeply that it caused that person's expression toward you to change? A look of pain or anger replaced the ready, affectionate smile you usually received. No doubt you longed for things to be right between the two of you again, because each time you looked into that face, you were reminded that your relationship was strained. The psalmist knew this was exactly what had happened between his people and God. Their continued disobedience and rebellion had resulted in God temporarily withdrawing His favor.

So twice, in verses 3 and 7, he prayed the same prayer: "Restore us, O God; cause Your face to shine." He was asking God to help them change their course so He could smile on them. He was praying God would help them live differently so He could bless them again. Throughout Scripture, we're reminded that God responds to this kind of prayer. He's ready to lead us in right paths if we are ready to follow (Prov. 3:5–6). He wants to smile on us with blessing.

Mark Hoover, NewSpring Church
Wichita, KS

MAY 16

The God Who Sees

Psalm 80:12–19

¹² Why have You broken down her hedges,
So that all who pass by the way pluck her
fruit?
¹³ The boar out of the woods uproots it,
And the wild beast of the field devours it.

¹⁴ Return, we beseech You, O God of hosts;
Look down from heaven and see,
And visit this vine
¹⁵ And the vineyard which Your right hand has
planted,
And the branch *that* You made strong for
Yourself.
¹⁶ *It is* burned with fire, *it is* cut down;
They perish at the rebuke of Your
countenance.
¹⁷ Let Your hand be upon the man of Your right
hand,
Upon the son of man *whom* You made strong
for Yourself.
¹⁸ Then we will not turn back from You;
Revive us, and we will call upon Your name.

¹⁹ Restore us, O Lord God of hosts;
Cause Your face to shine,
And we shall be saved!

DEVOTIONAL

One of the toughest assignments life ever hands us is to try to keep functioning while everything in our world is falling apart. If you've ever been there, or that's where you are today, you know how difficult it can be to try to do all the things you normally do when nothing is normal. The added pressure and pain piled on top of an already stressful life can bring us to the point of despair. We sometimes wonder, *Does anyone understand what I'm feeling? Does anyone even see me?*

Verse 14 is a comforting reminder that there is Someone who understands our exhaustion and pain. In the midst of billions of people, He sees us. He's watching every moment of our lives. That verse says He also comes to "visit" us in our troubles.

Genesis 16 tells the story of a desperate young woman, pregnant and temporarily homeless, who felt she had no one left who cared for her. God visited her in her moment of hopelessness. Even though all her problems didn't disappear, she was so encouraged to know that God was paying attention to her that the Bible says she called the name of the Lord, "You-Are-the-God-Who-Sees" (v. 13).

No matter what this day has in store for you, you can be assured that God is watching. Like the psalmist did, ask Him to come visit your circumstances with His awesome power.

Mark Hoover, NewSpring Church
Wichita, KS

MAY 17

An Appeal for Israel's Repentance

Psalm 81:1–16

S ING aloud to God our strength;
  Make a joyful shout to the God of Jacob.
2 Raise a song and strike the timbrel,
  The pleasant harp with the lute.

3 Blow the trumpet at the time of the New
      Moon,
  At the full moon, on our solemn feast day.
4 For this *is* a statute for Israel,
  A law of the God of Jacob.
5 This He established in Joseph *as* a testimony,
  When He went throughout the land of Egypt,
  Where I heard a language I did not
      understand.

6 "I removed his shoulder from the burden;
  His hands were freed from the baskets.
7 You called in trouble, and I delivered you;
  I answered you in the secret place of thunder;
  I tested you at the waters of Meribah.   Selah

8 "Hear, O My people, and I will admonish you!
  O Israel, if you will listen to Me!
9 There shall be no foreign god among you;
  Nor shall you worship any foreign god.
10 I *am* the LORD your God,
  Who brought you out of the land of Egypt;
  Open your mouth wide, and I will fill it.

11 "But My people would not heed My voice,
  And Israel would *have* none of Me.
12 So I gave them over to their own stubborn
      heart,
  To walk in their own counsels.

13 "Oh, that My people would listen to Me,
  That Israel would walk in My ways!
14 I would soon subdue their enemies,
  And turn My hand against their adversaries.
15 The haters of the LORD would pretend submis-
      sion to Him,
  But their fate would endure forever.
16 He would have fed them also with the finest of
      wheat;
  And with honey from the rock I would have
      satisfied you."

DEVOTIONAL

I n the second half of today's psalm, God pours out the feelings that responsible parents know all too well. If our children persist in stubbornly refusing to listen, the time may come when we have to allow them to feel the discomfort associated with unwise choices. In verses 11 and 12, God laments, "My people would not heed My voice . . . so I gave them over to their own stubborn heart, to walk in their own counsels."

But parents who reluctantly have to make such a decision know what it means to suffer right along with their children as they learn life's painful lessons. For all of us who, in seasons of our lives, have ignored God's will, it's comforting to know that He grieves when He has to take similar steps. In verse 13, He cries, "Oh, that my people would listen to Me." Just as we want what is best for our children, verse 16 encourages us that God wants us to experience the very best, which only comes from Him.

Mark Hoover, NewSpring Church
Wichita, KS

MAY 18

A Plea for Justice

Psalm 82:1–8

GOD stands in the congregation of the mighty;
He judges among the gods.

2 How long will you judge unjustly,
And show partiality to the wicked?   Selah

3 Defend the poor and fatherless;
Do justice to the afflicted and needy.

4 Deliver the poor and needy;
Free *them* from the hand of the wicked.

5 They do not know, nor do they understand;
They walk about in darkness;
All the foundations of the earth are unstable.

6 I said, "You *are* gods,
And all of you *are* children of the Most High.

7 But you shall die like men,
And fall like one of the princes."

8 Arise, O God, judge the earth;
For You shall inherit all nations.

DEVOTIONAL

Psalm 82 is a song that cries out for justice in a world of injustice. From the writer's vantage point, he saw the poor mistreated, the orphan disenfranchised, and the sufferer loaded down with even heavier burdens. And all of this was happening at the hands of those who had been given the responsibility to ensure fairness. Those trusted with power were abusing it.

Sadly, as we look at our world today, we're aware that too little in that regard has changed in three thousand years. Our Enemy, Satan, has demonstrated a frightful ability to worm his way into the power bases of society to use them for his own ends. Far too often, individuals with selfish motivations and questionable agendas rise to places of power. Our hearts are especially grieved for those who suffer persecution and abuse at the hands of such people.

Perhaps you are dealing with a measure of unfair treatment in your own situation. Someone with power or influence over your circumstances is making your life difficult. Whether, like the psalmist, you're saddened by the injustice in the world around you, or you're dealing with it up close and personal, the good news is that our God "stands in the congregation of the mighty," and rules among the judges of this world (v. 1)! Verse 1 also triumphantly proclaims that those who may be "gods" in the eyes of people are no gods to our God.

Keep in mind today that when we, who know the true God, encounter injustice and mistreatment at the hands of the powerful, we always have a *higher court* in which to plead our case. With even greater encouragement, verse 8 reveals to us that the day is coming when our Lord will rule over all the nations, for He will "judge the earth . . . [and] shall inherit all nations." This reminds us of the angel's proclamation in Revelation 11:15, "The kingdoms of this world have become the kingdoms of our Lord and of His Christ, and He shall reign forever and ever!"

Mark Hoover, NewSpring Church
Wichita, KS

MAY 19

Prayer to Frustrate Conspiracy

Psalm 83:1–8

D O not keep silent, O God!
Do not hold Your peace,
And do not be still, O God!

2 For behold, Your enemies make a tumult;
And those who hate You have lifted up their
head.

3 They have taken crafty counsel against Your
people,
And consulted together against Your sheltered
ones.

4 They have said, "Come, and let us cut them off
from *being* a nation,
That the name of Israel may be remembered
no more."

5 For they have consulted together with one
consent;
They form a confederacy against You:

6 The tents of Edom and the Ishmaelites;
Moab and the Hagrites;

7 Gebal, Ammon, and Amalek;
Philistia with the inhabitants of Tyre;

8 Assyria also has joined with them;
They have helped the children of Lot.   Selah

DEVOTIONAL

I n verses 2 and 3, the psalmist bemoans a
conspiracy consisting of many enemies and
draws a distinction that is helpful to us as we try
to understand the world in which we live. In verse
2, he identifies the conspirators as God's enemies.
And in verse 3, he reminds the Lord that those
who "hate You" are now coming against "Your
people." The way the psalmist saw it, the enemies
of God were attacking Him, and His people were
caught in the crossfire.

This happens in our lives as well. There will be
times when we face opposition merely because we
happen to be God's children. Our enemy, Satan,
is in a long-running battle with our God, and for
thousands of years he has waged warfare against
the Lord by attacking those who love Him.

So how do we respond when this happens?
First, like the psalmist, we can cry out to God for
His help. While Satan is a powerful adversary, he
is no match for God. When the psalmist prays, "Do
not keep silent, O God," in verse 1, he is asking God
to use His all-surpassing power.

Sometimes Satan uses people to advance his
agenda, and the opposition can turn personal.
When that happens, it's important to remember
Paul's words to the Ephesians in chapter 6 of that
book, "We do not wrestle against flesh and blood
but against principalities, against powers, against
the rulers of the darkness of this age, against spiritual hosts of wickedness in the heavenly places" (v.
12). Our fight is never against people. So often we
are tempted to make conflicts personal, but that
misdirects our focus. Paul also reminded us to
wear the "whole armor of God" (v. 13), because we
need every piece of God's arsenal to battle Satan
and his evil forces.

If you find yourself in a spiritual battle today,
you may not feel like rejoicing, but there is something to be very happy about. You know which
side you're on. And it's the winning side!

Mark Hoover, NewSpring Church
Wichita, KS

MAY 20

Describe a time in your life when you or someone you love stubbornly refused to listen.

_____

_____

_____

_____

_____

_____

_____

_____

_____

_____

_____

Recall a time in your life when God rescued you from Satan's attack.

_____

_____

_____

_____

_____

_____

_____

_____

_____

MAY 21

A Prayer Against Israel's Enemies

Psalm 83:9–18

9 Deal with them as *with* Midian,
As *with* Sisera,
As *with* Jabin at the Brook Kishon,

10 Who perished at En Dor,
Who became *as* refuse on the earth.

11 Make their nobles like Oreb and like Zeeb,
Yes, all their princes like Zebah and
Zalmunna,

12 Who said, "Let us take for ourselves
The pastures of God for a possession."

13 O my God, make them like the whirling dust,
Like the chaff before the wind!

14 As the fire burns the woods,
And as the flame sets the mountains on fire,

15 So pursue them with Your tempest,
And frighten them with Your storm.

16 Fill their faces with shame,
That they may seek Your name, O LORD.

17 Let them be confounded and dismayed
forever;
Yes, let them be put to shame and perish,

18 That they may know that You, whose name
alone *is* the LORD,
Are the Most High over all the earth.

DEVOTIONAL

Anyone who has a heart for honoring God and building His kingdom will face opposition. It should not come as a surprise when the forces of darkness marshal their attacks against us. God's people have dealt with opposition, oppression, and persecution for centuries. When you look back over two thousand years of history, the Enemy has come time and time again with the agenda to steal, kill, and destroy (John 10:10).

In our passage today, the psalmist cried out to God as Israel was about to be attacked by its enemies. This prayer reveals three ways to respond when you are under attack.

Don't be surprised when you come under attack for righteousness' sake. Our world is not friendly toward those who hold to the truth and stand for righteousness. You are not alone. There are many who have been attacked and are being attacked.

Remember, God is in control and is for you. The psalmist used examples of God shaming His enemies through supernatural acts and the faithfulness of servants like Debra, Barak (Judg. 4–5), and Gideon (Judg. 6–8). God is more than capable of dealing with opposition and any enemy that would stand before you. And those who stand in defiance of God's plan and righteous truth should beware.

Cry out to God and trust Him to accomplish His will. Ask for His power and strength. Remember, He blows the chaff away and sets the mountains on fire (vv. 13–14)! He can give you strength to stand during the attack. Ask Him to accomplish His purpose. Pray "that they may seek Your name, O LORD . . . [and] . . . that they may know . . . You, whose name alone is the LORD" (vv. 16, 18). Finally, praise Him for His sovereignty and for who He is: "the Most High over all the earth" (v. 18).

Dr. Lee Sheppard, Mabel White Baptist Church
Macon, GA

MAY 22

Dwelling in the House of God

Psalm 84:1–12

H OW lovely *is* Your tabernacle,
O LORD of hosts!

2 My soul longs, yes, even faints
For the courts of the LORD;
My heart and my flesh cry out for the living
God.

3 Even the sparrow has found a home,
And the swallow a nest for herself,
Where she may lay her young—
Even Your altars, O LORD of hosts,
My King and my God.

4 Blessed *are* those who dwell in Your house;
They will still be praising You. Selah

5 Blessed *is* the man whose strength *is* in You,
Whose heart *is* set on pilgrimage.

6 *As they* pass through the Valley of Baca,
They make it a spring;
The rain also covers it with pools.

7 They go from strength to strength;
Each one appears before God in Zion.

8 O LORD God of hosts, hear my prayer;
Give ear, O God of Jacob! Selah

9 O God, behold our shield,
And look upon the face of Your anointed.

10 For a day in Your courts *is* better than a
thousand.
I would rather be a doorkeeper in the house of
my God
Than dwell in the tents of wickedness.

11 For the LORD God *is* a sun and shield;

The LORD will give grace and glory;
No good *thing* will He withhold
From those who walk uprightly.

12 O LORD of hosts,
Blessed *is* the man who trusts in You!

DEVOTIONAL

T he psalmist gives us a snapshot of genuine worship in Psalm 84. Genuine worship is seeking God with everything we have; it is addictive because it reveals and results in life change!

So why worship? We worship because our heart is right. We realize that our strength for life is not our own and we must totally rely on God's strength. We worship because of God's faithfulness. We all journey through the "Valley of Baca" (v. 6), the valley of weeping. We endure hardships, trials, losses, and temptations, yet God proves His faithfulness by giving us strength to endure. We worship because He allows us to serve Him, and we are overcome by the fact that our great God would allow us to serve Him. We proclaim that one day of fellowship is a thousand times better than anything else. Finally, we worship because of His provision and protection—"for the LORD God is a sun and shield" (v. 11). God provides restoration and protection in the journey of life.

Are you weary and weak? Are you overwhelmed by life? Then worship Him and receive the power to overcome the things that are weighing you down.

Dr. Lee Sheppard, Mabel White Baptist Church
Macon, GA

MAY 23

Restore Favor to the Land

Psalm 85:1–13

LORD, You have been favorable to Your land;
    You have brought back the captivity of Jacob.

2 You have forgiven the iniquity of Your people;
    You have covered all their sin.   Selah

3 You have taken away all Your wrath;
    You have turned from the fierceness of
        Your anger.

4 Restore us, O God of our salvation,
    And cause Your anger toward us to cease.

5 Will You be angry with us forever?
    Will You prolong Your anger to all
        generations?

6 Will You not revive us again,
    That Your people may rejoice in You?

7 Show us Your mercy, LORD,
    And grant us Your salvation.

8 I will hear what God the LORD will speak,
    For He will speak peace
    To His people and to His saints;
    But let them not turn back to folly.

9 Surely His salvation *is* near to those who
        fear Him,
    That glory may dwell in our land.

10 Mercy and truth have met together;
    Righteousness and peace have kissed.

11 Truth shall spring out of the earth,
    And righteousness shall look down from
        heaven.

12 Yes, the LORD will give *what is* good;
    And our land will yield its increase.

13 Righteousness will go before Him,
    And shall make His footsteps *our* pathway.

DEVOTIONAL

Will You not revive us again, that Your people may rejoice in You?" (v. 6). How long has it been since you've prayed a prayer like this? Has your relationship with God become slack, your passion waned, your enthusiasm died, and your commitment to the things of God diminished? Do you need personal revival and renewal?

We are so busy and preoccupied by the things of this world that if we are not careful, we will get drawn away from God, misplace our passion, and pursue other things. So how can we know if we need revival in our lives? Well, we need revival when our salvation has lost its joy, when our sin does not break our heart, and when we make little to no effort to witness to the lost. We need revival when worship becomes boring, when we are at odds with other believers and see no need for reconciliation, and when we fail to believe God for the impossible. We need revival when we have to be begged to give and serve in the church and when we would rather make money than give money. We need revival when we have to be entertained to be drawn to church and when we are indifferent to the fact that there are 2.5 billion people on the planet who have never heard the name of Jesus. We need revival when we don't regularly see the supernatural evidence of God's power and when we lose our desire to fellowship with other believers.

Do you need revival? Ask God to show you and trust in Him to send it.

Dr. Lee Sheppard, Mabel White Baptist Church
Macon, GA

MAY 24

Prayer for Mercy

Psalm 86:1–10

B OW down Your ear, O Lord, hear me;
For I *am* poor and needy.

2 Preserve my life, for I *am* holy;
You are my God;
Save Your servant who trusts in You!

3 Be merciful to me, O Lord,
For I cry to You all day long.

4 Rejoice the soul of Your servant,
For to You, O Lord, I lift up my soul.

5 For You, Lord, *are* good, and ready to forgive,
And abundant in mercy to all those who call
upon You.

6 Give ear, O Lord, to my prayer;
And attend to the voice of my supplications.

7 In the day of my trouble I will call upon You,
For You will answer me.

8 Among the gods *there is* none like You, O Lord;
Nor *are there any works* like Your works.

9 All nations whom You have made
Shall come and worship before You, O Lord,
And shall glorify Your name.

10 For You *are* great, and do wondrous things;
You alone *are* God.

DEVOTIONAL

W hen it comes to your relationship with God,
what do you need the most? What is it that
you need above everything else as you approach
God? The answer is mercy. God's grace and mercy
are companions. You cannot experience the grace
of God without mercy, and you cannot experience

the mercy of God without grace. Mercy is God giving to us what we do not deserve. We need mercy. It
is at the heart of the Christian faith.

Mercy is a word Christians use a lot. We use
it in our prayers. We use it in the songs of worship that we sing. We've become so familiar with
the word that I wonder if we totally understand it
and if we have become desensitized to the impact
God's mercy has on our lives.

Twenty-seven psalms focus on mercy and our
need for it. Mercy is something we need every
time we sin (v. 5a), and it is something we need
every day of our lives. Thankfully, God's mercy has
no limit (v. 5b).

When we sin, we can cry out to God for mercy
and forgiveness (vv. 3, 5). Sin breaks our fellowship with a holy God, so we must confess our sin
and receive God's mercy for forgiveness (1 John
1:9). Each time we do this, God extends His mercy
to us. He washes us clean and completely removes
any record of wrong.

God's mercy is guaranteed to those who call out
to Him (v. 7). The truth is, there is very little guaranteed in the world in which we live. How refreshing that David gave us a glimpse of the character of
God when he said, "I will call upon You, for You will
answer me" (v. 7). There wasn't a doubt in his mind
that God would extend help, strength, assurance,
forgiveness, or whatever he needed. This should
drive us to our knees in worship of our great God
who does wondrous things (v. 10).

Dr. Lee Sheppard, Mabel White Baptist Church
Macon, GA

MAY 25

The Lord's Compassion

Psalm 86:11–17

11 Teach me Your way, O LORD;
   I will walk in Your truth;
   Unite my heart to fear Your name.
12 I will praise You, O Lord my God, with all my
      heart,
   And I will glorify Your name forevermore.
13 For great *is* Your mercy toward me,
   And You have delivered my soul from the
      depths of Sheol.

14 O God, the proud have risen against me,
   And a mob of violent *men* have sought my life,
   And have not set You before them.
15 But You, O Lord, *are* a God full of compassion,
      and gracious,
   Longsuffering and abundant in mercy and
      truth.
16 Oh, turn to me, and have mercy on me!
   Give Your strength to Your servant,
   And save the son of Your maidservant.
17 Show me a sign for good,
   That those who hate me may see *it* and be
      ashamed,
   Because You, LORD, have helped me and com-
      forted me.

DEVOTIONAL

Sometimes it is difficult to get our hearts around the truth that no matter what our circumstances may be, God is worthy of our praise. No matter what we may be going through, whether good or bad, prospering or experiencing adversity,

there is great comfort in knowing that God is the same, unchanging and ever present. He is a loving, kind, helpful, giving, and forgiving God. He uses everything that comes into our lives to shape us to look, sound, and act more like Jesus. He truly works all things for our good and His glory. That is called compassion.

Compassion is recognizing the suffering of others and then taking action to help. Because God is sovereign, He knows all things. He knows of our storms and victories, our hurts and fears, and He searches our hearts and knows exactly where we are in our faith journey. He is willing to help us in and through our times of suffering. However, for us to fully comprehend His great compassion, there are some things we must remember.

We must be *teachable* (v. 11). There is something to be learned through every trial we face. God wants us to look to Him, listen to Him, and live in such a way that honors Him.

We must *praise Him* for His compassion (v. 13). We recognize where He has brought us from and what He is doing in our lives. This results in worship.

We must *share our hearts* with Him (vv. 14, 17). We are to be transparent, because He loves us and cares about what we are experiencing.

We must *depend on Him* (vv. 15–16) and ask God to see us through our trials. When we confess our trust in and dependence on Him for help and comfort, He provides us with the strength we need.

Dr. Lee Sheppard, Mabel White Baptist Church
Macon, GA

MAY 26

The Glories of the City of God

Psalm 87:1–7

HIS foundation *is* in the holy mountains.
² The LORD loves the gates of Zion
More than all the dwellings of Jacob.
³ Glorious things are spoken of you,
O city of God!   Selah

⁴ "I will make mention of Rahab and Babylon to
those who know Me;
Behold, O Philistia and Tyre, with Ethiopia:
'This *one* was born there.'"

⁵ And of Zion it will be said,
"This *one* and that *one* were born in her;
And the Most High Himself shall establish her."
⁶ The LORD will record,
When He registers the peoples:
"This *one* was born there."   Selah

⁷ Both the singers and the players on instruments *say,*
"All my springs *are* in you."

DEVOTIONAL

Jerusalem, the "city of God" (v. 3), is a holy
place. The Jews consider its soil and even its
air to be holy and sacred. They mention the city's
name in prayers. They pray in its direction, close
the Passover service with the statement "Next year
in Jerusalem," and recall the city in the blessing at
the end of each meal.

Being a part of the chosen people is important
to them. However, to be born in Jerusalem is an
even greater honor (vv. 5–6), so their pedigree
matters immensely.

How much value do we put on being born
into the royal family of God? In Jerusalem, God
dwelled in the Holy Place. For the Christ-follower,
God dwells in the heart. Before Christ, only the
high priest could enter the Holy Place. However,
because of the atonement of Jesus, every believer
has access to the Father.

I wonder if we take our spiritual pedigree for
granted as Christians. How valuable is it for us to
know that we have been born into a royal family?
We are children of the King of kings and Lord of
lords. The apostle Paul said, "But you are a chosen
generation, a royal priesthood, a holy nation, His
own special people" (1 Pet. 2:9). What joy to know
God chose us because we are special to Him and
gave us the gift of a relationship with Him. What
freedom to know we can go to the Father in prayer
and He hears our prayers. What power is available
as we are filled with the Holy Spirit.

How long has it been since you sat quietly
and thought about the fact that God is with
you? Friend, He is with you! You are not alone.
Everywhere you go and every step you take, He is
there. He will lead you, guide you, and direct you
if you will allow Him to. He's a companion and
a friend. He will never leave you or forsake you,
regardless of where life takes you. He alone satisfies unlike anything else.

Retreat to your holy place and drink in the
presence and grace of our great God.

Dr. Lee Sheppard, Mabel White Baptist Church
Macon, GA

 # MAY 27

Are there specific things God has spoken to you about through your reading this week?

_____

_____

_____

_____

_____

_____

_____

_____

_____

_____

_____

_____

Take a few moments to record the ways God has demonstrated His grace and mercy in your life.

_____

_____

_____

_____

_____

_____

_____

_____

_____

_____

MAY 28

A Prayer for Help in Despondency

Psalm 88:1–9a

O LORD, God of my salvation,
  I have cried out day and night before You.
² Let my prayer come before You;
  Incline Your ear to my cry.

³ For my soul is full of troubles,
  And my life draws near to the grave.
⁴ I am counted with those who go down to
    the pit;
  I am like a man *who has* no strength,
⁵ Adrift among the dead,
  Like the slain who lie in the grave,
  Whom You remember no more,
  And who are cut off from Your hand.

⁶ You have laid me in the lowest pit,
  In darkness, in the depths.
⁷ Your wrath lies heavy upon me,
  And You have afflicted *me* with all Your waves.
                                              Selah
⁸ You have put away my acquaintances far
    from me;
  You have made me an abomination to them;
  I am shut up, and I cannot get out;
⁹ My eye wastes away because of affliction.

DEVOTIONAL

H ave you ever cried your eyes out? The writer of this psalm speaks of continual tears that lead to painful eyes. What could possibly make a person cry so much?

Theologians believe this individual suffered from leprosy since childhood. Day and night his ailment caused physical, emotional, relational, and even spiritual suffering. He was discouraged, hurting, weak, and lonely. His prayer makes this one of the saddest psalms in all of Scripture. Yet, in the midst of his painful circumstances, he consistently and persistently cried out to God.

God's Word never promises freedom from "the pit" (v. 4). In fact, the Bible is full of examples of God-fearing individuals who declare His goodness and trust His presence in spite of their difficulties. Just think, this may have been one of the psalms prayed by Jesus in the midst of His suffering.

As you begin this week, take a moment to ponder the different types of difficulty you could encounter. God's Word guarantees we will face various kinds of trials. Will your soul be full of troubles? Will you lose strength? Will your acquaintances seem far away from you? Any and all of these things could happen.

Determine to declare God's sovereignty regardless of the situations you face. God is still the God of your salvation, even in your sorrows. He is Jehovah God! Cry if you must, but in the midst of your tears, remember to always cry out to God. He will be present with you in your pain, even in the deepest, darkest pits of life.

Prayer may not change your circumstances, but prayer will definitely change you!

Paul Purvis, First Baptist Church Temple Terrace
Temple Terrace, FL

MAY 29

A Call to the Lord for Salvation

Psalm 88:9b–18

LORD, I have called daily upon You;
I have stretched out my hands to You.

10 Will You work wonders for the dead?
Shall the dead arise *and* praise You?   Selah

11 Shall Your lovingkindness be declared in the
grave?
Or Your faithfulness in the place of
destruction?

12 Shall Your wonders be known in the dark?
And Your righteousness in the land of
forgetfulness?

13 But to You I have cried out, O LORD,
And in the morning my prayer comes
before You.

14 LORD, why do You cast off my soul?
Why do You hide Your face from me?

15 I *have been* afflicted and ready to die from
my youth;
I suffer Your terrors;
I am distraught.

16 Your fierce wrath has gone over me;
Your terrors have cut me off.

17 They came around me all day long like water;
They engulfed me altogether.

18 Loved one and friend You have put far
from me,
And my acquaintances into darkness.

DEVOTIONAL

Shall Your wonders be known in the dark?" In verse 12, the psalmist poses the question asked by many in the midst of suffering and sorrow. Can I trust God's goodness in the bad seasons of life?

The answer is simple and straightforward: *yes!* God's powers are not diminished in the presence of your difficulties. His sovereignty is not challenged by your uncertainty. Your questions do not intimidate God. Ask questions, but honor Him by waiting expectantly for His response.

This writer began every day calling out to God. Why? Because he understood the power of persistent prayer. He knew that God did hear and would answer, so he prayed, and prayed, and prayed. This same avenue into God's presence is made available to you. Even in the darkest moments of life He is there, awaiting your call.

Once again, Scripture reminds us that God's presence does not equal pain's absence. However, because of God's presence, pain's potency is limited. Difficult times may certainly lead to dark days, but dark days need not mean defeat. Ask God to give you strength to call on Him, even in the darkest moments of life.

Begin this day crying out to the Lord. Wait expectantly for His answer and trust His presence.

Paul Purvis, First Baptist Church Temple Terrace
Temple Terrace, FL

MAY 30

Remembering the Covenant

Psalm 89:1–10

I WILL sing of the mercies of the LORD forever;
With my mouth will I make known Your faith-
    fulness to all generations.
2 For I have said, "Mercy shall be built up forever;
Your faithfulness You shall establish in the
    very heavens."
3 "I have made a covenant with My chosen,
I have sworn to My servant David:
4 'Your seed I will establish forever,
And build up your throne to all generations.'"
                    Selah

5 And the heavens will praise Your wonders,
    O LORD;
Your faithfulness also in the assembly of
    the saints.
6 For who in the heavens can be compared to
    the LORD?
Who among the sons of the mighty can be
    likened to the LORD?
7 God is greatly to be feared in the assembly of
    the saints,
And to be held in reverence by all *those*
    around Him.
8 O LORD God of hosts,
Who *is* mighty like You, O LORD?
Your faithfulness also surrounds You.
9 You rule the raging of the sea;
When its waves rise, You still them.
10 You have broken Rahab in pieces, as one who
    is slain;

You have scattered Your enemies with Your
    mighty arm.

DEVOTIONAL

God is faithful! While Psalm 88 ends with a chorus of despair, Psalm 89 begins with a melody declaring God's goodness. What is different? Though the writers of Psalm 88 and Psalm 89 are not the same individual, they wrote in the midst of similar circumstances, but with different perspectives. Perhaps this is why the writer of this psalm is compared to Solomon in his wisdom. Godly wisdom allows you to recognize that this world's fiery trials pale in comparison to God's otherworldly faithfulness. Godly wisdom allows you to sing of His mercies even when most believe the music has faded.

But beware. Scripture teaches that if we fail to walk in wisdom, if we fail to sing His praises, God's creation, from the rocks to the heavens, will praise His mighty name. His faithfulness is worthy to be praised. So praise Him.

Take a moment today and remember His faithfulness. Remember how He saved you, and remember a time His grace sustained you. Take a walk down memory lane and sing a melodious song of His mercy. Recall a time when He was faithful in spite of your faithlessness. Remember and praise today.

Paul Purvis, First Baptist Church Temple Terrace
Temple Terrace, FL

MAY 31

Testaments of Mercy and Truth

Psalm 89:11–23

11 The heavens *are* Yours, the earth also *is* Yours;
   The world and all its fullness, You have
      founded them.
12 The north and the south, You have created
      them;
   Tabor and Hermon rejoice in Your name.
13 You have a mighty arm;
   Strong is Your hand, *and* high is Your right
      hand.
14 Righteousness and justice *are* the foundation
      of Your throne;
   Mercy and truth go before Your face.
15 Blessed *are* the people who know the joyful
      sound!
   They walk, O Lᴏʀᴅ, in the light of Your
      countenance.
16 In Your name they rejoice all day long,
   And in Your righteousness they are exalted.
17 For You *are* the glory of their strength,
   And in Your favor our horn is exalted.
18 For our shield *belongs* to the Lᴏʀᴅ,
   And our king to the Holy One of Israel.

19 Then You spoke in a vision to Your holy one,
   And said: "I have given help to *one who is*
      mighty;
   I have exalted one chosen from the people.
20 I have found My servant David;
   With My holy oil I have anointed him,
21 With whom My hand shall be established;
   Also My arm shall strengthen him.

22 The enemy shall not outwit him,
   Nor the son of wickedness afflict him.
23 I will beat down his foes before his face,
   And plague those who hate him.

DEVOTIONAL

It all belongs to God! God is the owner, and we are simply managers. If we understand that truth, everything changes.

God's ownership not only affects how we view the possessions He's entrusted to us, but this truth also reminds us that we are in fact His prize possessions, and we begin to understand that God really cares for that which is His. The psalmist illustrates this truth by pointing to the most significant sites on the landscape of his day: two mountains, climbing high into the sky proclaiming the mercy and truth of God.

God's mercy and truth are two of His greatest provisions. In His mercy, God protects us from "what could have been." Rather than giving us what we actually deserve, He graces us with gifts that conform us to His image. In His truth, He points us to what should be. He does not use His superiority to confuse us or get us off track; we do that on our own. Because He is true, we can always count on Him to keep His word. As *the* Truth, He promises to guide our paths in the way that is right.

Remember, if you are a child of God, you are His. Just as He established David, He desires to raise you up as a trophy of His mercy and truth.

Paul Purvis, First Baptist Church Temple Terrace
Temple Terrace, FL

JUNE 1

God Will Remain True to His Word

Psalm 89:24–37

24 "But My faithfulness and My mercy *shall be* with him,
And in My name his horn shall be exalted.

25 Also I will set his hand over the sea,
And his right hand over the rivers.

26 He shall cry to Me, 'You *are* my Father,
My God, and the rock of my salvation.'

27 Also I will make him *My* firstborn,
The highest of the kings of the earth.

28 My mercy I will keep for him forever,
And My covenant shall stand firm with him.

29 His seed also I will make *to endure* forever,
And his throne as the days of heaven.

30 "If his sons forsake My law
And do not walk in My judgments,

31 If they break My statutes
And do not keep My commandments,

32 Then I will punish their transgression with the rod,
And their iniquity with stripes.

33 Nevertheless My lovingkindness I will not utterly take from him,
Nor allow My faithfulness to fail.

34 My covenant I will not break,
Nor alter the word that has gone out of My lips.

35 Once I have sworn by My holiness;
I will not lie to David:

36 His seed shall endure forever,
And his throne as the sun before Me;

37 It shall be established forever like the moon,
Even *like* the faithful witness in the sky." Selah

DEVOTIONAL

Have you ever stopped to think about all the "but God" moments in Scripture?

From the very beginning, man has always missed God's mark, making himself vulnerable to the consequences of sin, but time and time again the faithfulness and mercy of our Father God has allowed us to experience grace.

God certainly demonstrated grace in the case of David, but God also remained true to His word. God's covenant with David did not change as a result of David's sin. Though David faltered, God remained faithful.

It's hard to believe that elements of this same covenant are available to you and me. Yet Scripture clearly teaches that God loves us and desires a covenant relationship in spite of our sin. His faithfulness will not fail.

This does not mean our sin is without consequence. Sometimes we will experience the pain caused by our sin, while at other times we will not. Occasionally we will be able to make restitution for our wrong doings, but often this will not be an option. Either way, our sin has been punished. Jesus took our stripes, He was beaten with our rod, and He certainly is the rock of our salvation.

Let God know how grateful you are that His graciousness is not based on your goodness. Thank Him today for keeping His word even when you fail to keep yours.

Paul Purvis, First Baptist Church Temple Terrace
Temple Terrace, FL

JUNE 2

David Questions God's Promise

Psalm 89:38–52

38 But You have cast off and abhorred,
You have been furious with Your anointed.

39 You have renounced the covenant of Your
servant;
You have profaned his crown *by casting it* to
the ground.

40 You have broken down all his hedges;
You have brought his strongholds to ruin.

41 All who pass by the way plunder him;
He is a reproach to his neighbors.

42 You have exalted the right hand of his
adversaries;
You have made all his enemies rejoice.

43 You have also turned back the edge of his sword,
And have not sustained him in the battle.
You have made his glory cease,
And cast his throne down to the ground.

45 The days of his youth You have shortened;
You have covered him with shame.   Selah

46 How long, LORD?
Will You hide Yourself forever?
Will Your wrath burn like fire?

47 Remember how short my time is;
For what futility have You created all the children of men?

48 What man can live and not see death?
Can he deliver his life from the power of the
grave?   Selah

49 Lord, where *are* Your former lovingkindnesses,
Which You swore to David in Your truth?

50 Remember, Lord, the reproach of Your
servants—
How I bear in my bosom *the reproach of* all the
many peoples,

51 With which Your enemies have reproached,
O LORD,
With which they have reproached the
footsteps of Your anointed.

52 Blessed *be* the LORD forevermore!
Amen and Amen.

DEVOTIONAL

How do you move from pain to praise? You journey through your insecurity past your uncertainty and beyond your doubt. You make a conscious decision to trust God, period!

The psalmist transitions from anxiety about God's absence to adoration of His eternal presence. What changed?

In verses 47 and 48, the writer reminds us of the frailty of life. In light of death's certainty, we are challenged to make life matter regardless of the circumstances we encounter. His presence never changes, but sometimes our perspective must change.

Our perspective is even greater in light of the life, death, burial, and resurrection of Jesus Christ. The apostle Paul reminds us in 1 Corinthians 15 that even death was defeated on Calvary's cross.

What does this mean for you? Though life is frail, God is faithful! You can trust Him on the journey through pain to praise. Remember, God is at work in you for your good and His glory, but your faith walk with Him is an ongoing journey. Ask God to give you faith for the journey today!

Paul Purvis, First Baptist Church Temple Terrace
Temple Terrace, FL

JUNE 3

Have you cried out to the Lord this week? Do a quick inventory and spend any additional time necessary to let God know what's on your mind. Write down some of your deepest concerns. Then take time to listen expectantly and hear what He has to say in response.

_____

_____

_____

_____

_____

_____

_____

_____

_____

What are some times in your life where God's faithfulness has been most evident? Take a moment and record a few of your favorite spiritual markers of God's provision. Thank God specifically for His loyalty and love at different times in your life.

_____

_____

_____

_____

_____

_____

_____

_____

JUNE 4

The Eternity of God

Psalm 90:1–6

L ORD, You have been our dwelling place in all
generations.

2 Before the mountains were brought forth,
Or ever You had formed the earth and the
world,
Even from everlasting to everlasting, You *are*
God.

3 You turn man to destruction,
And say, "Return, O children of men."

4 For a thousand years in Your sight
Are like yesterday when it is past,
And *like* a watch in the night.

5 You carry them away *like* a flood;
They are like a sleep.
In the morning they are like grass *which*
grows up:

6 In the morning it flourishes and grows up;
In the evening it is cut down and withers.

DEVOTIONAL

P salm 90 is the oldest recorded psalm and was
written by Moses when the children of Israel
turned away from Canaan and headed back to the
wilderness they had just left (Num. 13–14). Israel
had come up to Kadesh-Barnea. They sent spies
into Canaan, and ten brought back a negative report.
The land was as God had promised, but they saw
giants and were confident they could not conquer
them. Two men, Joshua and Caleb, gave a different
assessment. It was a land flowing with milk and
honey. And as for the giants—"Who cares if there

are giants. God is on our side, and we cannot be
defeated" was their response. However, the majority
ruled, fear drove out faith, and the Israelites decided
to not even attempt to conquer the Promised Land.
As a result of their lack of faith, God decreed that
everyone over the age of twenty, except Joshua and
Caleb, would die in the wilderness.

Moses began this psalm with the Hebrew name
of God, *Adonai*, which speaks of God as master,
in control over everything. What an awesome and
wonderful God we have! Nothing can slip by Him
or take Him by surprise. We have a God who rules
over all.

He rules over the wrong choices of life. Forty
years after the children of Israel disobeyed God
and missed out on His blessing, the next generation
of Israelites walked into the Promised Land. This
world will not stop the plan and purposes of God.

God rules over the choices of others that impact
our lives. Joshua and Caleb desired to demonstrate
faith and obey God. Even though they spent forty
years in the wilderness because of the disobedience of the first generation, they saw God's promise fulfilled in their lifetime.

God even rules over death. The English
Standard Version translates verse 3, "You return
man to dust." Death is a reality for everyone, but for
the Christ follower there is something beyond the
grave. Even though we are going to return to the
dust, we are also promised to return *from* the dust.

Psalm 90 gives every Christ follower a perspective to remember: we have a sovereign God who is
in total control of not only this world but also our
lives. Nothing gets by Him.

Chris Dixon, Liberty Baptist Church
Dublin, GA

JUNE 5

Man Is Frail, God Is Eternal

Psalm 90:7–17

7 For we have been consumed by Your anger,
And by Your wrath we are terrified.

8 You have set our iniquities before You,
Our secret *sins* in the light of Your
countenance.

9 For all our days have passed away in Your wrath;
We finish our years like a sigh.

10 The days of our lives *are* seventy years;
And if by reason of strength *they are* eighty
years,
Yet their boast *is* only labor and sorrow;
For it is soon cut off, and we fly away.

11 Who knows the power of Your anger?
For as the fear of You, *so is* Your wrath.

12 So teach *us* to number our days,
That we may gain a heart of wisdom.

13 Return, O LORD!
How long?
And have compassion on Your servants.

14 Oh, satisfy us early with Your mercy,
That we may rejoice and be glad all our days!

15 Make us glad according to the days *in which*
You have afflicted us,
The years *in which* we have seen evil.

16 Let Your work appear to Your servants,
And Your glory to their children.

17 And let the beauty of the LORD our God be
upon us,
And establish the work of our hands for us;
Yes, establish the work of our hands.

DEVOTIONAL

On average, it is estimated that there are 130 million babies born in the world each year. Every one of us has a certain amount of days, hours, minutes, and seconds before we leave this playground called Earth. Each and every day we use up very precious and valuable moments. That reality is exactly what Moses had in mind as he thought about the death sentence on the Israelites. Moses brought to light two major problems that are still problems for us today.

First is the problem of sin. He wrote, "You have set our iniquities before You, our secret sins in the light of Your countenance" (v. 8). Even though life is short, sin is in no short supply. Moses reminds us there is no secret sin. Whatever you feel is hidden is already exposed with God. And in a world that excuses and abuses sin, God only judges sin. The words Moses used in regard to sin are "anger" and "wrath" (v. 7).

Second, Moses knew that their days were numbered and that they would perish in the desert. Their disobedience brought the judgment of God.

How did Moses respond? He prayed! What did he ask for? Mercy, joy, work, and God's presence.

Life is fleeting! But what makes for a good life is the mercy and forgiveness of God found in Jesus Christ. Find joy in the fact that God has a plan and purpose for your life in the work He has called you to do, and experience God's presence as you spend time with Him each day.

Chris Dixon, Liberty Baptist Church
Dublin, GA

JUNE 6

Abiding in the Presence of God

Psalm 91:1–16

HE who dwells in the secret place of the
    Most High
  Shall abide under the shadow of the Almighty.
2 I will say of the LORD, "*He is* my refuge and my
    fortress;
  My God, in Him I will trust."

3 Surely He shall deliver you from the snare of
    the fowler
  And from the perilous pestilence.
4 He shall cover you with His feathers,
  And under His wings you shall take refuge;
  His truth *shall be your* shield and buckler.
5 You shall not be afraid of the terror by night,
  Nor of the arrow *that* flies by day,
6 *Nor* of the pestilence *that* walks in darkness,
  Nor of the destruction *that* lays waste at noonday.

7 A thousand may fall at your side,
  And ten thousand at your right hand;
  But it shall not come near you.
8 Only with your eyes shall you look,
  And see the reward of the wicked.

9 Because you have made the LORD, *who is* my
    refuge,
  Even the Most High, your dwelling place,
10 No evil shall befall you,
  Nor shall any plague come near your dwelling;
11 For He shall give His angels charge over you,
  To keep you in all your ways.
12 In *their* hands they shall bear you up,
  Lest you dash your foot against a stone.

13 You shall tread upon the lion and the cobra,
  The young lion and the serpent you shall
    trample underfoot.

14 "Because he has set his love upon Me, therefore
    I will deliver him;
  I will set him on high, because he has known
    My name.
15 He shall call upon Me, and I will answer him;
  I *will be* with him in trouble;
  I will deliver him and honor him.
16 With long life I will satisfy him,
  And show him My salvation."

DEVOTIONAL

In verses 1 and 2, this psalmist used four names for God: *Elyon, Shaddai, Jehovah,* and *Elohim.* Each one of these names reveals to us the power and promise available to us in times of trouble.

"The Most High" (*Elyon*) refers to possession. We have a God who owns it all. Even if you were to add together the net worths of the world's richest people, God would still be richer!

"The Almighty" (*Shaddai*) refers to provision. God not only possesses, but He also gives. He is the One who supplies all of our needs according to His riches (Phil. 4:19).

"The LORD" (*Jehovah*) refers to God's promise to do exceedingly, abundantly above all we could ask or think according to the power at work within us (Eph. 3:20).

"My God" (*Elohim*) refers to the power of God the Creator. If God can create the world, He can create a way! How about that for a refuge and a fortress?

Chris Dixon, Liberty Baptist Church
Dublin, GA

JUNE 7

Praise to the Lord for His Love

Psalm 92:1–15

I T *is* good to give thanks to the LORD,
And to sing praises to Your name, O Most
High;

2 To declare Your lovingkindness in the
morning,
And Your faithfulness every night,

3 On an instrument of ten strings,
On the lute,
And on the harp,
With harmonious sound.

4 For You, LORD, have made me glad through
Your work;
I will triumph in the works of Your hands.

5 O LORD, how great are Your works!
Your thoughts are very deep.

6 A senseless man does not know,
Nor does a fool understand this.

7 When the wicked spring up like grass,
And when all the workers of iniquity flourish,
It is that they may be destroyed forever.

8 But You, LORD, *are* on high forevermore.

9 For behold, Your enemies, O LORD,
For behold, Your enemies shall perish;
All the workers of iniquity shall be scattered.

10 But my horn You have exalted like a wild ox;
I have been anointed with fresh oil.

11 My eye also has seen *my desire* on my
enemies;
My ears hear *my desire* on the wicked
Who rise up against me.

12 The righteous shall flourish like a palm tree,
He shall grow like a cedar in Lebanon.

13 Those who are planted in the house of the
LORD
Shall flourish in the courts of our God.

14 They shall still bear fruit in old age;
They shall be fresh and flourishing,

15 To declare that the LORD is upright;
He is my rock, and *there is* no unrighteousness
in Him.

DEVOTIONAL

*"I can safely say, on the authority of all that is
revealed in the Word of God, that any man or
woman on this earth who is bored and turned
off by worship is not ready for Heaven."*

—*A. W. Tozer*[1]

I love praise and worship, but too often my
attention turns to the day before it turns to
Jesus. I do the necessary without taking time for
the primary. Throughout the Bible we are told to
praise God, and nowhere do we see that challenge
greater than in the book of Psalms. Here we are
reminded to praise God for the great things He
has done, but we are also to praise Him for who
He is. We are to praise Him when life is good, and
we are to praise Him when life is challenging.

Today, let's prepare ourselves for heaven. Take
some time away from all the distractions life
throws at you, and don't just pray and read the
Bible—*praise Him!*

*Chris Dixon, Liberty Baptist Church
Dublin, GA*

JUNE 8

The Eternal Reign of the Lord

Psalm 93:1–5

T HE LORD reigns, He is clothed with majesty;
  The LORD is clothed,
He has girded Himself with strength.
Surely the world is established, so that it cannot be moved.

2 Your throne *is* established from of old;
You *are* from everlasting.

3 The floods have lifted up, O LORD,
The floods have lifted up their voice;
The floods lift up their waves.

4 The LORD on high *is* mightier
Than the noise of many waters,
Than the mighty waves of the sea.

5 Your testimonies are very sure;
Holiness adorns Your house,
O LORD, forever.

DEVOTIONAL

W hen I read verse 4 of Psalm 93, I can't help but think about the children of Israel, their deliverance from Egypt, and their life in the wilderness. There were anywhere from two to three million Israelites at this time. That's a lot of people!

The Bible says they crossed the Red Sea in one night. If they had crossed side by side in pairs of two, they would have formed a line over seven hundred miles long and it would have taken them thirty-five days and nights to cross. To get that many people across in one night, they would have had to march five thousand people side by side, which would have required God to open a path in the Red Sea three miles wide.

Once they crossed the sea, a crowd that big would require a camping area of 750 square miles. It would require 1,500 tons of food per day to keep them from starving. It would have taken two freight trains, each one mile long, to haul in the daily food supply. At today's prices, it would cost around $5 million a day to feed them. It would require 11 million gallons of water for the bare necessities every day. If you figured one quail to each family of five, it would have required around 750,000 quail each morning. There had to have been around 2 million gallons of manna that fell on the ground each morning. Yet none of these challenges were too big for God!

I am grateful we have a God who is mightier than our problems. No matter what you may be facing today, His promises are very sure. He is the God who is able!

Chris Dixon, Liberty Baptist Church
Dublin, GA

JUNE 9

God, the Refuge of the Righteous

Psalm 94:1–11

O LORD God, to whom vengeance belongs—
 O God, to whom vengeance belongs, shine
  forth!
2 Rise up, O Judge of the earth;
  Render punishment to the proud.
3 LORD, how long will the wicked,
  How long will the wicked triumph?

4 They utter speech, *and* speak insolent things;
  All the workers of iniquity boast in
   themselves.
5 They break in pieces Your people, O LORD,
  And afflict Your heritage.
6 They slay the widow and the stranger,
  And murder the fatherless.
7 Yet they say, "The Lord does not see,
  Nor does the God of Jacob understand."

8 Understand, you senseless among the people;
  And *you* fools, when will you be wise?
9 He who planted the ear, shall He not hear?
  He who formed the eye, shall He not see?
10 He who instructs the nations, shall He not
    correct,
  He who teaches man knowledge?
11 The LORD knows the thoughts of man,
  That they *are* futile.

DEVOTIONAL

The psalmist raises one of the challenging questions of life: Where is God when things are bad? The fact of the matter is, there are going to be times when the arithmetic of life is not going to add up. The hardest things in life to stand are the things you don't understand. Life is not always going to make sense to you. But there is a great truth to remember: just because things do not make sense to you does not mean they do not make sense to God. Everything He allows in our lives fits perfectly in His plan, even when we don't understand the timing or the "why" of our circumstances.

Frances Ridley Havergal said, "In perplexities—when we cannot tell what to do, when we cannot understand what is going on around us—let us be calmed and steadied and made patient by the thought that what is hidden from us is not hidden from Him."[2]

Where is God when things are bad? He is on His throne, watching over those who are His. God knows what He is doing! When things are bad, He will work out the situation for His glory and for our good.

Chris Dixon, Liberty Baptist Church
Dublin, GA

JUNE 10

In what areas of your life do you need to begin to trust God to be a refuge and fortress? What doubts, concerns, questions, and fears do you need to place in God's hands?

_____

_____

_____

_____

_____

_____

_____

_____

_____

_____

For what can you praise God today?

_____

_____

_____

_____

_____

_____

_____

_____

_____

JUNE II

God, Our Faithful Friend

Psalm 94:12–23

¹² Blessed *is* the man whom You instruct, O LORD,
And teach out of Your law,

¹³ That You may give him rest from the days of
adversity,
Until the pit is dug for the wicked.

¹⁴ For the LORD will not cast off His people,
Nor will He forsake His inheritance.

¹⁵ But judgment will return to righteousness,
And all the upright in heart will follow it.

¹⁶ Who will rise up for me against the evildoers?
Who will stand up for me against the workers
of iniquity?

¹⁷ Unless the Lord *had been* my help,
My soul would soon have settled in silence.

¹⁸ If I say, "My foot slips,"
Your mercy, O LORD, will hold me up.

¹⁹ In the multitude of my anxieties within me,
Your comforts delight my soul.

²⁰ Shall the throne of iniquity, which devises evil
by law,
Have fellowship with You?

²¹ They gather together against the life of the
righteous,
And condemn innocent blood.

²² But the LORD has been my defense,
And my God the rock of my refuge.

²³ He has brought on them their own iniquity,
And shall cut them off in their own
wickedness;
The LORD our God shall cut them off.

DEVOTIONAL

Do you think of God as your friend, as someone who wants to help you? Many people don't. And because they don't, they are not open and honest with Him. They don't really seek Him or share with Him their hopes and dreams, their failures and fears.

But the truth is, the Lord is the best friend a person could ever have. He is the One who hangs in with us when everyone else bails out on us (v. 14). He is the One who has all power and wants to help us. Even when you and I blow it big-time, God's mercy is there to hold us up (v. 18). Even when we are overwhelmed with worries and fears, God's comfort is there to calm our hearts and delight our souls (v. 19).

Without question, those who foolishly and arrogantly reject God's great love and amazing grace will face righteous judgment for their sins and rebellion against the King of kings. God is holy and cannot have fellowship with sin (v. 20). That is why Jesus died and rose again, to pay for all our sins so we could enjoy His presence now and live forever with Him in heaven one day. Those who refuse that gift of salvation will be cut off from the Lord (v. 23). How terrible, tragic, and utterly senseless. It need not be so for anyone.

The Lord wants to forgive, not judge. He wants to save, not condemn. He wants to be our redeemer, friend, and helper. Is He all that and more to you? Is He your rock of refuge? He can be right now if you will simply cry out to Him in repentance and faith.

Jeff Schreve, First Baptist Church
Texarkana, TX

JUNE 12

A Call to Worship and Obedience

Psalm 95:1–11

O H come, let us sing to the LORD!
Let us shout joyfully to the Rock of our
salvation.

2 Let us come before His presence with
thanksgiving;
Let us shout joyfully to Him with psalms.

3 For the LORD *is* the great God,
And the great King above all gods.

4 In His hand *are* the deep places of the earth;
The heights of the hills *are* His also.

5 The sea *is* His, for He made it;
And His hands formed the dry *land*.

6 Oh come, let us worship and bow down;
Let us kneel before the LORD our Maker.

7 For He *is* our God,
And we *are* the people of His pasture,
And the sheep of His hand.

Today, if you will hear His voice:

8 "Do not harden your hearts, as in the rebellion,
As *in* the day of trial in the wilderness,

9 When your fathers tested Me;
They tried Me, though they saw My work.

10 For forty years I was grieved with *that*
generation,
And said, 'It *is* a people who go astray in their
hearts,
And they do not know My ways.'

11 So I swore in My wrath,
'They shall not enter My rest.'"

DEVOTIONAL

H ave you ever met a beloved celebrity,
movie star, or sports hero who left you
starstruck—utterly paralyzed, speechless, overwhelmed, and in awe? I had that experience in
1996 when I met the man who played my favorite
movie character of all time, Rocky Balboa. I found
myself in stunned amazement when I shook
Sylvester Stallone's hand. Although just a man,
and a gracious man at that, he seemed larger than
life to me.

When is the last time you have been starstruck
before the Lord? How long has it been since you
have really seen Him for who He is, the great and
holy King of the universe? How long has it been
since you found yourself totally and completely
overwhelmed, speechless, and in awe of almighty
God? Perhaps it has been far too long.

Psalm 95 is a wonderful psalm of worship, adoration, and praise. It reminds us of who He is, "the
LORD our Maker," and who we are, "the people of His
pasture" (vv. 6–7). It brings us to our knees in gratitude and awe. Take time right now to worship the
Lord in spirit and truth. Focus on His greatness and
unfathomable wisdom, power, and grace. Believe
the truth that He is the Good Shepherd who really
loves you and wants what is best for you. The cross
proves it. Ask Him to open your ears and soften
your heart so you can hear His voice and obey.

God takes no pleasure in people who harden
their hearts to Him. But He takes *great* pleasure
in those who willingly bow their knees to His will
and ways.

Jeff Schreve, First Baptist Church
Texarkana, TX

JUNE 13

A Song of Praise to God

Psalm 96:1–13

O H, sing to the LORD a new song!
Sing to the LORD, all the earth.

2 Sing to the LORD, bless His name;
Proclaim the good news of His salvation from
day to day.

3 Declare His glory among the nations,
His wonders among all peoples.

4 For the LORD *is* great and greatly to be praised;
He *is* to be feared above all gods.

5 For all the gods of the peoples *are* idols,
But the LORD made the heavens.

6 Honor and majesty *are* before Him;
Strength and beauty *are* in His sanctuary.

7 Give to the LORD, O families of the peoples,
Give to the LORD glory and strength.

8 Give to the LORD the glory *due* His name;
Bring an offering, and come into His courts.

9 Oh, worship the LORD in the beauty of
holiness!
Tremble before Him, all the earth.

10 Say among the nations, "The LORD reigns;
The world also is firmly established,
It shall not be moved;
He shall judge the peoples righteously."

11 Let the heavens rejoice, and let the earth
be glad;
Let the sea roar, and all its fullness;

12 Let the field be joyful, and all that *is* in it.
Then all the trees of the woods will rejoice
before the LORD.

13 For He is coming, for He is coming to judge
the earth.
He shall judge the world with righteousness,
And the peoples with His truth.

DEVOTIONAL

G od loves it when we worship Him. He is glo-rified and honored when we turn our eyes upon His greatness and fully acknowledge who He is. Indeed, worship blesses God's heart, and it changes our hearts as we get our eyes off our problems and onto the Problem Solver.

Are you a worshiper? Do you really worship God in a way that pleases Him? The sad truth is that many who call themselves Christians go through the motions of worship and fail to truly worship the King.

Psalm 96 gives us a blueprint for worship. It tells us what worship really looks like. You see, when we are truly worshiping, we are fully engaged. We open our mouths and sing . . . or at least make a joyful noise. We proclaim the good news of salvation and unashamedly declare His glory and power. We bring a generous offering and give cheerfully to His kingdom's work on earth. We get our hearts right and rejoice in Him, acknowledging that He is the righteous Judge who is coming again.

True worship is filled with exuberance and joy as we focus on who God is and what He has done. Those who truly worship are truly changed as they experience a fresh encounter with the living God.

Do you need a fresh touch today? "Oh, worship the LORD in the beauty of holiness!" (v. 9).

Jeff Schreve, First Baptist Church
Texarkana, TX

JUNE 14

A Song of Praise to the Sovereign Lord

Psalm 97:1–12

THE LORD reigns;
Let the earth rejoice;
Let the multitude of isles be glad!

2 Clouds and darkness surround Him;
Righteousness and justice *are* the foundation
of His throne.

3 A fire goes before Him,
And burns up His enemies round about.

4 His lightnings light the world;
The earth sees and trembles.

5 The mountains melt like wax at the presence
of the LORD,
At the presence of the Lord of the whole earth.

6 The heavens declare His righteousness,
And all the peoples see His glory.

7 Let all be put to shame who serve carved images,
Who boast of idols.
Worship Him, all *you* gods.

8 Zion hears and is glad,
And the daughters of Judah rejoice
Because of Your judgments, O LORD.

9 For You, LORD, *are* most high above all the
earth;
You are exalted far above all gods.

10 You who love the LORD, hate evil!
He preserves the souls of His saints;
He delivers them out of the hand of the
wicked.

11 Light is sown for the righteous,
And gladness for the upright in heart.

12 Rejoice in the LORD, you righteous,
And give thanks at the remembrance of His
holy name.

DEVOTIONAL

Problems. We all have them. And the danger we face with regard to our problems is to get overwhelmed with them; to see our problems as big and our God as small. But the truth is this: all our seemingly big and bad problems are nothing more than a pimple on a flea compared to almighty God.

God is so great and glorious. You and I cannot even begin to think or imagine big enough when it comes to God. For example, our known universe is calculated by astronomers to be about 14 billion light-years, with a light-second equaling 186,000 miles. When you do the math and turn seconds into years, the final number is mind-boggling. What is even more mind-boggling is the fact that God measures the universe with a span, the distance between His thumb and little finger (see Isa. 40:12). The children's song says it best: "My God is so big, so strong, and so mighty; there's nothing my God cannot do."

Are your eyes on the Lord today? Do you see Him as the reigning King, the One who is more than able to handle anything that comes into your life?

Worship Him and Him alone. Put Him first and love Him with all your heart. As you do, you will see His glory. The evil and idolatrous things that so easily find a home in our hearts will be exposed and expelled. And you will be glad!

Jeff Schreve, First Baptist Church
Texarkana, TX

JUNE 15
The Lord's Salvation and Judgment

Psalm 98:1–9

OH, sing to the LORD a new song!
For He has done marvelous things;
His right hand and His holy arm have gained
Him the victory.

2 The LORD has made known His salvation;
His righteousness He has revealed in the sight
of the nations.

3 He has remembered His mercy and His faithfulness to the house of Israel;
All the ends of the earth have seen the salvation of our God.

4 Shout joyfully to the LORD, all the earth;
Break forth in song, rejoice, and sing praises.

5 Sing to the LORD with the harp,
With the harp and the sound of a psalm,

6 With trumpets and the sound of a horn;
Shout joyfully before the LORD, the King.

7 Let the sea roar, and all its fullness,
The world and those who dwell in it;

8 Let the rivers clap *their* hands;
Let the hills be joyful together before the LORD,

9 For He is coming to judge the earth.
With righteousness He shall judge the world,
And the peoples with equity.

DEVOTIONAL

Are you ready for the Lord to come? Are you ready to face the righteous Judge who will judge us all with fairness and equity? No human being can stand before the Lord on his own merits. If all our righteous deeds are filthy rags before Him, what of our unrighteous deeds? If God were to judge us based on the sweat of our brow and the work of our hands, we would all be destined for hell.

But the Lord has made His salvation known. Jesus shed His blood for us and paid for all our sins. What a marvelous thing He has done! And all we have to do is receive the gift He has so graciously and freely given.

For those who reject His salvation, the return of the King is not a time for rejoicing, but a time for fearing. God will judge righteously, and there will be no "grading on a curve." All those who reject His love will be damned forever. At the Great White Throne, they will hear Him say with sadness, "Not My will, but yours be done."

For those who receive the gift of salvation, the coming of the Lord is a time to rejoice. We will be judged, but it will be a judgment to determine eternal rewards, not eternal destination.

The Lord will have each one of His children appear before Him at the judgment seat of Christ. His main question: "What did you do with the Christian life I gave you? Did you walk with Me and live to please Me, or did you put Me on the back burner and live to please yourself?"

He is coming to judge. Are you ready for Him? If not, consider this your wakeup call from the Lord.

Jeff Schreve, First Baptist Church
Texarkana, TX

JUNE 16

Praise to the Lord for His Holiness

Psalm 99:1–9

THE LORD reigns;
Let the peoples tremble!
He dwells *between* the cherubim;
Let the earth be moved!

2   The LORD *is* great in Zion,
And He *is* high above all the peoples.

3   Let them praise Your great and awesome
name—
He *is* holy.

4   The King's strength also loves justice;
You have established equity;
You have executed justice and righteousness
in Jacob.

5   Exalt the LORD our God,
And worship at His footstool—
He *is* holy.

6   Moses and Aaron were among His priests,
And Samuel was among those who called
upon His name;
They called upon the LORD, and He answered
them.

7   He spoke to them in the cloudy pillar;
They kept His testimonies and the ordinance
He gave them.

8   You answered them, O LORD our God;
You were to them God-Who-Forgives,
Though You took vengeance on their deeds.

9   Exalt the LORD our God,
And worship at His holy hill;
For the LORD our God *is* holy.

DEVOTIONAL

If you had to come up with only one word that best describes God, what word would it be? Would it be *love*? He certainly is love. Would it be *truth*? He certainly is truth. Would it be *omnipotent*? He certainly has all power. What word would you come up with?

The angels around the throne of God speak a word continuously, and that word is *holy*. "Holy, holy, holy is the LORD of hosts" (Isa. 6:3). God is worthy to be worshiped and praised because He is holy—totally pure, morally perfect, and set apart.

God wants His people to be like He is, holy. "Be holy, for I am holy" (1 Pet. 1:16). We can't "worship the LORD in the beauty of holiness" (Ps. 96:9) if we have known sin in our hearts. We have to get right with Him, through confession and repentance, so we can truly worship holy God in holiness.

As we worship Him in holiness, with all our sins out from the shadows and under His blood, we can have great confidence as we pray. Prayer is not a waste of time, because God answers prayer. When we join with Moses and Samuel in calling on His name, we are given the promise that He will indeed answer us.

Are you facing tough times today? Does life seem to be caving in on you? Cry out to the Holy One from a repentant heart. Obey the Lord and get yourself on blessing ground. God does business with those who mean business ... so pray, believe, and get ready to receive.

Jeff Schreve, First Baptist Church
Texarkana, TX

JUNE 17

Since God has revealed Himself as your helper, where do you need help today? What sins are you struggling with? Bitterness? Jealousy? Lust? Greed? Selfishness? Pride? Fear of failure? Openly and honestly talk to your divine helper about these issues, and ask Him to make a real difference in you.

Our God is an awesome God. He is mighty and majestic, holy and exalted. We should be awestruck at the mere mention of His name. The truth is, we easily lose sight of His greatness and take Him for granted. Take some time to write down some of the wonderful attributes of God . . . and praise Him for being all that and more.

JUNE 18

The Lord's Faithfulness to His People

Psalm 100:1–5

MAKE a joyful shout to the LORD, all you lands!

2 Serve the LORD with gladness;
Come before His presence with singing.

3 Know that the LORD, He *is* God;
It is He *who* has made us, and not we ourselves;
We are His people and the sheep of His pasture.

4 Enter into His gates with thanksgiving,
And into His courts with praise.
Be thankful to Him, *and* bless His name.

5 For the LORD *is* good;
His mercy *is* everlasting,
And His truth *endures* to all generations.

Psalm 101:1–8

I WILL sing of mercy and justice;
To You, O LORD, I will sing praises.

2 I will behave wisely in a perfect way.
Oh, when will You come to me?
I will walk within my house with a perfect heart.

3 I will set nothing wicked before my eyes;
I hate the work of those who fall away;
It shall not cling to me.

4 A perverse heart shall depart from me;
I will not know wickedness.

5 Whoever secretly slanders his neighbor,
Him I will destroy;

The one who has a haughty look and a proud heart,
Him I will not endure.

6 My eyes *shall be* on the faithful of the land,
That they may dwell with me;
He who walks in a perfect way,
He shall serve me.

7 He who works deceit shall not dwell within my house;
He who tells lies shall not continue in my presence.

8 Early I will destroy all the wicked of the land,
That I may cut off all the evildoers from the city of the LORD.

DEVOTIONAL

What if, on your way into church next Sunday, you encountered people entering the building who were already shouting, singing, and praising God? All this before the choir had warmed up, one testimony had been shared, or one person had been baptized? Why this awesome expression of public praise? There can only be one explanation. The people cannot contain their praise of God in public because of Who they have encountered in private. David said, "I will walk within my house with a perfect heart" (Ps. 101:2).

Worship and service to God become dull when we neglect our time alone with Him. God is full of joy. When we are full of God, we are full of joy that cannot be contained. The key to joyful expressions of public worship is our private meetings with Him.

Scott Yirka, Hibernia Baptist Church
Fleming Island, FL

JUNE 19

The Lord's Eternal Love

Psalm 102:1–17

HEAR my prayer, O LORD,
  And let my cry come to You.
2 Do not hide Your face from me in the day of
      my trouble;
  Incline Your ear to me;
  In the day that I call, answer me speedily.
3 For my days are consumed like smoke,
  And my bones are burned like a hearth.
4 My heart is stricken and withered like grass,
  So that I forget to eat my bread.
5 Because of the sound of my groaning
  My bones cling to my skin.
6 I am like a pelican of the wilderness;
  I am like an owl of the desert.
7 I lie awake,
  And am like a sparrow alone on the housetop.
8 My enemies reproach me all day long;
  Those who deride me swear an oath
          against me.
9 For I have eaten ashes like bread,
  And mingled my drink with weeping,
10 Because of Your indignation and Your wrath;
  For You have lifted me up and cast me away.
11 My days *are* like a shadow that lengthens,
  And I wither away like grass.
12 But You, O LORD, shall endure forever,
  And the remembrance of Your name to all
          generations.
13 You will arise *and* have mercy on Zion;
  For the time to favor her,

Yes, the set time, has come.
14 For Your servants take pleasure in her stones,
  And show favor to her dust.
15 So the nations shall fear the name of the LORD,
  And all the kings of the earth Your glory.
16 For the LORD shall build up Zion;
  He shall appear in His glory.
17 He shall regard the prayer of the destitute,
  And shall not despise their prayer.

DEVOTIONAL

The Babylonians had attacked (Jer. 25:11–13), Jerusalem lay in ruins, and the psalmist was greatly distressed. Life had changed and much had been lost. He would have been overwhelmed by his grief were it not for his hope in God. Life changes, but God does not. "But You, O LORD, shall endure forever" (Ps. 102:12). This psalm not only points to a past event, but it is also a messianic psalm, which means it points to Jesus. Reading the psalm, you can hear Jesus pouring out His soul to His Father in the Garden of Gethsemane, knowing He will be forsaken by His own and delivered to His enemies. In His deep despair, Jesus demonstrated perfect trust in the Father and said, "Your will be done" (Matt. 26:42).

We will face difficult changes in life. What we need to remember is that God does not change; He is faithful and will arise at the set time and have mercy on us, His children. Even when we feel we are withering away like grass, our Lord will come to our aid. He hears our prayers.

Scott Yirka, Hibernia Baptist Church
Fleming Island, FL

JUNE 20

The Psalmist Remembers His Troubles

Psalm 102:18–28

18 This will be written for the generation to come,
That a people yet to be created may praise the LORD.

19 For He looked down from the height of His sanctuary;
From heaven the LORD viewed the earth,

20 To hear the groaning of the prisoner,
To release those appointed to death,

21 To declare the name of the LORD in Zion,
And His praise in Jerusalem,

22 When the peoples are gathered together,
And the kingdoms, to serve the LORD.

23 He weakened my strength in the way;
He shortened my days.

24 I said, "O my God,
Do not take me away in the midst of my days;
Your years *are* throughout all generations.

25 Of old You laid the foundation of the earth,
And the heavens *are* the work of Your hands.

26 They will perish, but You will endure;
Yes, they will all grow old like a garment;
Like a cloak You will change them,
And they will be changed.

27 But You *are* the same,
And Your years will have no end.

28 The children of Your servants will continue,
And their descendants will be established before You."

DEVOTIONAL

The last portion of this psalm is quoted in Hebrews 1:10–12. Creation is the handiwork of our Lord Jesus Christ. He is the Creator and Sustainer of all things (Col. 1:16–17). As wonderful as creation is, it is but a minute foretaste of what is to come. Creation is decaying. It is given to entropy and subjected to the second law of thermodynamics (Rom. 8:20–21). Therefore, we are living in a temporary world that is wearing out like an old T-shirt. All of creation is headed for re-creation. That's right; all will be changed one day by our Lord, including us (1 Cor. 15:50–58). We will put off this corrupted flesh and put on incorruption.

So here is the deal: heaven is ahead for us. Too many people are trying to create a heaven on earth. Do you see the problem with that approach to life? This life ebbs and flows like the tide from hurt to happiness; things change constantly. If we are anchored to the comforts in this world, we will drift into a dark sea of despair. If we are anchored in the unchanging Christ, we will be secure no matter what changes comes our way.

Scott Yirka, Hibernia Baptist Church
Fleming Island, FL

JUNE 21

Praise for the Lord's Mercies

Psalm 103:1–10

B LESS the LORD, O my soul;
And all that is within me, *bless* His holy
    name!
² Bless the LORD, O my soul,
    And forget not all His benefits:
³ Who forgives all your iniquities,
    Who heals all your diseases,
⁴ Who redeems your life from destruction,
    Who crowns you with lovingkindness and
        tender mercies,
⁵ Who satisfies your mouth with good *things,*
    So that your youth is renewed like the eagle's.

⁶ The LORD executes righteousness
    And justice for all who are oppressed.
⁷ He made known His ways to Moses,
    His acts to the children of Israel.
⁸ The LORD *is* merciful and gracious,
    Slow to anger, and abounding in mercy.
⁹ He will not always strive *with us,*
    Nor will He keep *His anger* forever.
¹⁰ He has not dealt with us according to our sins,
    Nor punished us according to our iniquities.

DEVOTIONAL

S omeone once quipped they suffered from
amnesia and déjà vu at the same time. I think
this is true of most believers. We sometimes find
ourselves saying, "I know I have forgotten this
before."

We certainly can forget the blessings of God, so
it is good to recount them. God is so gracious to
us that He even gave us a special way to remember our Lord's death until He comes back: the
Lord's Supper. He wants us to remember important things: He forgives all our iniquities, He heals
all our diseases, He redeems us, He loves us, He is
merciful to us, He satisfies us, and He renews our
strength.

God has given all these benefits to us through
His Son, Jesus (Eph. 1:3). Remember, God laid
our sins on Jesus so we would not be punished
"according to our iniquities" (Ps. 103:10). Sinners
must be punished and we are sinners. Our only
hope is that the "LORD is merciful and gracious" (v.
8) toward us and that He chose a worthy substitute to punish in our place. Jesus, God in the flesh,
is the substitute of God's choosing. Jesus went to
a criminal's cross, was crucified in agony, drank
every drop of God's wrath directed at sin from
the cup of suffering, and then gave up His life.
God dealt with Jesus, who knew no sin as a sinner, so that He could deal with sinners as though
they had no sin (Gal. 2:20). Praise the Lord now by
recounting the ways He has blessed you.

Scott Yirka, Hibernia Baptist Church
Fleming Island, FL

JUNE 22

The Lord Is Merciful

Psalm 103:11–22

11 For as the heavens are high above the earth,
   So great is His mercy toward those who
      fear Him;
12 As far as the east is from the west,
   So far has He removed our transgressions
      from us.
13 As a father pities *his* children,
   So the LORD pities those who fear Him.
14 For He knows our frame;
   He remembers that we *are* dust.

15 *As for* man, his days *are* like grass;
   As a flower of the field, so he flourishes.
16 For the wind passes over it, and it is gone,
   And its place remembers it no more.
17 But the mercy of the LORD *is* from everlasting
      to everlasting
   On those who fear Him,
   And His righteousness to children's
      children,
18 To such as keep His covenant,
   And to those who remember His
      commandments to do them.

19 The LORD has established His throne in
      heaven,
   And His kingdom rules over all.

20 Bless the LORD, you His angels,
   Who excel in strength, who do His word,
   Heeding the voice of His word.
21 Bless the LORD, all *you* His hosts,
   You ministers of His, who do His pleasure.

22 Bless the LORD, all His works,
   In all places of His dominion.

Bless the LORD, O my soul!

DEVOTIONAL

How far is the east from the west? A childhood Sunday school teacher taught me a lesson I will never forget. He said that if we were to travel north long enough, we would eventually arrive at the North Pole. That is the place North and South meet. However, if we launched out on an eastern latitude, we could travel around the world and never meet west. Maybe that is why the psalmist did not say God has removed our sin as far as the north is from the south. Because God's mercy is everlasting, we who have believed in His Son will never face condemnation because all our sin is completely forgiven. We have entered a blood covenant with God through Jesus and our sin has been totally cleansed (1 John 1:7).

All the saved can join heaven in rejoicing today because God is on His throne; He saves us and keeps us saved. Be assured that your salvation is secure because God keeps you not because you keep God.

Scott Yirka, Hibernia Baptist Church
Fleming Island, FL

JUNE 23

Praise to the Lord for His Creation

Psalm 104:1-9

B LESS the LORD, O my soul!
O LORD my God, You are very great:
You are clothed with honor and majesty,

2 Who cover *Yourself* with light as *with* a
garment,
Who stretch out the heavens like a curtain.

3 He lays the beams of His upper chambers in
the waters,
Who makes the clouds His chariot,
Who walks on the wings of the wind,

4 Who makes His angels spirits,
His ministers a flame of fire.

5 *You who* laid the foundations of the earth,
So *that* it should not be moved forever,

6 You covered it with the deep as *with* a
garment;
The waters stood above the mountains.

7 At Your rebuke they fled;
At the voice of Your thunder they hastened
away.

8 They went up over the mountains;
They went down into the valleys,
To the place which You founded for them.

9 You have set a boundary that they may not
pass over,
That they may not return to cover the earth.

DEVOTIONAL

A s the old hymn says, Oh Lord my God, when
I in awesome wonder, consider all the works
Thy hand hath made."[1] The psalmist wrote, "O
LORD my God, You are very great" (v. 1). This psalm
is divine fresh air in our stagnant atmosphere
of humanism and is a psalm of perfect praise. It
seems fitting simply to recount the greatness of
God here on display.

God is clothed with light, for what else could
clothe He who *is* light (1 Tim. 6:16)? No wonder
the sun will become obsolete (Rev. 21:23). He
uses the clouds as His chariot and angels swiftly
carry out His will everywhere He commands.
He alone laid out the earth and hung it on nothing (Job 26:7). He alone set the boundaries of the
oceans and raised the mountains to their place
(Job 38:11–12). He can be seen in creation: "For
since the creation of the world His invisible attributes are clearly seen, being understood by the
things that are made, even His eternal power and
Godhead, so that they are without excuse" (Rom.
1:20). He is known through His Son (Heb. 1:1–2).
He has been revealed through His Word.

The purpose of Scripture is to teach us about
God. The place to find God is in the Bible, not
signs, wonders, or experiences. When we learn
who God is from Holy Scripture, then sings our
soul, "How great Thou art."[2]

Scott Yirka, Hibernia Baptist Church
Fleming Island, FL

JUNE 24

The greatest blessing you can know is that a Holy God has offered salvation to you and will not deal with you the way you deserve because of your sin. Take a moment to recount your salvation and then write down your testimony. Would you write down the names of four or five people to whom you would like to relate your salvation story?

_____

_____

_____

_____

_____

_____

_____

_____

_____

_____

"Therefore by Him let us continually offer the sacrifice of praise to God, that is, the fruit of our lips, giving thanks to His name" (Heb. 13:15). Record some attributes of God, praise Him for who He is, and give thanks for what He has done.

_____

_____

_____

_____

_____

_____

_____

_____

JUNE 25

Creation Sings Praise

Psalm 104:10–23

¹⁰ He sends the springs into the valleys;
They flow among the hills.

¹¹ They give drink to every beast of the field;
The wild donkeys quench their thirst.

¹² By them the birds of the heavens have their
home;
They sing among the branches.

¹³ He waters the hills from His upper chambers;
The earth is satisfied with the fruit of Your
works.

¹⁴ He causes the grass to grow for the cattle,
And vegetation for the service of man,
That he may bring forth food from the earth,

¹⁵ And wine *that* makes glad the heart of man,
Oil to make *his* face shine,
And bread *which* strengthens man's heart.

¹⁶ The trees of the LORD are full *of sap,*
The cedars of Lebanon which He planted,

¹⁷ Where the birds make their nests;
The stork has her home in the fir trees.

¹⁸ The high hills *are* for the wild goats;
The cliffs are a refuge for the rock badgers.

¹⁹ He appointed the moon for seasons;
The sun knows its going down.

²⁰ You make darkness, and it is night,
In which all the beasts of the forest creep about.

²¹ The young lions roar after their prey,
And seek their food from God.

²² *When* the sun rises, they gather together
And lie down in their dens.

²³ Man goes out to his work
And to his labor until the evening.

DEVOTIONAL

When I was a teenager, I learned a song that is now a staple in many worship services that speaks to the beauty and majesty of God titled "I Stand in Awe of You." Sometimes when I'm alone and reflecting on all God is and all He has done, I sing that song of praise: "I stand, I stand in awe of You. I stand, I stand in awe of You. Holy God to whom all praise is due, I stand in awe of You."[1]

The beauty and power of the song has stuck in my head and heart for years. I can sing the lyrics of the verse and chorus word-for-word in my mind as a song of praise to God. Psalm 104 is also such a song. It is the recognition of God's glory through His provisions for all of creation.

Every detail of creation sings a song of praise to the Creator. Today, consider taking a walk and reflecting on what you see: birds, trees, water, fields. Take in the beauty of nature along a desolate road or look up in the sky in a downtown city. "Let all creation sing the wonders of His love."

God designed every detail of creation and every detail of man for His praise and glory. For a complementary testimony of praise to God, consider flipping a few pages to Psalm 139 and read it with Psalm 104 as the backdrop. The parallels of the two psalms work in concert to echo the praise of the Creator God.

May your heart sing with praise for who He is and for the garden of life in which He has placed you.

Dr. Richard Mark Lee, First Baptist Church
McKinney, TX

JUNE 26

God Created Everything

Psalm 104:24–35

24 O LORD, how manifold are Your works!
In wisdom You have made them all.
The earth is full of Your possessions—

25 This great and wide sea,
In which *are* innumerable teeming things,
Living things both small and great.

26 There the ships sail about;
There is that Leviathan
Which You have made to play there.

27 These all wait for You,
That You may give *them* their food in due
season.

28 *What* You give them they gather in;
You open Your hand, they are filled with
good.

29 You hide Your face, they are troubled;
You take away their breath, they die and return
to their dust.

30 You send forth Your Spirit, they are created;
And You renew the face of the earth.

31 May the glory of the LORD endure forever;
May the LORD rejoice in His works.

32 He looks on the earth, and it trembles;
He touches the hills, and they smoke.

33 I will sing to the LORD as long as I live;
I will sing praise to my God while I have my
being.

34 May my meditation be sweet to Him;
I will be glad in the LORD.

35 May sinners be consumed from the earth,
And the wicked be no more.

Bless the LORD, O my soul!
Praise the LORD!

DEVOTIONAL

The psalms are songs of praise to God. Verse 24 continues the praise of yesterday's reading (vv. 10–23) and echoes the praise found in Psalm 24: God designed all of creation.

From today's reading, how do we respond to who He is? The earth trembles at His focus (v. 32). The hills smoke. How do we respond to His attention? How often do we tremble in reverential awe and holy fear of God? Have we grown so arrogant as a people that we've forgotten the awe, wonder, fear, and respect for the greatness of God? Have we become complacent about His power and the majesty of His work? Our lives are to reflect the glory of God. We are to live in concert with His creation as a symphony of praise unto our Creator God, our King, our Lord, and our Savior.

Does the wonder of worship consume you, or are you too casual and comfortable in His presence? He is God, and we are His creation. Read verses 31–35 slowly, carefully, and with a reflective, reverential awe. Worship and praise the Lord our God. As I read this passage, my heart begins to sing, "Bless the Lord, O my soul, worship His holy name."[2]

Dr. Richard Mark Lee, First Baptist Church
McKinney, TX

JUNE 27

The Eternal Faithfulness of the Lord

Psalm 105:1–15

OH, give thanks to the LORD!
Call upon His name;
Make known His deeds among the peoples!

2 Sing to Him, sing psalms to Him;
Talk of all His wondrous works!

3 Glory in His holy name;
Let the hearts of those rejoice who seek the
LORD!

4 Seek the LORD and His strength;
Seek His face evermore!

5 Remember His marvelous works which He
has done,
His wonders, and the judgments of His mouth,

6 O seed of Abraham His servant,
You children of Jacob, His chosen ones!

7 He *is* the LORD our God;
His judgments *are* in all the earth.

8 He remembers His covenant forever,
The word *which* He commanded, for a
thousand generations,

9 *The covenant* which He made with Abraham,
And His oath to Isaac,

10 And confirmed it to Jacob for a statute,
To Israel *as* an everlasting covenant,

11 Saying, "To you I will give the land of Canaan
As the allotment of your inheritance,"

12 When they were few in number,
Indeed very few, and strangers in it.

13 When they went from one nation to another,
From *one* kingdom to another people,

14 He permitted no one to do them wrong;
Yes, He rebuked kings for their sakes,

15 *Saying,* "Do not touch My anointed ones,
And do My prophets no harm."

DEVOTIONAL

The verses from this psalm are repeated in 1 Chronicles 16:8–22 when King David gave instructions for instruments to be played and worship leaders to lead the people to praise God for His faithfulness. The setting is the procession of the ark of the covenant into the city of Jerusalem. David encouraged the people to praise God for both His faithfulness and His presence. The ark of the covenant served as a reminder of God's faithfulness to deliver His people from Egypt and of His continued active presence in their lives. It is wise for us to recall all that God has done in the past and proclaim His goodness, faithfulness, and provision.

Sing to the Lord and seek the Lord. May our hearts be filled with praise and prayer. God always comes through. Jerry Rankin has written, "His timing is seldom in line with our expectations but that's our problem, not His."[3] The lessons of history teach us that God will always keep His Word.

God's faithfulness in the past allows us to trust Him for our future. He's been faithful to provide for us even in the midst of our rebellion and wondering. He will fulfill His promise. Meditate on the first five verses and sing a new song of praise as you seek God's presence and power in your life. He's worthy! He's waiting! He's here!

As I reflect on this psalm, I sing in my mind the hymn "Great Is Thy Faithfulness."

Dr. Richard Mark Lee, First Baptist Church
McKinney, TX

JUNE 28

God's Faithfulness to His Covenant

Psalm 105:16–25

16 Moreover He called for a famine in the land;
He destroyed all the provision of bread.

17 He sent a man before them—
Joseph—*who* was sold as a slave.

18 They hurt his feet with fetters,
He was laid in irons.

19 Until the time that his word came to pass,
The word of the LORD tested him.

20 The king sent and released him,
The ruler of the people let him go free.

21 He made him lord of his house,
And ruler of all his possessions,

22 To bind his princes at his pleasure,
And teach his elders wisdom.

23 Israel also came into Egypt,
And Jacob dwelt in the land of Ham.

24 He increased His people greatly,
And made them stronger than their enemies.

25 He turned their heart to hate His people,
To deal craftily with His servants.

DEVOTIONAL

How do you respond when things seem to go from bad to worse? Oftentimes, responses of anger, frustration, bewilderment, and doubt consume our thoughts. And yet it just might be the work of God behind the scenes for a greater good. Such was the case with Joseph.

If you are familiar with the story of Joseph (Gen. 37–50), it might be tempting to gloss over this psalm and miss out on this song of thanksgiving and praise. Joseph endured trials and testing and passed every test! God was working in Joseph so that at the appointed time, He might work through Joseph. For thirteen years, Joseph was being prepared for his life of service. At the age of thirty, God promoted Joseph from a common slave to the second in command in all the land of Egypt.

God was fulfilling His covenant and promise to Abraham in Genesis 12 through Joseph, Jacob, and Egypt. God is in control. He is sovereign. Even when circumstances seem to be going in a different direction, God can be trusted. He has never failed. Years ago I learned a powerful principle: don't doubt in the dark what God has shown you in the light.

His Word is true. He does not change. He is faithful. He can be trusted. He fulfills His promises! Matt Redman's song "Blessed Be Your Name" expresses this psalm so well:

> Blessed be Your name
> On the road marked with suffering
> Though there's pain in the offering
> Blessed be Your name
> Every blessing You pour out
> I'll turn back to praise
> When the darkness closes in, Lord
> Still I will say
> Blessed be the name of the Lord.[4]

Dr. Richard Mark Lee, First Baptist Church
McKinney, TX

JUNE 29

A Celebration of God's Gift

Psalm 105:26–45

26 He sent Moses His servant,
And Aaron whom He had chosen.

27 They performed His signs among them,
And wonders in the land of Ham.

28 He sent darkness, and made *it* dark;
And they did not rebel against His word.

29 He turned their waters into blood,
And killed their fish.

30 Their land abounded with frogs,
Even in the chambers of their kings.

31 He spoke, and there came swarms of flies,
And lice in all their territory.

32 He gave them hail for rain,
And flaming fire in their land.

33 He struck their vines also, and their fig trees,
And splintered the trees of their territory.

34 He spoke, and locusts came,
Young locusts without number,

35 And ate up all the vegetation in their land,
And devoured the fruit of their ground.

36 He also destroyed all the firstborn in their
    land,
The first of all their strength.

37 He also brought them out with silver and gold,
And *there was* none feeble among His tribes.

38 Egypt was glad when they departed,
For the fear of them had fallen upon them.

39 He spread a cloud for a covering,
And fire to give light in the night.

40 *The people* asked, and He brought quail,

And satisfied them with the bread of heaven.

41 He opened the rock, and water gushed out;
It ran in the dry places *like* a river.

42 For He remembered His holy promise,
And Abraham His servant.

43 He brought out His people with joy,
His chosen ones with gladness.

44 He gave them the lands of the Gentiles,
And they inherited the labor of the nations,

45 That they might observe His statutes
And keep His laws.

Praise the LORD!

DEVOTIONAL

Today's reading reminds us of God's work through Moses to lead His people out from four hundred years of slavery. This portion of Psalm 105 recounts some of the plagues from Exodus 7–11 that were instrumental in the children of Israel's deliverance from Egypt's captivity. The ninth plague, referred to as "darkness" in Psalm 105:28, resulted in Pharaoh's acknowledgement of God's power.

So many times we get wrapped up in our present and ignore the lessons of the past. This psalm is a reminder of God's work in the past preparing and providing for His people. Based on God's faithfulness in the past, we can have faith for our future. God does not mismanage events or circumstances. His provision is the continuation of the fulfillment of His promise to Abraham. He is at work in all things. He brought out His people with joy and gladness (v. 43). He provided the land promised so they might observe His statutes and keep His laws!

Dr. Richard Mark Lee, First Baptist Church
McKinney, TX

JUNE 30

Joy in Forgiveness of Israel's Sins

Psalm 106:1–12

P RAISE the LORD!
    Oh, give thanks to the LORD, for *He is* good!
For His mercy *endures* forever.

2 Who can utter the mighty acts of the LORD?
    Who can declare all His praise?

3 Blessed *are* those who keep justice,
    And he who does righteousness at all times!

4 Remember me, O LORD, with the favor *You*
    have toward Your people.
    Oh, visit me with Your salvation,

5 That I may see the benefit of Your chosen
    ones,
    That I may rejoice in the gladness of Your
    nation,
    That I may glory with Your inheritance.

6 We have sinned with our fathers,
    We have committed iniquity,
    We have done wickedly.

7 Our fathers in Egypt did not understand Your
    wonders;
    They did not remember the multitude of Your
    mercies,
    But rebelled by the sea—the Red Sea.

8 Nevertheless He saved them for His name's
    sake,
    That He might make His mighty power
    known.

9 He rebuked the Red Sea also, and it dried up;
    So He led them through the depths,
    As through the wilderness.

10 He saved them from the hand of him who
    hated *them,*
    And redeemed them from the hand of the
    enemy.

11 The waters covered their enemies;
    There was not one of them left.

12 Then they believed His words;
    They sang His praise.

DEVOTIONAL

T he opening verse of Psalm 106 is repeated
  in Psalms 107, 118, and 136 and also in 1
Chronicles 16:34. A song by Chris Tomlin comes
to mind and causes me to pause and worship.
"Give thanks to the Lord our God and King, His
love endures forever."[5]

Sin has consequences that must be dealt with,
and yet God continues to extend His mercy to His
people. The psalmist reviews Israel's rebellion and
sin against God to show the mercy, faithfulness,
and forgiveness of God. Who of us would be so
faithful if those we loved had betrayed us? Many
of us have a short leash of forgiveness and can be
quick to write off those who repeatedly turn on
us. Not our great God! His mercy endures. God's
continued mercy is not a reason for us to sin and
presume upon His forgiveness, but rather a reason
to sing songs of praise because His love endures!

Those who have been forgiven know how to
rejoice in thanksgiving and praise. God's work in
our lives is to display His glory. Reread verse 8:
"Nevertheless He saved them for His name's sake,
that He might make His mighty power known."

God is always faithful. Sing your praise to Him!

Dr. Richard Mark Lee, First Baptist Church
McKinney, TX

JULY 1

Reflect upon this week's reading and write your own song of praise to God. Don't worry about the rhyme or rhythm. Worship God and praise Him for His faithfulness in your life.

_____

_____

_____

_____

_____

_____

_____

_____

_____

_____

_____

_____

Psalm 106:8 says, "He saved them for His name's sake, that He might make His mighty power known." How are you allowing God to use your life to display His glory?

_____

_____

_____

_____

_____

_____

_____

_____

_____

JULY 2

They Forgot God Their Savior

Psalm 106:13–23

¹³ They soon forgot His works;
They did not wait for His counsel,

¹⁴ But lusted exceedingly in the wilderness,
And tested God in the desert.

¹⁵ And He gave them their request,
But sent leanness into their soul.

¹⁶ When they envied Moses in the camp,
And Aaron the saint of the LORD,

¹⁷ The earth opened up and swallowed Dathan,
And covered the faction of Abiram.

¹⁸ A fire was kindled in their company;
The flame burned up the wicked.

¹⁹ They made a calf in Horeb,
And worshiped the molded image.

²⁰ Thus they changed their glory
Into the image of an ox that eats grass.

²¹ They forgot God their Savior,
Who had done great things in Egypt,

²² Wondrous works in the land of Ham,
Awesome things by the Red Sea.

²³ Therefore He said that He would destroy them,
Had not Moses His chosen one stood before
Him in the breach,
To turn away His wrath, lest He destroy *them.*

DEVOTIONAL

As you walk with the Lord, don't allow sinful attitudes to dominate your life. Pushing out memories of God's past graces from your mind is an invitation for wicked thoughts to take up residence. Sinful attitudes lead to sinful actions.

Israel thought, *I don't know what God is up to, but He is going to have to do better than this!* Surveying their circumstances caused them to complain that God's provision wasn't enough. Grumbling and complaining give evidence you have forgotten God's grace toward you. A critical attitude is a byproduct of a heart that is seeking satisfaction in life apart from God.

Dathan thought, *I don't like the authority of Moses. I think I should be in charge.* Dathan, along with others, rebelled against the authority of Moses and Aaron in Israel. Their inability to submit to the authority God had allowed was a direct rebellion against God. Submission to authority is a foundation for true worship. If you are rebelling against the authority structures in your life, you are rebelling against God.

A critical and rebellious attitude leads to idolatry. When we don't find our soul's rest in our relationship with God, we seek to satisfy our flesh with what the world provides. This is idolatry. When we defy those in authority over us, we are defying God. These sinful attitudes lead us to actively elevate something, someone, or even ourselves above God.

Sinful attitudes gain momentum when we forget what God has done with His people and us. Remembering God's grace elevates His glorious nature in our thoughts and strengthens our resolve to walk with Him daily. If you sense a critical or rebellious attitude taking up residence in your life, confess it to God as sin. Then spend time with Him in prayer recalling how He has worked in the lives of His people and yours. Don't fall into the pit of forgetfulness.

Dr. Levi Skipper, Concord Baptist Church
Clermont, GA

JULY 3
Stand for God's Glory

Psalm 106:24–33

24 Then they despised the pleasant land;
   They did not believe His word,
25 But complained in their tents,
   And did not heed the voice of the LORD.
26 Therefore He raised up His hand *in an oath*
      against them,
   To overthrow them in the wilderness,
27 To overthrow their descendants among the
      nations,
   And to scatter them in the lands.
28 They joined themselves also to Baal of Peor,
   And ate sacrifices made to the dead.
29 Thus they provoked *Him* to anger with their
      deeds,
   And the plague broke out among them.
30 Then Phinehas stood up and intervened,
   And the plague was stopped.
31 And that was accounted to him for
      righteousness
   To all generations forevermore.
32 They angered *Him* also at the waters of strife,
   So that it went ill with Moses on account of
      them;
33 Because they rebelled against His Spirit,
   So that he spoke rashly with his lips.

DEVOTIONAL

A group of ungrateful people turned their noses up to God in pride, continually complaining against God and dissatisfied with His provision and protection. They entered their tents at night grumbling about their situation in life. The Lord's anger burned greatly against the people of Israel. They had betrayed Him and chosen to worship idols. They were committing spiritual adultery against the Lord by bowing down to the false gods of Peor. God had had enough, and, in just wrath, He poured out a plague upon the people, which killed twenty-four thousand (see Num. 25:1–13).

However, in the midst of dissention was a great man of faith. In the midst of this great plague was a man who was passionate about the Lord. He is seldom mentioned today, but he had a massive impact on the history of the Jewish people. His name was Phinehas. Phinehas was zealous for the glory of God. He was appalled at the way the people of Israel had turned their backs on the one true and living God. He stood for the truth, and the Lord honored him. God stopped the plague against Israel.

We are encouraged by this great man of faith in the Old Testament. Like Phinehas, we must stand for the truth of God in the midst of rebellion. When there is grumbling against God in our homes, our churches, or our workplaces, we must boldly stand for the Lord. We must not allow the culture or crowd to press us into its mold. Instead, by the Spirit's empowerment we should honor God publicly and passionately.

Which person are you? Are you the one who continually complains about your situation? Do you find a critical attitude always displaying itself in your life? Or are you like Phinehas, standing for the glory of God regardless of outward circumstances?

*Dr. Levi Skipper, Concord Baptist Church
Clermont, GA*

JULY 4

Keep Your Heart True

Psalm 106:34–48

34 They did not destroy the peoples,
Concerning whom the Lord had commanded them,

35 But they mingled with the Gentiles
And learned their works;

36 They served their idols,
Which became a snare to them.

37 They even sacrificed their sons
And their daughters to demons,

38 And shed innocent blood,
The blood of their sons and daughters,
Whom they sacrificed to the idols of Canaan;
And the land was polluted with blood.

39 Thus they were defiled by their own works,
And played the harlot by their own deeds.

40 Therefore the wrath of the Lord was kindled against His people,
So that He abhorred His own inheritance.

41 And He gave them into the hand of the Gentiles,
And those who hated them ruled over them.

42 Their enemies also oppressed them,
And they were brought into subjection under their hand.

43 Many times He delivered them;
But they rebelled in their counsel,
And were brought low for their iniquity.

44 Nevertheless He regarded their affliction,
When He heard their cry;

45 And for their sake He remembered His covenant,

And relented according to the multitude of His mercies.

46 He also made them to be pitied
By all those who carried them away captive.

47 Save us, O Lord our God,
And gather us from among the Gentiles,
To give thanks to Your holy name,
To triumph in Your praise.

48 Blessed *be* the Lord God of Israel
From everlasting to everlasting!
And let all the people say, "Amen!"

Praise the Lord!

DEVOTIONAL

The people of Israel were not to marry those who were outside the covenant promises of God. The reason was that in doing so, their hearts would be carried off by false gods introduced by pagan spouses. But they disobeyed God's instruction and fell so far into idolatry that they were committing nauseating acts before the Lord. Even though the Lord brought them deliverance on many occasions, they eventually rebelled again, following their own personal wisdom.

Like the Israelites, we are not to give ourselves to this world's system (Jas. 4:4; 1 John 2:15). If we give ourselves to the lusts of the world, we will be drawn away from the authentic love of Jesus and will be bowing down to something or someone other than God. Our lives cannot be a blessing to Him if we are caught up in this great sin.

As you take inventory of your life, are you a friend of the current world system?

Dr. Levi Skipper, Concord Baptist Church
Clermont, GA

JULY 5

Thanksgiving to the Lord

Psalm 107:1–16

OH, give thanks to the LORD, for *He is* good!
For His mercy *endures* forever.

2 Let the redeemed of the LORD say *so,*
Whom He has redeemed from the hand of
the enemy,

3 And gathered out of the lands,
From the east and from the west,
From the north and from the south.

4 They wandered in the wilderness in a
desolate way;
They found no city to dwell in.

5 Hungry and thirsty,
Their soul fainted in them.

6 Then they cried out to the LORD in their trouble,
And He delivered them out of their distresses.

7 And He led them forth by the right way,
That they might go to a city for a dwelling place.

8 Oh, that *men* would give thanks to the LORD *for*
His goodness,
And *for* His wonderful works to the children
of men!

9 For He satisfies the longing soul,
And fills the hungry soul with goodness.

10 Those who sat in darkness and in the shadow
of death,
Bound in affliction and irons—

11 Because they rebelled against the words of God,
And despised the counsel of the Most High,

12 Therefore He brought down their heart with
labor;

They fell down, and *there was* none to help.

13 Then they cried out to the LORD in their trouble,
And He saved them out of their distresses.

14 He brought them out of darkness and the
shadow of death,
And broke their chains in pieces.

15 Oh, that *men* would give thanks to the LORD *for*
His goodness,
And *for* His wonderful works to the children
of men!

16 For He has broken the gates of bronze,
And cut the bars of iron in two.

DEVOTIONAL

Have you ever taken a rock and skipped it across a pond? I am tempted to do this every time I stand before a flat body of water. The goal is obviously to see how many times I can get the rock to skip. The more, the better.

The psalmist encourages us to give thanks to the Lord. The same word used for giving thanks is also used to describe the act of throwing or casting something, like a rock. Today, imagine that you stand at the edge of the vast riches of God's blessings in your life. Beside you is a pile of smooth rocks. In prayer, pick up those rocks and skip your thanksgiving to the throne of God. See how often you can thank God for what He has done in your life, through your life, and all around you.

We cast our thanksgiving to the Lord because He is good. The mercy that God has bestowed upon us is worthy of a million rocks of praise. So get to skipping!

Dr. Levi Skipper, Concord Baptist Church
Clermont, GA

JULY 6

God Hears Our Cries

Psalm 107:17–32

17 Fools, because of their transgression,
And because of their iniquities, were afflicted.

18 Their soul abhorred all manner of food,
And they drew near to the gates of death.

19 Then they cried out to the LORD in their
trouble,
And He saved them out of their distresses.

20 He sent His word and healed them,
And delivered *them* from their destructions.

21 Oh, that *men* would give thanks to the LORD *for*
His goodness,
And *for* His wonderful works to the children
of men!

22 Let them sacrifice the sacrifices of
thanksgiving,
And declare His works with rejoicing.

23 Those who go down to the sea in ships,
Who do business on great waters,

24 They see the works of the LORD,
And His wonders in the deep.

25 For He commands and raises the stormy wind,
Which lifts up the waves of the sea.

26 They mount up to the heavens,
They go down again to the depths;
Their soul melts because of trouble.

27 They reel to and fro, and stagger like a
drunken man,
And are at their wits' end.

28 Then they cry out to the LORD in their trouble,
And He brings them out of their distresses.

29 He calms the storm,
So that its waves are still.

30 Then they are glad because they are quiet;
So He guides them to their desired haven.

31 Oh, that *men* would give thanks to the LORD *for*
His goodness,
And *for* His wonderful works to the children
of men!

32 Let them exalt Him also in the assembly of the
people,
And praise Him in the company of the elders.

DEVOTIONAL

I recently told my daughter not to ride her bike barefoot. It seemed obvious to me that if she did, eventually she would scrape her feet. Apparently she didn't see the danger and went out barefoot anyway. Not long after that, we heard the scream. Looking through the window, I could see her hobbling toward us with tears rushing down her big rosy cheeks. She had scraped her big toe. Instead of saying to my four-year-old, "I told you so!" we quickly took her inside to bandage her wound.

The Lord gives His law to us really to say, "Don't hurt yourself." He knows if we walk barefoot in this world system, we will scrape our feet. Thankfully, just as Israel experienced the healing Word of the Lord, you and I can experience it too. Like a bandage, God's Word soothes our wounds and nurses us back to health.

How many times have you experienced the healing touch of the Lord in your life? An unthankful heart is a blinded heart to the mercy of God. His healing should motivate us to thankfulness.

Dr. Levi Skipper, Concord Baptist Church
Clermont, GA

JULY 7

Difficulties Reveal God's Goodness

Psalm 107:33–43

33 He turns rivers into a wilderness,
And the watersprings into dry ground;

34 A fruitful land into barrenness,
For the wickedness of those who dwell in it.

35 He turns a wilderness into pools of water,
And dry land into watersprings.

36 There He makes the hungry dwell,
That they may establish a city for a dwelling
place,

37 And sow fields and plant vineyards,
That they may yield a fruitful harvest.

38 He also blesses them, and they multiply
greatly;
And He does not let their cattle decrease.

39 When they are diminished and brought low
Through oppression, affliction and sorrow,

40 He pours contempt on princes,
And causes them to wander in the wilderness
where there is no way;

41 Yet He sets the poor on high, far from
affliction,
And makes *their* families like a flock.

42 The righteous see *it* and rejoice,
And all iniquity stops its mouth.

43 Whoever *is* wise will observe these *things,*
And they will understand the lovingkindness
of the LORD.

DEVOTIONAL

The psalmist has described many trials that a person can face in this life. These trials can actually become trails that lead people closer to the Lord. In fact, the darker the trial, the brighter the love of God shines.

Think about those who wandered in the wilderness. Without the wandering, they would never have experienced the deliverance of God. Those who were oppressed in bondage would not have experienced the release of God without the bondage. Those who are sick would not know the mercy of God without the sickness. Those lost at sea would not know the Lord's direction if they had never become lost. Most of God's character would never be known by His people if trials were not allowed to touch us.

I was walking my young son to his room one night. We walked up the stairs into a dark hallway, and the closer we got to his room, the darker it became. I noticed the darker it got, the tighter his hand gripped my finger. He kept moving forward, trusting me to protect him.

As you walk with the Lord into and through the darkness of trials, remember that the darker it gets, the tighter you should grip His hand. As you grip His hand, you will become more and more aware of His everlasting lovingkindness.

Don't allow your trials to sideline you. Give thanks to the Lord for the trial, knowing that this difficulty in your life will eventually reveal more of God's lovingkindness toward you.

Dr. Levi Skipper, Concord Baptist Church
Clermont, GA

JULY 8

Write two sinful attitudes the Lord may have brought to your mind this week and journal how you plan to overcome them by God's grace.

_____

_____

_____

_____

_____

_____

_____

_____

_____

List the characteristics of God that you have learned through the trials in your life.

_____

_____

_____

_____

_____

_____

_____

_____

_____

JULY 9

Assurance of God's Victory

Psalm 108:1–13

O GOD, my heart is steadfast;
I will sing and give praise, even with my
glory.

2 Awake, lute and harp!
I will awaken the dawn.

3 I will praise You, O LORD, among the
peoples,
And I will sing praises to You among the
nations.

4 For Your mercy *is* great above the heavens,
And Your truth *reaches* to the clouds.

5 Be exalted, O God, above the heavens,
And Your glory above all the earth;

6 That Your beloved may be delivered,
Save *with* Your right hand, and hear me.

7 God has spoken in His holiness:
"I will rejoice;
I will divide Shechem
And measure out the Valley of Succoth.

8 Gilead *is* Mine; Manasseh *is* Mine;
Ephraim also *is* the helmet for My head;
Judah *is* My lawgiver.

9 Moab *is* My washpot;
Over Edom I will cast My shoe;
Over Philistia I will triumph."

10 Who will bring me *into* the strong city?
Who will lead me to Edom?

11 *Is it* not You, O God, *who* cast us off?
And You, O God, *who* did not go out with our
armies?

12 Give us help from trouble,
For the help of man is useless.

13 Through God we will do valiantly,
For *it is* He *who* shall tread down our enemies.

DEVOTIONAL

In Psalm 108, the psalmist was writing from a position of strength and confidence—something not always seen in the psalms. In this writing, David's praise came from a truly sincere place. It appears to burst forth from inside him in a rush of spontaneous joy.

The praise was so enthusiastic and heartfelt that David was looking for a variety of ways to express it: with instruments, in the morning, and among the people. David was also clarifying the qualitative nature of his praise. His exaltation for God was above that for any human being. It was above the heavens and the earth. And it was given against the backdrop of previous deliverances. The psalm culminates with a final request of help and sovereign intervention.

The value of the psalms is not just in their historic significance. They also provide a model for our own praise. Their example provokes another level of praise from us.

- Do you share David's enthusiasm for God?
- Are you looking for a variety of mediums to express it?
- Is your praise specific?
- Do you spend time expressing gratitude for what He has already done before you make a new set of requests?

Let your praises ring!

Pieter Van Waarde, Woodcrest Chapel
Columbia, MO

JULY 10

Plea for Judgment of False Accusers

Psalm 109:1–13

DO not keep silent,
O God of my praise!

2 For the mouth of the wicked and the mouth of
the deceitful
Have opened against me;
They have spoken against me with a lying
tongue.

3 They have also surrounded me with words of
hatred,
And fought against me without a cause.

4 In return for my love they are my accusers,
But I *give myself to* prayer.

5 Thus they have rewarded me evil for good,
And hatred for my love.

6 Set a wicked man over him,
And let an accuser stand at his right hand.

7 When he is judged, let him be found guilty,
And let his prayer become sin.

8 Let his days be few,
And let another take his office.

9 Let his children be fatherless,
And his wife a widow.

10 Let his children continually be vagabonds,
and beg;
Let them seek *their bread* also from their
desolate places.

11 Let the creditor seize all that he has,
And let strangers plunder his labor.

12 Let there be none to extend mercy to him,
Nor let there be any to favor his fatherless
children.

13 Let his posterity be cut off,
And in the generation following let their name
be blotted out.

DEVOTIONAL

Sometimes people grow up with an impression that God cannot or will not tolerate our complaints or frustrations. Sometimes there is the perception that God is only interested in flowery prayers that talk about sunshine and daises. Sometimes we assume that God is like a heavenly parent who says, "If you don't have something nice to say, don't say anything at all!"

David, in his psalms, wrote what he felt. There was no holding back. In this instance, he had been wronged and cheated, and that treatment was undeserved. He called out to God for His intervention, and he got quite specific about the ways he hoped God would bring retribution. Is that allowed?

Perhaps the real lesson to be learned from this psalm is that there is nothing you can't express to God. God is ready to hear our complaints. He wants to know what is on our hearts—even if it isn't all that pretty.

- Do you believe God is ready and willing to hear what is really on your heart?
- Is there something you have been holding back that probably needs to be expressed to God?

He is waiting to hear it.

Pieter Van Waarde, Woodcrest Chapel
Columbia, MO

JULY 11

David's Request for Judgment

Psalm 109:14–20

¹⁴ Let the iniquity of his fathers be remembered
before the LORD,
And let not the sin of his mother be blotted
out.

¹⁵ Let them be continually before the LORD,
That He may cut off the memory of them from
the earth;

¹⁶ Because he did not remember to show mercy,
But persecuted the poor and needy man,
That he might even slay the broken in heart.

¹⁷ As he loved cursing, so let it come to him;
As he did not delight in blessing, so let it be
far from him.

¹⁸ As he clothed himself with cursing as with his
garment,
So let it enter his body like water,
And like oil into his bones.

¹⁹ Let it be to him like the garment which covers
him,
And for a belt with which he girds himself
continually.

²⁰ *Let* this *be* the LORD's reward to my accusers,
And to those who speak evil against my
person.

DEVOTIONAL

David was a warrior king. He was a man
of action and a dynamic leader. He bat-
tled Goliath as a teenager and fended off Saul's
attacks. He led his men into battle. If something
wasn't right, he wasn't hesitant about interven-
ing. Therefore, one might assume that he was also
headstrong, cocky, and impulsive. And history
suggests he was at times. Yet in this psalm, the
curtain is pulled back, and we are given a behind-
the-scenes look at his prayers.

Even though David was not afraid to act, he
was also a man who understood the power of
prayer. Whatever great thing might occur on the
battlefield, he put his trust first and foremost
in what God would do on his behalf. Whatever
God accomplished would be significantly more
impressive than anything David could accomplish
in his own strength.

- Are there ways in which you find yourself acting out of your own strength?
- Is there a situation you have been wrestling
with that you need to hold before God in
prayer?
- David wrote out his prayers. Would it be helpful to write out your own?

God's intervention is more powerful than anything we can accomplish on our own.

Pieter Van Waarde, Woodcrest Chapel
Columbia, MO

JULY 12

David Begs for God's Mercy

Psalm 109:21–31

21 But You, O GOD the Lord,
   Deal with me for Your name's sake;
   Because Your mercy *is* good, deliver me.

22 For I *am* poor and needy,
   And my heart is wounded within me.

23 I am gone like a shadow when it lengthens;
   I am shaken off like a locust.

24 My knees are weak through fasting,
   And my flesh is feeble from lack of fatness.

25 I also have become a reproach to them;
   When they look at me, they shake their heads.

26 Help me, O LORD my God!
   Oh, save me according to Your mercy,

27 That they may know that this *is* Your hand—
   That You, LORD, have done it!

28 Let them curse, but You bless;
   When they arise, let them be ashamed,
   But let Your servant rejoice.

29 Let my accusers be clothed with shame,
   And let them cover themselves with their own
      disgrace as with a mantle.

30 I will greatly praise the LORD with my mouth;
   Yes, I will praise Him among the multitude.

31 For He shall stand at the right hand of the
      poor,
   To save *him* from those who condemn him.

DEVOTIONAL

I have a personal confession. I don't like appearing weak. I don't like how it makes me feel. More importantly, I imagine that people will think less of me if they think I am weak. So I pretend. I act and talk stronger than I really am. I live by the motto, "Never let them see you sweat!"

David had no taste for such self-aggrandizement. He was weak and poor and he knew it. He said it outright. No illusions of grandeur. No pretending. No hiding. Just gut-level honesty. He even suggested that his attempts to follow God had made him so: "My knees are weak through fasting" (v. 24).

After his authentic personal proclamation of weakness, David cried out to God for help, and his closing refrain of praise suggests an expectant positive response from God.

- Is it possible that your willingness to confess your own weakness is the key to experiencing God's redemptive provision?

- Are there places where you are pretending to be stronger than you really are, a posture that creates a barrier to God's deliverance?

- Could you give yourself permission to name your weakness in God's presence and see if that opens the door to what you most need from Him?

When we are weak, then we are strong.

Pieter Van Waarde, Woodcrest Chapel
Columbia, MO

JULY 13

Announcement of the Messiah's Reign

Psalm 110:1–7

THE LORD said to my Lord,
  "Sit at My right hand,
  Till I make Your enemies Your footstool."

2 The LORD shall send the rod of Your strength
    out of Zion.
  Rule in the midst of Your enemies!

3 Your people *shall be* volunteers
  In the day of Your power;
  In the beauties of holiness, from the womb of
    the morning,
  You have the dew of Your youth.

4 The LORD has sworn
  And will not relent,
  "You *are* a priest forever
  According to the order of Melchizedek."

5 The Lord *is* at Your right hand;
  He shall execute kings in the day of His wrath.

6 He shall judge among the nations,
  He shall fill *the places* with dead bodies,
  He shall execute the heads of many countries.

7 He shall drink of the brook by the wayside;
  Therefore He shall lift up the head.

DEVOTIONAL

This psalm of David's is a prophetic proclamation regarding the reign of Christ. It is a piece that has been cited by generations as a profound prediction of the divinity of Christ. That fact alone puts this passage in a very unique place.

However, beyond that, I can't help but wonder how it must have felt to David to be entrusted with these words. Did he have any hesitation about writing them? Did it feel like he was going out on a limb to make such bold proclamations? We will never know this side of heaven, but I would imagine so.

One could note the accuracy of the predictions and be in awe of the passage for that reason alone. But perhaps another layer of application is to take courage from David's boldness. He was inspired to write something, through the work of God's Spirit inside him, and his cooperation has inspired generations.

- Is God asking you to cooperate with Him in a way that is moving you out of your comfort zone?
- How can what you read today serve as an encouragement to you to be faithful in your own cooperative work with God's Spirit?
- Can you begin to imagine how your own obedience to God's calling, even in small ways, can be a blessing to people in generations to come?

Do not discount the significance of your own obedience to Christ.

Pieter Van Waarde, Woodcrest Chapel
Columbia, MO

JULY 14

God's Faithfulness and Justice

Psalm 111:1–10

PRAISE the LORD!
I will praise the LORD with *my* whole heart,
In the assembly of the upright and *in the*
congregation.

2 The works of the LORD *are* great,
Studied by all who have pleasure in them.

3 His work *is* honorable and glorious,
And His righteousness endures forever.

4 He has made His wonderful works to be
remembered;
The LORD *is* gracious and full of compassion.

5 He has given food to those who fear Him;
He will ever be mindful of His covenant.

6 He has declared to His people the power of His
works,
In giving them the heritage of the nations.

7 The works of His hands *are* verity and justice;
All His precepts *are* sure.

8 They stand fast forever and ever,
And are done in truth and uprightness.

9 He has sent redemption to His people;
He has commanded His covenant forever:
Holy and awesome *is* His name.

10 The fear of the LORD *is* the beginning of
wisdom;
A good understanding have all those who do
His commandments.
His praise endures forever.

DEVOTIONAL

This week began with a psalm of praise, and it ends in praise as well. These words are so expressive and eloquent; I am inspired by them. Are you?

That said, I often wonder if these words came from a heart full of praise, or if David wrote them to remind himself of who God was—even when his heart was having a hard time believing. Is authentic praise solely the product of a heart that is full of awe, or does praise in faith fill the heart with awe? I suspect both are true. Perhaps they build on each other.

- Can you imagine yourself giving God enthusiastic praise for who He is regardless of what is happening in your life?
- How does what David wrote connect to what you need to know about God today?
- Even if you don't have the words to express your praise to God, how can you use these words to aid your own praise efforts?

Praise and worship of God are always appropriate responses, no matter what the circumstances of our life might be.

Pieter Van Waarde, Woodcrest Chapel
Columbia, MO

JULY 15

In light of David's enthusiastic praise, how could you creatively express your own worship of God?

_____

_____

_____

_____

_____

_____

_____

_____

_____

_____

Given God's faithfulness (illustrated in David's experience and praise), what can you confidently entrust to God this week?

_____

_____

_____

_____

_____

_____

_____

_____

JULY 16

The Blessed State of the Righteous

Psalm 112:1–10

PRAISE the LORD!
Blessed *is* the man *who* fears the LORD,

Who delights greatly in His commandments.

2 His descendants will be mighty on earth;
The generation of the upright will be blessed.

3 Wealth and riches *will be* in his house,
And his righteousness endures forever.

4 Unto the upright there arises light in the
darkness;
He is gracious, and full of compassion, and
righteous.

5 A good man deals graciously and lends;
He will guide his affairs with discretion.

6 Surely he will never be shaken;
The righteous will be in everlasting
remembrance.

7 He will not be afraid of evil tidings;
His heart is steadfast, trusting in the LORD.

8 His heart *is* established;
He will not be afraid,
Until he sees *his desire* upon his enemies.

9 He has dispersed abroad,
He has given to the poor;
His righteousness endures forever;
His horn will be exalted with honor.

10 The wicked will see *it* and be grieved;
He will gnash his teeth and melt away;
The desire of the wicked shall perish.

DEVOTIONAL

Fear God and fear nothing else" is a quote from Elisabeth Elliot that really summarizes our reading for today. Failing to fear God will lead us to fear everything. Is your life characterized by fear and anxiety? How can you break the chains of fear and begin to walk in freedom?

The fear the psalmist called us to is not the paralyzing fear that the world knows, but a type of fear that is a healthy respect for the majesty of God. When our lives are characterized by this type of fear, we find ourselves being freed from all other fears. In verse 7, we read, "He will not be afraid of evil tidings." Living life with a proper fear of God releases us from unhealthy debilitating fears that have hounded us for years. What a great promise!

But how is this type of God-honoring fear cultivated? Verse 1 teaches us that worship and the Word will develop a healthy fear of God. These two commands are a blueprint for spiritual freedom. As you praise God for His past goodness in your life, your reverence for Him grows. Perhaps you began studying scripture out of duty, but soon found that the Word was your delight. As you fed on it, those nagging fears were farther and farther away in your rearview mirror. Who would have thought that the key to overcoming the fears of the world is a byproduct of being overcome with the fear of God?

Brady Cooper, New Vision Baptist Church
Murfreesboro, TN

JULY 17
The Majesty and Condescension of God

Psalm 113:1–9

PRAISE the LORD!
Praise, O servants of the LORD,
Praise the name of the LORD!

2 Blessed be the name of the LORD
From this time forth and forevermore!

3 From the rising of the sun to its going down
The LORD's name *is* to be praised.

4 The LORD *is* high above all nations,
His glory above the heavens.

5 Who *is* like the LORD our God,
Who dwells on high,

6 Who humbles Himself to behold
The things that are in the heavens and in the
earth?

7 He raises the poor out of the dust,
And lifts the needy out of the ash heap,

8 That He may seat *him* with princes—
With the princes of His people.

9 He grants the barren woman a home,
Like a joyful mother of children.

Praise the LORD!

DEVOTIONAL

Praising the name of the Lord sounds good, but what does that really mean? God has many different names in the scriptures. I would invite you to think about a name as if it were a diamond with many facets. To praise the name of the Lord is to look at each individual facet of God's nature and be captivated by its brilliance.

In today's reading, the psalmist reminds us that God is eternal. This facet is too brilliant for our eyes to take in, but as we get a glimpse of it, we don't fear the future because our God resides there. This leads us to praise Him, and then we begin to understand what it means to praise the name of the Lord.

The psalmist then draws our attention to another facet of God's name—His sovereignty. He is over all things. He is directing all things to a glorious end for His children. "A man's heart plans his way, but the LORD directs his steps" (Prov. 16:9). When tyrants rattle their sabers with threats of war, when financial experts predict collapse, we are reminded that God is sovereign over all and we praise His name.

Another facet to which the psalmist alludes for our practice in praising the name of the Lord is that He is our *Redeemer*. That means no matter how deep you are in the ash heap, you are not there without hope. God redeems broken marriages from the ash heap. God redeems broken bodies from the ash heap. I love how this psalm ends: "He grants the barren woman a home."

The psalmist polishes off another facet of God's great name for us to gaze upon—the grace of God, the undeserved favor of the King. Our God is a God of grace, from creation to the final consummation of the kingdom. When we reflect on the grace of God in our lives, we can't help but praise Him. In ancient cultures, a barren woman was seen as an outcast or accursed. We were outcasts and accursed due to sin, but God's grace brought us in. What a name!

Brady Cooper, New Vision Baptist Church
Murfreesboro, TN

JULY 18

God's Deliverance of Israel

Psalm 114:1–8

W HEN Israel went out of Egypt,
The house of Jacob from a people of
strange language,
² Judah became His sanctuary,
And Israel His dominion.

³ The sea saw *it* and fled;
Jordan turned back.
⁴ The mountains skipped like rams,
The little hills like lambs.
⁵ What ails you, O sea, that you fled?
O Jordan, *that* you turned back?
⁶ O mountains, *that* you skipped like rams?
O little hills, like lambs?

⁷ Tremble, O earth, at the presence of the Lord,
At the presence of the God of Jacob,
⁸ Who turned the rock *into* a pool of water,
The flint into a fountain of waters.

DEVOTIONAL

T he exodus is a story of God's miraculous saving power from beginning to end. It is also
a beautiful picture of God's redemption of us in
Jesus Christ. Today's reading describes in beautiful poetry God's sovereign workings in the exodus. We are reminded that we have a God who
goes ahead of us. He parts the seas, brings down
mountains, and turns rocks into pools of water.

As we think about our lives in light of the exodus, we realize that through faith in the crucified
and risen Christ, we are brought out of slavery. We
trust God's provision for our salvation, but many

times as we start our new journey we struggle.
Just as the children of Israel were to drive out the
inhabitants that were residents in Canaan, God, as
we grow in our relationship with Christ, desires
to drive out those deep-seated strongholds in our
lives. Lust and greed, jealousy and bitterness. Many
believers find themselves saved and stuck.

Today, let Psalm 114 remind us that we serve
a God who goes ahead of us, making personal
sanctification possible. As God parted the sea and
brought low the mountains or obstacles for the
Israelites, He is able to bring us spiritual victory in
our lives by driving out the obstacles that keep us
from enjoying His blessings and glorifying Him.

Today, can you see your life as Canaan with
many fortified cities that need to be conquered
for the glory of God? Would you first believe that
no stronghold, no matter how long it has resided
in you, is beyond the power of God to be trans-
formed? Second, what would it look like for you
to stop trying to overcome your stronghold and
really start trusting God to break the chains and
give you new desires?

Let verse 2 be your prayer today: Father, make
my life Your sanctuary, that You would have
dominion over all that I am for Your glory!

Brady Cooper, New Vision Baptist Church
Murfreesboro, TN

JULY 19

The Futility of Idols

Psalm 115:1–18

N OT unto us, O LORD, not unto us,
But to Your name give glory,
Because of Your mercy,
Because of Your truth.

2 Why should the Gentiles say,
"So where *is* their God?"

3 But our God *is* in heaven;
He does whatever He pleases.

4 Their idols *are* silver and gold,
The work of men's hands.

5 They have mouths, but they do not speak;
Eyes they have, but they do not see;

6 They have ears, but they do not hear;
Noses they have, but they do not smell;

7 They have hands, but they do not handle;
Feet they have, but they do not walk;
Nor do they mutter through their throat.

8 Those who make them are like them;
So is everyone who trusts in them.

9 O Israel, trust in the LORD;
He *is* their help and their shield.

10 O house of Aaron, trust in the LORD;
He *is* their help and their shield.

11 You who fear the LORD, trust in the LORD;
He *is* their help and their shield.

12 The LORD has been mindful of *us;*
He will bless us;
He will bless the house of Israel;
He will bless the house of Aaron.

13 He will bless those who fear the LORD,
Both small and great.

14 May the LORD give you increase more and more,
You and your children.

15 *May* you *be* blessed by the LORD,
Who made heaven and earth.

16 The heaven, *even* the heavens, *are* the LORD's;
But the earth He has given to the children of men.

17 The dead do not praise the LORD,
Nor any who go down into silence.

18 But we will bless the LORD
From this time forth and forevermore.

Praise the LORD!

DEVOTIONAL

T his psalm may have been sung at the opening of the second temple (Ezra 6:16). Verse 2 reveals confusion on the part of the Gentile neighbors because they couldn't see any god in the temple. The Gentiles' temples and homes were filled with gods.

Isaiah 44:9 warns, "Those who make an image, all of them are useless, and their precious things shall not profit." What are the idols in your life today? Great places to search for idols in your life are your checkbook and calendar. How you spend your time and money reveal what is really important to you. "For where your treasure is, there your heart will be also" (Luke 12:34).

As God begins to reveal the idols in our lives, may we die to trying to create a life with our hands and start trusting in Him, allowing Him to produce His life in us. He is our help and our shield!

Brady Cooper, New Vision Baptist Church
Murfreesboro, TN

JULY 20

Deliverance from Death

Psalm 116:1–19

I LOVE the LORD, because He has heard
My voice *and* my supplications.

2 Because He has inclined His ear to me,
Therefore I will call *upon Him* as long as I live.

3 The pains of death surrounded me,
And the pangs of Sheol laid hold of me;
I found trouble and sorrow.

4 Then I called upon the name of the LORD:
"O LORD, I implore You, deliver my soul!"

5 Gracious *is* the LORD, and righteous;
Yes, our God *is* merciful.

6 The LORD preserves the simple;
I was brought low, and He saved me.

7 Return to your rest, O my soul,
For the LORD has dealt bountifully with you.

8 For You have delivered my soul from death,
My eyes from tears,
And my feet from falling.

9 I will walk before the LORD
In the land of the living.

10 I believed, therefore I spoke,
"I am greatly afflicted."

11 I said in my haste,
"All men *are* liars."

12 What shall I render to the LORD
For all His benefits toward me?

13 I will take up the cup of salvation,
And call upon the name of the LORD.

14 I will pay my vows to the LORD
Now in the presence of all His people.

15 Precious in the sight of the LORD
Is the death of His saints.

16 O LORD, truly I *am* Your servant;
I *am* Your servant, the son of Your
maidservant;
You have loosed my bonds.

17 I will offer to You the sacrifice of thanksgiving,
And will call upon the name of the LORD.

18 I will pay my vows to the LORD
Now in the presence of all His people,

19 In the courts of the LORD's house,
In the midst of you, O Jerusalem.

Praise the LORD!

DEVOTIONAL

The psalmist cried out to the Lord in the midst of trials he feared might cost him his life. Dishonest men were pursuing him like hounds and death seemed imminent, but God answered his prayer and rescued him from his adversaries. The psalmist was freed from another dangerous situation in this psalm.

The fear of death is an inner foe we struggle with all of our lives. In verse 15, we see these external trials have also been tools of God to release the psalmist from his inner trial. Getting God's perspective on death is liberating in our lives. Like the psalmist, we often do not get this perspective without going through the fire of trials. In God's sight, death is a beautiful thing because in heaven His children see that His glory far outweighs anything in this life. Christ has defeated death, so this ancient adversary is no longer to be feared.

Brady Cooper, New Vision Baptist Church
Murfreesboro, TN

JULY 21

Let All Peoples Praise the Lord

Psalm 117:1–2

P RAISE the LORD, all you Gentiles!
Laud Him, all you peoples!
2 For His merciful kindness is great toward us,
And the truth of the LORD *endures* forever.
Praise the LORD!

Psalm 118:1–14

O H, give thanks to the LORD, for *He is* good!
For His mercy *endures* forever.

2 Let Israel now say,
"His mercy *endures* forever."
3 Let the house of Aaron now say,
"His mercy *endures* forever."
4 Let those who fear the LORD now say,
"His mercy *endures* forever."
5 I called on the LORD in distress;
The LORD answered me *and set me* in a broad
place.
6 The LORD *is* on my side;
I will not fear.
What can man do to me?
7 The LORD is for me among those who help me;
Therefore I shall see *my desire* on those who
hate me.
8 *It is* better to trust in the LORD
Than to put confidence in man.
9 *It is* better to trust in the LORD
Than to put confidence in princes.
10 All nations surrounded me,
But in the name of the LORD I will destroy them.

11 They surrounded me,
Yes, they surrounded me;
But in the name of the LORD I will destroy them.
12 They surrounded me like bees;
They were quenched like a fire of thorns;
For in the name of the LORD I will destroy them.
13 You pushed me violently, that I might fall,
But the LORD helped me.
14 The LORD *is* my strength and song,
And He has become my salvation.

DEVOTIONAL

O ne common truth is that we are all broken
and hurting. Hurting people usually end up
hurting others, and we have all experienced the
bitter pill of being hurt by others. But there is one
who will never harm us—our Lord.

In today's reading, verse 8 gives us a life truth
that has to be learned. Scripture says, "I will not
leave you nor forsake you" (Josh. 1:5), and "There
is a friend who sticks closer than a brother" (Prov.
18:24). We may know intellectually that God is all
we need, but we do not know Him well enough to
allow Him to meet those needs. The secret of life
is found in where you place your confidence. The
psalmist is reminding us that at a foundational
level, people can't deliver the goods. Our hope for
our salvation is Christ! Our hope for our families
is Christ! Our hope for our nation is Christ!

Father, reveal to us any area of our lives where
our confidence lies in anyone other than You.
Allow us to serve others, not look to them for our
security.

Brady Cooper, New Vision Baptist Church
Murfreesboro, TN

 JULY 22

What do your check registry and calendar reveal about the priorities in your life?

_____

_____

_____

_____

_____

_____

_____

_____

_____

_____

_____

What are some characteristics of God's nature that are most meaningful to you during this season of your life?

_____

_____

_____

_____

_____

_____

_____

_____

_____

_____

_____

JULY 23

Prophecy About the Coming Savior

Psalm 118:15–29

15 The voice of rejoicing and salvation
Is in the tents of the righteous;
The right hand of the LORD does valiantly.

16 The right hand of the LORD is exalted;
The right hand of the LORD does valiantly.

17 I shall not die, but live,
And declare the works of the LORD.

18 The LORD has chastened me severely,
But He has not given me over to death.

19 Open to me the gates of righteousness;
I will go through them,
And I will praise the LORD.

20 This is the gate of the LORD,
Through which the righteous shall enter.

21 I will praise You,
For You have answered me,
And have become my salvation.

22 The stone *which* the builders rejected
Has become the chief cornerstone.

23 This was the LORD's doing;
It *is* marvelous in our eyes.

24 This *is* the day the LORD has made;
We will rejoice and be glad in it.

25 Save now, I pray, O LORD;
O LORD, I pray, send now prosperity.

26 Blessed *is* he who comes in the name of the
LORD!
We have blessed you from the house of the
LORD.

27 God *is* the LORD,
And He has given us light;
Bind the sacrifice with cords to the horns of
the altar.

28 You *are* my God, and I will praise You;
You are my God, I will exalt You.

29 Oh, give thanks to the LORD, for *He is* good!
For His mercy *endures* forever.

DEVOTIONAL

In these verses, we see a prophecy of the humiliation and exaltation of Jesus and the suffering and glory that will follow.

In verse 19, David asked for permission to enter through the gates of heaven. In verse 21, we see him thanking God for granting him admission. He thanked God for the "gate of the LORD," through which the righteous enter. We know this gate is Jesus! In John 14:6, Jesus said, "I am the way, the truth, and the life. No one comes to the Father except through Me."

He is the only gate, but He is not only the gate. Jesus is also the cornerstone, which the builders rejected. In Acts 4:10, Peter accused the priests and religious scribes of being the ones who rejected Jesus. The One who was rejected became the chief cornerstone (v. 11). The humiliated was exalted, as we see in Philippians 2. Ultimately, we also see that God will reject those who reject Jesus.

Have you received Jesus or rejected Him? I pray you'll receive Him.

Dr. Alex Himaya, theChurch.at
Tulsa, OK

JULY 24

The Excellencies of the Word of God

Psalm 119:1–16

B LESSED *are* the undefiled in the way,
Who walk in the law of the LORD!

2 Blessed *are* those who keep His testimonies,
Who seek Him with the whole heart!

3 They also do no iniquity;
They walk in His ways.

4 You have commanded *us*
To keep Your precepts diligently.

5 Oh, that my ways were directed
To keep Your statutes!

6 Then I would not be ashamed,
When I look into all Your commandments.

7 I will praise You with uprightness of heart,
When I learn Your righteous judgments.

8 I will keep Your statutes;
Oh, do not forsake me utterly!

9 How can a young man cleanse his way?
By taking heed according to Your word.

10 With my whole heart I have sought You;
Oh, let me not wander from Your
commandments!

11 Your word I have hidden in my heart,
That I might not sin against You.

12 Blessed *are* You, O LORD!
Teach me Your statutes.

13 With my lips I have declared
All the judgments of Your mouth.

14 I have rejoiced in the way of Your testimonies,
As *much as* in all riches.

15 I will meditate on Your precepts,
And contemplate Your ways.

16 I will delight myself in Your statutes;
I will not forget Your word.

DEVOTIONAL

P salm 119 is the longest passage of scripture in the Bible. It is a collection of David's soul cries to God. It is like a daily journal that David kept, and consequently, there seems to be little coherence between the verses. Matthew Henry calls Psalm 119 a chest of gold rings instead of a chain of gold links.[1] This psalm is divided into twenty-two parts, one part (each eight verses long) for each of the letters in the Hebrew alphabet. Some call it the "saint's alphabet."

In this first part, the psalmist emphasized that godly people are a happy and blessed people. In verse 5, David declared, "Oh, that my ways were directed to keep Your statutes!" That is a prayer to pray, isn't it? The Word of God, the law of the Lord, and His statutes are life giving. In the Word, we find divine revelation, clear direction, and a path to live on.

Verse 11, I think, is the key to spiritual warfare. If we are to beat the Enemy, we must do it in the same fashion that Jesus did when He faced Satan. At every temptation and attack, Jesus responded with, "It is written" (Matt. 4).

Are you ready to beat your Enemy with an "It is written" on the tip of your tongue at a moment's notice? If not, ask God to show you a verse to memorize right now.

Dr. Alex Himaya, theChurch.at
Tulsa, OK

JULY 25

A Call for Obedience

Psalm 119:17–32

17 Deal bountifully with Your servant,
   That I may live and keep Your word.

18 Open my eyes, that I may see
   Wondrous things from Your law.

19 I *am* a stranger in the earth;
   Do not hide Your commandments from me.

20 My soul breaks with longing
   For Your judgments at all times.

21 You rebuke the proud—the cursed,
   Who stray from Your commandments.

22 Remove from me reproach and contempt,
   For I have kept Your testimonies.

23 Princes also sit *and* speak against me,
   But Your servant meditates on Your statutes.

24 Your testimonies also *are* my delight
   And my counselors.

25 My soul clings to the dust;
   Revive me according to Your word.

26 I have declared my ways, and You answered me;
   Teach me Your statutes.

27 Make me understand the way of Your
        precepts;
   So shall I meditate on Your wonderful works.

28 My soul melts from heaviness;
   Strengthen me according to Your word.

29 Remove from me the way of lying,
   And grant me Your law graciously.

30 I have chosen the way of truth;
   Your judgments I have laid *before me.*

31 I cling to Your testimonies;
   O Lord, do not put me to shame!

32 I will run the course of Your commandments,
   For You shall enlarge my heart.

DEVOTIONAL

Jesus often prayed for His followers' eyes to be opened. Clearly, He was not referring to physical eyes. He was asking the Father to give His followers spiritual eyes. If Jesus felt the need to pray that for us, don't you think we should ask the Father for the same thing?

In verse 18, David asked God to open his eyes that he might see the wonders in the Word of God. He also prayed, "Do not hide Your commandments from me" (v. 19), "teach me Your statutes" (v. 26), "revive me according to Your word" (v. 25), "make me understand the way of Your precepts" (v. 26), and "grant me Your law graciously" (v. 29).

David clearly understood that his relationship with God was directly connected to the Word, and his relationship to the Word was clearly dependent upon his relationship with God. He made request after request of the Father to help him understand, obey, and follow the Word.

In this year of looking at the Wisdom Literature in the Bible, perhaps the wisest thing we can learn to practice is asking God for His wisdom related to His very Word.

Lord, would You please open our eyes to all You want to show us and tell us today in Your Word?

Dr. Alex Himaya, theChurch.at
Tulsa, OK

JULY 26

Dedication to the Lord

Psalm 119:33–48

33 Teach me, O LORD, the way of Your statutes,
   And I shall keep it *to* the end.
34 Give me understanding, and I shall keep
      Your law;
   Indeed, I shall observe it with *my* whole
      heart.
35 Make me walk in the path of Your
      commandments,
   For I delight in it.
36 Incline my heart to Your testimonies,
   And not to covetousness.
37 Turn away my eyes from looking at
      worthless things,
   And revive me in Your way.
38 Establish Your word to Your servant,
   Who *is devoted* to fearing You.
39 Turn away my reproach which I dread,
   For Your judgments *are* good.
40 Behold, I long for Your precepts;
   Revive me in Your righteousness.
41 Let Your mercies come also to me, O LORD—
   Your salvation according to Your word.
42 So shall I have an answer for him who
      reproaches me,
   For I trust in Your word.
43 And take not the word of truth utterly out of
      my mouth,
   For I have hoped in Your ordinances.
   So shall I keep Your law continually,
   Forever and ever.

45 And I will walk at liberty,
   For I seek Your precepts.
46 I will speak of Your testimonies also before
      kings,
   And will not be ashamed.
47 And I will delight myself in Your
      commandments,
   Which I love.
48 My hands also I will lift up to Your
      commandments,
   Which I love,
   And I will meditate on Your statutes.

DEVOTIONAL

Eight times in today's reading David said, "I shall" or "I will." David alternated between asking God for something and making commitments to God.

In verse 33, the psalmist asked the Lord to teach him and give him understanding. Think about the prophets and wise teachers to which David had access to. Yet he longed for God to be his teacher and the instructor of his life. He said, "Teach me, oh LORD, the way of Your statutes" (v. 33). David asked for understanding from the Lord, and he promised he would observe God's law with his "whole heart" (v. 34). David wanted God to use the Word to change his life.

God, would You teach us Your Word and Your way? Use Your Word to change our lives today. We will listen and obey.

Dr. Alex Himaya, theChurch.at
Tulsa, OK

JULY 27

The Comfort of God's Word

Psalm 119:49–64

⁴⁹ Remember the word to Your servant,
Upon which You have caused me to hope.

⁵⁰ This *is* my comfort in my affliction,
For Your word has given me life.

⁵¹ The proud have me in great derision,
Yet I do not turn aside from Your law.

⁵² I remembered Your judgments of old,
O LORD,
And have comforted myself.

⁵³ Indignation has taken hold of me
Because of the wicked, who forsake Your law.

⁵⁴ Your statutes have been my songs
In the house of my pilgrimage.

⁵⁵ I remember Your name in the night, O LORD,
And I keep Your law.

⁵⁶ This has become mine,
Because I kept Your precepts.

⁵⁷ *You are* my portion, O LORD;
I have said that I would keep Your words.

⁵⁸ I entreated Your favor with *my* whole heart;
Be merciful to me according to Your word.

⁵⁹ I thought about my ways,
And turned my feet to Your testimonies.

⁶⁰ I made haste, and did not delay
To keep Your commandments.

⁶¹ The cords of the wicked have bound me,
But I have not forgotten Your law.

⁶² At midnight I will rise to give thanks to You,
Because of Your righteous judgments.

⁶³ I *am* a companion of all who fear You,
And of those who keep Your precepts.

⁶⁴ The earth, O LORD, is full of Your mercy;
Teach me Your statutes.

DEVOTIONAL

David asked God to "remember the word to Your servant." The New Living Bible translates verse 49 as, "Remember your promise to me." Not just any promise, but the one God had caused him to hope in.

What promises of God do you hope in? For which ones are you claiming, asking, and believing God to accomplish?

David listed some of the benefits the very Word of God had in his life. It had served as his hope and his comfort and created a song in his heart. What are some of the benefits the Word of God has had in your life? For example, has there been an affliction you were comforted in by the Word of God? As you think through some of those benefits, list them and thank God for them.

Every time we face new challenges in life, remembering comforts God has provided in the past and the times He has proven Himself faithful can comfort us in the present.

God, remind us of Your constant presence and ministry in our lives. Remind us of all of Your precious promises to us. Would You use Your Word to comfort us today?

Dr. Alex Himaya, theChurch.at
Tulsa, OK

JULY 28

The Delight of God's Kindness

Psalm 119:65–80

65 You have dealt well with Your servant,
O LORD, according to Your word.

66 Teach me good judgment and knowledge,
For I believe Your commandments.

67 Before I was afflicted I went astray,
But now I keep Your word.

68 You *are* good, and do good;
Teach me Your statutes.

69 The proud have forged a lie against me,
But I will keep Your precepts with *my* whole
heart.

70 Their heart is as fat as grease,
But I delight in Your law.

71 *It is* good for me that I have been afflicted,
That I may learn Your statutes.

72 The law of Your mouth *is* better to me
Than thousands of *coins of* gold and silver.

73 Your hands have made me and fashioned me;
Give me understanding, that I may learn Your
commandments.

74 Those who fear You will be glad when they see
me,
Because I have hoped in Your word.

75 I know, O LORD, that Your judgments *are* right,
And *that* in faithfulness You have afflicted me.

76 Let, I pray, Your merciful kindness be for my
comfort,
According to Your word to Your servant.

77 Let Your tender mercies come to me, that I
may live;
For Your law *is* my delight.

78 Let the proud be ashamed,
For they treated me wrongfully with
falsehood;
But I will meditate on Your precepts.

79 Let those who fear You turn to me,
Those who know Your testimonies.

80 Let my heart be blameless regarding Your
statutes,
That I may not be ashamed.

DEVOTIONAL

David began this section of the psalm with a thankful acknowledgment that God had "dealt well with him" (v. 65). I can't think of a greater truth for us to not only realize but to understand and believe. No matter what God has done, not done, or allowed in your life, He has "dealt well" with you. He has been, is, and will be there for you. He has always acted for your good. The devil has no greater or more subtle trick in our lives than to cause us to believe that God is not for us or not acting on our behalf. Our theology demands that no matter what happens in our lives, we have received more than we deserve, we are always loved, and God can and will use all things for our good.

David asked God to teach him good judgment and knowledge (v. 73). When we are tempted to believe that God is not acting on our behalf, we need Him to give us good judgment and knowledge to see the truth.

God is good and greatly to be praised.

Thank You, God, for Your goodness to us.

Dr. Alex Himaya, theChurch.at
Tulsa, OK

JULY 29

What areas of temptation in your life do you need an "It is written" for? Ask God to give you eyes to see the areas that so easily trip you up and to show you some scripture to memorize to equip you for victory in those specific areas.

_____

_____

_____

_____

_____

_____

_____

_____

_____

_____

What are some scriptural promises you need to memorize and stand on?

_____

_____

_____

_____

_____

_____

_____

_____

_____

_____

_____

JULY 30

A Request for Revival

Psalm 119:81–96

81 My soul faints for Your salvation,
But I hope in Your word.

82 My eyes fail *from searching* Your word,
Saying, "When will You comfort me?"

83 For I have become like a wineskin in smoke,
Yet I do not forget Your statutes.

84 How many *are* the days of Your servant?
When will You execute judgment on those who
persecute me?

85 The proud have dug pits for me,
Which *is* not according to Your law.

86 All Your commandments *are* faithful;
They persecute me wrongfully;
Help me!

87 They almost made an end of me on earth,
But I did not forsake Your precepts.

88 Revive me according to Your lovingkindness,
So that I may keep the testimony of Your
mouth.

89 Forever, O LORD,
Your word is settled in heaven.

90 Your faithfulness *endures* to all generations;
You established the earth, and it abides.

91 They continue this day according to Your
ordinances,
For all *are* Your servants.

92 Unless Your law *had been* my delight,
I would then have perished in my affliction.

93 I will never forget Your precepts,
For by them You have given me life.

94 I *am* Yours, save me;
For I have sought Your precepts.

95 The wicked wait for me to destroy me,
But I will consider Your testimonies.

96 I have seen the consummation of all
perfection,
But Your commandment *is* exceedingly broad.

DEVOTIONAL

They clash sometimes. Or at least they seem to. The commandments of God and the circumstances of life. God speaks, but so do people, and if we're not careful, the voices around us can drown out the voice above us or within us.

The voices around us speak harm, deceit, and discouragement. The voices around us attack us and tell us we are forgotten and unloved. The voices around us make us afraid of the future and anxious about today.

But the voice of God tells us something different. His words tell us we are loved by the Father. They tell us we have a future and a hope and that God's purposes in and around us will surely prevail.

So the next time someone's words seek to destroy you emotionally and spiritually, consider His testimony. Remember what God says and what He commands. Trust His Word and build upon His principles. When the small, tired voices around you are silenced, God's Word will still endure. What He says is true. It is settled in heaven, so let it be settled in your heart.

Dr. Willy Rice, Calvary Baptist Church
Clearwater, FL

JULY 31

The Guiding Light of God's Word

Psalm 119:97–112

97 Oh, how I love Your law!
It *is* my meditation all the day.

98 You, through Your commandments, make me wiser than my enemies;
For they *are* ever with me.

99 I have more understanding than all my teachers,
For Your testimonies *are* my meditation.

100 I understand more than the ancients,
Because I keep Your precepts.

101 I have restrained my feet from every evil way,
That I may keep Your word.

102 I have not departed from Your judgments,
For You Yourself have taught me.

103 How sweet are Your words to my taste,
Sweeter than honey to my mouth!

104 Through Your precepts I get understanding;
Therefore I hate every false way.

105 Your word *is* a lamp to my feet
And a light to my path.

106 I have sworn and confirmed
That I will keep Your righteous judgments.

107 I am afflicted very much;
Revive me, O Lord, according to Your word.

108 Accept, I pray, the freewill offerings of my mouth, O Lord,
And teach me Your judgments.

109 My life *is* continually in my hand,
Yet I do not forget Your law.

110 The wicked have laid a snare for me,
Yet I have not strayed from Your precepts.

111 Your testimonies I have taken as a heritage forever,
For they *are* the rejoicing of my heart.

112 I have inclined my heart to perform Your statutes
Forever, to the very end.

DEVOTIONAL

A lamp to my feet and a light to my path." It's a familiar verse (v. 105), memorized by thousands of children. It's a comforting reminder, because we need such a light and we are desperate for such a lamp.

Have you ever walked in darkness? No doubt you have at some point. Outside on a moonless night. Awakened at night in a strange place. When there is no light, you stumble around. You stump your toe, bump into the wall, or, even worse, trip and fall. It's a bad thing to take a spill in a room, but far worse to take a fall in life.

Without God's truth, without the light of His revelation, we are blinded like a man walking in darkness. We take a wrong turn. We make a bad choice. We do what seems best, but quickly learn that sometimes what seems best can end up very wrong.

You can either go through life guessing, making decisions based on a hunch or something you've heard, or you can turn the light on. God's Word gives us wisdom and guidance for every situation in life. His truth lights our path and shows us where to go. If you find yourself walking in darkness, you reach for a flashlight. In life, reach for God's Word. Trust His truth, follow His principles, and walk in the light.

Dr. Willy Rice, Calvary Baptist Church
Clearwater, FL

AUGUST 1

Trust in God in All Things

Psalm 119:113–128

¹¹³ I hate the double-minded,
But I love Your law.

¹¹⁴ You *are* my hiding place and my shield;
I hope in Your word.

¹¹⁵ Depart from me, you evildoers,
For I will keep the commandments of my God!

¹¹⁶ Uphold me according to Your word, that I
may live;
And do not let me be ashamed of my hope.

¹¹⁷ Hold me up, and I shall be safe,
And I shall observe Your statutes continually.

¹¹⁸ You reject all those who stray from Your
statutes,
For their deceit *is* falsehood.

¹¹⁹ You put away all the wicked of the earth *like*
dross;
Therefore I love Your testimonies.

¹²⁰ My flesh trembles for fear of You,
And I am afraid of Your judgments.

¹²¹ I have done justice and righteousness;
Do not leave me to my oppressors.

¹²² Be surety for Your servant for good;
Do not let the proud oppress me.

¹²³ My eyes fail *from seeking* Your salvation
And Your righteous word.

¹²⁴ Deal with Your servant according to Your
mercy,
And teach me Your statutes.

¹²⁵ I *am* Your servant;
Give me understanding,
That I may know Your testimonies.

¹²⁶ *It is* time for *You* to act, O LORD,
For they have regarded Your law as void.

¹²⁷ Therefore I love Your commandments
More than gold, yes, than fine gold!

¹²⁸ Therefore all *Your* precepts *concerning* all *things*
I consider *to be* right;
I hate every false way.

DEVOTIONAL

It's called "spatial disorientation." It's what happens when pilots become disoriented while they are flying. Every pilot learns early on that you can't always trust your senses. Every year tragic plane accidents happen because of pilot error. Often a pilot, especially a novice, becomes confused and disoriented. Suddenly they can't tell what is up and what is down. Their eyes play tricks on them. Pilots have flown their planes into the ground believing they were pulling them higher into the air. Experienced pilots know that you don't trust your senses; you trust the instruments. The plane's instruments can tell you how high you are, whether you're flying level or spinning dangerously out of control, and whether you're gaining or losing altitude.

In life, you can go by your senses if you want to. You can go by what seems right, but be warned, you can quickly get into trouble. The psalmist chose to trust something greater and wiser than himself; he chose to trust God. He said, "Therefore all Your precepts concerning all things I consider to be right" (v. 128). The choice is yours. You can trust yourself, or you can trust Someone greater. Put your trust in God.

Dr. Willy Rice, Calvary Baptist Church
Clearwater, FL

AUGUST 2

God's Word Brings Freedom

Psalm 119:129–144

129 Your testimonies are wonderful;
Therefore my soul keeps them.

130 The entrance of Your words gives light;
It gives understanding to the simple.

131 I opened my mouth and panted,
For I longed for Your commandments.

132 Look upon me and be merciful to me,
As Your custom *is* toward those who love Your
name.

133 Direct my steps by Your word,
And let no iniquity have dominion over me.

134 Redeem me from the oppression of man,
That I may keep Your precepts.

135 Make Your face shine upon Your servant,
And teach me Your statutes.

136 Rivers of water run down from my eyes,
Because *men* do not keep Your law.

137 Righteous *are* You, O LORD,
And upright *are* Your judgments.

138 Your testimonies, *which* You have commanded,
Are righteous and very faithful.

139 My zeal has consumed me,
Because my enemies have forgotten Your
words.

140 Your word *is* very pure;
Therefore Your servant loves it.

141 I *am* small and despised,
Yet I do not forget Your precepts.

142 Your righteousness *is* an everlasting
righteousness,
And Your law *is* truth.

143 Trouble and anguish have overtaken me,
Yet Your commandments *are* my delights.

144 The righteousness of Your testimonies *is*
everlasting;
Give me understanding, and I shall live.

DEVOTIONAL

Slavery. It's an ugly word and an even uglier reality. Most of us know something about the history of slavery. We at least know there was a time when people were denied freedom and basic rights due to their ethnicity. We abhor it today. We know people are made to be free. But are we really free?

Slavery takes many forms, and perhaps spiritual oppression is the worst. Free people are not always free, not when they are bound to addictions, enslaved to habitual patterns, and trapped in deceptive lies.

The psalmist knew about the oppression of men, and he knew about the dominion of sin. He knew sin can enslave worse than any human master. So he prayed, "Let no iniquity have dominion over me" (v. 133). So what is the path to freedom? It is to be directed by the truth of God's Word. The psalmist prayed, "Direct my steps by Your word" (v. 133). He had confidence that God would guide him into freedom if he would only listen and obey. He knew he would be freed from oppression if he followed God's principles.

God's Word leads us away from oppression and bondage and into spiritual freedom. Trust Him today and step into the freedom He has for you.

Dr. Willy Rice, Calvary Baptist Church
Clearwater, FL

AUGUST 3
God's Word Is Truth

Psalm 119:145–160

¹⁴⁵ I cry out with *my* whole heart;
Hear me, O LORD!
I will keep Your statutes.

¹⁴⁶ I cry out to You;
Save me, and I will keep Your testimonies.

¹⁴⁷ I rise before the dawning of the morning,
And cry for help;
I hope in Your word.

¹⁴⁸ My eyes are awake through the *night*
watches,
That I may meditate on Your word.

¹⁴⁹ Hear my voice according to Your
lovingkindness;
O LORD, revive me according to Your justice.

¹⁵⁰ They draw near who follow after wickedness;
They are far from Your law.

¹⁵¹ You *are* near, O LORD,
And all Your commandments *are* truth.

¹⁵² Concerning Your testimonies,
I have known of old that You have founded
them forever.

¹⁵³ Consider my affliction and deliver me,
For I do not forget Your law.

¹⁵⁴ Plead my cause and redeem me;
Revive me according to Your word.

¹⁵⁵ Salvation *is* far from the wicked,
For they do not seek Your statutes.

¹⁵⁶ Great *are* Your tender mercies, O LORD;
Revive me according to Your judgments.

¹⁵⁷ Many *are* my persecutors and my enemies,
Yet I do not turn from Your testimonies.

¹⁵⁸ I see the treacherous, and am disgusted,
Because they do not keep Your word.

¹⁵⁹ Consider how I love Your precepts;
Revive me, O LORD, according to Your
lovingkindness.

¹⁶⁰ The entirety of Your word *is* truth,
And every one of Your righteous judgments
endures forever.

DEVOTIONAL

They are near. The voices that confuse, deceive, and attack. They are near. As near as the remote control. As near as the radio. As near as the next social media post. We are surrounded by voices, and so many of those voices despise God's truth, mock His existence, and disparage His promises.

It's easy to get overwhelmed and discouraged. The voices seem to be everywhere, and it's hard to escape, hard to be grounded in truth. The voices that discourage are near, but there is Someone who is nearer still. He is as close as your next breath, your next heartbeat, your next thoughts. He is with us, in us, and for us. "You are near, O LORD, and all Your commandments are truth" (v. 151).

Yes, our world is full of noisy voices, and you'll probably hear some today. But isn't it good to know that God is near and that it is His voice that will ultimately prevail? It is His truth that will stand for all time. His truth endures forever. So all those voices of doubt and discouragement? They will soon be gone like the morning mist. But God's Word is true, and His promises for you will endure forever.

Dr. Willy Rice, Calvary Baptist Church
Clearwater, FL

AUGUST 4

The Hope of Salvation

Psalm 119:161–176

¹⁶¹ Princes persecute me without a cause,
But my heart stands in awe of Your word.

¹⁶² I rejoice at Your word
As one who finds great treasure.

¹⁶³ I hate and abhor lying,
But I love Your law.

¹⁶⁴ Seven times a day I praise You,
Because of Your righteous judgments.

¹⁶⁵ Great peace have those who love Your law,
And nothing causes them to stumble.

¹⁶⁶ Lord, I hope for Your salvation,
And I do Your commandments.

¹⁶⁷ My soul keeps Your testimonies,
And I love them exceedingly.

¹⁶⁸ I keep Your precepts and Your testimonies,
For all my ways *are* before You.

¹⁶⁹ Let my cry come before You, O Lord;
Give me understanding according to Your word.

¹⁷⁰ Let my supplication come before You;
Deliver me according to Your word.

¹⁷¹ My lips shall utter praise,
For You teach me Your statutes.

¹⁷² My tongue shall speak of Your word,
For all Your commandments *are*
righteousness.

¹⁷³ Let Your hand become my help,
For I have chosen Your precepts.

¹⁷⁴ I long for Your salvation, O Lord,
And Your law *is* my delight.

¹⁷⁵ Let my soul live, and it shall praise You;
And let Your judgments help me.

¹⁷⁶ I have gone astray like a lost sheep;
Seek Your servant,
For I do not forget Your commandments.

DEVOTIONAL

Have you ever found a treasure? Maybe you've fantasized about being one of those people who stumble across something extraordinary: a shipwreck discovered, a buried chest uncovered, or a priceless antique procured on a lark. We dream of striking it rich, of finding a treasure.

But there is a treasure to be uncovered that is more valuable than any pot of gold. It is the treasure of God's Word, the storehouse of His timeless principles for life. The psalmist rejoiced at God's Word "as one who finds great treasure" (v. 162).

Years later Jesus would compare the kingdom of God to a treasure a man stumbled across while walking in a field. The man, Jesus said, would go and sell all he had to buy the field and own the treasure (Matt. 13:44). Whatever he lost would not compare to the enormity of what he gained.

Such is God's kingdom. It is a great treasure. When you see it is true, you will willingly sacrifice whatever you must to lay hold of the treasure. You will repent and turn away from an old way of life and embrace a new life that God offers.

The Bible we hold and the truth it contains is a great treasure. Give thanks for the treasure and dive in to discover its truth today.

Dr. Willy Rice, Calvary Baptist Church
Clearwater, FL

AUGUST 5

Do God's commands limit your freedom or protect your freedom? Can you remember a time when God's commands seemed restrictive at the moment, but later you saw how God was protecting you and preparing you for something better?

_____

_____

_____

_____

_____

_____

_____

_____

_____

_____

What sin or pattern of behavior threatens to enslave you? What are the lies that threaten to blind and deceive you? What steps do you need to take to clearly hear and obey God's voice and reject the lies that lead to destruction?

_____

_____

_____

_____

_____

_____

_____

_____

AUGUST 6

Plea for Relief from Bitter Foes

Psalm 120:1–7

I N my distress I cried to the LORD,
And He heard me.

2 Deliver my soul, O LORD, from lying lips
And from a deceitful tongue.

3 What shall be given to you,
Or what shall be done to you,
You false tongue?

4 Sharp arrows of the warrior,
With coals of the broom tree!

5 Woe is me, that I dwell in Meshech,
That I dwell among the tents of Kedar!

6 My soul has dwelt too long
With one who hates peace.

7 I *am for* peace;
But when I speak, they *are* for war.

Psalm 121:1–8

I WILL lift up my eyes to the hills—
From whence comes my help?

2 My help *comes* from the LORD,
Who made heaven and earth.

3 He will not allow your foot to be moved;
He who keeps you will not slumber.

4 Behold, He who keeps Israel
Shall neither slumber nor sleep.

5 The LORD *is* your keeper;
The LORD *is* your shade at your right hand.

6 The sun shall not strike you by day,
Nor the moon by night.

7 The LORD shall preserve you from all evil;
He shall preserve your soul.

8 The LORD shall preserve your going out and
your coming in
From this time forth, and even forevermore.

DEVOTIONAL

S ticks and stones may break my bones, but words will never hurt me." Most of us spoke these words as children when someone said unkind things about us. Unfortunately, this popular rhyme isn't true. Hurtful words hurt.

The psalmist knew the pain of having lies told about him, but he didn't respond with vicious statements of his own. The author instead "cried to the LORD" (120:1) and expressed his displeasure at the desire others had for constant conflict.

His heavenly Father responded by reminding the author that the lies being told were like "arrows" and "coals of the broom tree" (120:4). These two word pictures illustrate the boomerang effect of lying lips. Lies damage the character and reputation of those telling them more than their intended targets.

Our heavenly Father knows the truth about us. He sovereignly works to ensure our integrity before others. In Psalm 121, the author uses six different expressions to show the Lord "keeps" or "preserves" His children. And this protection occurs all the time, day and night.

As believers, we should seek to live peacefully with others. But when they wound us with their words or tell untruthful things about us, we should lift our "eyes to the hills" (121:1) and remember the Lord protects us from all untruth.

Phil Waldrep, Phil Waldrep Ministries
Decatur, AL

AUGUST 7

Going to the House of the Lord

Psalm 122:1–9

I WAS glad when they said to me,
"Let us go into the house of the LORD."
2 Our feet have been standing
Within your gates, O Jerusalem!

3 Jerusalem is built
As a city that is compact together,
4 Where the tribes go up,
The tribes of the LORD,
To the Testimony of Israel,
To give thanks to the name of the LORD.
5 For thrones are set there for judgment,
The thrones of the house of David.

6 Pray for the peace of Jerusalem:
"May they prosper who love you.
7 Peace be within your walls,
Prosperity within your palaces."
8 For the sake of my brethren and companions,
I will now say, "Peace *be* within you."
9 Because of the house of the LORD our God
I will seek your good.

Psalm 123:1–4

U NTO You I lift up my eyes,
O You who dwell in the heavens.
2 Behold, as the eyes of servants *look* to the
hand of their masters,
As the eyes of a maid to the hand of her
mistress,
So our eyes *look* to the LORD our God,
Until He has mercy on us.

3 Have mercy on us, O LORD, have mercy on us!
For we are exceedingly filled with contempt.
4 Our soul is exceedingly filled
With the scorn of those who are at ease,
With the contempt of the proud.

DEVOTIONAL

I wonder if one of the reasons church attendance is declining is because it's so easy to attend and therefore isn't viewed as special. Today we can get into our car, drive a few miles, and arrive for services minutes later. For the Jews many years ago, going to the temple in Jerusalem often took days. Because of the planning that was necessary, they treasured their time there.

The "house of the LORD" (122:1) represented more than a place of fellowship; it housed the presence of God. There they felt secure from their enemies. Together the Jews lifted their voices in thanksgiving for the blessings of God and prayed together for the continued peace and prosperity of Israel.

As Christians it isn't necessary for us to visit Jerusalem to experience God. Yes, we should sense His presence and power each time we attend a church service. But we should experience His presence every day. Like the psalmist in the temple, we should voice our praise for who God is. We should offer thanksgiving for His blessings in our lives. And we should share our heart's desires with Him.

An amazing thing happens when we experience the real presence of God. We begin to be like Him. And we desire more and more to spend time with Him. And then, like the Jews, we are "glad" when we can enter the presence of our heavenly Father.

Phil Waldrep, Phil Waldrep Ministries
Decatur, AL

AUGUST 8

The Lord, the Defense of His People

Psalm 124:1–8

I F it had not been the LORD who was on our side,"
Let Israel now say—

2 "If it had not been the LORD who was on our side,
When men rose up against us,

3 Then they would have swallowed us alive,
When their wrath was kindled against us;

4 Then the waters would have overwhelmed us,
The stream would have gone over our soul;

5 Then the swollen waters
Would have gone over our soul."

6 Blessed *be* the LORD,
Who has not given us *as* prey to their teeth.

7 Our soul has escaped as a bird from the snare
of the fowlers;
The snare is broken, and we have escaped.

8 Our help *is* in the name of the LORD,
Who made heaven and earth.

Psalm 125:1–5

T HOSE who trust in the LORD
Are like Mount Zion,
Which cannot be moved, *but* abides forever.

2 As the mountains surround Jerusalem,
So the LORD surrounds His people
From this time forth and forever.

3 For the scepter of wickedness shall not rest
On the land allotted to the righteous,
Lest the righteous reach out their hands to
iniquity.

4 Do good, O LORD, to *those who are* good,
And to *those who are* upright in their hearts.

5 As for such as turn aside to their crooked ways,
The LORD shall lead them away
With the workers of iniquity.

Peace *be* upon Israel!

DEVOTIONAL

H ave you ever taken time to look back over your life to identify experiences that you can explain only by saying that the Lord intervened? Maybe you remember an accident that should have occurred but didn't. Or maybe you recall a time when doctors gave a family member little chance of healing from an illness but that person recovered. Many times in our lives we can say with the Israelites, "If it had not been the LORD who was on our side" (124:1).

The psalmist took time to list things that could have happened if God wasn't for them. Some were physical. The nations opposed to the Israelites would have destroyed them and taken them prisoners of war. Others were emotional in nature. Circumstances in our lives sometimes can overwhelm us. The author of Psalm 124 used the image of a flood drowning people. But the Lord gives emotional strength when it seems we cannot take anymore. Best of all, our heavenly Father provides all our spiritual needs.

Psalm 125 reminds us of the eternal stability we have in Christ. Earthly kingdoms existed for a period of time, but His kingdom is "from this time forth and forever" (v. 2) Therefore, the wicked will not prevail and God's people shall triumph.

Phil Waldrep, Phil Waldrep Ministries
Decatur, AL

AUGUST 9

A Joyful Return to Zion

Psalm 126:1–6

WHEN the LORD brought back the captivity of Zion,
We were like those who dream.

2 Then our mouth was filled with laughter,
And our tongue with singing.
Then they said among the nations,
"The LORD has done great things for them."

3 The LORD has done great things for us,
And we are glad.

4 Bring back our captivity, O LORD,
As the streams in the South.

5 Those who sow in tears
Shall reap in joy.

6 He who continually goes forth weeping,
Bearing seed for sowing,
Shall doubtless come again with rejoicing,
Bringing his sheaves *with him.*

Psalm 127:1–5

UNLESS the LORD builds the house,
They labor in vain who build it;
Unless the LORD guards the city,
The watchman stays awake in vain.

2 *It is* vain for you to rise up early,
To sit up late,
To eat the bread of sorrows;
For so He gives His beloved sleep.

3 Behold, children *are* a heritage from
the LORD,
The fruit of the womb *is* a reward.

4 Like arrows in the hand of a warrior,
So *are* the children of one's youth.

5 Happy *is* the man who has his quiver full
of them;
They shall not be ashamed,
But shall speak with their enemies in the gate.

DEVOTIONAL

While sitting in traffic recently I saw a bumper sticker that read, "I am blessed to be a blessing." Those words prompted me to realize all blessings from God are to encourage us to be a blessing to others.

Most Bible scholars believe Psalm 126 was a song sung by the Israelites after Jerusalem was delivered from the Assyrian army. This victory, recorded in 2 Kings 18–19, was swift and quick. Even the other nations upon hearing of the Jewish victory had to admit "the LORD has done great things for them" (v. 2). Deliverance, however, brought a responsibility with it. The Jews who were blessed with freedom from the Assyrians were to be a blessing to others. The psalmist used the metaphor of a farmer plowing his fields, sowing his seeds, and reaping a harvest as a picture of Israel's responsibility to bless others.

As believers we have experienced deliverance from sin. The bondage of sin no longer exists. Now we have a responsibility to lift our voices in praise and to share the gospel. Psalm 127 reminds us, however, that we are to live our lives empowered by the Lord. Only then will we effectively make an impact on others and our children.

Phil Waldrep, Phil Waldrep Ministries
Decatur, AL

AUGUST 10

Blessings of Those Who Fear the Lord

Psalm 128:1–6

BLESSED *is* every one who fears the LORD,
Who walks in His ways.

2 When you eat the labor of your hands,
You *shall be* happy, and *it shall be* well
    with you.
3 Your wife *shall be* like a fruitful vine
In the very heart of your house,
Your children like olive plants
All around your table.
4 Behold, thus shall the man be blessed
Who fears the LORD.

5 The LORD bless you out of Zion,
And may you see the good of Jerusalem
All the days of your life.
6 Yes, may you see your children's children.

Peace *be* upon Israel!

Psalm 129:1–8

MANY a time they have afflicted me from
    my youth,"
Let Israel now say—
2 "Many a time they have afflicted me from my
    youth;
Yet they have not prevailed against me.
3 The plowers plowed on my back;
They made their furrows long."
4 The LORD *is* righteous;
He has cut in pieces the cords of the wicked.

5 Let all those who hate Zion
Be put to shame and turned back.

6 Let them be as the grass *on* the housetops,
Which withers before it grows up,
7 With which the reaper does not fill his hand,
Nor he who binds sheaves, his arms.
8 Neither let those who pass by them say,
"The blessing of the LORD *be* upon you;
We bless you in the name of the LORD!"

DEVOTIONAL

I hate my job!"
"What is wrong with my family?"
"When will everyone get off my back?!"
    Have you made these remarks or felt like making them? At some point most of us have.

In these two psalms, the author addressed these emotions. At the outset he wanted us to know the key to handling emotional outbursts is obedience to God's Word. Obedience changes our perspective on life. We begin to see everything as a ministry rather than a chore. Our occupation, for example, becomes a mission field instead of a dreaded routine. We see our fellow employees as people in need of Christ or believers needing our encouragement. The change of perspective turns our job into a joy because we see a higher calling in what we do.

The psalmist extends the effects of our obedience to our family. Our spouse and our children will see and feel the positive results of our obedience to our heavenly Father. Ultimately, our obedience to biblical teachings blesses our community and our country.

The psalmist assures those who are obedient that the Lord will deal justly with those who repress the godly.

Phil Waldrep, Phil Waldrep Ministries
Decatur, AL

AUGUST 11

Waiting for the Redemption of the Lord

Psalm 130:1–8

O UT of the depths I have cried to You, O LORD;
  ² Lord, hear my voice!
Let Your ears be attentive
To the voice of my supplications.

³ If You, LORD, should mark iniquities,
  O Lord, who could stand?
⁴ But *there is* forgiveness with You,
  That You may be feared.

⁵ I wait for the LORD, my soul waits,
  And in His word I do hope.
⁶ My soul *waits* for the Lord
  More than those who watch for the
      morning—
  Yes, more than those who watch for the
      morning.

⁷ O Israel, hope in the LORD;
  For with the LORD *there is* mercy,
  And with Him *is* abundant redemption.
⁸ And He shall redeem Israel
  From all his iniquities.

Psalm 131:1–3

L ORD, my heart is not haughty,
  Nor my eyes lofty.
Neither do I concern myself with great
      matters,
Nor with things too profound for me.

² Surely I have calmed and quieted my soul,
  Like a weaned child with his mother;
  Like a weaned child *is* my soul within me.

³ O Israel, hope in the LORD
  From this time forth and forever.

DEVOTIONAL

W hen Paul wrote to the church at Corinth, he encouraged the believers to "put away childish things" (1 Cor. 13:11). Maturity demands it. In Psalm 131, the psalmist used the word picture of a child being weaned from his mother to illustrate spiritual maturity. Just as babies go through a period of transition when they are weaned from their mother's milk, so Christians go through a transition from a baby Christian to a mature believer who can handle the weightier matters of life and faith.

Psalm 130 lists some of the things we feel as the growing pains of maturity. The author says we sometimes cry out to the Lord when we are overwhelmed by life's events. Our heavenly Father often allows us to see our need for Him, and we realize we can't face life's difficulties alone. The writer also reminds us maturity is occurring when we feel the guilt of our sin. Spiritual growth requires us to see the depths of our sin and the forgiveness we have in Christ.

Sometimes the Lord allows us to go through experiences when we cannot see His hand or sense His purpose. These times prompt us to trust Him. At all times our Lord is growing us into the likeness of His Son.

Phil Waldrep, Phil Waldrep Ministries
Decatur, AL

AUGUST 12

An old hymn says we should "count our many blessings," naming them "one by one." What specific blessings has the Lord given you? Make a list and take a moment to praise Him for them.

Think of a specific time when you felt overwhelmed by life's circumstances. How did our heavenly Father help you during that time? What can you see looking back that matured you spiritually during that time?

AUGUST 13

The Eternal Dwelling of God in Zion

Psalm 132:1–18

Lord, remember David
And all his afflictions;

2 How he swore to the Lord,
And vowed to the Mighty One of Jacob:

3 "Surely I will not go into the chamber of my
house,
Or go up to the comfort of my bed;

4 I will not give sleep to my eyes
Or slumber to my eyelids,

5 Until I find a place for the Lord,
A dwelling place for the Mighty One of Jacob."

6 Behold, we heard of it in Ephrathah;
We found it in the fields of the woods.

7 Let us go into His tabernacle;
Let us worship at His footstool.

8 Arise, O Lord, to Your resting place,
You and the ark of Your strength.

9 Let Your priests be clothed with
righteousness,
And let Your saints shout for joy.

10 For Your servant David's sake,
Do not turn away the face of Your Anointed.

11 The Lord has sworn in truth to David;
He will not turn from it:
"I will set upon your throne the fruit of your
body.

12 If your sons will keep My covenant
And My testimony which I shall teach them,
Their sons also shall sit upon your throne
forevermore."

13 For the Lord has chosen Zion;
He has desired it for His dwelling place:

14 "This is My resting place forever;
Here I will dwell, for I have desired it.

15 I will abundantly bless her provision;
I will satisfy her poor with bread.

16 I will also clothe her priests with salvation,
And her saints shall shout aloud for joy.

17 There I will make the horn of David grow;
I will prepare a lamp for My Anointed.

18 His enemies I will clothe with shame,
But upon Himself His crown shall flourish."

DEVOTIONAL

David began this psalm with a simple request, "Lord, remember David." I'm sure David knew this was a strange request because our God never forgets! He knows all that we do, and He even knows why we do it.

God remembered David, and because of God's Word, we all remember David, both the good and the bad. David was known as a man after God's own heart, and it shows here in our scriptures. David wants to build God a dwelling place on earth. He has an earthly home, and he desires for God to have one as well.

What about you? If you know the Lord, you are His temple! Never forget this truth.

Dr. Jerry Walls, Southside Baptist Church
Warner Robins, GA

AUGUST 14

Blessed Unity of the People of God

Psalm 133:1–3

B EHOLD, how good and how pleasant *it is*
For brethren to dwell together in unity!

2 *It is* like the precious oil upon the head,
Running down on the beard,
The beard of Aaron,
Running down on the edge of his garments.

3 *It is* like the dew of Hermon,
Descending upon the mountains of Zion;
For there the LORD commanded the blessing—
Life forevermore.

Psalm 134:1–3

B EHOLD, bless the LORD,
All *you* servants of the LORD,
Who by night stand in the house of the LORD!

2 Lift up your hands *in* the sanctuary,
And bless the LORD.

3 The LORD who made heaven and earth
Bless you from Zion!

DEVOTIONAL

I think some people confuse unity with uniformity, but they are actually not alike in the least.
Uniformity is when everyone looks alike, talks
alike, dresses alike, and thinks alike. Unity, on
the other hand, is when everyone looks, sounds,
dresses, and thinks differently, but still comes
together as one for the greater good. Uniformity
is when everyone agrees on everything, while
unity is when everyone agrees on the main
thing. In other words, unity is when people who
don't necessarily have anything in common join
together for something that they do have in common. As the people of God, we are to be unified in
purpose. This doesn't mean that God wants us all
to be the same. Instead, His desire is to take all of
us, who are very different, and make us one.

I cannot express to you how important it is
to recognize the differences between these two
words! If you fail to understand what unity really
is, you will impose your preferences upon those
you come in contact with. But if you truly understand unity, you can accept people who are different from you, and when you do, it becomes a
wonderful experience.

Choose unity, not uniformity!

Dr. Jerry Walls, Southside Baptist Church
Warner Robins, GA

AUGUST 15

Praise in Creation and Redemption

Psalm 135:1–21

P RAISE the LORD!
  Praise the name of the LORD;
  Praise *Him,* O you servants of the LORD!
2 You who stand in the house of the LORD,
  In the courts of the house of our God,
3 Praise the LORD, for the LORD *is* good;
  Sing praises to His name, for *it is* pleasant.
4 For the LORD has chosen Jacob for Himself,
  Israel for His special treasure.

5 For I know that the LORD *is* great,
  And our Lord *is* above all gods.
6 Whatever the LORD pleases He does,
  In heaven and in earth,
  In the seas and in all deep places.
7 He causes the vapors to ascend from the ends
      of the earth;
  He makes lightning for the rain;
  He brings the wind out of His treasuries.

8 He destroyed the firstborn of Egypt,
  Both of man and beast.
9 He sent signs and wonders into the midst of
      you, O Egypt,
  Upon Pharaoh and all his servants.
10 He defeated many nations
  And slew mighty kings—
11 Sihon king of the Amorites,
  Og king of Bashan,
  And all the kingdoms of Canaan—
12 And gave their land *as* a heritage,
  A heritage to Israel His people.

13 Your name, O LORD, *endures* forever,
  Your fame, O LORD, throughout all generations.
14 For the LORD will judge His people,
  And He will have compassion on His servants.

15 The idols of the nations *are* silver and gold,
  The work of men's hands.
16 They have mouths, but they do not speak;
  Eyes they have, but they do not see;
17 They have ears, but they do not hear;
  Nor is there *any* breath in their mouths.
18 Those who make them are like them;
  So is everyone who trusts in them.

19 Bless the LORD, O house of Israel!
  Bless the LORD, O house of Aaron!
20 Bless the LORD, O house of Levi!
  You who fear the LORD, bless the LORD!
21 Blessed be the LORD out of Zion,
  Who dwells in Jerusalem!

  Praise the LORD!

DEVOTIONAL

E verybody worships something. We all live
  with this desire to worship, and if we don't
guard ourselves, we will find ourselves opening the door for something else or someone else
to take the place of God in our lives. It may be a
relationship. It may be a hobby. We may even worship ourselves. And when we make these things
the priority of our lives, not only do we worship
the wrong thing, but by default, we stiff-arm the
only One who is actually worthy of our worship.
We push away our heavenly Father.

Dr. Jerry Walls, Southside Baptist Church
Warner Robins, GA

AUGUST 16

Thanks to God for His Enduring Mercy

Psalm 136:1–9

O H, give thanks to the Lord, for *He is* good!
For His mercy *endures* forever.

2 Oh, give thanks to the God of gods!
For His mercy *endures* forever.

3 Oh, give thanks to the Lord of lords!
For His mercy *endures* forever:

4 To Him who alone does great wonders,
For His mercy *endures* forever;

5 To Him who by wisdom made the heavens,
For His mercy *endures* forever;

6 To Him who laid out the earth above the
waters,
For His mercy *endures* forever;

7 To Him who made great lights,
For His mercy *endures* forever—

8 The sun to rule by day,
For His mercy *endures* forever;

9 The moon and stars to rule by night,
For His mercy *endures* forever.

DEVOTIONAL

W hen my children were growing up, I was constantly prompting them to do all kinds of things. I would prompt them to open doors for people, prompt them to wash their hands and brush their teeth, and prompt them every other day to clean their rooms. On some days, it seemed like all I was doing was prompting them.

But more than anything else, I was constantly prompting my children to say thank you. And I prompted them the same way every parent in the history of the world prompted their children.

When I saw that they might have missed an opportunity to say thanks, I would simply remind them by saying, "What do you say?" When I said, "What do you say?" my children knew that this really wasn't a question. I would have been surprised if one of them had said something like, "It's about time" or "See you later." My children knew that the answer was, "Thank you." So let me ask you a question. In light of all that God has done for you, what should you say to Him today?

Dr. Jerry Walls, Southside Baptist Church
Warner Robins, GA

AUGUST 17

God's Enduring Mercy

Psalm 136:10–26

¹⁰ To Him who struck Egypt in their firstborn,
   For His mercy *endures* forever;

¹¹ And brought out Israel from among them,
   For His mercy *endures* forever;

¹² With a strong hand, and with an outstretched arm,
   For His mercy *endures* forever;

¹³ To Him who divided the Red Sea in two,
   For His mercy *endures* forever;

¹⁴ And made Israel pass through the midst of it,
   For His mercy *endures* forever;

¹⁵ But overthrew Pharaoh and his army in the Red Sea,
   For His mercy *endures* forever;

¹⁶ To Him who led His people through the wilderness,
   For His mercy *endures* forever;

¹⁷ To Him who struck down great kings,
   For His mercy *endures* forever;

¹⁸ And slew famous kings,
   For His mercy *endures* forever—

¹⁹ Sihon king of the Amorites,
   For His mercy *endures* forever;

²⁰ And Og king of Bashan,
   For His mercy *endures* forever—

²¹ And gave their land as a heritage,
   For His mercy *endures* forever;

²² A heritage to Israel His servant,
   For His mercy *endures* forever.

²³ Who remembered us in our lowly state,
   For His mercy *endures* forever;

²⁴ And rescued us from our enemies,
   For His mercy *endures* forever;

²⁵ Who gives food to all flesh,
   For His mercy *endures* forever.

²⁶ Oh, give thanks to the God of heaven!
   For His mercy *endures* forever.

DEVOTIONAL

I don't know if you noticed, but the Lord's mercy endures forever.

The psalmist makes it clear to anyone questioning whether or not the Lord's mercy is always going to be around that it most definitely is not going anywhere at all. The same God whose mercy was so well known in the Old Testament demonstrated His mercy in a magnificent way when He sent Jesus into the world to save sinners like you and me. We did nothing to deserve this extraordinary gift. Our response to His wonderful mercy should be thanksgiving and worship.

I don't know how you've been the recipient of His mercy recently, but I do know that you have been. Let our God know today how thankful you are for it!

Dr. Jerry Walls, Southside Baptist Church
Warner Robins, GA

AUGUST 18

Longing for Zion in a Foreign Land

Psalm 137:1–9

BY the rivers of Babylon,
There we sat down, yea, we wept
When we remembered Zion.

2   We hung our harps
Upon the willows in the midst of it.

3   For there those who carried us away captive
      asked of us a song,
And those who plundered us *requested* mirth,
Saying, "Sing us *one* of the songs of Zion!"

4   How shall we sing the LORD's song
In a foreign land?

5   If I forget you, O Jerusalem,
Let my right hand forget *its skill!*

6   If I do not remember you,
Let my tongue cling to the roof of my
      mouth—
If I do not exalt Jerusalem
Above my chief joy.

7   Remember, O LORD, against the sons of Edom
The day of Jerusalem,
Who said, "Raze *it*, raze *it*,
To its very foundation!"

8   O daughter of Babylon, who are to be
      destroyed,
Happy the one who repays you as you have
      served us!

9   Happy the one who takes and dashes
Your little ones against the rock!

DEVOTIONAL

Our text today finds God's people in Babylon. Babylon represents a place of judgment. God's people are there for one reason: they have refused to obey His commandments and to walk in His ways!

When we read this psalm, we realize that the Israelites recognized that the path they had chosen was not the right path. They had followed the path that they desired, and now they were suffering the consequences! Realization of what their decision had brought them caused them to weep.

We who are God's children can often find ourselves in the same position as Israel. We follow our own paths rather than God's and end up in a spiritual desert. Let's exercise spiritual discipline. Let's stay away from Babylon and experience the joy of walking with God. Let's listen to the right voice so that we might rejoice!

Dr. Jerry Walls, Southside Baptist Church
Warner Robins, GA

AUGUST 19

We are God's temple! How can you live out this truth today?

_____

_____

_____

_____

_____

_____

_____

_____

_____

How long has it been since you took some time to say thank you to your heavenly Father? Write down some of your more recent blessings.

_____

_____

_____

_____

_____

_____

_____

_____

_____

_____

AUGUST 20

The Lord's Goodness to the Faithful

Psalm 138:1–8

I WILL praise You with my whole heart;
Before the gods I will sing praises to You.

2 I will worship toward Your holy temple,
And praise Your name
For Your lovingkindness and Your truth;
For You have magnified Your word above all
Your name.

3 In the day when I cried out, You answered me,
And made me bold *with* strength in my soul.

4 All the kings of the earth shall praise You,
O Lord,
When they hear the words of Your mouth.

5 Yes, they shall sing of the ways of the Lord,
For great *is* the glory of the Lord.

6 Though the Lord *is* on high,
Yet He regards the lowly;
But the proud He knows from afar.

7 Though I walk in the midst of trouble, You will
revive me;
You will stretch out Your hand
Against the wrath of my enemies,
And Your right hand will save me.

8 The Lord will perfect *that which* concerns me;
Your mercy, O Lord, *endures* forever;
Do not forsake the works of Your hands.

DEVOTIONAL

God is good! Pause for a moment and consider that statement. It has become so familiar that it may have lost its power. But believe me, this is an amazing truth—God is good!

Some would say, "God cannot be good. Have you seen all the evil in our world today? A good God would not allow that to happen." Yet all of the wickedness in the world cannot change this fact: even when times are bad, God is good! Others would say, "God cannot be good. If He is good, then why do we encounter sickness and suffering?" Even when health is bad, God is good!

How good is God? Verse 3 tells us that God is so good He hears us when we call and He answers us. God speaks through Jeremiah the prophet and says, "Call to Me, and I will answer you, and show you great and mighty things, which you do not know" (Jer. 33:3). God is good!

God is so good that He deserves our love and praise. David said, "They shall sing of the ways of the Lord, for great is the glory of the Lord" (Ps. 138:5). David offered praise to God because of His "lovingkindness" and "truth" (v. 2). God is good!

God is so good that even though He is "on high," He "regards the lowly" (v. 6). This is an amazing truth. God is good! God is so good that He promises to finish what He has started in His children. "The Lord will perfect that which concerns me" (v. 8). Paul wrote, "He who has begun a good work in you will complete it" (Phil. 1:6).

Maybe for some reason you have doubted God's goodness and love. Remember once again that His mercy endures forever and He is good!

Dr. Jim Perdue, Second Baptist Church
Warner Robins, GA

AUGUST 21

God's Perfect Knowledge of Man

Psalm 139:1–12

O LORD, You have searched me and known *me*.
² You know my sitting down and my
    rising up;
You understand my thought afar off.
³ You comprehend my path and my lying down,
And are acquainted with all my ways.
⁴ For *there is* not a word on my tongue,
But behold, O LORD, You know it altogether.
⁵ You have hedged me behind and before,
And laid Your hand upon me.
⁶ *Such* knowledge *is* too wonderful for me;
It is high, I cannot *attain* it.

⁷ Where can I go from Your Spirit?
Or where can I flee from Your presence?
⁸ If I ascend into heaven, You *are* there;
If I make my bed in hell, behold, You *are there*.
⁹ *If* I take the wings of the morning,
And dwell in the uttermost parts of the sea,
¹⁰ Even there Your hand shall lead me,
And Your right hand shall hold me.
¹¹ If I say, "Surely the darkness shall fall on me,"
Even the night shall be light about me;
¹² Indeed, the darkness shall not hide from You,
But the night shines as the day;
The darkness and the light *are* both alike
    to You.

DEVOTIONAL

God knows you perfectly and completely—and He loves you anyway. There are things about myself that I don't like. There are things that displease me. There are things about my past that I wish I could change. But God loves me anyway.

No one knows you better than God. He knows when you go to sleep and when you wake up. He knows your every thought. He sees everywhere you go and everything you do. He knows every word that comes to your mind and out of your mouth. He sees you in the light, and He sees you in the dark.

If that kind of knowledge amazes you, then you are in good company. David was amazed too. He said, "Such knowledge is too wonderful for me; it is high, I cannot attain it" (v. 6). God's omniscience is hard for us to fathom.

God knows you. There is nowhere you can hide from Him. There are no secrets you can keep from Him. A Bible teacher once said, "There is nothing around the corner which is beyond God's view." The author of Hebrews reminds us that "no creature [is] hidden from His sight" (4:13). He sees all and knows all.

At first, this thought might frighten you, and rightfully so. There is nowhere to hide from God. But then, this thought should comfort you. You are never out of His sight, and you are never out of His hands. He sees you completely. He knows you thoroughly. And He loves you perfectly.

Dr. Jim Perdue, Second Baptist Church
Warner Robins, GA

AUGUST 22

God's Perfect Knowledge of Man

Psalm 139:13–24

13 For You formed my inward parts;
You covered me in my mother's womb.

14 I will praise You, for I am fearfully *and*
wonderfully made;
Marvelous are Your works,
And *that* my soul knows very well.

15 My frame was not hidden from You,
When I was made in secret,
And skillfully wrought in the lowest parts of
the earth.

16 Your eyes saw my substance, being yet unformed.
And in Your book they all were written,
The days fashioned for me,
When *as yet there were* none of them.

17 How precious also are Your thoughts to me,
O God!
How great is the sum of them!

18 *If* I should count them, they would be more in
number than the sand;
When I awake, I am still with You.

19 Oh, that You would slay the wicked, O God!
Depart from me, therefore, you bloodthirsty
men.

20 For they speak against You wickedly;
Your enemies take *Your name* in vain.

21 Do I not hate them, O Lord, who hate You?
And do I not loathe those who rise up
against You?

22 I hate them with perfect hatred;
I count them my enemies.

23 Search me, O God, and know my heart;
Try me, and know my anxieties;

24 And see if *there is any* wicked way in me,
And lead me in the way everlasting.

DEVOTIONAL

The great Bible commentator Matthew Henry said, "[God] not only sees [men], but He sees through them."[1] He sees your outward actions, but He also knows your inward motivations. He sees your deeds, but He also knows your heart.

There is nothing about you that God does not see and know. David says that God knew you even when you were in your mother's womb. "For You formed my inward parts; You covered me in my mother's womb" (v. 13). Although you were "yet unformed" (v. 16), God knew everything about you and every one of your days.

Before your first breath, God knew exactly how many you would breathe. Before your first word, God knew exactly how many you would speak. Before your first step, God knew exactly how many you would take. Before your first moment, God knew exactly how many you would live. God's knowledge is simply amazing!

Beyond that, His thoughts toward you are "precious" and "great" (v. 17). God knows your thoughts and words, your motives and actions, your friends and enemies. Nothing is hidden from Him. This should motivate you to worship Him. It should lead you to prayer. And why don't you do that right now? Read aloud the last two verses of this chapter and let that be the sincere prayer of your heart.

Dr. Jim Perdue, Second Baptist Church
Warner Robins, GA

AUGUST 23

Prayer for Deliverance from Evil Men

Psalm 140:1-13

D ELIVER me, O LORD, from evil men;
Preserve me from violent men,

2 Who plan evil things in *their* hearts;
They continually gather together *for* war.

3 They sharpen their tongues like a serpent;
The poison of asps *is* under their lips.　　Selah

4 Keep me, O LORD, from the hands of the wicked;
Preserve me from violent men,
Who have purposed to make my steps stumble.

5 The proud have hidden a snare for me, and cords;
They have spread a net by the wayside;
They have set traps for me.　　Selah

6 I said to the LORD: "You *are* my God;
Hear the voice of my supplications, O LORD.

7 O GOD the Lord, the strength of my salvation,
You have covered my head in the day of battle.

8 Do not grant, O LORD, the desires of the wicked;
Do not further his *wicked* scheme,
Lest they be exalted.　　Selah

9 "*As for* the head of those who surround me,
Let the evil of their lips cover them;

10 Let burning coals fall upon them;
Let them be cast into the fire,
Into deep pits, that they rise not up again.

11 Let not a slanderer be established in the earth;
Let evil hunt the violent man to overthrow *him*."

12 I know that the LORD will maintain
The cause of the afflicted,
And justice for the poor.

13 Surely the righteous shall give thanks to Your name;
The upright shall dwell in Your presence.

DEVOTIONAL

M aybe you have heard the story of the little boy who had been consistently misbehaving in church. Finally, his father snatched him up and hurried him out to receive his punishment. No one really paid any attention until the little boy cried out, "Y'all pray for me now!"

In times of trouble, it seems that our first instinct is to pray. In fact, some people treat God like they would a trial attorney. They only go to Him when they are in trouble. But the reality is that this world is a wicked and violent place. There is trouble and pain all around us. We must be faithful in coming to the Father in prayer.

David cried out to God in a time of distress. He asked the Lord to protect him from "evil" and "violent men" (vv. 1, 4). Many scholars believe that David wrote this psalm while he was an official in King Saul's court, when some of Saul's officers were spreading lies and setting traps for David.

The Bible tells us that our Enemy is a liar and deceiver. God's people face the same problems today that David encountered. In times of distress, and at all times, run to God in prayer. E. M. Bounds wrote, "The more praying there is in the world the better the world will be, the mightier the forces against evil everywhere."[2]

Dr. Jim Perdue, Second Baptist Church
Warner Robins, GA

AUGUST 24
Prayer for Safekeeping from Wickedness

Psalm 141:1–10

LORD, I cry out to You;
Make haste to me!
Give ear to my voice when I cry out to You.

2 Let my prayer be set before You *as* incense,
The lifting up of my hands *as* the evening
sacrifice.

3 Set a guard, O LORD, over my mouth;
Keep watch over the door of my lips.

4 Do not incline my heart to any evil thing,
To practice wicked works
With men who work iniquity;
And do not let me eat of their delicacies.

5 Let the righteous strike me;
It shall be a kindness.
And let him rebuke me;
It shall be as excellent oil;
Let my head not refuse it.

For still my prayer *is* against the deeds of the
wicked.

6 Their judges are overthrown by the sides of
the cliff,
And they hear my words, for they are sweet.

7 Our bones are scattered at the mouth of the
grave,
As when one plows and breaks up the earth.

8 But my eyes *are* upon You, O GOD the Lord;
In You I take refuge;
Do not leave my soul destitute.

9 Keep me from the snares they have laid for me,
And from the traps of the workers of iniquity.

10 Let the wicked fall into their own nets,
While I escape safely.

DEVOTIONAL

Jesus taught in Matthew 6 that we should avoid evil. "And do not lead us into temptation, but deliver us from the evil one" (v. 13). In today's psalm, David prayed that God would protect him from wickedness. The Enemy will ensure that sin will find you, and you have to know what to do when it knocks on your door. Opportunities for evil abound, but how do faithful followers of Christ prepare to face temptation when it comes?

First, we have to pray. David went to the Lord with a sincere request. He said, "LORD, I cry out to you! . . . Set a guard, O LORD, over my mouth; keep watch over the door of my lips" (v. 1, 3). This is a request we should all make.

Second, we must keep our hearts in check so that sin cannot find a foothold. David prayed, "Do not incline my heart to any evil thing" (v. 4).

Third, we must be willing to listen to the counsel of godly people who want to help us walk in the paths of righteousness. David said that when the righteous strike us it is a good thing (v. 5). It helps us stay on the right path.

Finally, no matter what we face, we must keep our eyes upon God and trust in Him. "But my eyes are upon You, O GOD the Lord; in You I take refuge" (v. 8). Avoiding sin doesn't just happen by accident. You have to be vigilant to identify and overcome temptation when it comes. Only God can give you the strength to do that.

Dr. Jim Perdue, Second Baptist Church
Warner Robins, GA

AUGUST 25

A Plea for Relief from Persecutors

Psalm 142:1–7

I CRY out to the LORD with my voice;
With my voice to the LORD I make my
   supplication.

2 I pour out my complaint before Him;
   I declare before Him my trouble.

3 When my spirit was overwhelmed within me,
   Then You knew my path.
   In the way in which I walk
   They have secretly set a snare for me.

4 Look on *my* right hand and see,
   For *there is* no one who acknowledges me;
   Refuge has failed me;
   No one cares for my soul.

5 I cried out to You, O LORD:
   I said, "You *are* my refuge,
   My portion in the land of the living.

6 Attend to my cry,
   For I am brought very low;
   Deliver me from my persecutors,
   For they are stronger than I.

7 Bring my soul out of prison,
   That I may praise Your name;
   The righteous shall surround me,
   For You shall deal bountifully with me."

DEVOTIONAL

Have you ever felt completely overwhelmed? Have you ever felt like you were at the end of your rope and you weren't sure where to turn?

There is never a problem that is too small for God to care about or too big for Him to handle.

David was being hunted and pursued by the angry and impetuous King Saul. Crying out to God, David described his situation with words like these: "trouble," "prison," and "snare." He said, "My spirit was overwhelmed within me. . . . Refuge has failed me; no one cares for my soul. . . . I am brought very low" (vv. 3–4, 6).

Have you ever felt this way before? Have you ever felt like your life was falling apart and the world was caving in upon you? Most likely you have. What are we to do in times like these? We see the answer in these words from the pen of David. He said in verse 1, "I cry out to the LORD with my voice; with my voice to the LORD I make my supplication." David understood where to turn in times of trouble. Even in the midst of danger and difficulty David looked to God for deliverance. He said, "Bring my soul out of prison, that I may praise Your name; the righteous shall surround me, for You shall deal bountifully with me" (v. 7).

No matter what you face right now, God can bring you through it. No matter what surrounds you, God can cover you in His righteousness. No matter what life has dealt you, you can say, "You shall deal bountifully with me" (v. 7).

Remember, you will learn more from life's trials than life's triumphs. God will teach you and grow you through persecution. The great preacher Charles Haddon Spurgeon said, "I am sure I have derived more real benefit and permanent strength and growth in grace, and every precious thing, from the furnace of affliction, than I have ever derived from prosperity."[3]

Dr. Jim Perdue, Second Baptist Church
Warner Robins, GA

AUGUST 26

It is easy to forget how good God is to His children. List some ways you have experienced the goodness of God in your life. Write a prayer of praise and gratitude for the good things with which God has blessed you.

Are you able to look back on some of the trials of your life and realize that they were really blessings in disguise? Take some time to list some difficulties you have faced and how you have experienced God's faithfulness even in the midst of trouble.

AUGUST 27

Appeal for Guidance and Deliverance

Psalm 143:1–12

HEAR my prayer, O LORD,
Give ear to my supplications!
In Your faithfulness answer me,
And in Your righteousness.

2 Do not enter into judgment with Your servant,
For in Your sight no one living is righteous.

3 For the enemy has persecuted my soul;
He has crushed my life to the ground;
He has made me dwell in darkness,
Like those who have long been dead.

4 Therefore my spirit is overwhelmed within
me;
My heart within me is distressed.

5 I remember the days of old;
I meditate on all Your works;
I muse on the work of Your hands.

6 I spread out my hands to You;
My soul *longs* for You like a thirsty land. Selah

7 Answer me speedily, O LORD;
My spirit fails!
Do not hide Your face from me,
Lest I be like those who go down into the pit.

8 Cause me to hear Your lovingkindness in the
morning,
For in You do I trust;
Cause me to know the way in which I should
walk,
For I lift up my soul to You.

9 Deliver me, O LORD, from my enemies;
In You I take shelter.

10 Teach me to do Your will,
For You *are* my God;
Your Spirit *is* good.
Lead me in the land of uprightness.

11 Revive me, O LORD, for Your name's sake!
For Your righteousness' sake bring my soul out
of trouble.

12 In Your mercy cut off my enemies,
And destroy all those who afflict my soul;
For I *am* Your servant.

DEVOTIONAL

The condition of David's heart is evident. In a state of brokenness and desperation, he expressed his longing for cleansing and fellowship. Intimacy with his heavenly Father was the desire of his heart. His distress provides a great example of the recognition that David was unable to accomplish anything apart from the Lord. What tremendous teaching this is for us today! Until we humble ourselves and acknowledge our need for our heavenly Father, we will not experience the true joy, peace, and fellowship that He graciously provides for His children. David expressed a deep longing for the Lord and recognized his need for revival. I am challenged by the attitude of his heart and long to mirror that in my own.

Lord, may we long for You above all else and may You revive the hearts of Your people.

Eddie Middleton, Eddie Middleton Ministries
Acworth, GA

AUGUST 28

The Lord Who Preserves

Psalm 144:1–15

B LESSED *be* the LORD my Rock,
Who trains my hands for war,
And my fingers for battle—
2 My lovingkindness and my fortress,
My high tower and my deliverer,
My shield and *the One* in whom I take refuge,
Who subdues my people under me.

3 LORD, what *is* man, that You take knowledge of
him?
Or the son of man, that You are mindful of
him?
4 Man is like a breath;
His days *are* like a passing shadow.

5 Bow down Your heavens, O LORD, and come
down;
Touch the mountains, and they shall smoke.
6 Flash forth lightning and scatter them;
Shoot out Your arrows and destroy them.
7 Stretch out Your hand from above;
Rescue me and deliver me out of great waters,
From the hand of foreigners,
8 Whose mouth speaks lying words,
And whose right hand *is* a right hand of
falsehood.

9 I will sing a new song to You, O God;
On a harp of ten strings I will sing praises to
You,
10 *The One* who gives salvation to kings,
Who delivers David His servant
From the deadly sword.

11 Rescue me and deliver me from the hand of
foreigners,
Whose mouth speaks lying words,
And whose right hand *is* a right hand of
falsehood—
12 That our sons *may be* as plants grown up in
their youth;
That our daughters *may be* as pillars,
Sculptured in palace style;
13 *That* our barns *may be* full,
Supplying all kinds of produce;
That our sheep may bring forth thousands
And ten thousands in our fields;
14 *That* our oxen *may be* well laden;
That there be no breaking in or going out;
That there be no outcry in our streets.
15 Happy *are* the people who are in such a state;
Happy *are* the people whose God *is* the LORD!

DEVOTIONAL

D avid confessed the greatness of his Lord,
praised Him for equipping him to be victorious in battle, and spoke of His lovingkindness.
David was a shepherd and therefore concerned for
his flock. He provided the reminder that as powerful and awesome as the Lord is, He still cares for
each of His children compassionately. David spoke
to God's display of power and gave Him all of the
glory. The Lord was his fortress, his shield, and
the One in whom he took refuge. We often look to
others for protection and provision, but when the
Lord is our Deliverer, an attitude of praise and an
ability to rest in Him follows.

Eddie Middleton, Eddie Middleton Ministries
Acworth, GA

AUGUST 29

A Song of God's Majesty and Love

Psalm 145:1–21

I WILL extol You, my God, O King;
And I will bless Your name forever and ever.

2 Every day I will bless You,
And I will praise Your name forever and ever.

3 Great *is* the LORD, and greatly to be praised;
And His greatness *is* unsearchable.

4 One generation shall praise Your works to
another,
And shall declare Your mighty acts.

5 I will meditate on the glorious splendor of
Your majesty,
And on Your wondrous works.

6 *Men* shall speak of the might of Your awesome
acts,
And I will declare Your greatness.

7 They shall utter the memory of Your great
goodness,
And shall sing of Your righteousness.

8 The LORD *is* gracious and full of compassion,
Slow to anger and great in mercy.

9 The LORD *is* good to all,
And His tender mercies *are* over all His works.

10 All Your works shall praise You, O LORD,
And Your saints shall bless You.

11 They shall speak of the glory of Your kingdom,
And talk of Your power,

12 To make known to the sons of men His
mighty acts,
And the glorious majesty of His kingdom.

13 Your kingdom *is* an everlasting kingdom,
And Your dominion *endures* throughout all
generations.

14 The LORD upholds all who fall,
And raises up all *who are* bowed down.

15 The eyes of all look expectantly to You,
And You give them their food in due season.

16 You open Your hand
And satisfy the desire of every living thing.

17 The LORD *is* righteous in all His ways,
Gracious in all His works.

18 The LORD *is* near to all who call upon Him,
To all who call upon Him in truth.

19 He will fulfill the desire of those who fear Him;
He also will hear their cry and save them.

20 The LORD preserves all who love Him,
But all the wicked He will destroy.

21 My mouth shall speak the praise of the LORD,
And all flesh shall bless His holy name
Forever and ever.

DEVOTIONAL

What an incredible description of the Father's heart for His children! We are reminded that He is gracious and full of compassion. He is slow to anger and great in mercy. For those who struggle with the need to perform well in order to earn the love, grace, and approval of God, these truths provide great freedom. The Lord extends acceptance and demonstrates that His love is unconditional. David's cry of praise and thanksgiving for the Lord's goodness fueled his heart in worship. May we also remember to reflect on and trust in His promises while gratefully calling upon Him who is always near.

Eddie Middleton, Eddie Middleton Ministries
Acworth, GA

AUGUST 30

Hope Is in the Lord

Psalm 146:1–10

P RAISE the LORD!
  Praise the LORD, O my soul!
2 While I live I will praise the LORD;
  I will sing praises to my God while I have
    my being.

3 Do not put your trust in princes,
  Nor in a son of man, in whom *there is* no help.
4 His spirit departs, he returns to his earth;
  In that very day his plans perish.

5 Happy *is he* who *has* the God of Jacob for
    his help,
  Whose hope *is* in the LORD his God,
6 Who made heaven and earth,
  The sea, and all that *is* in them;
  Who keeps truth forever,
7 Who executes justice for the oppressed,
  Who gives food to the hungry.
  The LORD gives freedom to the prisoners.

8 The LORD opens *the eyes of* the blind;
  The LORD raises those who are bowed down;
  The LORD loves the righteous.
9 The LORD watches over the strangers;
  He relieves the fatherless and widow;
  But the way of the wicked He turns upside
    down.

10 The LORD shall reign forever—
  Your God, O Zion, to all generations.

  Praise the LORD!

DEVOTIONAL

The psalmist rejoices in the trust he finds in the Lord. The faithfulness and capability of his God allow him to place his confidence in Him alone. His hope is in the Lord, and he confidently proclaims all of the ways His God intercedes on behalf of his own.

Joy comes from knowing you can trust in a loving Father who will always be faithful to care for you. He knows your needs, desires, and struggles, and you can depend on His provision and timing. When we are not trusting in Him, and we are trusting in ourselves or others, we will be left lacking. He uses others in our lives as tools of His care, but we must make every effort not to look to anyone above Him. He cares for you because He loves you. He provides for you because He assured you He would. He is worthy to be praised, just like David did, by you and me today.

Eddie Middleton, Eddie Middleton Ministries
Acworth, GA

AUGUST 31

Praise to God for His Word

Psalm 147:1–20

P RAISE the LORD!
For *it is* good to sing praises to our God;
For *it is* pleasant, *and* praise is beautiful.

2 The LORD builds up Jerusalem;
He gathers together the outcasts of Israel.

3 He heals the brokenhearted
And binds up their wounds.

4 He counts the number of the stars;
He calls them all by name.

5 Great *is* our Lord, and mighty in power;
His understanding *is* infinite.

6 The LORD lifts up the humble;
He casts the wicked down to the ground.

7 Sing to the LORD with thanksgiving;
Sing praises on the harp to our God,

8 Who covers the heavens with clouds,
Who prepares rain for the earth,
Who makes grass to grow on the mountains.

9 He gives to the beast its food,
And to the young ravens that cry.

10 He does not delight in the strength of the
horse;
He takes no pleasure in the legs of a man.

11 The LORD takes pleasure in those who fear
Him,
In those who hope in His mercy.

12 Praise the LORD, O Jerusalem!
Praise your God, O Zion!

13 For He has strengthened the bars of your gates;
He has blessed your children within you.

14 He makes peace *in* your borders,
And fills you with the finest wheat.

15 He sends out His command *to the* earth;
His word runs very swiftly.

16 He gives snow like wool;
He scatters the frost like ashes;

17 He casts out His hail like morsels;
Who can stand before His cold?

18 He sends out His word and melts them;
He causes His wind to blow, *and* the waters flow.

19 He declares His word to Jacob,
His statutes and His judgments to Israel.

20 He has not dealt thus with any nation;
And *as for His* judgments, they have not
known them.
Praise the LORD!

DEVOTIONAL

T he Father knows all about our smallest
hurts, yet He also knows the stars by name!
This psalm powerfully displays the Father's heart
toward those whose hearts have been broken. He is
the Great Physician, who offers healing and comfort. He's busy at work caring for, ministering to,
and meeting the needs of His children, even when
His actions aren't yet evidenced. The psalmist
notes that the Lord will find pleasure in those who
fear Him. The admonition to fear the Lord is not
indicating that we should be afraid of Him but that
we should revere Him. We should be captivated by
a reverential awe as we recognize and acknowledge
that He is worthy of all honor and praise. Fearing
the Lord requires personal worship that will enable
a heart to truly revere God above all others.

Eddie Middleton, Eddie Middleton Ministries
Acworth, GA

SEPTEMBER 1

Praise to the Lord from Creation

Psalm 148:1–14

Praise the LORD!

Praise the LORD from the heavens;
Praise Him in the heights!

2 Praise Him, all His angels;
Praise Him, all His hosts!

3 Praise Him, sun and moon;
Praise Him, all you stars of light!

4 Praise Him, you heavens of heavens,
And you waters above the heavens!

5 Let them praise the name of the LORD,
For He commanded and they were created.

6 He also established them forever and ever;
He made a decree which shall not pass away.

7 Praise the LORD from the earth,
You great sea creatures and all the depths;

8 Fire and hail, snow and clouds;
Stormy wind, fulfilling His word;

9 Mountains and all hills;
Fruitful trees and all cedars;

10 Beasts and all cattle;
Creeping things and flying fowl;

11 Kings of the earth and all peoples;
Princes and all judges of the earth;

12 Both young men and maidens;
Old men and children.

13 Let them praise the name of the LORD,
For His name alone is exalted;
His glory *is* above the earth and heaven.

14 And He has exalted the horn of His people,
The praise of all His saints—

Of the children of Israel,
A people near to Him.

Praise the LORD!

DEVOTIONAL

In this psalm, the psalmist sings the praises of the Lord from the highest of the heavens to the lowest parts of the sea. We don't worship the sun, moon, or stars—we worship the One who created them all. His beautiful and incredible creation ought to evoke worship and awe in our hearts over His power and might. He allows us to enjoy His creation, but desires that our hearts would always remain focused on the Creator. I've appreciated the challenge to always be ready to praise the Lord for who He is, what He has done, and all that He assures me in His Word that He will do no matter what is going on in my life. When our perspectives are right, our hearts will echo that of the psalmists.

Eddie Middleton, Eddie Middleton Ministries
Acworth, GA

SEPTEMBER 2

Do you trust in the Father's love for you, provision for you, and compassion toward you? If not, spend some time reflecting on the truths of Scripture that assure you of each.

_____

_____

_____

_____

_____

_____

_____

_____

_____

_____

_____

Does praise flow from your heart like that of the psalmist's? Take a moment to search your heart and ask what prohibits you from praising Him the way He deserves to be praised.

_____

_____

_____

_____

_____

_____

_____

_____

_____

_____

SEPTEMBER 3

Praise to God for His Salvation

Psalm 149:1–9

PRAISE the LORD!

Sing to the LORD a new song,
And His praise in the assembly of saints.

2 Let Israel rejoice in their Maker;
Let the children of Zion be joyful in their King.

3 Let them praise His name with the dance;
Let them sing praises to Him with the timbrel
and harp.

4 For the LORD takes pleasure in His people;
He will beautify the humble with salvation.

5 Let the saints be joyful in glory;
Let them sing aloud on their beds.

6 *Let* the high praises of God *be* in their mouth,
And a two-edged sword in their hand,

7 To execute vengeance on the nations,
And punishments on the peoples;

8 To bind their kings with chains,
And their nobles with fetters of iron;

9 To execute on them the written judgment—
This honor have all His saints.

Praise the LORD!

Psalm 150:1–6

PRAISE the LORD!

Praise God in His sanctuary;
Praise Him in His mighty firmament!

2 Praise Him for His mighty acts;
Praise Him according to His excellent
greatness!

3 Praise Him with the sound of the trumpet;
Praise Him with the lute and harp!

4 Praise Him with the timbrel and dance;
Praise Him with stringed instruments and
flutes!

5 Praise Him with loud cymbals;
Praise Him with clashing cymbals!

6 Let everything that has breath praise the LORD.

Praise the LORD!

DEVOTIONAL

Four thoughts on worship.

1. *The Place of Worship.* Corporately: "in the assembly of the saints" (149:1); "in His sanctuary" (150:1). Individually: "sing aloud on their beds" (149:5). Some excuse themselves from corporate worship, saying they can worship as well privately. Some only worship in church and not in private. Both views are wrong.

2. *The Perspective of Worship.* Creatively: We are to sing a "new song." Our worship and adoration of God should grow and expand, causing news songs to arise. Dance was a creative expression of worship for King David (2 Sam. 6:16). Musically: Singing is mentioned twice (149:3, 5). Seven different instruments are mentioned (149:3; 150:3–5).

3. *The Passion of Worship.* Joyfully: Joy occurs three times (149:2, 5). Verbally: Worship is expressive (149:6; 150:6). Worship is used too much as a noun and not enough as a verb!

4. *The Point of Worship.* "Praise the LORD." These two chapters contain fifteen verses, and praise is mentioned nineteen times! The point is obvious—we are to "Praise the LORD!"

Allan Taylor, Minister of Education
First Baptist Church Woodstock, Woodstock, GA

SEPTEMBER 4

The Beginning of Knowledge

Proverbs 1:1–19

THE proverbs of Solomon the son of David, king of Israel:

2 To know wisdom and instruction,
To perceive the words of understanding,

3 To receive the instruction of wisdom,
Justice, judgment, and equity;

4 To give prudence to the simple,
To the young man knowledge and
discretion—

5 A wise *man* will hear and increase learning,
And a man of understanding will attain wise
counsel,

6 To understand a proverb and an enigma,
The words of the wise and their riddles.

7 The fear of the LORD *is* the beginning of
knowledge,
But fools despise wisdom and instruction.

8 My son, hear the instruction of your father,
And do not forsake the law of your mother;

9 For they *will be* a graceful ornament on your
head,
And chains about your neck.

10 My son, if sinners entice you,
Do not consent.

11 If they say, "Come with us,
Let us lie in wait to *shed* blood;
Let us lurk secretly for the innocent without
cause;

12 Let us swallow them alive like Sheol,
And whole, like those who go down to the Pit;

13 We shall find all *kinds* of precious possessions,
We shall fill our houses with spoil;

14 Cast in your lot among us,
Let us all have one purse"—

15 My son, do not walk in the way with them,
Keep your foot from their path;

16 For their feet run to evil,
And they make haste to shed blood.

17 Surely, in vain the net is spread
In the sight of any bird;

18 But they lie in wait for their *own* blood,
They lurk secretly for their *own* lives.

19 So *are* the ways of everyone who is greedy for
gain;
It takes away the life of its owners.

DEVOTIONAL

Proverbs is a book about wisdom. Its purpose is to help one discern the best course of action for better living. Solomon, the wisest man who ever lived, wrote most of this book.

It has been said that we are one decision away from stupid. Well, the proverbs are written to get the stupid out of us!

The key verse in the book is found in verse 7 of today's text. We can only find true wisdom when we acknowledge God, because He is the source of all wisdom. All logic, reasoning, and religious reckoning that is not built on the foundation of the fear, reverence, and awe of God will be empty, for it has the wrong starting point. If God is indeed God, then He should be revered. If He is not, then quit reading this book because it doesn't matter.

Allan Taylor, Minister of Education,
First Baptist Church Woodstock, Woodstock, GA

SEPTEMBER 5

The Call of Wisdom

Proverbs 1:20–33

20 Wisdom calls aloud outside;
   She raises her voice in the open squares.
21 She cries out in the chief concourses,
   At the openings of the gates in the city
   She speaks her words:
22 "How long, you simple ones, will you love
       simplicity?
   For scorners delight in their scorning,
   And fools hate knowledge.
23 Turn at my rebuke;
   Surely I will pour out my spirit on you;
   I will make my words known to you.
24 Because I have called and you refused,
   I have stretched out my hand and no one
       regarded,
25 Because you disdained all my counsel,
   And would have none of my rebuke,
26 I also will laugh at your calamity;
   I will mock when your terror comes,
27 When your terror comes like a storm,
   And your destruction comes like a
       whirlwind,
   When distress and anguish come upon you.
28 "Then they will call on me, but I will not
       answer;
   They will seek me diligently, but they will not
       find me.
29 Because they hated knowledge
   And did not choose the fear of the LORD,
30 They would have none of my counsel
   And despised my every rebuke.

31 Therefore they shall eat the fruit of their own
       way,
   And be filled to the full with their own fancies.
32 For the turning away of the simple will slay
       them,
   And the complacency of fools will destroy
       them;
33 But whoever listens to me will dwell safely,
   And will be secure, without fear of evil."

DEVOTIONAL

Wisdom pleads for us to enroll in Wisdom University. Wisdom "calls aloud," "raises her voice," "cries out," "speaks her words," and stretches out her hand (vv. 20–21, 24). Wisdom is not secret or evasive. She goes public, like a fiery prophet, thundering her voice for all to hear. Wisdom has made every effort to convince us. What more can she do? She even asks, "How long, you simple ones, will you love simplicity?" (v. 22). *Simple* means stupid. Wisdom wants to know just how long we plan to stay stupid. Her statement implies we should have seen the error of our foolish ways by now, but we have "refused" and "disdained" her. (vv. 24–25) Stupidity despises wisdom, and the results are . . .

Derision: (v. 26).

Devastation: (v. 27).

Destruction: (v. 27).

Distress: (v. 27).

Desperation: (v. 28).

Desolation: (v. 28).

"How long will you be stupid?" Wisdom is pleading! Will you heed her voice?

Allan Taylor, Minister of Education,
First Baptist Church Woodstock, Woodstock, GA

SEPTEMBER 6

The Value of Wisdom

Proverbs 2:1–22

MY son, if you receive my words,
And treasure my commands within you,

2 So that you incline your ear to wisdom,
And apply your heart to understanding;

3 Yes, if you cry out for discernment,
And lift up your voice for understanding,

4 If you seek her as silver,
And search for her as *for* hidden treasures;

5 Then you will understand the fear of the LORD,
And find the knowledge of God.

6 For the LORD gives wisdom;
From His mouth *come* knowledge and
understanding;

7 He stores up sound wisdom for the upright;
He is a shield to those who walk uprightly;

8 He guards the paths of justice,
And preserves the way of His saints.

9 Then you will understand righteousness and
justice,
Equity *and* every good path.

10 When wisdom enters your heart,
And knowledge is pleasant to your soul,

11 Discretion will preserve you;
Understanding will keep you,

12 To deliver you from the way of evil,
From the man who speaks perverse things,

13 From those who leave the paths of uprightness
To walk in the ways of darkness;

14 Who rejoice in doing evil,
And delight in the perversity of the wicked;

15 Whose ways *are* crooked,
And *who are* devious in their paths;

16 To deliver you from the immoral woman,
From the seductress *who* flatters with her words,

17 Who forsakes the companion of her youth,
And forgets the covenant of her God.

18 For her house leads down to death,
And her paths to the dead;

19 None who go to her return,
Nor do they regain the paths of life—

20 So you may walk in the way of goodness,
And keep *to* the paths of righteousness.

21 For the upright will dwell in the land,
And the blameless will remain in it;

22 But the wicked will be cut off from the earth,
And the unfaithful will be uprooted from it.

DEVOTIONAL

A young man asked an old wise man to teach him wisdom. The old man took him out into a river. The elder then held him under the water. Upon letting him up the elder asked, "Do you want air?" "Yes," cried the young man. The old man plunged him under once again, held him longer, and upon bringing him up, asked, "Do you want air?" "Yes," he cried, panting for oxygen. One last time the old man thrust him under and held him until the young man was kicking and fighting. He came up gasping desperately for air. The young man said in disgust, "Are you trying to drown me?" The old man calmly asked, "Do you want air?" "Well, of course, you old fool," was his reply. The old wise man said, "When you want wisdom as much as you want air, you will get it!"

Allan Taylor, Minister of Education,
First Baptist Church Woodstock, Woodstock, GA

SEPTEMBER 7

Guidance for the Young

Proverbs 3:1–20

M Y son, do not forget my law,
 But let your heart keep my commands;
2 For length of days and long life
 And peace they will add to you.

3 Let not mercy and truth forsake you;
 Bind them around your neck,
 Write them on the tablet of your heart,
4 *And* so find favor and high esteem
 In the sight of God and man.

5 Trust in the LORD with all your heart,
 And lean not on your own understanding;
6 In all your ways acknowledge Him,
 And He shall direct your paths.

7 Do not be wise in your own eyes;
 Fear the LORD and depart from evil.
8 It will be health to your flesh,
 And strength to your bones.

9 Honor the LORD with your possessions,
 And with the firstfruits of all your increase;
10 So your barns will be filled with plenty,
 And your vats will overflow with new wine.

11 My son, do not despise the chastening of
 the LORD,
 Nor detest His correction;
12 For whom the LORD loves He corrects,
 Just as a father the son *in whom* he delights.

13 Happy *is* the man *who* finds wisdom,
 And the man *who* gains understanding;

14 For her proceeds *are* better than the profits
 of silver,
 And her gain than fine gold.
15 She *is* more precious than rubies,
 And all the things you may desire cannot
 compare with her.
16 Length of days *is* in her right hand,
 In her left hand riches and honor.
17 Her ways *are* ways of pleasantness,
 And all her paths *are* peace.
18 She *is* a tree of life to those who take hold of her,
 And happy *are all* who retain her.

19 The LORD by wisdom founded the earth;
 By understanding He established the heavens;
20 By His knowledge the depths were broken up,
 And clouds drop down the dew.

DEVOTIONAL

W isdom affects the head, but it must also affect the heart (v. 1). With our heads we have knowledge of God's Word, but with our hearts we keep God's commandments. God instructed us to write His commandments on the tablets of our hearts (v. 3), that we "might not sin against" Him (Ps. 119:11).

"Trust in the LORD with all your heart" (Prov. 3:5). Trust is a big deal, for relationships are built upon it. The Bible says we can trust in the Lord for He is trustworthy.

Do you know why we don't "honor the LORD with [our] possessions" (v. 9)? It's a heart issue! Do you know why we "despise the chastening of the LORD" (v. 11)? It's a heart issue!

Allan Taylor, Minister of Education,
First Baptist Church Woodstock, Woodstock, GA

SEPTEMBER 8

Keep Your Faith with Wisdom

Proverbs 3:21–35

21 My son, let them not depart from your eyes—
Keep sound wisdom and discretion;

22 So they will be life to your soul
And grace to your neck.

23 Then you will walk safely in your way,
And your foot will not stumble.

24 When you lie down, you will not be afraid;
Yes, you will lie down and your sleep will be
sweet.

25 Do not be afraid of sudden terror,
Nor of trouble from the wicked when it comes;

26 For the LORD will be your confidence,
And will keep your foot from being caught.

27 Do not withhold good from those to whom it
is due,
When it is in the power of your hand to
do *so*.

28 Do not say to your neighbor,
"Go, and come back,
And tomorrow I will give *it*,"
When you have it with you.

29 Do not devise evil against your neighbor,
For he dwells by you for safety's sake.

30 Do not strive with a man without cause,
If he has done you no harm.

31 Do not envy the oppressor,
And choose none of his ways;

32 For the perverse *person is* an abomination to
the LORD,
But His secret counsel *is* with the upright.

33 The curse of the LORD *is* on the house of the
wicked,
But He blesses the home of the just.

34 Surely He scorns the scornful,
But gives grace to the humble.

35 The wise shall inherit glory,
But shame shall be the legacy of fools.

DEVOTIONAL

As a former high school football coach, I used to teach my players the Two Rules for Winning: (1) Don't beat yourself. At least make your opponent beat you and earn the win. Don't just hand the game to them. (2) Practice the fundamental disciplines of the game. This is exactly what Proverbs does. Wisdom teaches us how to avoid defeat—how to keep from beating ourselves. Wisdom also teaches us how to practice the basic disciplines of character. Our text provides these two rules for winning in life:

1. Do not withhold good from others. "Do not devise evil against your neighbor" (v. 29). "Do not strive without cause" (v. 30). "Do not envy" (v. 31).

2. Guard wisdom. Keep sound wisdom and discretion. What does a "win" look like? Life to your soul. A beautiful ornament around your neck. You will walk safely in the way. Your sleep will be sweet. The Lord will be your confidence. God blesses the home of the just. God gives grace to the humble. The wise shall inherit glory.

So, guard wisdom and WIN!

Allan Taylor, Minister of Education,
First Baptist Church Woodstock, Woodstock, GA

SEPTEMBER 9

How would you describe "the fear of the LORD" (Prov. 1:7)? In what ways do you fear the Lord? How does your fear of God direct your life?

_____

_____

_____

_____

_____

_____

_____

_____

_____

_____

_____

The psalmist was continually praising God. How do you corporately and individually worship and praise God?

_____

_____

_____

_____

_____

_____

_____

_____

_____

SEPTEMBER 10

Security in Wisdom

Proverbs 4:1–12

Hear, *my* children, the instruction of a
    father,
    And give attention to know understanding;

2 For I give you good doctrine:
    Do not forsake my law.

3 When I was my father's son,
    Tender and the only one in the sight of my
        mother,

4 He also taught me, and said to me:
    "Let your heart retain my words;
    Keep my commands, and live.

5 Get wisdom! Get understanding!
    Do not forget, nor turn away from the words
        of my mouth.

6 Do not forsake her, and she will preserve you;
    Love her, and she will keep you.

7 Wisdom *is* the principal thing;
    Therefore get wisdom.
    And in all your getting, get understanding.

8 Exalt her, and she will promote you;
    She will bring you honor, when you embrace
        her.

9 She will place on your head an ornament of
        grace;
    A crown of glory she will deliver to you."

10 Hear, my son, and receive my sayings,
    And the years of your life will be many.

11 I have taught you in the way of wisdom;
    I have led you in right paths.

12 When you walk, your steps will not be hindered,
    And when you run, you will not stumble.

DEVOTIONAL

In Ephesians 5:17, the apostle Paul declared, "Therefore do not be unwise." His admonition has been tossed aside today. We live in an unwise world. There is no shortage of talking or even shouting by opinionated people, but there is an absence of wisdom. As a result, foolishness has become the norm. We live in the manifestation of Romans 1:22: "Professing to be wise, they became fools."

Our text for today informs us that wisdom is something to be sought. Verse 5 says, "Get wisdom!" That idea is repeated in verse 7: "Therefore get wisdom." Wisdom is not something with which we are born, nor is it something we acquire simply by growing older. It does not even come as a result of higher education.

Verse 1 intimates that wisdom can be gleaned by listening to the instruction of a father. James 1:5 tells us, "If any of you lacks wisdom, let him ask of God, who gives to all liberally and without reproach, and it will be given to him." True wisdom is available, but it only comes from God. Only godly parents can impart the wisdom they have received from God to their children.

Wisdom has many benefits for the child of God. Wisdom keeps the child of God out of sin (v. 6), brings honor (vv. 8–9), and keeps him going in the right direction (v. 11). No wonder this text exhorts us to get wisdom, to give attention to it (v. 1), to retain it (v. 4), and to love it and not forsake it (v. 6).

Allow God to teach you wisdom. He will, if you seek Him. Make this your life's priority. Remember, "wisdom is the principal thing" (v. 7).

Dr. Bob Pitman, Bob Pitman Ministries
Muscle Shoals, AL

SEPTEMBER 11

Walk in the Way of Wisdom

Proverbs 4:13–27

13 Take firm hold of instruction, do not let go;
Keep her, for she *is* your life.

14 Do not enter the path of the wicked,
And do not walk in the way of evil.

15 Avoid it, do not travel on it;
Turn away from it and pass on.

16 For they do not sleep unless they have
done evil;
And their sleep is taken away unless they
make *someone* fall.

17 For they eat the bread of wickedness,
And drink the wine of violence.

18 But the path of the just *is* like the
shining sun,
That shines ever brighter unto the perfect day.

19 The way of the wicked *is* like darkness;
They do not know what makes them stumble.

20 My son, give attention to my words;
Incline your ear to my sayings.

21 Do not let them depart from your eyes;
Keep them in the midst of your heart;

22 For they *are* life to those who find them,
And health to all their flesh.

23 Keep your heart with all diligence,
For out of it *spring* the issues of life.

24 Put away from you a deceitful mouth,
And put perverse lips far from you.

25 Let your eyes look straight ahead,
And your eyelids look right before you.

26 Ponder the path of your feet,
And let all your ways be established.

27 Do not turn to the right or the left;
Remove your foot from evil.

DEVOTIONAL

A children's chorus tells us, "O be careful little eyes what you see, O be careful little eyes what you see; for the Father up above is looking down in love, O be careful little eyes what you see."[1] It goes on to warn little ears, little mouths, and little feet as well. The writer of that song must have had today's text in mind.

As children of God, we are not *of* this world, but we live *in* this world. We walk in it, we see it, we hear it, and we speak to it. As we walk in this world, wisdom is the staff to which we must take firm hold and not let go so that we will take the right path (v. 13). Unfortunately, there is a wrong path. It is a path of wickedness and evil (v. 14), violence (v. 17), and darkness (v. 19). The wisdom of God warns us to stay off this path. Look at the flashing warning lights in verses 14–15: "Do not enter," "do not walk," "avoid," "do not travel," "turn away from it," and "pass on."

The path that wisdom brings is a path of justice and light (v. 18), a sharp contrast to the other one. The path of the wise is not always easy, but it is noble and will bring satisfaction to the believer and glory to God.

Our feet, eyes, ears, and mouths behave as they do out of the dictates of our hearts. The most important thing is to "keep your heart" (v. 23). That means to guard your heart. Guard your heart by going to the right places, looking at the right things, listening to the right voices, and speaking the right words. Guard your heart!

Dr. Bob Pitman, Bob Pitman Ministries
Muscle Shoals, AL

SEPTEMBER 12

The Peril of Adultery

Proverbs 5:1–14

M Y son, pay attention to my wisdom;
Lend your ear to my understanding,

2 That you may preserve discretion,
And your lips may keep knowledge.

3 For the lips of an immoral woman drip honey,
And her mouth *is* smoother than oil;

4 But in the end she is bitter as wormwood,
Sharp as a two-edged sword.

5 Her feet go down to death,
Her steps lay hold of hell.

6 Lest you ponder *her* path of life—
Her ways are unstable;
You do not know *them.*

7 Therefore hear me now, *my* children,
And do not depart from the words of my mouth.

8 Remove your way far from her,
And do not go near the door of her house,

9 Lest you give your honor to others,
And your years to the cruel *one;*

10 Lest aliens be filled with your wealth,
And your labors *go* to the house of a foreigner;

11 And you mourn at last,
When your flesh and your body are consumed,

12 And say:
"How I have hated instruction,
And my heart despised correction!

13 I have not obeyed the voice of my teachers,
Nor inclined my ear to those who instructed me!

14 I was on the verge of total ruin,
In the midst of the assembly and
congregation."

DEVOTIONAL

T he first two chapters of Genesis reveal the creative activity of God. We are told in chapter 1 that He created light and saw that "it was good" (v. 4). He created the dry land and the seas and saw that "it was good" (v. 10). He created the trees, grass, fruit, and vegetables, and saw that "it was good" (v. 12). He created the heavenly lights, including the sun and moon, and once again saw that "it was good" (v. 18). Then God made the birds in the air and the creatures in the waters and saw that "it was good" (v. 21). Then He created the animals that live on land, and once again He saw that "it was good" (v. 25). However, when God made man, we read these unexpected words: "It is not good" (2:18).

The problem was not that there was a flaw in God's creation of man. After all, man was made in the image of God. The full declaration of Genesis 2:18 states, "It is not good that the man should be alone." So God created woman. Thus, the first marriage was between Adam and Eve, the first two people God ever made.

The writer of Hebrews stated, "Marriage is honorable in all, and the bed undefiled" (13:4). However, there is nothing that dishonors and defiles marriage more than adultery. Read the Scripture for today again and see words like *immoral, bitter, death, hell, unstable, cruel, mourn, hated, despised,* and *ruin.* These are not happy words. These are words of sadness, dishonor, and defilement. Concerning adultery, Proverbs says, "Remove your way far from her" (5:8).

Dr. Bob Pitman, Bob Pitman Ministries
Muscle Shoals, AL

SEPTEMBER 13
Warning Against Immorality

Proverbs 5:15–23

¹⁵ Drink water from your own cistern,
And running water from your own well.

¹⁶ Should your fountains be dispersed abroad,
Streams of water in the streets?

¹⁷ Let them be only your own,
And not for strangers with you.

¹⁸ Let your fountain be blessed,
And rejoice with the wife of your youth.

¹⁹ *As a* loving deer and a graceful doe,
Let her breasts satisfy you at all times;
And always be enraptured with her love.

²⁰ For why should you, my son, be enraptured by
an immoral woman,
And be embraced in the arms of a seductress?

²¹ For the ways of man *are* before the eyes of
the LORD,
And He ponders all his paths.

²² His own iniquities entrap the wicked *man*,
And he is caught in the cords of his sin.

²³ He shall die for lack of instruction,
And in the greatness of his folly he shall
go astray.

DEVOTIONAL

Marriage is a very special relationship between a man and a woman. God created marriage as a gift to humanity. Godly marriages are based on love, trust, and mutual respect. When these are not in place, marriages often fail.

The writer of Proverbs used the word *immoral* in verse 20. The word literally means "to turn aside." It speaks of turning aside from your wife or husband in order to find sexual satisfaction with another.

Immorality is first and foremost an act of infidelity. It is a forsaking of one's own cistern and a departure from one's own well (v. 15). Unfaithfulness is the most difficult sin to forgive in a marriage relationship. It is a spear in the heart of the wounded spouse. It brings hurt that cannot easily be removed. More than that, long after the hurt dissipates, the lack of trust lingers on. Sometimes that trust is never regained. Distrust can become a cancer that eats away at a relationship.

Second, immorality ruins your witness for the Lord. In verse 16, the "fountains being dispersed abroad" speak of the outflow of the marriage relationship toward others. When a marriage is healthy, it reaches out and blesses the children, the neighbors, the church, and the community. However, when a marriage is corrupted by immorality, what flows out to others is sadness, regret, and disappointment.

Third, immorality robs the offender of joy. You cannot "rejoice with the wife of your youth" when living in immorality (v. 18). Temporary lustful satisfaction is a poor substitute for lifelong joy.

Finally, immorality brings judgment. God sees all (v. 21) and allows sinfulness to bring its own punishment of bondage (v. 22). This world is full of men and women who have been "caught in the cords" of their sin.

Choose a better path! Do not allow Satan to deceive you and rob you of the best things in life.

Dr. Bob Pitman, Bob Pitman Ministries
Muscle Shoals, AL

SEPTEMBER 14

Dangerous Promises

Proverbs 6:1–19

My son, if you become surety for your friend,
If you have shaken hands in pledge for a
    stranger,

2 You are snared by the words of your mouth;
You are taken by the words of your mouth.

3 So do this, my son, and deliver yourself;
For you have come into the hand of your
    friend:
Go and humble yourself;
Plead with your friend.

4 Give no sleep to your eyes,
Nor slumber to your eyelids.

5 Deliver yourself like a gazelle from the hand *of*
    the hunter,
And like a bird from the hand of the fowler.

6 Go to the ant, you sluggard!
Consider her ways and be wise,

7 Which, having no captain,
Overseer or ruler,

8 Provides her supplies in the summer,
And gathers her food in the harvest.

9 How long will you slumber, O sluggard?
When will you rise from your sleep?

10 A little sleep, a little slumber,
A little folding of the hands to sleep—

11 So shall your poverty come on you like a
    prowler,
And your need like an armed man.

12 A worthless person, a wicked man,
Walks with a perverse mouth;

13 He winks with his eyes,
He shuffles his feet,
He points with his fingers;

14 Perversity *is* in his heart,
He devises evil continually,
He sows discord.

15 Therefore his calamity shall come suddenly;
Suddenly he shall be broken without remedy.

16 These six *things* the LORD hates,
Yes, seven *are* an abomination to Him:

17 A proud look,
A lying tongue,
Hands that shed innocent blood,

18 A heart that devises wicked plans,
Feet that are swift in running to evil,

19 A false witness *who* speaks lies,
And one who sows discord among brethren.

DEVOTIONAL

The life of faith has both a vertical and a horizontal relationship. Vertically, we have a relationship with God. Horizontally, we have a relationship with other people. Our families, friends, schoolmates, and work associates are people with whom we have vital relationships.

The way we treat people is an indication of how we stand with God. We should be diligent in seeing to it that we are right with those around us.

The seven sins listed in this text are sins that a person commits against other people. The way we look at others, the way we talk to them, the way we talk about them, and the way we treat them should exemplify our walk with God.

Dr. Bob Pitman, Bob Pitman Ministries
Muscle Shoals, AL

SEPTEMBER 15

Beware of Adultery

Proverbs 6:20–35

20 My son, keep your father's command,
And do not forsake the law of your mother.

21 Bind them continually upon your heart;
Tie them around your neck.

22 When you roam, they will lead you;
When you sleep, they will keep you;
And *when* you awake, they will speak with you.

23 For the commandment *is* a lamp,
And the law a light;
Reproofs of instruction *are* the way of life,

24 To keep you from the evil woman,
From the flattering tongue of a seductress.

25 Do not lust after her beauty in your heart,
Nor let her allure you with her eyelids.

26 For by means of a harlot
A man is reduced to a crust of bread;
And an adulteress will prey upon his precious
life.

27 Can a man take fire to his bosom,
And his clothes not be burned?

28 Can one walk on hot coals,
And his feet not be seared?

29 So *is* he who goes in to his neighbor's wife;
Whoever touches her shall not be innocent.

30 *People* do not despise a thief
If he steals to satisfy himself when he is
starving.

31 Yet *when* he is found, he must restore sevenfold;
He may have to give up all the substance of his
house.

32 Whoever commits adultery with a woman
lacks understanding;
He *who* does so destroys his own soul.

33 Wounds and dishonor he will get,
And his reproach will not be wiped away.

34 For jealousy *is* a husband's fury;
Therefore he will not spare in the day of
vengeance.

35 He will accept no recompense,
Nor will he be appeased though you give
many gifts.

DEVOTIONAL

Once again Solomon turns to the marriage relationship. Truly, it is the highest of all human relationships. It is so significant to God that Jesus used the relationship between a husband and wife as an illustration of His own relationship to His church (Eph. 5:22–25).

One out of every two marriages in America today ends in divorce. That ratio is the same inside the church as it is outside the church. The heart of God must grieve at that statistic.

God's people must remember His Word. It should be forever tied around our necks (Prov. 6:21), which means close to our hearts. His Word guides us when we are awake and asleep. It gives us light in the darkness and lifts us up when we fall. It gives us strength to stand against temptations that would lead us astray. It provides protection for our families and serves as a rebuke to those who would seek to destroy that which is precious to us. Remember His Word!

Dr. Bob Pitman, Bob Pitman Ministries
Muscle Shoals, AL

SEPTEMBER 16

What is wisdom and from whence does it come?

_____

_____

_____

_____

_____

_____

_____

_____

_____

_____

How does godly wisdom manifest itself in our daily lives?

_____

_____

_____

_____

_____

_____

_____

_____

_____

_____

SEPTEMBER 17

The Wiles of a Harlot

Proverbs 7:1–9

MY son, keep my words,
   And treasure my commands within you.

2 Keep my commands and live,
   And my law as the apple of your eye.

3 Bind them on your fingers;
   Write them on the tablet of your heart.

4 Say to wisdom, "You *are* my sister,"
   And call understanding *your* nearest kin,

5 That they may keep you from the immoral
        woman,
   From the seductress *who* flatters with her
        words.

6 For at the window of my house
   I looked through my lattice,

7 And saw among the simple,
   I perceived among the youths,
   A young man devoid of understanding,

8 Passing along the street near her corner;
   And he took the path to her house

9 In the twilight, in the evening,
   In the black and dark night.

DEVOTIONAL

Proverbs is clear and concise and does not mince words. This passage tells us that there is nothing like a torrid affair in the beginning. It is the end that's nasty. Solomon, writing to his son, knew a lot about adultery. Solomon's parents were the most celebrated adulterers who had ever lived—David and Bathsheba (2 Sam. 11–12). Solomon knew the destruction that it can bring.

The world is very good at telling us about the beginning, but not the ending. When David committed adultery, Nathan the prophet did not tell him that he should not have the passion or desire for a woman. He told him to look at what he had done to this family—this woman, this man. Sin eventually destroys. An affair is living out a short-term fantasy. It gives moments of pleasure simply because it is not reality.

The world convinces us that we can find a perfect person to meet all of our needs. Society feeds that image with models and sexual ads. The reality is that no one looks good all the time or forever. There is no senior tour for models. We have a choice in life. We can tear up the fantasy that does not exist and accept our mate as a gift of God, or we can tear up our mate trying to make them look like a fantasy that does not exist.

Remember the lady at the well who had been married five times and was living with a man (John 4:1–26)? Jesus said to her and He says to us that trying to get our needs met by another person will always leave us thirsty. Jesus wanted to give her living water that would truly satisfy her deepest needs. Jesus wants to love and treasure us, which frees us to love and treasure others.

Charles Lowery, Ph.D., Psychologist
Dallas, TX

SEPTEMBER 18

The Crafty Harlot

Proverbs 7:10–27

10 And there a woman met him,
With the attire of a harlot, and a crafty heart.

11 She *was* loud and rebellious,
Her feet would not stay at home.

12 At times *she was* outside, at times in the open square,
Lurking at every corner.

13 So she caught him and kissed him;
With an impudent face she said to him:

14 "*I have* peace offerings with me;
Today I have paid my vows.

15 So I came out to meet you,
Diligently to seek your face,
And I have found you.

16 I have spread my bed with tapestry,
Colored coverings of Egyptian linen.

17 I have perfumed my bed
With myrrh, aloes, and cinnamon.

18 Come, let us take our fill of love until morning;
Let us delight ourselves with love.

19 For my husband *is* not at home;
He has gone on a long journey;

20 He has taken a bag of money with him,
And will come home on the appointed day."

21 With her enticing speech she caused him to yield,
With her flattering lips she seduced him.

22 Immediately he went after her, as an ox goes to the slaughter,
Or as a fool to the correction of the stocks,

23 Till an arrow struck his liver.

As a bird hastens to the snare,
He did not know it *would cost* his life.

24 Now therefore, listen to me, *my* children;
Pay attention to the words of my mouth:

25 Do not let your heart turn aside to her ways,
Do not stray into her paths;

26 For she has cast down many wounded,
And all who were slain by her were strong *men*.

27 Her house *is* the way to hell,
Descending to the chambers of death.

DEVOTIONAL

All sin is rooted in the basic assumption that God is not good. When we understand God, we know that He wants what is best for us and we will have the self-control to follow His commands. Most of the time we try to solve our spiritual problems with a physical solution. We are lonely because we try to fill God's place in our hearts with another person. The Bible teaches us that there is a vacuum inside of us that only God can fill. No matter what perfect partner you think you can find, that person will not satisfy.

Remember the lady caught in the act of adultery (John 8:1–12)? Jesus said to the people around her that if they were without sin to cast the first stone. They all left, but she stayed. That took courage. She could have walked off with them, but she knew Jesus could help her. She knew there was hope—Jesus did not condemn her. He told her to go and sin no more. Ask God's forgiveness and move on. It is never too late for God's best. God does not keep sex from you; He saves sex for you.

Charles Lowery, Ph.D., Psychologist
Dallas, TX

SEPTEMBER 19

The Excellence of Wisdom

Proverbs 8:1–21

D OES not wisdom cry out,
And understanding lift up her voice?

2 She takes her stand on the top of the high hill,
Beside the way, where the paths meet.

3 She cries out by the gates, at the entry of the city,
At the entrance of the doors:

4 "To you, O men, I call,
And my voice *is* to the sons of men.

5 O you simple ones, understand prudence,
And you fools, be of an understanding heart.

6 Listen, for I will speak of excellent things,
And from the opening of my lips *will come* right things;

7 For my mouth will speak truth;
Wickedness *is* an abomination to my lips.

8 All the words of my mouth *are* with righteousness;
Nothing crooked or perverse *is* in them.

9 They *are* all plain to him who understands,
And right to those who find knowledge.

10 Receive my instruction, and not silver,
And knowledge rather than choice gold;

11 For wisdom *is* better than rubies,
And all the things one may desire cannot be compared with her.

12 "I, wisdom, dwell with prudence,
And find out knowledge *and* discretion.

13 The fear of the LORD *is* to hate evil;
Pride and arrogance and the evil way
And the perverse mouth I hate.

14 Counsel *is* mine, and sound wisdom;
I *am* understanding, I have strength.

15 By me kings reign,
And rulers decree justice.

16 By me princes rule, and nobles,
All the judges of the earth.

17 I love those who love me,
And those who seek me diligently will find me.

18 Riches and honor *are* with me,
Enduring riches and righteousness.

19 My fruit *is* better than gold, yes, than fine gold,
And my revenue than choice silver.

20 I traverse the way of righteousness,
In the midst of the paths of justice,

21 That I may cause those who love me to inherit wealth,
That I may fill their treasuries.

DEVOTIONAL

T oday's topic is the excellence of wisdom. The book of Proverbs is truth compressed into short sayings that are extremely practical. For example, Exodus teaches that we should not commit adultery, but Proverbs teaches us that if we commit adultery we could lose our life.

We try to trust Jesus with church life and eternal life. But we often don't practice His principles because we think we know better than God. Faith is trusting God's promises for heaven, but wisdom is trusting God's principles for a great life.

Practice wisdom, and you will have all you need and even have some left over for the ones you love. It is not just what you leave to them but, more importantly, what you leave in them.

Charles Lowery, Ph.D., Psychologist
Dallas, TX

SEPTEMBER 20

God, the Wise Creator

Proverbs 8:22–36

22 "The LORD possessed me at the beginning of
His way,
Before His works of old.

23 I have been established from everlasting,
From the beginning, before there was ever
an earth.

24 When *there were* no depths I was brought forth,
When *there were* no fountains abounding
with water.

25 Before the mountains were settled,
Before the hills, I was brought forth;

26 While as yet He had not made the earth or the
fields,
Or the primal dust of the world.

27 When He prepared the heavens, I *was* there,
When He drew a circle on the face of the deep,

28 When He established the clouds above,
When He strengthened the fountains of
the deep,

29 When He assigned to the sea its limit,
So that the waters would not transgress His
command,
When He marked out the foundations of
the earth,

30 Then I was beside Him *as* a master craftsman;
And I was daily *His* delight,
Rejoicing always before Him,

31 Rejoicing in His inhabited world,
And my delight *was* with the sons of men.

32 "Now therefore, listen to me, *my* children,
For blessed *are those who* keep my ways.

33 Hear instruction and be wise,
And do not disdain *it*.

34 Blessed is the man who listens to me,
Watching daily at my gates,
Waiting at the posts of my doors.

35 For whoever finds me finds life,
And obtains favor from the LORD;

36 But he who sins against me wrongs his own
soul;
All those who hate me love death."

DEVOTIONAL

When I read the passage today, I am reminded of Job and the problems he endured. Job questioned and argued with God about his difficulties and God showed up! God then questioned Job about creation. In our day, God would ask Job if he had ever watched the Discovery Channel, and then God would say that He created all of that! Proverbs teaches us that He is not just the Creator, He is also the wise and wonderful Creator. He created us as His daily delight.

Proverbs is an instruction book to us from God. We are sons and daughters of the King. Proverbs is God's wisdom preserved so that we can live like the King's son or daughter. God used Solomon as the messenger to show us His divine truth. He gave us something on which to base our lives.

Charles Lowery, Ph.D., Psychologist
Dallas, TX

SEPTEMBER 21

Wisdom's Invitation

Proverbs 9:1–18

WISDOM has built her house,
    She has hewn out her seven pillars;
2 She has slaughtered her meat,
    She has mixed her wine,
    She has also furnished her table.
3 She has sent out her maidens,
    She cries out from the highest places of the
      city,
4 "Whoever *is* simple, let him turn in here!"
    As for him who lacks understanding, she says
      to him,
5 "Come, eat of my bread
    And drink of the wine I have mixed.
6 Forsake foolishness and live,
    And go in the way of understanding.

7 "He who corrects a scoffer gets shame for
      himself,
    And he who rebukes a wicked *man only*
      harms himself.
8 Do not correct a scoffer, lest he hate you;
    Rebuke a wise *man,* and he will love you.
9 Give *instruction* to a wise *man,* and he will be
      still wiser;
    Teach a just *man,* and he will increase in
      learning.
10 "The fear of the LORD *is* the beginning of wisdom,
    And the knowledge of the Holy One *is*
      understanding.
11 For by me your days will be multiplied,
    And years of life will be added to you.

12 If you are wise, you are wise for yourself,
    And *if* you scoff, you will bear *it* alone."

13 A foolish woman is clamorous;
    She is simple, and knows nothing.
14 For she sits at the door of her house,
    On a seat *by* the highest places of the city,
15 To call to those who pass by,
    Who go straight on their way:
16 "Whoever *is* simple, let him turn in here";
    And *as for* him who lacks understanding, she
      says to him,
17 "Stolen water is sweet,
    And bread *eaten* in secret is pleasant."
18 But he does not know that the dead *are* there,
    That her guests *are* in the depths of hell.

DEVOTIONAL

Wisdom is looking at life from God's perspective, and wisdom is different from knowledge. You can get knowledge from looking around, but you get wisdom only from looking up. Our scripture today teaches that wisdom is a personal call: "[Wisdom] cries out" (v. 3). God is always personal with us, and He ultimately becomes personal through His Son, Jesus Christ. Wisdom's invitation involves a choice. We must purposely choose wisdom. The good news of verse 1 is, "Wisdom has built her house." We have a wealthy God who spares no expense. Have enough wisdom to allow Him to build you a great house.

Charles Lowery, Ph.D., Psychologist
Dallas, TX

SEPTEMBER 22

A Wise Son and a Foolish Son

Proverbs 10:1–14

THE proverbs of Solomon:

A wise son makes a glad father,
But a foolish son *is* the grief of his mother.

2 Treasures of wickedness profit nothing,
But righteousness delivers from death.

3 The LORD will not allow the righteous soul to
famish,
But He casts away the desire of the wicked.

4 He who has a slack hand becomes poor,
But the hand of the diligent makes rich.

5 He who gathers in summer *is* a wise son;
He who sleeps in harvest *is* a son who causes
shame.

6 Blessings *are* on the head of the righteous,
But violence covers the mouth of the wicked.

7 The memory of the righteous *is* blessed,
But the name of the wicked will rot.

8 The wise in heart will receive commands,
But a prating fool will fall.

9 He who walks with integrity walks securely,
But he who perverts his ways will become
known.

10 He who winks with the eye causes trouble,
But a prating fool will fall.

11 The mouth of the righteous *is* a well of life,
But violence covers the mouth of the wicked.

12 Hatred stirs up strife,
But love covers all sins.

13 Wisdom is found on the lips of him who has
understanding,
But a rod *is* for the back of him who is devoid
of understanding.

14 Wise *people* store up knowledge,
But the mouth of the foolish *is* near
destruction.

DEVOTIONAL

Our scripture today is about passing wisdom to the next generation. As I observe family life in America, it seems that we may be passing down more foolishness than wisdom. Are we producing a Peter Pan generation in which no one grows up?

A dignitary visiting America commented that he was quite impressed by how well parents obeyed the children. When we allow God to have His rightful place in our homes, children will feel secure in their place. Wisdom teaches that they will not always get their way and that consequences are powerful. At home, a child is disciplined with love, but the world will discipline without love. Your children may lose their marriages or even their lives. Learning to say no is only half of the battle. It is more important to know when to say yes. The boundary becomes a blessing when children realize the benefit of a better way to live.

The family is God's way of passing down His wisdom from generation to generation. Wisdom will also be the difference between the wise and the foolish. Take the time and energy to invest in passing down wisdom to the next generation.

Charles Lowery, Ph.D., Psychologist
Dallas, TX

SEPTEMBER 23

Think about your family of origin. When you were growing up, what wisdom was passed down to you from your parents?

What wisdom are you passing down to the next generation?

SEPTEMBER 24

The Righteous Way of Life

Proverbs 10:15–32

15 The rich man's wealth *is* his strong city;
The destruction of the poor *is* their poverty.

16 The labor of the righteous *leads* to life,
The wages of the wicked to sin.

17 He who keeps instruction *is in* the way of life,
But he who refuses correction goes astray.

18 Whoever hides hatred *has* lying lips,
And whoever spreads slander *is* a fool.

19 In the multitude of words sin is not lacking,
But he who restrains his lips *is* wise.

20 The tongue of the righteous *is* choice silver;
The heart of the wicked *is worth* little.

21 The lips of the righteous feed many,
But fools die for lack of wisdom.

22 The blessing of the LORD makes *one* rich,
And He adds no sorrow with it.

23 To do evil *is* like sport to a fool,
But a man of understanding has wisdom.

24 The fear of the wicked will come upon him,
And the desire of the righteous will be granted.

25 When the whirlwind passes by, the wicked *is*
no *more*,
But the righteous *has* an everlasting
foundation.

26 As vinegar to the teeth and smoke to the eyes,
So *is* the lazy *man* to those who send him.

27 The fear of the LORD prolongs days,
But the years of the wicked will be shortened.

28 The hope of the righteous *will be* gladness,
But the expectation of the wicked will perish.

29 The way of the LORD *is* strength for the upright,
But destruction *will come* to the workers of
iniquity.

30 The righteous will never be removed,
But the wicked will not inhabit the earth.

31 The mouth of the righteous brings forth
wisdom,
But the perverse tongue will be cut out.

32 The lips of the righteous know what is
acceptable,
But the mouth of the wicked *what is* perverse.

DEVOTIONAL

The righteous way of life is available to us through Christ (2 Cor. 5:21). Thus, it is possible for us to be the salt and light that the world yearns for and to make a difference in the places we occupy. Being righteous, therefore, is much more than deeds alone; it encompasses our attitude toward others and ourselves as well.

The righteous know their standing with God and are able to walk within the boundaries of their God-given authority to bring about change in the world around them. Their vision is much broader and higher than that of the world, and they are willing to act accordingly.

Fear is displaced by God's perfect love (1 John 4:18), which enables the righteous to enter into His redemptive plan for the earth and its inhabitants. The righteous way of life is a tool God uses to reveal His love, His power, and His desire for everyone to come to Him.

Tim DeTellis, New Missions
Orlando, FL

SEPTEMBER 25

The Folly of Wickedness

Proverbs 11:1–11

DISHONEST scales *are* an abomination to the LORD,
But a just weight *is* His delight.

2 When pride comes, then comes shame;
But with the humble *is* wisdom.

3 The integrity of the upright will guide them,
But the perversity of the unfaithful will destroy them.

4 Riches do not profit in the day of wrath,
But righteousness delivers from death.

5 The righteousness of the blameless will direct his way aright,
But the wicked will fall by his own wickedness.

6 The righteousness of the upright will deliver them,
But the unfaithful will be caught by *their* lust.

7 When a wicked man dies, *his* expectation will perish,
And the hope of the unjust perishes.

8 The righteous is delivered from trouble,
And it comes to the wicked instead.

9 The hypocrite with *his* mouth destroys his neighbor,
But through knowledge the righteous will be delivered.

10 When it goes well with the righteous, the city rejoices;
And when the wicked perish, *there is* jubilation.

11 By the blessing of the upright the city is exalted,
But it is overthrown by the mouth of the wicked.

DEVOTIONAL

The definition of *folly* is "the state or quality of being foolish; the lack of understanding or sense; a foolish action or practice."

Wickedness means "the state of being wicked; evil disposition; immorality; a wicked or sinful thing or act; morally bad or objectionable behavior."

These two dispositions are bad enough alone, but put together they result in tragic consequences. The word *fool* as used in Proverbs means "a morally deficient person." When a fool resorts to wicked behavior, the truth of today's scripture becomes clearer.

The contrast drawn between the righteous and the wicked reveals how wicked behavior is bound to darkness. Take a moment to reflect upon the condition of the world today. Do you see evidence of the folly of wickedness in action? Now consider the contrasting view. Do you see how righteousness counteracts it?

Every day you are faced with choices of how to engage the world around you. Spend time today reflecting on the difference your decisions will make in the lives of those around you. Will there be rejoicing (v. 10)?

Ask God for wisdom to make righteous choices today.

Tim DeTellis, New Missions
Orlando, FL

SEPTEMBER 26

The Pursuit of Righteousness

Proverbs 11:12–21

¹² He who is devoid of wisdom despises his
neighbor,
But a man of understanding holds his peace.

¹³ A talebearer reveals secrets,
But he who is of a faithful spirit conceals a
matter.

¹⁴ Where *there is* no counsel, the people fall;
But in the multitude of counselors *there is*
safety.

¹⁵ He who is surety for a stranger will suffer,
But one who hates being surety is secure.

¹⁶ A gracious woman retains honor,
But ruthless *men* retain riches.

¹⁷ The merciful man does good for his own soul,
But *he who is* cruel troubles his own flesh.

¹⁸ The wicked *man* does deceptive work,
But he who sows righteousness *will have* a
sure reward.

¹⁹ As righteousness *leads* to life,
So he who pursues evil *pursues it* to his own
death.

²⁰ Those who are of a perverse heart *are* an
abomination to the Lord,
But *the* blameless in their ways *are* His delight.

²¹ *Though they join* forces, the wicked will not go
unpunished;
But the posterity of the righteous will be
delivered.

DEVOTIONAL

The apostle Paul pursued righteousness intentionally, and he encouraged other believers to do the same. He wrote, "That I may know Him and the power of His resurrection, and the fellowship of His sufferings, being conformed to His death, if, by any means, I may attain to the resurrection from the dead. Not that I have already attained, or am already perfected; but I press on, that I may lay hold of that for which Christ Jesus has also laid hold of me" (Phil. 3:10–12).

The pursuit of righteousness is a lifelong journey that is filled with discovery. Often the lessons we learn are the result of bad decisions we have made. Nevertheless, God has a way of changing the value of poor choices when we honestly try to live according to His Word.

God will help you overcome anything that blocks your way if you will incline your heart toward Him. Paul said that he had not yet reached the point of perfection, so he kept pressing on to take hold of Christ. Likewise, your journey in the pursuit of righteousness will require perseverance in order to reach the prize. "I press toward the goal for the prize of the upward call of God in Christ Jesus" (Phil. 3:14).

Spend some time reflecting on your desire to grow in Christ. What stands between you and the fulfillment of that desire? If you identified something blocking your path, ask God to help you overcome it so that you can gain victory over it.

Tim DeTellis, New Missions
Orlando, FL

SEPTEMBER 27

Wealth Is a Gift to Be Shared

Proverbs 11:22–31

²² *As* a ring of gold in a swine's snout,
So is a lovely woman who lacks discretion.

²³ The desire of the righteous *is* only good,
But the expectation of the wicked *is* wrath.

²⁴ There is *one* who scatters, yet increases more;
And there is *one* who withholds more than is
right,
But it *leads* to poverty.

²⁵ The generous soul will be made rich,
And he who waters will also be watered
himself.

²⁶ The people will curse him who withholds
grain,
But blessing *will be* on the head of him who
sells *it*.

²⁷ He who earnestly seeks good finds favor,
But trouble will come to him who seeks *evil*.

²⁸ He who trusts in his riches will fall,
But the righteous will flourish like foliage.

²⁹ He who troubles his own house will inherit
the wind,
And the fool *will be* servant to the wise of
heart.

³⁰ The fruit of the righteous *is a* tree of life,
And he who wins souls *is* wise.

³¹ If the righteous will be recompensed on the
earth,
How much more the ungodly and the sinner.

DEVOTIONAL

To have great wealth means far more than having a large amount of money or possessions. Great wealth can also include having wisdom, knowledge, and common sense, among other things. What is notable about this list, however, is how the worth of each is magnified when it is shared.

When Moses told Israel that God gave them the power to get wealth, he assured them that it was so that God's covenant could be established (Deut. 8:18). It was not so they could hoard the wealth and keep it all for themselves. Likewise, we are not to hoard wealth of any kind but are to use it for God's purposes. Whether it is financial blessing or receiving words of wisdom, knowledge, or common sense, when wealth is shared, lives are enriched.

When you are entrusted by God with wealth, your first responsibility is to Him in how you use it. Are you a conduit that He can use to enrich others? Or are you a reservoir that keeps getting fuller and fuller?

What has God entrusted to you? If money, how are you using it? If wisdom, do you share it? If knowledge, do you make it available for others so they can learn? If common sense, are you a mentor to those who need it?

Wealth is to be shared, so start sharing.

Tim DeTellis, New Missions
Orlando, FL

SEPTEMBER 28

The Righteous Shall Stand

Proverbs 12:1–11

WHOEVER loves instruction loves knowledge,
But he who hates correction *is* stupid.

2 A good *man* obtains favor from the LORD,
But a man of wicked intentions He will
condemn.

3 A man is not established by wickedness,
But the root of the righteous cannot be moved.

4 An excellent wife *is* the crown of her husband,
But she who causes shame *is* like rottenness in
his bones.

5 The thoughts of the righteous *are* right,
But the counsels of the wicked *are* deceitful.

6 The words of the wicked *are,* "Lie in wait for
blood,"
But the mouth of the upright will deliver them.

7 The wicked are overthrown and *are* no more,
But the house of the righteous will stand.

8 A man will be commended according to his
wisdom,
But he who is of a perverse heart will be despised.

9 Better *is the one* who is slighted but has a
servant,
Than he who honors himself but lacks bread.

10 A righteous *man* regards the life of his animal,
But the tender mercies of the wicked *are* cruel.

11 He who tills his land will be satisfied with bread,
But he who follows frivolity *is* devoid of
understanding.

Today's theme comes from verse 7 of the reading: "The wicked are overthrown and are no more, but the house of the righteous will stand." Sometimes it seems that just the opposite is true: the wicked rule while the righteous are maligned and mistreated.

Cruelty and oppression are facts of life today in many parts of the world. Christian martyrdom worldwide is at an all-time high as oppressive governments turn a blind eye to the persecution and death of righteous people. Some people wonder why God allows this if He really cares for His own.

Two thousand years ago Jesus saw the same thing and was subject to it Himself, but He never wavered. Jesus said something that we have difficulty apprehending: "Destroy this temple, and in three days I will raise it up" (John 2:19). Jesus knew that He was of the house of God. His focus was set in heaven, not on earth. Unlike Him, we often focus on the temporary things of this life instead of the permanence of our eternal home.

The scripture is true: the house of the righteous *will* stand because it is the house of God, and His kingdom is everlasting. Today, recognize and celebrate your position in the house of the righteous and share your strength. Pray for believers who are suffering persecution.

Tim DeTellis, New Missions
Orlando, FL

SEPTEMBER 29

Whatever a Man Sews He Will Reap

Proverbs 12:12–28

12 The wicked covet the catch of evil *men*,
But the root of the righteous yields *fruit*.

13 The wicked is ensnared by the transgression
of *his* lips,
But the righteous will come through trouble.

14 A man will be satisfied with good by the fruit
of *his* mouth,
And the recompense of a man's hands will be
rendered to him.

15 The way of a fool *is* right in his own eyes,
But he who heeds counsel *is* wise.

16 A fool's wrath is known at once,
But a prudent *man* covers shame.

17 He *who* speaks truth declares righteousness,
But a false witness, deceit.

18 There is one who speaks like the piercings of
a sword,
But the tongue of the wise *promotes* health.

19 The truthful lip shall be established forever,
But a lying tongue *is* but for a moment.

20 Deceit is in the heart of those who devise
evil,
But counselors of peace have joy.

21 No grave trouble will overtake the righteous,
But the wicked shall be filled with evil.

22 Lying lips *are* an abomination to the LORD,
But those who deal truthfully *are* His delight.

23 A prudent man conceals knowledge,
But the heart of fools proclaims foolishness.

24 The hand of the diligent will rule,
But the lazy *man* will be put to forced labor.

25 Anxiety in the heart of man causes depression,
But a good word makes it glad.

26 The righteous should choose his friends carefully,
For the way of the wicked leads them astray.

27 The lazy *man* does not roast what he took in
hunting,
But diligence *is* man's precious possession.

28 In the way of righteousness *is* life,
And in *its* pathway *there is* no death.

DEVOTIONAL

The principle of sowing and reaping is found throughout Scripture. From the beginning we see how God established this in the natural world: "Then God said, 'Let the earth bring forth grass, the herb that yields seed, and the fruit tree that yields fruit according to its kind, whose seed is in itself, on the earth'; and it was so" (Gen. 1:11).

This same principle applies to everyday life in your behavior, attitudes, thoughts, and speech. If you sow anger, you will reap anger; sow mercy, reap mercy.

Paul said to meditate on what is true, noble, just, pure, lovely, virtuous, and of good report (Phil. 4:8). Why? To sow good seed in your mind so that you will reap a bountiful harvest of good.

Today, be aware of what is good around you and thank God for it. Compliment another person; help someone; leave a generous tip. Then look back on the day and see the difference your attitude made.

Tim DeTellis, New Missions
Orlando, FL

SEPTEMBER 30

List the challenges you face in living a righteous life. How can God help you overcome them?

_____

_____

_____

_____

_____

_____

_____

_____

_____

_____

_____

_____

Think back on times when you reaped what you had sown. What did you learn from each experience?

_____

_____

_____

_____

_____

_____

_____

_____

_____

_____

_____

OCTOBER 1

Wisdom Loves Righteousness

Proverbs 13:1–12

A WISE son *heeds* his father's instruction,
But a scoffer does not listen to rebuke.

2 A man shall eat well by the fruit of *his* mouth,
But the soul of the unfaithful feeds on
violence.

3 He who guards his mouth preserves his life,
But he who opens wide his lips shall have
destruction.

4 The soul of a lazy *man* desires, and *has*
nothing;
But the soul of the diligent shall be made rich.

5 A righteous *man* hates lying,
But a wicked *man* is loathsome and comes to
shame.

6 Righteousness guards *him whose* way is
blameless,
But wickedness overthrows the sinner.

7 There is one who makes himself rich, yet *has*
nothing;
And one who makes himself poor, yet *has*
great riches.

8 The ransom of a man's life *is* his riches,
But the poor does not hear rebuke.

9 The light of the righteous rejoices,
But the lamp of the wicked will be put out.

10 By pride comes nothing but strife,
But with the well-advised *is* wisdom.

11 Wealth *gained by* dishonesty will be diminished,
But he who gathers by labor will increase.

12 Hope deferred makes the heart sick,
But *when* the desire comes, *it is* a tree of life.

DEVOTIONAL

Rest in Jesus' righteousness; it is His gift to you. The psalmist tells us, "Delight yourself also in the LORD, and He shall give you the desires of your heart. Commit your way to the LORD, trust also in Him, and He shall bring it [the desires of your heart] to pass. He shall bring forth your righteousness [His gift in you] as the light, and your justice as the noonday" (Ps. 37:4–7). When we desire Jesus, He becomes our "tree of life" (Prov. 13:12). Every desire of our hearts is satisfied in Him.

What are we to do while we wait for His desire to be fulfilled in us? We are to rest in the Lord and wait patiently for Him. However, resting in the Lord is not the same as being lazy. Verse 4 warns us that a lazy person has desires but is never satisfied.

The South American sloth hangs inverted, seemingly disorientated, in the trees. It spends most of the day asleep, it only wakes to eat, and it rarely ever moves. Likewise, a slothful man is also disorientated, moving so slowly you cannot tell if he is coming or going. He wants riches without labor, wisdom without study, respect without being respectable, and love without time given to building relationships.

Rest in the knowledge that Christ is at work in you, but work with diligence in all your assignments for His glory. We must concern ourselves first with His righteous work in us before we consider our righteous work. For we are His workmanship, not the other way around.

Roy Mack, Grace Fellowship Church
Warren, OH

OCTOBER 2

The Law of the Wise

Proverbs 13:13–25

13 He who despises the word will be destroyed,
But he who fears the commandment will be
rewarded.

14 The law of the wise *is* a fountain of life,
To turn *one* away from the snares of death.

15 Good understanding gains favor,
But the way of the unfaithful *is* hard.

16 Every prudent *man* acts with knowledge,
But a fool lays open *his* folly.

17 A wicked messenger falls into trouble,
But a faithful ambassador *brings* health.

18 Poverty and shame *will come* to him who
disdains correction,
But he who regards a rebuke will be honored.

19 A desire accomplished is sweet to the soul,
But *it is* an abomination to fools to depart
from evil.

20 He who walks with wise *men* will be wise,
But the companion of fools will be destroyed.

21 Evil pursues sinners,
But to the righteous, good shall be repaid.

22 A good *man* leaves an inheritance to his
children's children,
But the wealth of the sinner is stored up for
the righteous.

23 Much food *is in* the fallow *ground* of
the poor,
And for lack of justice there is waste.

24 He who spares his rod hates his son,
But he who loves him disciplines him promptly.

25 The righteous eats to the satisfying of his soul,
But the stomach of the wicked shall be in want.

DEVOTIONAL

The Proverbs were written in part to be a fountain of life and to help us avoid the snares of death. Proverbs 13:24 is perhaps one of the most misunderstood verses. It may appear that the writer is speaking of beating a child with a rod. That is not the intent or the teaching of the verse. Children were not made to be abused, and child abuse is not of God. Children are a gift from God and should be enjoyed, not tolerated. But parents are to correct and discipline bad behavior. It is easy to identify parents who do not do this. Their children are the ones who are running away from them, ignoring all instructions, and are quite bothersome to everyone around them.

Discipleship begins in the home. Being a disciple of Jesus has much to do with being a disciplined person. Correcting behavior is only half the job. Parents are to be to their children what Jesus is to the Christian, a Shepherd. Our Great Shepherd desires our hearts be right, not just our actions. The shepherd's "rod" is used to correct a stray. Often the Shepherd uses the rod to get our attention to listen to His voice.

Parents need to raise children who respect and listen to them. A parent's word should mean something. Children must be taught to respect and obey their parents' words. A disciplined child has the best opportunity to find the fountain of life and avoid the snares of death.

Roy Mack, Grace Fellowship Church
Warren, OH

OCTOBER 3

The Ways of Life and Death

Proverbs 14:1–14

THE wise woman builds her house,
But the foolish pulls it down with her hands.

2 He who walks in his uprightness fears the
LORD,
But *he who is* perverse in his ways despises
Him.

3 In the mouth of a fool *is* a rod of pride,
But the lips of the wise will preserve them.

4 Where no oxen *are,* the trough *is* clean;
But much increase *comes* by the strength of
an ox.

5 A faithful witness does not lie,
But a false witness will utter lies.

6 A scoffer seeks wisdom and does not *find it,*
But knowledge *is* easy to him who
understands.

7 Go from the presence of a foolish man,
When you do not perceive *in him* the lips of
knowledge.

8 The wisdom of the prudent *is* to understand
his way,
But the folly of fools *is* deceit.

9 Fools mock at sin,
But among the upright *there is* favor.

10 The heart knows its own bitterness,
And a stranger does not share its joy.

11 The house of the wicked will be overthrown,
But the tent of the upright will flourish.

12 There is a way *that seems* right to a man,
But its end *is* the way of death.

13 Even in laughter the heart may sorrow,
And the end of mirth *may be* grief.

14 The backslider in heart will be filled with his
own ways,
But a good man *will be satisfied* from above.

DEVOTIONAL

Jeremiah 17:9 tells us, "The heart is deceitful above all things, and desperately wicked; who can know it?" A person's heart can deceive him into believing that something seems right, but its end is the "way of death" (v. 12). If it's contrary to the Word of God, it cannot be right. Some people reason that since others bend the rules, cut corners, and employ situational ethics, why shouldn't they? Verse 12 does not teach that these people will physically die for doing such things. However, conducting oneself contrary to the Word of God will bring a different kind of death. It may bring the death of self-respect, relationships, finances, or a preferred future in God's will for your life.

Most importantly, there is only one way to God, which is through Christ (John 14:6). It would "seem right" that a person could live a good life—be a good neighbor, family member, and citizen, do thousands of good deeds—and reach heaven. But these things, though commendable, all end in death outside of Christ. If we could reach heaven by doing good, we would be our own savior. Only saving faith in the sacrifice of Jesus Christ makes a way to eternal life.

Roy Mack, Grace Fellowship Church
Warren, OH

OCTOBER 4

The Fountain of Life

Proverbs 14:15–35

15 The simple believes every word,
But the prudent considers well his steps.

16 A wise *man* fears and departs from evil,
But a fool rages and is self-confident.

17 A quick-tempered *man* acts foolishly,
And a man of wicked intentions is hated.

18 The simple inherit folly,
But the prudent are crowned with knowledge.

19 The evil will bow before the good,
And the wicked at the gates of the righteous.

20 The poor *man* is hated even by his own
neighbor,
But the rich *has* many friends.

21 He who despises his neighbor sins;
But he who has mercy on the poor, happy *is* he.

22 Do they not go astray who devise evil?
But mercy and truth *belong* to those who
devise good.

23 In all labor there is profit,
But idle chatter *leads* only to poverty.

24 The crown of the wise is their riches,
But the foolishness of fools *is* folly.

25 A true witness delivers souls,
But a deceitful *witness* speaks lies.

26 In the fear of the LORD *there is* strong
confidence,
And His children will have a place of refuge.

27 The fear of the LORD *is* a fountain of life,
To turn *one* away from the snares of death.

28 In a multitude of people *is* a king's honor,
But in the lack of people *is* the downfall of a
prince.

29 *He who is* slow to wrath has great
understanding,
But *he who is* impulsive exalts folly.

30 A sound heart *is* life to the body,
But envy *is* rottenness to the bones.

31 He who oppresses the poor reproaches his
Maker,
But he who honors Him has mercy on the needy.

32 The wicked is banished in his wickedness,
But the righteous has a refuge in his death.

33 Wisdom rests in the heart of him who has
understanding,
But *what is* in the heart of fools is made known.

34 Righteousness exalts a nation,
But sin *is* a reproach to *any* people.

35 The king's favor *is* toward a wise servant,
But his wrath *is against* him who causes shame.

DEVOTIONAL

To be rich in God's economy is not what we have but who we have. Those who have Christ are rich. A pauper who knows Jesus is as wealthy as a king. Spiritual riches are eternal; all else is temporary. We who know the One who was rich and for our sakes became poor should be witnesses as instructed in verse 25. Go and share the One who gave us all things through His poverty. Lead them to the fountain of life.

Roy Mack, Grace Fellowship Church
Warren, OH

OCTOBER 5

A Soft Answer Turns Away Wrath

Proverbs 15:1–18

A SOFT answer turns away wrath,
But a harsh word stirs up anger.

2 The tongue of the wise uses knowledge rightly,
But the mouth of fools pours forth foolishness.

3 The eyes of the LORD *are* in every place,
Keeping watch on the evil and the good.

4 A wholesome tongue *is* a tree of life,
But perverseness in it breaks the spirit.

5 A fool despises his father's instruction,
But he who receives correction is prudent.

6 *In* the house of the righteous *there is* much treasure,
But in the revenue of the wicked is trouble.

7 The lips of the wise disperse knowledge,
But the heart of the fool *does* not *do* so.

8 The sacrifice of the wicked *is* an abomination to the LORD,
But the prayer of the upright *is* His delight.

9 The way of the wicked *is* an abomination to the LORD,
But He loves him who follows righteousness.

10 Harsh discipline *is* for him who forsakes the way,
And he who hates correction will die.

11 Hell and Destruction *are* before the LORD;
So how much more the hearts of the sons of men.

12 A scoffer does not love one who corrects him,
Nor will he go to the wise.

13 A merry heart makes a cheerful countenance,
But by sorrow of the heart the spirit is broken.

14 The heart of him who has understanding seeks knowledge,
But the mouth of fools feeds on foolishness.

15 All the days of the afflicted *are* evil,
But he who is of a merry heart *has* a continual feast.

16 Better *is* a little with the fear of the LORD,
Than great treasure with trouble.

17 Better *is* a dinner of herbs where love is,
Than a fatted calf with hatred.

18 A wrathful man stirs up strife,
But *he who is* slow to anger allays contention.

DEVOTIONAL

O ur tongues, according to James 3, are powerful little instruments—like a rudder to a ship, able to change our direction and alter our course. Our tongues can steer us into shallow rocks of destruction or speak of the depths of God. Our tongues can be on fire and set blazes fueled by the wind of gossip. Words can break a heart and shatter a soul, or they can be used as a tool to build people up. Our tongues can be harsh, stirring up anger, or they can be soft, turning away wrath.

The use of our tongues is a reliable gauge to help us know our own hearts. The thoughts of the heart will eventually spill out of the mouth. God is looking on the heart. May your tongue be a tree of life producing sweet fruit in a world that is full of perverse, rotten words.

Roy Mack, Grace Fellowship Church
Warren, OH

OCTOBER 6

Honor Your Father and Your Mother

Proverbs 15:19–33

19 The way of the lazy man *is* like a hedge of thorns,
But the way of the upright *is* a highway.

20 A wise son makes a father glad,
But a foolish man despises his mother.

21 Folly *is* joy *to him who is* destitute of discernment,
But a man of understanding walks uprightly.

22 Without counsel, plans go awry,
But in the multitude of counselors they are established.

23 A man has joy by the answer of his mouth,
And a word *spoken* in due season, how good *it is!*

24 The way of life *winds* upward for the wise,
That he may turn away from hell below.

25 The LORD will destroy the house of the proud,
But He will establish the boundary of the widow.

26 The thoughts of the wicked *are* an abomination to the LORD,
But *the words* of the pure *are* pleasant.

27 He who is greedy for gain troubles his own house,
But he who hates bribes will live.

28 The heart of the righteous studies how to answer,
But the mouth of the wicked pours forth evil.

29 The LORD *is* far from the wicked,
But He hears the prayer of the righteous.

30 The light of the eyes rejoices the heart,
And a good report makes the bones healthy.

31 The ear that hears the rebukes of life
Will abide among the wise.

32 He who disdains instruction despises his own soul,
But he who heeds rebuke gets understanding.

33 The fear of the LORD *is* the instruction of wisdom,
And before honor *is* humility.

DEVOTIONAL

I am grateful for my mom and dad. They have truly blessed my life. Not every person can readily say that. However, the Word does not make a distinction between good parents and bad parents; it just simply commands us to honor them. Many families cannot be in the same room without an argument breaking out. Often there is ongoing conflict that just picks up where it left off.

Think about how you are going to give an answer before you speak. Don't let your mouth pour forth hateful and hurtful words. Love is a decision. Decide to give honor. Verse 33 says, "Before honor is humility." When there have been harsh words spoken, decide with humility to demonstrate honor and respect. This leads to healing.

When it comes to family, there is always something for which to be thankful. People who think can always be thankful. Honor one another as a family, especially your parents. After all, you wouldn't be here without them.

Roy Mack, Grace Fellowship Church
Warren, OH

OCTOBER 7

Prayerfully list some people you will take time to bless this coming week with your words or actions. Perhaps there's a friend who is struggling in a trial or a test of faith. Maybe a family member needs your forgiveness or an aging parent needs honoring. Words have power. God created the universe by His Word. Choose your words wisely and prayerfully, and then use them to bless those whom God reveals to you.

The wise lead people to the Fountain of Life. Make a list of the people in your life whom you need to share Christ with. It may be that you are God's chosen person to go and lead them to the Fountain of Life. It is great when you can take God's Word and share your faith, but it also effective to simply share your testimony, to tell your story of faith. As Christians, all of our stories are His story in us. He is the Author and Finisher of our faith.

OCTOBER 8

God's Plan, Your Purpose

Proverbs 16:1–17

T HE preparations of the heart *belong* to man,
But the answer of the tongue *is* from the LORD.

2 All the ways of a man *are* pure in his own eyes,
But the LORD weighs the spirits.

3 Commit your works to the LORD,
And your thoughts will be established.

4 The LORD has made all for Himself,
Yes, even the wicked for the day of doom.

5 Everyone proud in heart *is* an abomination to
the LORD;
Though they join forces, none will go unpunished.

6 In mercy and truth
Atonement is provided for iniquity;
And by the fear of the LORD *one* departs from
evil.

7 When a man's ways please the LORD,
He makes even his enemies to be at peace
with him.

8 Better *is* a little with righteousness,
Than vast revenues without justice.

9 A man's heart plans his way,
But the LORD directs his steps.

10 Divination *is* on the lips of the king;
His mouth must not transgress in judgment.

11 Honest weights and scales *are* the LORD's;
All the weights in the bag *are* His work.

12 *It is* an abomination for kings to commit
wickedness,
For a throne is established by righteousness.

13 Righteous lips *are* the delight of kings,
And they love him who speaks *what is* right.

14 As messengers of death *is* the king's wrath,
But a wise man will appease it.

15 In the light of the king's face *is* life,
And his favor *is* like a cloud of the latter rain.

16 How much better to get wisdom than gold!
And to get understanding is to be chosen
rather than silver.

17 The highway of the upright *is* to depart from
evil;
He who keeps his way preserves his soul.

DEVOTIONAL

Y ou have probably heard it many times: "Failing to plan is planning to fail." Perhaps this principle is more biblical than you imagined. Obviously, a great deal in life occurs for which it is impossible to prepare, such as a natural disaster, a tragic death, a layoff at work, or an unexpected illness. For such instances, we pray for grace and trust the providence of God. However, God is honored when we commit our personal plans to Him. Jesus said, "Which of you, intending to build a tower, does not sit down first and count the cost, whether he has enough to finish it" (Luke 14:28).

Notice the language of today's passage: "the preparations of the heart . . . commit your works . . . a man's heart plans his way" (vv. 1, 3, 9). Do you see a pattern? God desires your heart to be so connected with Him that your daily plans are the overflow of His will. Ask God to make His precise plan the purpose of your very existence! You won't regret it!

Jeremy Morton, Cross Point Baptist Church
Perry, GA

OCTOBER 9

The Weight of Your Words

Proverbs 16:18–33

¹⁸ Pride *goes* before destruction,
And a haughty spirit before a fall.

¹⁹ Better *to be* of a humble spirit with the lowly,
Than to divide the spoil with the proud.

²⁰ He who heeds the word wisely will find good,
And whoever trusts in the LORD, happy *is* he.

²¹ The wise in heart will be called prudent,
And sweetness of the lips increases learning.

²² Understanding *is* a wellspring of life to him
who has it.
But the correction of fools *is* folly.

²³ The heart of the wise teaches his mouth,
And adds learning to his lips.

²⁴ Pleasant words *are like* a honeycomb,
Sweetness to the soul and health to the bones.

²⁵ There is a way *that seems* right to a man,
But its end *is* the way of death.

²⁶ The person who labors, labors for himself,
For his *hungry* mouth drives him *on*.

²⁷ An ungodly man digs up evil,
And *it is* on his lips like a burning fire.

²⁸ A perverse man sows strife,
And a whisperer separates the best of friends.

²⁹ A violent man entices his neighbor,
And leads him in a way *that is* not good.

³⁰ He winks his eye to devise perverse things;
He purses his lips *and* brings about evil.

³¹ The silverhaired head *is* a crown of glory,
If it is found in the way of righteousness.

³² *He who is* slow to anger *is* better than the mighty,
And he who rules his spirit than he who takes
a city.

³³ The lot is cast into the lap,
But its every decision *is* from the LORD.

DEVOTIONAL

Numerous studies indicate the average person speaks between five thousand and twenty thousand words a day! Now that's a lot of talking! No wonder James authored an entire chapter of the Bible encouraging believers to use godly discretion when speaking. He said, "No man can tame the tongue. It is an unruly evil, full of deadly poison" (Jas. 3:8). Just imagine how much conflict in your home would be eliminated if each family member chose their words more carefully? How many problems at work would disappear if every member of the office made a vow not to gossip or backbite? How much more power would our churches be infused with if believers shared the gospel more and repeated nonsensical hearsay less?

According to Solomon, this should be our aim. "The heart of the wise teaches his mouth, and adds learning to his lips" (Prov. 16:23). Scripture tells us to feast our hearts on the Bible so when our mouths open, profitable, helpful remarks will follow. "Pleasant words are like a honeycomb, sweetness to the soul and health to the bones" (v. 24). Ask God to give you wise, edifying speech. Before you speak, pray and think about the weight of your words. And remember James's counsel, "Let every man be swift to hear, slow to speak" (Jas. 1:19).

Jeremy Morton, Cross Point Baptist Church
Perry, GA

OCTOBER 10

A Teachable Spirit

Proverbs 17:1–14

B ETTER *is* a dry morsel with quietness,
Than a house full of feasting *with* strife.

2 A wise servant will rule over a son who causes
shame,
And will share an inheritance among the
brothers.

3 The refining pot *is* for silver and the furnace
for gold,
But the LORD tests the hearts.

4 An evildoer gives heed to false lips;
A liar listens eagerly to a spiteful tongue.

5 He who mocks the poor reproaches his Maker;
He who is glad at calamity will not go
unpunished.

6 Children's children *are* the crown of old men,
And the glory of children *is* their father.

7 Excellent speech is not becoming to a fool,
Much less lying lips to a prince.

8 A present *is* a precious stone in the eyes of its
possessor;
Wherever he turns, he prospers.

9 He who covers a transgression seeks love,
But he who repeats a matter separates friends.

10 Rebuke is more effective for a wise *man*
Than a hundred blows on a fool.

11 An evil *man* seeks only rebellion;
Therefore a cruel messenger will be sent
against him.

12 Let a man meet a bear robbed of her cubs,
Rather than a fool in his folly.

13 Whoever rewards evil for good,
Evil will not depart from his house.

14 The beginning of strife *is like* releasing water;
Therefore stop contention before a quarrel starts.

DEVOTIONAL

O n June 2, 2010, at Comerica Park, Detroit Tigers pitcher Armando Galarraga came within one out of completing a perfect game. Cleveland Indians batter Jason Donald hit the ball into the infield. Video footage actually proves Donald was thrown out at first base, but Major League umpire Jim Joyce incorrectly called Donald safe. Not only did it ruin Galarraga's perfect game, but it goes down as one of the worst umpiring blunders in baseball history. After viewing the video evidence, a tearful Joyce publicly apologized to Galarraga and admitted his call was a terrible mistake. Galarraga graciously accepted the apology and quickly came to Joyce's defense, calling for the national media to cut him slack. "After all," Galarraga said, "no one is perfect."

For many, nothing is more difficult than acknowledging a mistake. Something deep within us seeks to cover the error, or minimize it, or make an excuse. But the fact is, no one is perfect (Rom. 3:10, 23). Developing a teachable spirit is perhaps the godliest form of humility. The gospel of Christ can flourish in people who humbly acknowledge they do not have all the answers! Receive the wisdom of Solomon: "Rebuke is more effective for a wise man than a hundred blows on a fool" (Prov. 17:10).

Jeremy Morton, Cross Point Baptist Church
Perry, GA

OCTOBER 11

True Friends

Proverbs 17:15–28

15 He who justifies the wicked, and he who con-
demns the just,
Both of them alike *are* an abomination to the
LORD.

16 Why *is there* in the hand of a fool the purchase
price of wisdom,
Since *he has* no heart *for it?*

17 A friend loves at all times,
And a brother is born for adversity.

18 A man devoid of understanding shakes hands
in a pledge,
And becomes surety for his friend.

19 He who loves transgression loves strife,
And he who exalts his gate seeks destruction.

20 He who has a deceitful heart finds no good,
And he who has a perverse tongue falls into
evil.

21 He who begets a scoffer *does so* to his sorrow,
And the father of a fool has no joy.

22 A merry heart does good, *like* medicine,
But a broken spirit dries the bones.

23 A wicked *man* accepts a bribe behind the back
To pervert the ways of justice.

24 Wisdom *is* in the sight of him who has
understanding,
But the eyes of a fool *are* on the ends of the
earth.

25 A foolish son *is* a grief to his father,
And bitterness to her who bore him.

26 Also, to punish the righteous *is* not good,
Nor to strike princes for *their* uprightness.

27 He who has knowledge spares his words,
And a man of understanding is of a calm spirit.

28 Even a fool is counted wise when he holds his
peace;
When he shuts his lips, *he is considered*
perceptive.

DEVOTIONAL

When you hear the word *friend*, what immediately comes to mind? Unfortunately, due
to the fast-paced times in which we live, many of
our relationships never get beyond the surface.
The demand at work is high, the number of proj-
ects and tasks is great, and many of the meaningful friendships God desires for us are put on hold.
Yet Proverbs 17:17 says, "A friend loves at all times,
and a brother is born for adversity."

Are you familiar with the story of David and
Jonathan? If ever there was a friendship defined
by consistent love, selflessness, and support during times of crisis, it was the bond between David
and Jonathan. Jonathan's father, Saul, became
envious of David's achievements. His jealousy led
to a morbid obsession with trying to kill David.
But time and time again, God used Jonathan to
bring encouragement and hope to David's heart
when David needed it most!

Who are your best friends? The ones who
inspire your walk with God, will always love you,
and stay committed when times are tough!

Jeremy Morton, Cross Point Baptist Church
Perry, GA

OCTOBER 12

The Penalty of Pride

Proverbs 18:1–12

A MAN who isolates himself seeks his own desire;
He rages against all wise judgment.

2 A fool has no delight in understanding,
But in expressing his own heart.

3 When the wicked comes, contempt comes also;
And with dishonor *comes* reproach.

4 The words of a man's mouth *are* deep waters;
The wellspring of wisdom *is* a flowing brook.

5 *It is* not good to show partiality to the wicked,
Or to overthrow the righteous in judgment.

6 A fool's lips enter into contention,
And his mouth calls for blows.

7 A fool's mouth *is* his destruction,
And his lips *are* the snare of his soul.

8 The words of a talebearer *are* like tasty trifles,
And they go down into the inmost body.

9 He who is slothful in his work
Is a brother to him who is a great destroyer.

10 The name of the LORD *is* a strong tower;
The righteous run to it and are safe.

11 The rich man's wealth *is* his strong city,
And like a high wall in his own esteem.

12 Before destruction the heart of a man is haughty,
And before honor *is* humility.

DEVOTIONAL

Perhaps nothing is more lethal to the human heart than pride. Think about it: Pride banished Lucifer from heaven. Pride was the stumbling block to Adam and Eve in the garden. When King Uzziah, who was a believer, walked in humility before the Lord, God prospered him. However, 2 Chronicles 26 tells how Uzziah became proud toward the end of his life. Instead of respecting the office of the priests and allowing them to burn incense on the altar, Uzziah took matters into his own hands. The Bible describes the foolishness of his pride this way: "But when he was strong his heart was lifted up, to his destruction, for he transgressed against the LORD his God by entering the temple of the LORD to burn incense on the altar" (2 Chron. 26:16).

Pride causes us to fall headfirst down the slippery slope of self-reliance instead of trusting in God. How about Ananias and Sapphira in Acts 5? Pride caused them to lie to the Holy Spirit about the true nature of their financial gift to the church. Having prideful hearts literally killed Ananias and Sapphira as God executed judgment.

Scripture is full of vivid examples of God's total disdain for the wickedness of pride. Ironically, in beautiful fashion, the hallmark of Jesus' ministry was humility. Jesus taught, "Everyone who exalts himself will be humbled, and he who humbles himself will be exalted" (Luke 18:14). Paul described the lowly incarnation of Jesus this way: "[He] made Himself of no reputation, taking the form of a bondservant.... He humbled himself and became obedient to the point of death" (Phil. 2:6–8). John Stott said pride is your greatest enemy, but humility is your greatest friend. Take time to clothe yourself in true humility today.

Jeremy Morton, Cross Point Baptist Church
Perry, GA

OCTOBER 13

Seek Unity with Others

Proverbs 18:13–24

13 He who answers a matter before he hears *it,*
It *is* folly and shame to him.

14 The spirit of a man will sustain him in sickness,
But who can bear a broken spirit?

15 The heart of the prudent acquires knowledge,
And the ear of the wise seeks knowledge.

16 A man's gift makes room for him,
And brings him before great men.

17 The first *one* to plead his cause *seems* right,
Until his neighbor comes and examines him.

18 Casting lots causes contentions to cease,
And keeps the mighty apart.

19 A brother offended *is harder to win* than a
strong city,
And contentions *are* like the bars of a castle.

20 A man's stomach shall be satisfied from the
fruit of his mouth;
From the produce of his lips he shall be filled.

21 Death and life *are* in the power of the tongue,
And those who love it will eat its fruit.

22 *He who* finds a wife finds a good *thing,*
And obtains favor from the LORD.

23 The poor *man* uses entreaties,
But the rich answers roughly.

24 A man *who has* friends must himself be friendly,
But there is a friend *who* sticks closer than a
brother.

DEVOTIONAL

When Jesus was asked by the scribes to summarize the entire Law of God, he stated the chief objective for believers is to wholly love God and to devotedly love people (Mark 12:28–34). In fact, Jesus taught there were no commandments greater than these. Therefore, it is obvious God wants His children to walk in love and unity. But as anyone can attest, our earthly relationships are often characterized by distrust, gossip, envy, bitterness, and an overall lack of love.

Perhaps there is friction between you and a loved one. Even if you do not feel personally at fault over the issue, keep in mind God is honored when we clothe ourselves in humility and a gentle spirit. In fact, God even said He wants us to remember those among us who are less mature in their faith and to do everything in our power to not become a stumbling block for them (Rom. 14:13).

In a similar passage, God commands us to go to great lengths to live at peace with everyone we encounter (Rom. 12:18). Do you remember how Paul explained it? He said behaviors such as anger, wrath, malice, and slander are consistent with the old life—the life we lived prior to salvation in Christ. But when Christ enters the heart, we put on a new self. This new life is characterized by compassion, kindness, humility, meekness, and patience. Furthermore, our primary motivation to forgive others is the fact that Christ has forgiven us (Col. 3:13)!

Do you have an offended brother or sister? Is there friction in a relationship? By God's grace, clear it up today! You will be glad you did!

Jeremy Morton, Cross Point Baptist Church
Perry, GA

OCTOBER 14

As you seek to grow in godly wisdom this week, consider the various roles and responsibilities you have. For example, think of the specific areas you need God's wisdom. As an individual. As a marriage partner. As a parent. As an employee. As a friend.

If the Proverbs of Solomon have made anything plain, it's the principle of growing deeper with God as the pathway to increased wisdom. In other words, you cannot grow in wisdom until you immerse yourself in self-abandonment to God. What disciplines are being incorporated into your life for the overall purpose of growing in wisdom?

OCTOBER 15

The Fear of the Lord Leads to Life

Proverbs 19:1–10

BETTER *is* the poor who walks in his integrity
Than *one who is* perverse in his lips, and is
a fool.

2 Also it is not good *for* a soul *to be* without
knowledge,
And he sins who hastens with *his* feet.

3 The foolishness of a man twists his way,
And his heart frets against the LORD.

4 Wealth makes many friends,
But the poor is separated from his friend.

5 A false witness will not go unpunished,
And *he who* speaks lies will not escape.

6 Many entreat the favor of the nobility,
And every man *is* a friend to one who gives
gifts.

7 All the brothers of the poor hate him;
How much more do his friends go far from him!
He may pursue *them with* words, *yet* they
abandon *him*.

8 He who gets wisdom loves his own soul;
He who keeps understanding will find good.

9 A false witness will not go unpunished,
And *he who* speaks lies shall perish.

10 Luxury is not fitting for a fool,
Much less for a servant to rule over princes.

DEVOTIONAL

What does it mean to fear the Lord?
Unfortunately, far too many people in our world seem to have an attitude about God that is fear based. That is, they are scared to death of Him. They see Him not as a loving Father who has their best interest in mind, but as someone who is just waiting to catch them messing up in some area of life. That is *not* what it means to fear the Lord.

To fear the Lord means we hold Him in awe, reverence, and respect. We understand that He loves us, and because He does, He has given us His Word filled with wisdom that will enhance our lives and teach us how to live with purpose and meaning.

In this opening verse of Proverbs 19, He tells us that walking in integrity is one of the most important things we can ever do in life. *Integrity* means perfect, complete, or blameless. It describes a person who is honest and lives life as we should. It is set in contrast with one who is "perverse in his lips," dishonest, or a liar (v. 1).

Fearing the Lord, showing reverence and humility before His Word, leads to wise decisions and wisdom in life. I fear Him not because I am continually scared of Him. I fear Him because I know that He loves me and has given me a pathway in life. Everything He says to me in His word is going to lead to life and freedom.

Today, choose life. Walk in integrity with Him.

*Rick White, The People's Church
Franklin, TN*

OCTOBER 16

Patience Is a Virtue

Proverbs 19:11–20

11 The discretion of a man makes him slow to
 anger,
 And his glory *is* to overlook a transgression.

12 The king's wrath *is* like the roaring of a lion,
 But his favor *is* like dew on the grass.

13 A foolish son *is* the ruin of his father,
 And the contentions of a wife *are* a continual
 dripping.

14 Houses and riches *are* an inheritance from
 fathers,
 But a prudent wife *is* from the LORD.

15 Laziness casts *one* into a deep sleep,
 And an idle person will suffer hunger.

16 He who keeps the commandment keeps his soul,
 But he who is careless of his ways will die.

17 He who has pity on the poor lends to the LORD,
 And He will pay back what he has given.

18 Chasten your son while there is hope,
 And do not set your heart on his destruction.

19 *A man of* great wrath will suffer punishment;
 For if you rescue *him,* you will have to do it
 again.

20 Listen to counsel and receive instruction,
 That you may be wise in your latter days.

DEVOTIONAL

Lord, give me patience, and give it to me right
now. Have you ever felt that way? Most of us
have shared that common experience. I think it
has a lot to do with that great illusion in life we
call "control." And oh, how we like to think we are
in control.

When life feels out of control, we will usually
default to one of two positions: either we trust
and wait for God to act on our behalf or we take
matters into our own hands. When we choose the
latter, we always run the risk of acting in anger,
somehow believing that forcing our agenda is
going to change things. God says we are to be slow
to anger, and if we are able to actually overlook
an offense, that is even better. James 1:20 declares
that our anger never brings about the righteous
life that God desires. In fact, it usually makes matters worse. I can think about some very painful
times in my life and ministry when I chose the
option of anger rather than patiently waiting on
the Lord to work His ways in His time.

Notice how the writer of Proverbs contrasts
wrath and favor in verse 12. Wrath is the roaring
of a lion; it breeds fear and anxiety in others. Dew
is life-giving to plants and is pictured as the favor
or gift of God. When we are willing to wait on the
Lord to work on our behalf, He promises renewed
strength and energy (Isa. 40:31).

Easy to write, but sometimes hard to live out.
Does life seem to be out of control right now? Don't
take matters into your own hands. Remember, His
time table differs from ours, so ask God to help
you wait for Him.

Rick White, The People's Church
Franklin, TN

OCTOBER 17

Fear of the Lord Leads to Life

Proverbs 19:21–29

21 There are many plans in a man's heart,
Nevertheless the LORD's counsel—that will stand.

22 What is desired in a man is kindness,
And a poor man is better than a liar.

23 The fear of the LORD *leads* to life,
And *he who has it* will abide in satisfaction;
He will not be visited with evil.

24 A lazy *man* buries his hand in the bowl,
And will not so much as bring it to his mouth
again.

25 Strike a scoffer, and the simple will become
wary;
Rebuke one who has understanding, *and* he
will discern knowledge.

26 He who mistreats *his* father *and* chases away
his mother
Is a son who causes shame and brings reproach.

27 Cease listening to instruction, my son,
And you will stray from the words of
knowledge.

28 A disreputable witness scorns justice,
And the mouth of the wicked devours iniquity.

29 Judgments are prepared for scoffers,
And beatings for the backs of fools.

DEVOTIONAL

P lans—we all have them, we all make them. Proverbs says that there are many plans in our hearts. Most of us live with computers, planners, and devices to help us stay on track with our plans. There's nothing wrong with any of that unless we forget that ultimately only the plans and purposes of God will stand. We may make lots of plans, but the Lord will do what He has decided.

We experience the fullness of life when we submit our plans to Him for His approval. James writes that all of our plans need to start with the preface, if it is the Lord's will.[1] It is a constant reminder that He alone is sovereign and He holds our lives in His hands.

God wants us to live in accordance with His plan and will for our lives. We have all heard lots of talks about the will of God, and sometimes it's a mystery to us. While it is not always clear what the will of God may be in a given situation, we are not left without direction and purpose. Two things are certain about the plans of God. We are to live in obedience to that which He has clearly revealed in Scripture, and we are to glorify Him in all things. As long as we are willing to live with those two principles, then I believe God will graciously lead us through those times when His plan may not seem as clear as we desire.

I believe that God gives us strength and grace to live just one day at a time. Revealing His plans to us in daily living is part of the true mercies of God. Make a plan, submit it to the Lord, stick to it, and trust Him with the outcome.

Rick White, The People's Church
Franklin, TN

OCTOBER 18

Wine Is a Mocker

Proverbs 20:1–10

WINE *is* a mocker,
Strong drink *is* a brawler,
And whoever is led astray by it is not wise.

2   The wrath of a king *is* like the roaring of a lion;
Whoever provokes him to anger sins *against*
his own life.

3   *It is* honorable for a man to stop striving,
Since any fool can start a quarrel.

4   The lazy *man* will not plow because of winter;
He will beg during harvest and *have* nothing.

5   Counsel in the heart of man *is like* deep water,
But a man of understanding will draw it out.

6   Most men will proclaim each his own
goodness,
But who can find a faithful man?

7   The righteous *man* walks in his integrity;
His children *are* blessed after him.

8   A king who sits on the throne of judgment
Scatters all evil with his eyes.

9   Who can say, "I have made my heart clean,
I am pure from my sin"?

10   Diverse weights *and* diverse measures,
They *are* both alike, an abomination to the
LORD.

DEVOTIONAL

Sometimes the decisions we make in life are
not always between right and wrong. There
are times when we are deciding about what is
wise and unwise. There are issues regarding the
Christian life that believers may have different
views about. These are not matters that are primary to the gospel but are secondary or tertiary
issues. We have to be careful how we state our
convictions on these issues lest we build walls that
divide us instead of promoting unity in the body.
Perhaps no other issue has proven to be more
inflammatory than the use of alcohol. It has been
hotly debated through the ages.

For some it is a clear violation and therefore
sin, while for others it is not quite as clear. I happen to be one of those Christians who practice
abstinence when it comes to alcohol. I reached this
decision not because I felt there was an absolute
biblical prohibition against it but because I realized for me it would not be a wise decision. Not
every decision comes down to just right or wrong,
but they do often come down to wise and unwise.

Scripture makes a compelling case that anything that leads us astray in our walk with the
Lord and our relationship with others is not wise,
and that is not limited to the issue of alcohol. The
whole of Proverbs is about gaining wisdom that
leads us to a fuller experience in life. We would be
foolish to participate in anything that might rob
us of God's best for us.

Never make these issues a test of fellowship
with those who differ with you, but encourage all
to follow after wisdom.

Rick White, The People's Church
Franklin, TN

OCTOBER 19

Commit Our Cause to God

Proverbs 20:11–21

¹¹ Even a child is known by his deeds,
Whether what he does *is* pure and right.

¹² The hearing ear and the seeing eye,
The LORD has made them both.

¹³ Do not love sleep, lest you come to poverty;
Open your eyes, *and* you will be satisfied with
bread.

¹⁴ "*It is* good for nothing," cries the buyer;
But when he has gone his way, then he boasts.

¹⁵ There is gold and a multitude of rubies,
But the lips of knowledge *are* a precious jewel.

¹⁶ Take the garment of one who is surety *for* a
stranger,
And hold it as a pledge *when it* is for a
seductress.

¹⁷ Bread gained by deceit *is* sweet to a man,
But afterward his mouth will be filled with
gravel.

¹⁸ Plans are established by counsel;
By wise counsel wage war.

¹⁹ He who goes about *as* a talebearer reveals
secrets;
Therefore do not associate with one who flatters with his lips.

²⁰ Whoever curses his father or his mother,
His lamp will be put out in deep darkness.

²¹ An inheritance gained hastily at the beginning
Will not be blessed at the end.

DEVOTIONAL

We live in a causal generation. It would be interesting to determine how many days on the calendar are dedicated to the recognition of causes. Peace, poverty, hunger, education, and climate control are just a few that top the lists of today's most popular causes. There are lots of good causes to which we can give our energy, influence, and resources.

The writer of Proverbs does not single out causes that we are to commit to God; rather, we are to commit ourselves to Him. We are known by our deeds, attitudes, and actions that make up our character. This is not about speaking up or standing up for single-issues causes, but it is about living a life filled with character that reflects glory to God and honor to Christ.

Just take a look at the verses on your left and observe all the things that the writer mentions: work ethic, honesty, planning, truth telling, caring for parents. All of these can come under the umbrella of character. What God desires is that we commit the totality of our lives to Him. He knows that if we are people of character we are going to honor Him and make a positive impact on those around us.

Looking for a cause to get excited about? Commit your life and your character to Him. Search for wisdom in His Word and from His Spirit. Think about living your life today in such a way that honors Him in all you do. The hearing ear and the seeing eye, the Lord has made them both. Commit all your ways unto Him.

Rick White, The People's Church
Franklin, TN

OCTOBER 20

A Man's Steps Are of the Lord

Proverbs 20:22–30

22 Do not say, "I will recompense evil";
Wait for the LORD, and He will save you.

23 Diverse weights *are* an abomination to the
LORD,
And dishonest scales *are* not good.

24 A man's steps *are* of the LORD;
How then can a man understand his own way?

25 *It is* a snare for a man to devote rashly
something as holy,
And afterward to reconsider *his* vows.

26 A wise king sifts out the wicked,
And brings the threshing wheel over them.

27 The spirit of a man *is* the lamp of the LORD,
Searching all the inner depths of his heart.

28 Mercy and truth preserve the king,
And by lovingkindness he upholds his throne.

29 The glory of young men *is* their strength,
And the splendor of old men *is* their gray
head.

30 Blows that hurt cleanse away evil,
As *do* stripes the inner depths of the heart.

DEVOTIONAL

I am the proud grandfather of five, soon to be six, grandchildren. Yes, I always have pictures, and I am more than happy to share them with anyone willing to give me a minute. They are the joy of my life. It has been fun to watch them from birth until the time they each took their first steps.

There were lots of false starts, stumbles, and falls, but each one was taken in the sight of loving parents who were always there to catch, love, and guide them.

The steps of the men and women of God are ordered by the Lord. The entire story of Scripture is about a loving Father who created us and redeemed for Himself sons and daughters. He has provided for our every need and guided each step of our journey. Even during those times when we were not aware of His presence, He has been there with us. When we cannot see our way, He is always there. When we cannot understand our own way, He is always there. He is the one who orders our steps.

I would encourage you take your Bible and slowly read Hebrews 11. It gives a long list of ordinary people like you and me whom God used in extraordinary ways. Much of the time they could not see what was before them, and they definitely could not understand all the ways that God worked in their lives.

The one thing that these men and women had in common was their faith and trust in God. The scripture says that the world was not even worthy of them. These people remained true to the end. They did not receive the things promised, but saw them and welcomed them from a distance. They were looking for a better country, a heavenly one that only God could prepare for them.

If you are in Christ, your steps have been ordered by the Lord. He will not leave you or forsake you. He will be with you each step of the way. Blessings!

Rick White, The People's Church
Franklin, TN

OCTOBER 21

After spending this week in Proverbs 19–20, what are the specific ways you have seen the wisdom of the Lord applied in your life?

_____

_____

_____

_____

_____

_____

_____

_____

_____

_____

_____

_____

How have your steps been ordered by the Lord? Who are the people and what are the circumstances that God has used to bring you to where you are today?

_____

_____

_____

_____

_____

_____

_____

_____

_____

_____

OCTOBER 22

The Lord Considers the Heart

Proverbs 21:1–10

THE king's heart *is* in the hand of the LORD,
Like the rivers of water;
He turns it wherever He wishes.

2 Every way of a man *is* right in his own eyes,
But the LORD weighs the hearts.

3 To do righteousness and justice
Is more acceptable to the LORD than sacrifice.

4 A haughty look, a proud heart,
And the plowing of the wicked *are* sin.

5 The plans of the diligent *lead* surely to plenty,
But *those of* everyone *who is* hasty, surely to
poverty.

6 Getting treasures by a lying tongue
Is the fleeting fantasy of those who seek death.

7 The violence of the wicked will destroy them,
Because they refuse to do justice.

8 The way of a guilty man *is* perverse;
But *as for* the pure, his work *is* right.

9 Better to dwell in a corner of a housetop,
Than in a house shared with a contentious
woman.

10 The soul of the wicked desires evil;
His neighbor finds no favor in his eyes.

DEVOTIONAL

Hello, my friend. As you journey through another day, the Lord Jesus has an encouraging word for you. Consider your heart. Not the beat of your heart; rather, consider the content of your heart.

This proverb goes right to the heart of the matter. God reminds us up front that He holds us in the palm of His hand. Even a king is not exempt from the sovereign touch of the King of kings and the Lord of lords. Like a meandering river winding its way across the land, God will never leave us nor forsake us (Deut. 31:6).

My favorite river in Africa is the Umngazana River in Zululand where I was born. It winds its way from its source and finally empties itself into the Indian Ocean accompanied by all the debris it has picked up along the way. This proverb identifies much of that debris in our lives as we wander sinfully and aimlessly toward our final destination. Though our way seems so right in our own eyes, our plans and our desires can bring so much heartache to ourselves and to others. Thankfully, God holds our hearts in the palm of His hand.

Perhaps this is a day when you have sensed the load you carry is weighing you down to the point of exhaustion? Perhaps you find yourself at somewhat of a dead-end road? Let the Spirit of the Lord speak to you. This is what He does through His Word. Deep in your heart you know that God loves you so much. So be encouraged today.

Pray this prayer with me: Dear heavenly Father, thank You for all You mean to me today. Thank You most of all for the Lord Jesus Christ. I am so grateful for my salvation and the forgiveness of all of my sin. Where would I be and what would I do without You? You have not only set me free, but You have also given me such encouragement for my journey today. I worship You. In Jesus' name I pray. Amen.

Dr. Don Wilton, First Baptist Church
Spartanburg, SC

OCTOBER 23

Living a Life of Worth

Proverbs 21:11–20

11 When the scoffer is punished, the simple is made wise;
But when the wise is instructed, he receives knowledge.

12 The righteous *God* wisely considers the house of the wicked,
Overthrowing the wicked for *their* wickedness.

13 Whoever shuts his ears to the cry of the poor
Will also cry himself and not be heard.

14 A gift in secret pacifies anger,
And a bribe behind the back, strong wrath.

15 *It is* a joy for the just to do justice,
But destruction *will come* to the workers of iniquity.

16 A man who wanders from the way of understanding
Will rest in the assembly of the dead.

17 He who loves pleasure *will be* a poor man;
He who loves wine and oil will not be rich.

18 The wicked *shall be* a ransom for the righteous,
And the unfaithful for the upright.

19 Better to dwell in the wilderness,
Than with a contentious and angry woman.

20 *There is* desirable treasure,
And oil in the dwelling of the wise,
But a foolish man squanders it.

I cannot tell you how many times I have found myself at a point in my life when I really needed a special word from the Lord to pick me up. It always amazes me that God seems to know just what I need to hear!

So, for a few moments, think about the subject of worth. Worth will help you define your "win" in life's journey. Personally, I want my life to really count. I am sure you feel the same way. The older I get, the more I want to lay aside those things that really do not matter and pick up those things that make a difference—for me, yes; for others, certainly! But most of all for the Lord Jesus Christ. I no longer want to waste away valuable time and effort. Many things I have done are good and a whole lot of fun, but I do not want to be like a "foolish man" squandering the treasures of life God has afforded me (v. 20).

Life is too short, and there are too many people who do not know the Lord Jesus as their Savior. My son, Greg, a missionary with his family, reminds me often of the great English cricketer and missionary pioneer C. T. Studd, who put it like this: "Only one life, 'twill soon be past. Only what's done for Christ will last."[1]

Pray this prayer with me: Dear heavenly Father, how blessed I am to know the Lord Jesus Christ as my Savior and Lord. Thank You for all You have done for me, even though I am so undeserving of Your grace and mercy. Today, I renew my life of total surrender to You. I pray this in Jesus' name. Amen.

Dr. Don Wilton, First Baptist Church
Spartanburg, SC

OCTOBER 24
Victory Is in God's Hands

Proverbs 21:21–31

²¹ He who follows righteousness and mercy
Finds life, righteousness and honor.

²² A wise *man* scales the city of the mighty,
And brings down the trusted stronghold.

²³ Whoever guards his mouth and tongue
Keeps his soul from troubles.

²⁴ A proud *and* haughty *man*—"Scoffer" *is* his
name;
He acts with arrogant pride.

²⁵ The desire of the lazy *man* kills him,
For his hands refuse to labor.

²⁶ He covets greedily all day long,
But the righteous gives and does not spare.

²⁷ The sacrifice of the wicked *is* an abomination;
How much more *when* he brings it with
wicked intent!

²⁸ A false witness shall perish,
But the man who hears *him* will speak
endlessly.

²⁹ A wicked man hardens his face,
But *as for* the upright, he establishes his way.

³⁰ *There is* no wisdom or understanding
Or counsel against the LORD.

³¹ The horse *is* prepared for the day of battle,
But deliverance *is* of the LORD.

DEVOTIONAL

Yes, victory is in the hands of the Lord. I love that fact. I cannot imagine how many times I have determined to gain the upper hand over my life, my circumstances, and my fears. And yet I fail time and again. This is not to suggest there are not times the great human spirit rises to the occasion. Our individual abilities are amazing, really. Just think of all of the great accomplishments of mankind. We send rockets to the moon, climb the Mount Everests of our lives, solve mathematical problems, and forge new inventions on a daily basis. Technological know-how is changing almost every day, and possibilities are endless.

But just as we are warned in this proverb, no matter how much "the horse" is prepared for the "day of battle," deliverance is of the Lord (v. 31). What a word of encouragement! In other words, at the end of the day, God is the One who comes through and gives to His children all that is necessary to win the battle. The key words used in this proverb provide the key to our success in the Lord Jesus. Here is what we are exhorted to do: we must follow after His righteousness, act with wisdom, guard our mouths, give unsparingly, and listen carefully—just to highlight a few. The bottom line is this: God is on your side. Don't get in the way!

Pray this prayer with me: Dear heavenly Father, thank You for loving me so much. In Jesus' name I pray. Amen.

Dr. Don Wilton, First Baptist Church
Spartanburg, SC

OCTOBER 25
The Value of a Good Name

Proverbs 22:1–11

A GOOD name is to be chosen rather than
great riches,
Loving favor rather than silver and gold.

2 The rich and the poor have this in common,
The LORD *is* the maker of them all.

3 A prudent *man* foresees evil and hides himself,
But the simple pass on and are punished.

4 By humility *and* the fear of the LORD
Are riches and honor and life.

5 Thorns *and* snares *are* in the way of the perverse;
He who guards his soul will be far from them.

6 Train up a child in the way he should go,
And when he is old he will not depart from it.

7 The rich rules over the poor,
And the borrower *is* servant to the lender.

8 He who sows iniquity will reap sorrow,
And the rod of his anger will fail.

9 He who has a generous eye will be blessed,
For he gives of his bread to the poor.

10 Cast out the scoffer, and contention will leave;
Yes, strife and reproach will cease.

11 He who loves purity of heart
And has grace on his lips,
The king *will be* his friend.

DEVOTIONAL

What's in a name? Just think about this
question.

One of the great joys of my life is the fact that I
now have six grandsons and another on the way!
We love them so much and take such joy in watching
them grow up. When they are all in one place
at one time, things get rather interesting, to say the
least. Activity is putting it mildly. Each one of their
names is connected to specific significant people
in their parents' lives. Just their names alone bring
a whole frame of reference to their character and
disposition. My sons and daughter always called
me "Chief" when they were growing up, so guess
what? I am "Chief" to my grandkids. But my given
name is Donald, which means "big chief" or "world
ruler"—and I have always wanted to be!

In this proverb, the Lord reminds us of our personal
identity. And, more importantly, God lets us
know that how much our name is associated with
His goodness is in direct proportion to the choices
we make to live according to His standards and
expectations. The word *choices* is very critical
because you and I can make some pretty terrible
choices in life. In other words, be careful what you
"sow" because only "sorrow" can come from a
life of disobedience to the Lord (v. 8). Praise God,
however—Jesus Christ is King! And His forgiveness
and guidance guarantee His friendship.

Pray this prayer with me: Dear heavenly Father,
thank You for giving me life and making me who
I am in You. Help me live for You in every way, and
thank You for being my friend. In Jesus' name I
pray. Amen.

Dr. Don Wilton, First Baptist Church
Spartanburg, SC

OCTOBER 26

The Words of the Wise

Proverbs 22:12–21

¹² The eyes of the LORD preserve knowledge,
But He overthrows the words of the faithless.

¹³ The lazy *man* says, "*There is* a lion outside!
I shall be slain in the streets!"

¹⁴ The mouth of an immoral woman *is* a deep pit;
He who is abhorred by the LORD will fall there.

¹⁵ Foolishness *is* bound up in the heart of a child;
The rod of correction will drive it far from him.

¹⁶ He who oppresses the poor to increase his
riches,
And he who gives to the rich, *will* surely *come*
to poverty.

¹⁷ Incline your ear and hear the words of the wise,
And apply your heart to my knowledge;

¹⁸ For *it is* a pleasant thing if you keep them
within you;
Let them all be fixed upon your lips,

¹⁹ So that your trust may be in the LORD;
I have instructed you today, even you.

²⁰ Have I not written to you excellent things
Of counsels and knowledge,

²¹ That I may make you know the certainty of
the words of truth,
That you may answer words of truth
To those who send to you?

DEVOTIONAL

Perhaps begin this devotion with a short prayer like this: Dear God, I bow my head in Your presence, believing You have a very specific and special word for me today. I confess my sin to You and ask that You would speak to my heart. In Jesus' name I pray. Amen.

Just as Solomon knew the Lord was watching over him, so it is we are reminded of the deep and wonderful truth that He is watching over us. In fact, think about your eyes. The Bible reminds us that our eyes are the entrance to our hearts. God's eyes have the divine capability to preserve in us all the riches of His knowledge because they bring forth all the fragrance of His divine character. God's eyes are the windows to His heart, and through them He leads us into the vast resources of His matchless grace and mercy. This is the very reason why you and I can place our trust in the Lord and do so with absolute confidence. The result is "the certainty of the words of truth" (v. 21).

Our television ministry, The Encouraging Word, seeks to "share God's truth with a searching world" because people want to know the truth. The instructions in Proverbs all find their root in the truth of who God is. They are written down for us and are "excellent" for counsel and knowledge (v. 20). Shake off the things of the world and stand on His truth.

Pray this prayer with me: Dear heavenly Father, thank You for the truth of Your Word. Help me fix them on my lips. Help me heed Your words. Please help me take my stand for You today. I commend myself to Your grace and to Your wisdom in my life. In Jesus' name I pray. Amen.

Dr. Don Wilton, First Baptist Church
Spartanburg, SC

OCTOBER 27

Trust in the Lord

Proverbs 22:22–29

²² Do not rob the poor because he *is* poor,
Nor oppress the afflicted at the gate;
²³ For the LORD will plead their cause,
And plunder the soul of those who plunder
them.

²⁴ Make no friendship with an angry man,
And with a furious man do not go,
²⁵ Lest you learn his ways
And set a snare for your soul.

²⁶ Do not be one of those who shakes hands in
a pledge,
One of those who is surety for debts;
²⁷ If you have nothing *with which* to pay,
Why should he take away your bed from
under you?

²⁸ Do not remove the ancient landmark
Which your fathers have set.

²⁹ Do you see a man *who* excels in his work?
He will stand before kings;
He will not stand before unknown *men.*

DEVOTIONAL

Hello, my friend. As you journey through another day, the Lord Jesus has an encouraging word for you. He always does. This is why it is so important to have this daily devotional time with Him. I have often found myself wrung out and in need of a special infusion of the Lord's presence and His grace. I am sure you have felt the same way. You are not alone in your struggles and desires.

This proverb, in fact, invokes the mass of humanity. All of us are in the battlefields of life. The word *gate* is used to describe that place where so many come and go. Every year I lead wonderful groups of people to Israel. We have so much fun and fellowship, and we learn so much more about the land where our Savior was born, died, and rose again. Jerusalem is surrounded by gates. Each gate represents seething masses of people—all people for whom Christ died.

How easy it is to become one of many! How easy it is to simply get in the line and "go with the flow." How easy it is to take advantage of others, especially the poor, helpless, and downtrodden. How easy it is to lower the standards set by those who have been found faithful to the Lord. How easy it is to give way to bad behavior.

What the Lord wants us to know is that He is watching out. He is watching and caring for the poor as much as He is watching and caring for all those who love Him. Our challenge is to live up to all Christ is in us rather than down to a world lost in their trespasses and sins.

Pray this prayer with me: Dear heavenly Father, I am so grateful that I can walk through this day with You in my heart and in my life. I do not know how I could manage to please You without Your abiding presence. I am challenged in my witness for You at every turn of life and in every way. I confess before You and ask You to give me strength for this journey. In Jesus' name I pray. Amen.

Dr. Don Wilton, First Baptist Church
Spartanburg, SC

OCTOBER 28

In what specific ways does your living out the life of Christ reflect the fruit of the Spirit in Galatians 5:22?

_____

_____

_____

_____

_____

_____

_____

_____

_____

_____

How does the fruit of the Spirit in Galatians 5:22 apply to all the Lord has shown you about yourself in the devotional study in Proverbs?

_____

_____

_____

_____

_____

_____

_____

_____

_____

_____

OCTOBER 29

Seek Wisdom and Knowledge

Proverbs 23:1–12

W HEN you sit down to eat with a ruler,
Consider carefully what *is* before you;

2 And put a knife to your throat
If you *are* a man given to appetite.

3 Do not desire his delicacies,
For they *are* deceptive food.

4 Do not overwork to be rich;
Because of your own understanding, cease!

5 Will you set your eyes on that which is not?
For *riches* certainly make themselves wings;
They fly away like an eagle *toward* heaven.

6 Do not eat the bread of a miser,
Nor desire his delicacies;

7 For as he thinks in his heart, so *is* he.
"Eat and drink!" he says to you,
But his heart is not with you.

8 The morsel you have eaten, you will vomit up,
And waste your pleasant words.

9 Do not speak in the hearing of a fool,
For he will despise the wisdom of your words.

10 Do not remove the ancient landmark,
Nor enter the fields of the fatherless;

11 For their Redeemer *is* mighty;
He will plead their cause against you.

12 Apply your heart to instruction,
And your ears to words of knowledge.

DEVOTIONAL

B eginning in Proverbs 22:22, Solomon compiles thirty instructions that empower readers to know and live according to the truth. In today's reading, verses 6 through 8 caution us about the dangers associated with riches, particularly the wealth of others.

Never assume that the generosity of a stranger doesn't have a price tag attached (vv. 1–3). Usually, the wealthy do not lavish others without expecting something in return. Despite occasional exceptions, exercising restraint as a beneficiary ensures our obligation to the Lord alone. To protect yourself further, refuse to live with the goal of getting rich (vv. 4–5). Like a mirage that is always just out of reach, the wealth we desire is unattainable due to the insatiable appetite of our flesh (1 Tim. 6:9). Thus, befriending those with abundance is not only futile but also endangering (Prov. 23:6–8). While having wealthy friends is never prohibited, we should not seek them because of a desire for personal benefit.

The priority of wisdom and truth serves as the theme of admonitions nine through eleven. Though often counterintuitive, not everyone deserves to hear godly wisdom (v. 9). Believers should neither feel obligated to nor responsible for those who hate the truth. Regarding business, Christians should protect the weak with fairness and precedent, knowing that God defends based upon the truth rather than one's status or power (vv. 10–11). Because wisdom in these matters and many others is not always readily apparent, we should seek out instruction and knowledge with diligence (v. 12).

Dr. Adam Dooley, Dauphin Way Baptist Church
Mobile, AL

OCTOBER 30

Listen to Your Father

Proverbs 23:13–22

¹³ Do not withhold correction from a child,
    For *if* you beat him with a rod, he will not die.
¹⁴ You shall beat him with a rod,
    And deliver his soul from hell.

¹⁵ My son, if your heart is wise,
    My heart will rejoice—indeed, I myself;
¹⁶ Yes, my inmost being will rejoice
    When your lips speak right things.

¹⁷ Do not let your heart envy sinners,
    But *be zealous* for the fear of the Lord all
        the day;
¹⁸ For surely there is a hereafter,
    And your hope will not be cut off.

¹⁹ Hear, my son, and be wise;
    And guide your heart in the way.
²⁰ Do not mix with winebibbers,
    Or with gluttonous eaters of meat;
²¹ For the drunkard and the glutton will come to
        poverty,
    And drowsiness will clothe *a man* with rags.

²² Listen to your father who begot you,
    And do not despise your mother when she
        is old.

DEVOTIONAL

Do you ever feel overwhelmed as a parent? Do your inadequacies leave you feeling defeated in your attempts to prepare your family to remain godly in a sinful world? Every parent wants the best for his or her children, yet the pressures of life give us little time to debate strategy. Thankfully, Solomon offers practical insights for sowing the seed of wisdom into the people we love.

Continuing a previous theme (Prov. 13:24; 22:6), verses 13–14 remind us of the corporal punishment that children need to thrive. Though special care must be given to make certain this is not excessive or abusive (Eph. 6:4), loving discipline helps produce spiritual character. Because lifelong habits form early, any deviation from a path of godliness must be promptly corrected.

This does not mean, however, that guidance and support end after a child reaches adulthood. Hopefully, the rejoicing of their parents will motivate grown children to make godly choices (vv. 15–16). In addition, the continued counsel and guidance of spiritually seasoned moms and dads will aide any Christian struggling with more weighty matters. Refusing to be envious despite the apparent prosperity of the wicked will require continued fear of the Lord and confidence in His eternal rewards for the faithful (vv. 17–18). Avoiding drunkards and gluttons will protect believers from the poverty of laziness and drowsiness (vv. 19–21). No wonder verse 22 encourages continued respect and attention toward those who brought us into this world as they seek to guide us away from harmful temptations such as these.

Take a moment and thank God for the guidance of your parents over the years. If the Lord has given you children, ask for His help as you seek to lead them. Pray for each child by name and ask God to protect him or her from the pitfalls of these passages.

Dr. Adam Dooley, Dauphin Way Baptist Church
Mobile, AL

OCTOBER 31
The Downfall of the Drunkard

Proverbs 23:23–35

23 Buy the truth, and do not sell *it,*
  Also wisdom and instruction and
    understanding.

24 The father of the righteous will greatly
    rejoice,
  And he who begets a wise *child* will delight
    in him.

25 Let your father and your mother be glad,
  And let her who bore you rejoice.

26 My son, give me your heart,
  And let your eyes observe my ways.

27 For a harlot *is* a deep pit,
  And a seductress *is* a narrow well.

28 She also lies in wait as *for* a victim,
  And increases the unfaithful among men.

29 Who has woe?
  Who has sorrow?
  Who has contentions?
  Who has complaints?
  Who has wounds without cause?
  Who has redness of eyes?

30 Those who linger long at the wine,
  Those who go in search of mixed wine.

31 Do not look on the wine when it is red,
  When it sparkles in the cup,
  When it swirls around smoothly;

32 At the last it bites like a serpent,
  And stings like a viper.

33 Your eyes will see strange things,
  And your heart will utter perverse things.

34 Yes, you will be like one who lies down in the
    midst of the sea,
  Or like one who lies at the top of the mast,
    saying:

35 "They have struck me, *but* I was not hurt;
  They have beaten me, but I did not feel *it.*
  When shall I awake, that I may seek
    another *drink?*"

DEVOTIONAL

Because nothing brings godly parents more joy than the success and faithfulness of their children, living according to the truth of God and refusing to relinquish it at any cost are the keys to making them proud (vv. 23–25). Showing respect to parents requires words and deeds. In addition, parents must be willing to set a righteous example (v. 26). Two pitfalls are mentioned specifically in order.

First is the problem of promiscuity. Solomon describes the entanglement of a prostitute and adulteress as a pit and a narrow well. Once entrapped by the enticement of sexual sin, it is very difficult to break the pattern due to the idol of pleasure.

And second, addiction to alcohol ruins both the quality and reputation of a person's life. Aside from bringing sorrow, complaints, and wounds, the serpent of alcohol bites and stings unsuspecting victims with the immediacy of a hangover and often the permanency of lifelong heartache and destruction (vv. 29–34). Parents and children alike should protect their hearts (v. 26) to avoid these snares altogether.

Dr. Adam Dooley, Dauphin Way Baptist Church
Mobile, AL

NOVEMBER 1

Do Not Envy Evil Men

Proverbs 24:1–12

D O not be envious of evil men,
Nor desire to be with them;

2 For their heart devises violence,
And their lips talk of troublemaking.

3 Through wisdom a house is built,
And by understanding it is established;

4 By knowledge the rooms are filled
With all precious and pleasant riches.

5 A wise man *is* strong,
Yes, a man of knowledge increases strength;

6 For by wise counsel you will wage your own war,
And in a multitude of counselors *there is* safety.

7 Wisdom *is* too lofty for a fool;
He does not open his mouth in the gate.

8 He who plots to do evil
Will be called a schemer.

9 The devising of foolishness *is* sin,
And the scoffer *is* an abomination to men.

10 *If* you faint in the day of adversity,
Your strength *is* small.

11 Deliver *those who* are drawn toward death,
And hold back *those* stumbling to the slaughter.

12 If you say, "Surely we did not know this,"
Does not He who weighs the hearts consider *it?*
He who keeps your soul, does He *not* know *it?*
And will He *not* render to *each* man according to his deeds?

DEVOTIONAL

W hat does it look like when a person genuinely fears the Lord? What are signs that we are walking in the truth? Solomon continues his thirty sayings to help us answer questions like these. He warns Christians to be cautious about whom they allow to influence their lives (v. 1). The wickedness of evil men should not be envied or emulated (v. 2). Exercising wisdom such as this allows us to build lives, families, and legacies that are fulfilling and honoring to the Lord (vv. 3–4). In fact, real strength and success in any arena of life is the direct result of godly wisdom (v. 5). Thus, surrounding ourselves with like-minded people who fear the Lord empowers us to make spiritual decisions in light of the collective wisdom of God's people (v. 6).

Wisdom will also protect us from developing a reputation for plotting evil (vv. 8–9). We should work hard to preserve the characteristics of truthfulness and integrity. Doing so requires trusting God rather than our own schemes during times of adversity (v. 10). Relying on God when we are hurting often speaks the loudest to those who do not know Jesus. Our greatest platform to influence people for Christ is when we live with the hope of spiritual wisdom. Doing so may very well be the means God uses to deliver those who are marching toward eternal death (v. 11). Because we cannot claim ignorance and forfeit our mission to reach the lost, we dare not waste our adversity (v. 12).

Dr. Adam Dooley, Dauphin Way Baptist Church
Mobile, AL

NOVEMBER 2

The Conduct of the Righteous

Proverbs 24:13–22

13 My son, eat honey because *it is* good,
And the honeycomb *which is* sweet to your taste;
14 So *shall* the knowledge of wisdom *be* to your
soul;
If you have found *it,* there is a prospect,
And your hope will not be cut off.

15 Do not lie in wait, O wicked *man,* against the
dwelling of the righteous;
Do not plunder his resting place;
16 For a righteous *man* may fall seven times
And rise again,
But the wicked shall fall by calamity.

17 Do not rejoice when your enemy falls,
And do not let your heart be glad when he
stumbles;
18 Lest the LORD see *it,* and it displease Him,
And He turn away His wrath from him.

19 Do not fret because of evildoers,
Nor be envious of the wicked;
20 For there will be no prospect for the evil *man;*
The lamp of the wicked will be put out.

21 My son, fear the LORD and the king;
Do not associate with those given to change;
22 For their calamity will rise suddenly,
And who knows the ruin those two can bring?

DEVOTIONAL

Do you ever find yourself frustrated with others (and even with God) because of how they treat you? Have you wondered why those who blaspheme God seem to have it so good? If so, you're not alone. Far from useless spiritual theory, Solomon's discussion of wisdom paints a picture for us of righteous living in the context of questions like these. Much like honey, which is satisfying to the taste, wisdom offers the reward of a nurtured, happy soul that rests secure in the promises of God (vv. 13–14). Even though at times it seems as if the wicked prosper and take advantage of the righteous, ultimately evildoers will face the eternal judgment of God while the redeemed of the earth will be exalted in their humility (vv. 15–16).

After this reassuring declaration, Solomon cautions us against two extremes. First, lest we be tempted to gloat over the condemnation of others, we should remember that God takes no pleasure in the death of sinners (Ezek. 33:11) and neither should we (Prov. 24:17–18).

Equally important but vastly different is that we do not grow weary as we await God's intervention on our behalf. Because God determines the destiny of those who reject Him, we need not fret over the temporary injustices of this life (vv. 19–20). Has someone treated you unfairly? Don't despair! Do you feel abused, wounded, or defeated? Let God handle it! Settling the score with others is unnecessary, and celebrating their demise is impermissible. Wisdom reminds us that delayed victory does not equal permanent defeat. Believers should only fear God and His eternal Davidic King, the Lord Jesus, knowing that He will deal with those who do otherwise (vv. 21–22).

Dr. Adam Dooley, Dauphin Way Baptist Church
Mobile, AL

NOVEMBER 3
The Golden Rule of the Wise

Proverbs 24:23–34

23 These *things* also *belong* to the wise:

It *is* not good to show partiality in judgment.

24 He who says to the wicked, "You *are* righteous,"
Him the people will curse;
Nations will abhor him.

25 But those who rebuke *the wicked* will have
delight,
And a good blessing will come upon them.

26 He who gives a right answer kisses the lips.

27 Prepare your outside work,
Make it fit for yourself in the field;
And afterward build your house.

28 Do not be a witness against your neighbor
without cause,
For would you deceive with your lips?

29 Do not say, "I will do to him just as he has
done to me;
I will render to the man according to his
work."

30 I went by the field of the lazy *man*,
And by the vineyard of the man devoid of
understanding;

31 And there it was, all overgrown with thorns;
Its surface was covered with nettles;
Its stone wall was broken down.

32 When I saw *it*, I considered *it* well;
I looked on *it and* received instruction:

33 A little sleep, a little slumber,
A little folding of the hands to rest;

34 So shall your poverty come *like* a prowler,
And your need like an armed man.

DEVOTIONAL

What do honesty and hard work have in common? According to Solomon, both are expressions of wisdom that indicate our walking in the fear of the Lord.

Verses 23–26 remind us that dishonest partiality in a court of law is universally rejected. Those who acquit the wicked are cursed (v. 24), and those who condemn the wicked are blessed (v. 25). Honest answers show the respect to others that God requires of believers (v. 26). Seems simple enough, but lest we think we would never violate this important principle, verses 28 and 29 give a second example to personalize the dilemma. The scenario of getting even with a neighbor who wronged us might tempt us to make an exception to the standard of honesty. Trusting God to deal with those who hurt us requires speaking the truth even when it is not expedient (vv. 28–29). Wisdom means that we allow God to deal with others in His time rather than seeking to do it with our tongue.

The virtue of hard work should also characterize a Christian. For example, a person who builds a house should work hard, save resources, and carefully plan before construction begins (v. 27). To contrast, the text presents the devastation of laziness with a picture of one who does not labor in his field or vineyard (vv. 30–34). This is not the path of wisdom (see also Prov. 6:10–11).

Dr. Adam Dooley, Dauphin Way Baptist Church
Mobile, AL

November 4

How have riches, or the lack thereof, affected your relationship with God? Is it difficult for you to be content? How should we treat those who are financially blessed?

_____

_____

_____

_____

_____

_____

_____

_____

_____

_____

How do you respond to those who hurt you? Are you content to let God handle situations like these or do you take matters into your own hands? How should those who fear the Lord respond?

_____

_____

_____

_____

_____

_____

_____

_____

NOVEMBER 5

Rule Your Spirit

Proverbs 25:1–10

T HESE also are proverbs of Solomon which the men of Hezekiah king of Judah copied:

2 *It is* the glory of God to conceal a matter,
But the glory of kings *is* to search out a matter.

3 *As* the heavens for height and the earth for depth,
So the heart of kings *is* unsearchable.

4 Take away the dross from silver,
And it will go to the silversmith *for* jewelry.

5 Take away the wicked from before the king,
And his throne will be established in righteousness.

6 Do not exalt yourself in the presence of the king,
And do not stand in the place of the great;

7 For *it is* better that he say to you,
"Come up here,"
Than that you should be put lower in the presence of the prince,
Whom your eyes have seen.

8 Do not go hastily to court;
For what will you do in the end,
When your neighbor has put you to shame?

9 Debate your case with your neighbor,
And do not disclose the secret to another;

10 Lest he who hears *it* expose your shame,
And your reputation be ruined.

DEVOTIONAL

H ave you ever gotten mad and said something that you regretted immediately? Have you ever tweeted something, posted something on your Facebook page, or fired off an e-mail when you were frustrated only to regret it later? I certainly have. It is so easy to make an impulsive decision in the heat of the moment without putting any thought or prayer into it.

How many times do you really stop and take time to assess the situation? *Do I have all the facts? Am I taking this personally? Am I reacting out of emotion? Have I slept on this decision?*

What about prayer? *Have I diligently sought the Father for His answer? Do I know His heart on the matter?*

If we are not careful, we will seek to get others on our side. *Do you know what he (or she) said?* We want others to agree with our sin and bad decisions.

We must use wisdom (as the Proverbs teach) to think before we act. Ask the Lord to rule your spirit and to allow you to walk in wisdom.

Steve Flockhart, New Season Church
Hiram, GA

NOVEMBER 6

The Words and Ways of the Wise

Proverbs 25:11–18

11 A word fitly spoken *is like* apples of gold
   In settings of silver.
12 *Like* an earring of gold and an ornament of
      fine gold
   Is a wise rebuker to an obedient ear.
13 Like the cold of snow in time of harvest
   Is a faithful messenger to those who send him,
   For he refreshes the soul of his masters.
14 Whoever falsely boasts of giving
   Is like clouds and wind without rain.
15 By long forbearance a ruler is persuaded,
   And a gentle tongue breaks a bone.
16 Have you found honey?
   Eat only as much as you need,
   Lest you be filled with it and vomit.
17 Seldom set foot in your neighbor's house,
   Lest he become weary of you and hate you.
18 A man who bears false witness against his
      neighbor
   Is like a club, a sword, and a sharp arrow.

DEVOTIONAL

What we say affects more people than any other action we take. Our words carry tremendous weight and reveal the very nature of our hearts. Most of us have no idea how powerful our words are. Each of us can reflect on unkind words that were spoken to us at some point in our lives. Words may not leave a physical mark, but they certainly leave emotional wounds. When we communicate unkind or hateful words, we run the risk of damaging someone for life.

Positive communication is beneficial to your life and the lives of other people. Your words can refresh, empower, encourage, provide hope, build security, and share love. Your words can also communicate, "You are stupid," "You are fat," "You are ugly," "You will never change," "I do not know why I ever married you," "You are just like your father," "You will never amount to anything," etc. These words have the ability to crush a person's feelings, leave emotional scars, and devastate that person for life. We must think before speaking and choose to use words saturated with wisdom.

Steve Flockhart, New Season Church
Hiram, GA

NOVEMBER 7

How to Treat Our Enemies

Proverbs 25:19–28

¹⁹ Confidence in an unfaithful *man* in time of
trouble
Is like a bad tooth and a foot out of joint.

²⁰ *Like* one who takes away a garment in cold
weather,
And like vinegar on soda,
Is one who sings songs to a heavy heart.

²¹ If your enemy is hungry, give him bread to eat;
And if he is thirsty, give him water to drink;

²² For *so* you will heap coals of fire on his head,
And the LORD will reward you.

²³ The north wind brings forth rain,
And a backbiting tongue an angry
countenance.

²⁴ *It is* better to dwell in a corner of a housetop,
Than in a house shared with a contentious
woman.

²⁵ *As* cold water to a weary soul,
So *is* good news from a far country.

²⁶ A righteous *man* who falters before the wicked
Is like a murky spring and a polluted well.

²⁷ *It is* not good to eat much honey;
So to seek one's own glory *is not* glory.

²⁸ Whoever *has* no rule over his own spirit
Is like a city broken down, without walls.

Everyone has wounds and scars caused by someone else's hurtful actions or words. Whether it was a lie, betrayal, rejection, insult, or abuse, the pain is real and can cause deep wounds.

It can be difficult to overcome this type of hurt. I bet while reading these verses you were able to reflect on pain in your own life and the specific person or situation that caused it. Human nature wants to hold on to the grudge.

In Romans 12:20, we see the apostle Paul quoting this proverb about how we deal with our enemies. Paul instructs us not to seek revenge but to trust God to avenge any wrongdoing. Heaping coals of fire on our enemies' heads sounds good to us, but the picture in the Eastern culture is quite different from what we imagine. People carried things on their heads—buckets of water, fruit, etc.—so to the Eastern mind, heaping coals on someone's head would mean to provide some type of food, water, or shelter. To do this for an enemy would actually indicate a blessing for them. It would also indicate forgiveness.

Jesus put a new twist on relationships. He said that our relationship with God hinges on our relationships with other people.

Steve Flockhart, New Season Church
Hiram, GA

NOVEMBER 8

Honor Is Not Fitting for a Fool

Proverbs 26:1–12

AS snow in summer and rain in harvest,
So honor is not fitting for a fool.

2 Like a flitting sparrow, like a flying swallow,
So a curse without cause shall not alight.

3 A whip for the horse,
A bridle for the donkey,
And a rod for the fool's back.

4 Do not answer a fool according to his folly,
Lest you also be like him.

5 Answer a fool according to his folly,
Lest he be wise in his own eyes.

6 He who sends a message by the hand of a fool
Cuts off *his own* feet *and* drinks violence.

7 *Like* the legs of the lame that hang limp
Is a proverb in the mouth of fools.

8 Like one who binds a stone in a sling
Is he who gives honor to a fool.

9 *Like* a thorn *that* goes into the hand of a
drunkard
Is a proverb in the mouth of fools.

10 The great *God* who formed everything
Gives the fool *his* hire and the transgressor *his*
wages.

11 As a dog returns to his own vomit,
So a fool repeats his folly.

12 Do you see a man wise in his own eyes?
There is more hope for a fool than for him.

Have you ever met a person who is extremely stubborn and close-minded? Perhaps he or she is a rebel and will not follow the advice of anyone. This person does not seem to care about anyone else and does not consider the consequences of the actions that he or she takes. The same behavior and the same bad choices are made repeatedly with no effort or desire to change. Solomon calls this type of person a fool. These kinds of people do not admit when they are wrong, and it is a waste of time to attempt to rationalize with them.

We all make foolish choices and bad decisions. We all have acted like a fool at some point. The question today is, how can I learn to be wise and not be drawn to make foolish decisions? Jesus tells us in the Beatitudes that a foolish person builds his life on the sand (Matt. 7:24–27). There is no honor, no blessing, and no reward for the fool.

Steve Flockhart, New Season Church
Hiram, GA

NOVEMBER 9

Laziness Is Not an Option

Proverbs 26:13–19

¹³ The lazy *man* says, "*There is* a lion in the road!
A fierce lion *is* in the streets!"

¹⁴ *As* a door turns on its hinges,
So *does* the lazy *man* on his bed.

¹⁵ The lazy *man* buries his hand in the bowl;
It wearies him to bring it back to his mouth.

¹⁶ The lazy *man is* wiser in his own eyes
Than seven men who can answer sensibly.

¹⁷ He who passes by *and* meddles in a quarrel
not his own
Is like one who takes a dog by the ears.

¹⁸ Like a madman who throws firebrands,
arrows, and death,

¹⁹ *Is* the man *who* deceives his neighbor,
And says, "I was only joking!"

DEVOTIONAL

You may love the gym. You enjoy working out, pumping iron, walking on the treadmill, and staying fit. I do not enjoy these things. Whenever I feel the need to exercise, I lie down until that feeling passes! I have several reasons why I do not go to the gym. I have used these excuses for so long that I have started to believe them myself. I am sure you have heard your fair share of excuses, and you have probably come up with a few yourself.

This proverb tells us that this lazy person was afraid there was a lion roaming the streets. Do lions normally run down streets in a busy city? This guy is so lazy he won't even lift his food on a fork from his plate to his mouth. The lazy person has made excuses for so long that he now believes them. We all know lazy people who will not work and will not take care of their families. They allow their homes, cars, and even their lives to go without proper maintenance.

Are you lazy? Before you answer that too quickly, what about spiritual laziness? Do you read God's Word every day? Do you have a prayer time? Does your daily life reflect intimacy with God or have you been making excuses? Laziness cannot be an option!

Steve Flockhart, New Season Church
Hiram, GA

NOVEMBER 10

The Consequences of Wicked Words

Proverbs 26:20–28

²⁰ Where *there is* no wood, the fire goes out;
And where *there is* no talebearer, strife ceases.
²¹ *As* charcoal *is* to burning coals, and wood to fire,
So *is* a contentious man to kindle strife.
²² The words of a talebearer *are* like tasty trifles,
And they go down into the inmost body.
²³ Fervent lips with a wicked heart
Are like earthenware covered with silver dross.
²⁴ He who hates, disguises *it* with his lips,
And lays up deceit within himself;
²⁵ When he speaks kindly, do not believe him,
For *there are* seven abominations in his heart;
²⁶ *Though his* hatred is covered by deceit,
His wickedness will be revealed before the assembly.
²⁷ Whoever digs a pit will fall into it,
And he who rolls a stone will have it roll back on him.
²⁸ A lying tongue hates *those who are* crushed by it,
And a flattering mouth works ruin.

DEVOTIONAL

My wife has a sweet tooth. She loves any type of sweets, but especially anything chocolate. She bakes many delicious desserts, but her cookies are my favorite, specifically peanut butter cookies. Before I know it, I find myself enjoying those warm, delicious, "melt in your mouth" peanut butter cookies. I just cannot stop at one; I know I should, but I can't. I tell myself to eat one cookie, and eight cookies later, I finally stop. Even with the knowledge that these cookies are not good for me, the temptation overcomes me.

Gossip is like these delicious cookies that are so tempting. It is hard not to listen when someone starts sharing, and before you know it, you have repeated what you heard to someone else. It is hard to turn down "one more" cookie. In the same way, gossip offers one more "delicious tidbit" of a rumor or malicious chatter.

A person's character is revealed by what he or she says. Jesus tells us in Matthew 12:34–37 that words reveal your heart. The heart is the major issue in what you share. From the heart, wicked words overflow, which results in a miserable life for you and the people on the receiving end of your words.

Steve Flockhart, New Season Church
Hiram, GA

 # November 11

The book of Proverbs is a combination of bullet points or one-line sermons that get directly to the point. Paraphrase a proverb from this week in your own words.

Wisdom is the art of living skillfully. What areas of your life have you been challenged to live more skillfully?

NOVEMBER 12

My Son, Be Wise

Proverbs 27:1–9

DO not boast about tomorrow,
For you do not know what a day may bring
forth.

2 Let another man praise you, and not your own
mouth;
A stranger, and not your own lips.

3 A stone *is* heavy and sand *is* weighty,
But a fool's wrath *is* heavier than both of them.

4 Wrath *is* cruel and anger a torrent,
But who *is* able to stand before jealousy?

5 Open rebuke *is* better
Than love carefully concealed.

6 Faithful *are* the wounds of a friend,
But the kisses of an enemy *are* deceitful.

7 A satisfied soul loathes the honeycomb,
But to a hungry soul every bitter thing *is*
sweet.

8 Like a bird that wanders from its nest
Is a man who wanders from his place.

9 Ointment and perfume delight the heart,
And the sweetness of a man's friend *gives
delight* by hearty counsel.

DEVOTIONAL

One of the most difficult things in life is finding your place. I speak to a lot of young people each year about the importance of making wise choices. I often tell them there are three crucial decisions everyone must make. (1) Choose Jesus or you will go to hell. (2) Choose the right spouse or you will feel like your living in it. (3) Choose carefully what you will do for a living because you will spend a significant part of your life in your vocation. If you have a passionate desire to do what you do, it will not feel like work.

Making these important life choices starts with realizing you are a sinner in desperate need of a Savior and accepting that Jesus is who He says He is: the way, the truth, and the life. Choose Jesus and choose to live your life for Him. Then marry the one you love and love the person he or she becomes. Give yourself completely to that person and make every effort to grow together.

Lastly, do what you are gifted by God to do. Identify your gift set. When I was in grade school, I had to write, "I will not talk in class" thousands of times. Ironically, now speaking is my vocation, profession, and calling. I'm a preacher. You could have identified my gift set as a child. I love what I do. I was created by God in my mother's womb to be an evangelist.

You have a gift set and a purpose too. You will never be fulfilled or complete until you fill that God-sized void in your heart with a right relationship with Jesus and use your gifts for God's glory. Do what you do with passion, desire, and confidence. Be busy about the Father's business. You will be a blessing to others and you will be blessed. True wisdom comes from trusting in the Lord daily and allowing Him to guide your steps.

*Brian Fossett, Fossett Evangelistic Ministries
Dalton, GA*

NOVEMBER 13

Iron Sharpens Iron

Proverbs 27:10–17

10 Do not forsake your own friend or your
father's friend,
Nor go to your brother's house in the day of
your calamity;
Better *is* a neighbor nearby than a brother far
away.

11 My son, be wise, and make my heart glad,
That I may answer him who reproaches me.

12 A prudent *man* foresees evil *and* hides himself;
The simple pass on *and* are punished.

13 Take the garment of him who is surety for a
stranger,
And hold it in pledge *when* he is surety for a
seductress.

14 He who blesses his friend with a loud voice,
rising early in the morning,
It will be counted a curse to him.

15 A continual dripping on a very rainy day
And a contentious woman are alike;

16 Whoever restrains her restrains the wind,
And grasps oil with his right hand.

17 *As* iron sharpens iron,
So a man sharpens the countenance of his
friend.

DEVOTIONAL

One of the most dangerous places to be is the
back door of an average American church
on Sunday morning at noon. It often looks like a
stampede. However, I have observed that healthy
churches have members who like to linger. They
desire fellowship with one another.

One of the greatest gifts we have in this life is
our relationships. We learn, grow, and become better by mirroring the strengths we admire or desire
in others; or we notice weaknesses in others, see
them in ourselves, and try to change ourselves.

One of the most dangerous things you can
ever do is become disconnected or isolated. No
man is an island. You become lonely and bitter
alone. You become unfriendly and unhealthy. Be
proactive in making relationships. Be a people
person. Most people respond to you in a positive
manner after you initiate with a smile, greeting, or
handshake. Be approachable. Be in the room and
in the moment. Be sensitive to the opportunities
for relationships and new friendships all around
you and nurture those relationships. Treat others
like you want to be treated. Speak encouragement,
kindness, and love into all of those around you. Be
genuinely complimentary and liberal with praise.

Every year our family makes resolutions. Last
year I said I want to be a better listener. My middle
daughter said, "Dad, that has been your resolution
for the last three years." I said, "Honey, God's not
through with me. He is still working on all of us."

We grow from all of our relationships. Be
involved; get connected; build relationships; make
new friends. We draw strength from one another.
Seek to spend time with people of strong character as they will make you stronger.

Brian Fossett, Fossett Evangelistic Ministries
Dalton, GA

NOVEMBER 14

Know Your Responsibilities

Proverbs 27:18–27

¹⁸ Whoever keeps the fig tree will eat its fruit;
So he who waits on his master will be
honored.

¹⁹ As in water face *reflects* face,
So a man's heart *reveals* the man.

²⁰ Hell and Destruction are never full;
So the eyes of man are never satisfied.

²¹ The refining pot *is* for silver and the furnace
for gold,
And a man *is valued* by what others say of him.

²² Though you grind a fool in a mortar with a
pestle along with crushed grain,
Yet his foolishness will not depart from him.

²³ Be diligent to know the state of your flocks,
And attend to your herds;

²⁴ For riches *are* not forever,
Nor does a crown *endure* to all generations.

²⁵ *When* the hay is removed, and the tender grass
shows itself,
And the herbs of the mountains are gathered
in,

²⁶ The lambs *will provide* your clothing,
And the goats the price of a field;

²⁷ *You shall have* enough goats' milk for your
food,
For the food of your household,
And the nourishment of your maidservants.

DEVOTIONAL

The mantra of my church, Salem Baptist in Dalton, Georgia, is "Others." That is one of the main things that attracted our family there. I have always had the goal in my personal life that others would say, "I am a better person for Brian Fossett having walked through my life." I have not always achieved that goal, but I truly desire to add value to people's lives. We should invest our time, talent, and treasure in others.

One thing our American culture has bred is a strong emphasis on self. I do believe you should be the best you can possibly be, spiritually, physically, and emotionally. However, you should not become selfish, self-centered, or stingy. You are never happier than when you are giving to others of your time, talent, or treasure. Most are far more excited when giving a gift than receiving one. Whether it be serving in your church, volunteering in your community, or giving to a family in need, you will be blessed when you bless others. God never ministers through you without ministering to you. Today, commit to making a difference to the others in your life.

Brian Fossett, Fossett Evangelistic Ministries
Dalton, GA

NOVEMBER 15

The Righteous Are Bold as a Lion

Proverbs 28:1–9

T HE wicked flee when no one pursues,
  But the righteous are bold as a lion.

2 Because of the transgression of a land, many
    are its princes;
  But by a man of understanding *and* knowledge
  Right will be prolonged.

3 A poor man who oppresses the poor
  Is like a driving rain which leaves no food.

4 Those who forsake the law praise the wicked,
  But such as keep the law contend with them.

5 Evil men do not understand justice,
  But those who seek the LORD understand all.

6 Better *is* the poor who walks in his integrity
  Than one perverse *in his* ways, though he
    be rich.

7 Whoever keeps the law *is* a discerning son,
  But a companion of gluttons shames his
    father.

8 One who increases his possessions by usury
    and extortion
  Gathers it for him who will pity the poor.

9 One who turns away his ear from hearing
    the law,
  Even his prayer *is* an abomination.

DEVOTIONAL

O ne of the things the church is missing today is boldness. We have become timid. We are afraid of others thinking we are too zealous. I have always admired dreamers and visionaries, people with courage, boldness, and conviction.

God tells us without vision, people perish. Families, churches, and businesses need bold leaders with vision. My simplest definition of vision is "boldness of mind." God created us to be creative. We should think outside the box. We need to clearly get a word from God; then we need to be strong, consistent, and steadfast in building and fleshing out that vision. God did not call us to quit. We are not going to get to heaven and get extra credit for being apathetic or boring. The reason others are critical of you for being on fire for the Lord and "bold as a lion" (v. 1) is because it exposes their backslidden condition.

We need to be bold in action as well as in speech. Pray bold and live bold! If we seek to be more like Jesus, we should be bold for Jesus. He is the Lion of Judah! I have never heard of anyone leaving a church because of it was too on fire for Jesus. One day I asked my wife, "Do you know why you married me?" She replied, "No, why?" I said, "Because you knew life would never be boring." Live BOLD!

Brian Fossett, Fossett Evangelistic Ministries
Dalton, GA

NOVEMBER 16

The Pitfall of Evil

Proverbs 28:10–19

10 Whoever causes the upright to go astray in an evil way,
He himself will fall into his own pit;
But the blameless will inherit good.

11 The rich man *is* wise in his own eyes,
But the poor who has understanding searches him out.

12 When the righteous rejoice, *there is* great glory;
But when the wicked arise, men hide themselves.

13 He who covers his sins will not prosper,
But whoever confesses and forsakes *them* will have mercy.

14 Happy *is* the man who is always reverent,
But he who hardens his heart will fall into calamity.

15 *Like* a roaring lion and a charging bear
Is a wicked ruler over poor people.

16 A ruler who lacks understanding *is* a great oppressor,
But he who hates covetousness will prolong *his* days.

17 A man burdened with bloodshed will flee into a pit;
Let no one help him.

18 Whoever walks blamelessly will be saved,
But *he who is* perverse *in his* ways will suddenly fall.

19 He who tills his land will have plenty of bread,
But he who follows frivolity will have poverty enough!

DEVOTIONAL

Sometimes the Lord marks or sears something into your memory. I remember one such time during a church revival. There was a certain young man in attendance who had been in an accident that left him with some lasting effects of brain trauma. On the last night, I noticed the young man sitting on the front row barefooted. I pointed to his feet and said, "What's up?" He said he was on holy ground.

I began to feel convicted as the as the choir sang the song "We Are Standing on Holy Ground." He fervently looked through his Bible until he found the story of Moses standing on holy ground. He pointed to my shoes and said, "We are on holy ground." I said, "I'm with you." He bent over and said, "If you were really with me, you'd take off your shoes."

I fell under such great conviction, and the Lord reminded me it would be better to have a millstone tied around my neck and to be thrown into the deepest sea than to cause one of these little ones to struggle. I said, "Lord, I want to be obedient. If You want me to preach barefooted in a suit and tie, I will." The pressure was on. I was being introduced. I stood up and asked the church to wait while I unlaced my shoes. I explained to them that I did not want to be disrespectful but obedient.

The Lord richly blessed that night. Many were saved. Sometimes the Lord will take us out of our comfort zone in order to keep our hearts tender. But we must be sensitive to His Spirit.

Brian Fossett, Fossett Evangelistic Ministries
Dalton, GA

NOVEMBER 17

Choose Your Words Carefully

Proverbs 28:20–28

20 A faithful man will abound with blessings,
But he who hastens to be rich will not go
     unpunished.

21 To show partiality *is* not good,
Because for a piece of bread a man will
     transgress.

22 A man with an evil eye hastens after riches,
And does not consider that poverty will come
     upon him.

23 He who rebukes a man will find more favor
     afterward
Than he who flatters with the tongue.

24 Whoever robs his father or his mother,
And says, "*It is* no transgression,"
The same *is* companion to a destroyer.

25 He who is of a proud heart stirs up strife,
But he who trusts in the LORD will be
     prospered.

26 He who trusts in his own heart is a fool,
But whoever walks wisely will be delivered.

27 He who gives to the poor will not lack,
But he who hides his eyes will have many
     curses.

28 When the wicked arise, men hide themselves;
But when they perish, the righteous increase.

DEVOTIONAL

Words matter. Words can build up or tear down. Everyone has heard the old saying "Sticks and stones can break my bones, but words will never hurt me." The truth is, they can. Words matter. Words can encourage. I have a cousin, Brett Yaeger, who always told me when we were growing up, "You're a winner!" That always meant so much to me. Words matter. We need to let our "yes" be "yes" and our "no" be "no." The greatest word some never learn is *no*. Remember, it is better to over-deliver than to over-commit. Words matter. Think about the magnitude of commitment in the two little words *I do* at a wedding ceremony.

I have always told my family that I love them often. One day, when my middle daughter was five, I shouted through the house, "Kenzey, come here." A few moments later she appeared around the corner, hands on her hips, and said, "I know, Dad. You love me!" I still laugh to this day thinking about it, but I would rather tell them ad nauseam than for them to never be able to remember those important words from me. Words matter.

Brian Fossett, Fossett Evangelistic Ministries
Dalton, GA

NOVEMBER 18

What are you doing to bless others with this wonderful gift of life God has given you?

If today was the last day you had on earth before meeting Jesus face-to-face, how would you spend it?

NOVEMBER 19

Happy Is He Who Keeps the Law

Proverbs 29:1–9

HE who is often rebuked, *and* hardens *his* neck,

Will suddenly be destroyed, and that without remedy.

2 When the righteous are in authority, the people rejoice;
But when a wicked *man* rules, the people groan.

3 Whoever loves wisdom makes his father rejoice,
But a companion of harlots wastes *his* wealth.

4 The king establishes the land by justice,
But he who receives bribes overthrows it.

5 A man who flatters his neighbor
Spreads a net for his feet.

6 By transgression an evil man is snared,
But the righteous sings and rejoices.

7 The righteous considers the cause of the poor,
But the wicked does not understand *such* knowledge.

8 Scoffers set a city aflame,
But wise *men* turn away wrath.

9 *If* a wise man contends with a foolish man,
Whether *the fool* rages or laughs, *there is* no peace.

DEVOTIONAL

Is he coachable?" This seemed like an odd question for our head coach to ask. I was serving as a graduate assistant football coach, and we were watching video of a high-school recruit. This recruit was an exceptional athlete and had proven himself adequate in the classroom. It was a joy to watch him make tackles that no one else on his team could make. He was a great combination of size and speed. He could cover sideline to sideline and take on blockers yet still make the play. There was, however, one issue with this player. Because of his tremendous ability, there were times when he was not disciplined in his techniques and would get out of position. He thought his athletic ability could make up for his poor technique. The coach knew that once this player was at the college level with players who were just as fast and strong as he was, it would be imperative for him to allow coaches to speak into his life and then be able to carry out the proper techniques that were taught. Would he be a coachable athlete?

Verse 1 says it is possible to harden your neck when someone rebukes you. If we harden our hearts when someone loves us enough to show us our error based on God's Word, we are heading for destruction. We must ask ourselves if we are allowing others to confront us with God's precepts and if we are willing to confess and repent when we need to. We must ask ourselves, are we coachable?

Dr. Marty Jacumin, Bay Leaf Baptist Church
Raleigh, NC

NOVEMBER 20

Every Child Needs Correction

Proverbs 29:10–17

¹⁰ The bloodthirsty hate the blameless,
But the upright seek his well-being.

¹¹ A fool vents all his feelings,
But a wise *man* holds them back.

¹² If a ruler pays attention to lies,
All his servants *become* wicked.

¹³ The poor *man* and the oppressor have this
in common:
The LORD gives light to the eyes of both.

¹⁴ The king who judges the poor with truth,
His throne will be established forever.

¹⁵ The rod and rebuke give wisdom,
But a child left *to himself* brings shame to his
mother.

¹⁶ When the wicked are multiplied, transgression
increases;
But the righteous will see their fall.

¹⁷ Correct your son, and he will give you rest;
Yes, he will give delight to your soul.

DEVOTIONAL

I've heard it said that our lives are the loudest sermons we will ever preach. This simply means that people will not only hear our words but will also watch our lives. They desire to see if our lives match the words we proclaim. We must realize that because people are watching us, we are an example to them.

In the case of our text today, Solomon reminds parents that our children are watching us and we are to be an example to them. We must ask ourselves if we are being a good example or a bad example. Do they see in us a Christ-like attitude and devotion to our Savior? I've often heard it said that a child will not often accept God as their Father if they do not see their father following God. Solomon gives us several examples that we must set for our children.

First, we should seek to be peacemakers. He writes that the bloodthirsty hate the blameless. Are we modeling a respect and Christ-like love for those around us? Second, he writes that the fool vents his feelings, but a wise man holds them back. This is not comparing the introvert and the extrovert. It means that there are those who feel they must say everything that comes to mind no matter how it affects those around them.

Third, Solomon speaks to the discerning of truth. Are we seeking truth or are we seeking what is most beneficial for us? What are we modeling for our children? We read that when we rebuke and correct our children, they will give us rest. With this, we also must remember that they are watching our lives while we are teaching them. If we are bloodthirsty and consistently attack people, they will tend to do the same thing. If we can't control our tongues, they will not hear our words of self-discipline. If we ignore truth, they will do the same.

As we examine our witness to our children, are we a good example or a bad example of what it means to follow Jesus with a surrendered life?

Dr. Marty Jacumin, Bay Leaf Baptist Church
Raleigh, NC

November 21

There Is Safety in the Lord

Proverbs 29:18–27

¹⁸ Where *there is* no revelation, the people cast
off restraint;
But happy *is* he who keeps the law.

¹⁹ A servant will not be corrected by mere words;
For though he understands, he will not
respond.

²⁰ Do you see a man hasty in his words?
There is more hope for a fool than for him.

²¹ He who pampers his servant from childhood
Will have him as a son in the end.

²² An angry man stirs up strife,
And a furious man abounds in transgression.

²³ A man's pride will bring him low,
But the humble in spirit will retain honor.

²⁴ Whoever is a partner with a thief hates his
own life;
He swears to tell the truth, but reveals nothing.

²⁵ The fear of man brings a snare,
But whoever trusts in the LORD shall be safe.

²⁶ Many seek the ruler's favor,
But justice for man *comes* from the LORD.

²⁷ An unjust man *is* an abomination to the
righteous,
And *he who is* upright in the way *is* an abomination to the wicked.

DEVOTIONAL

Proverbs 29:18 may be one of the most mis-quoted verses in the Bible. It is often trans-lated this way, "Where there is no vision, the people perish." This is often used by leaders as they cast their vision for the group they are lead-ing. The problem with this is that it is possible to cast a vision that does not match God's will. Adolf Hitler was a man of vision and millions perished. Men like Jim Jones and David Koresh said they had "religious" visions, but many perished. I pre-fer the translation we read today, "Where there is no revelation," which refers to God's prophetic revelation. God has revealed Himself to us and makes His will for our lives known to us. He has given us His precepts that should guide our lives and set the direction that we will follow.

For leaders, God's will should always be the determining factor for how we lead the people entrusted to us. When we fail to lead according to God's Word, we and those who follow us are cast-ing off the restraints that God has laid out for us.

We are fallen humans and must realize that we are capable of wickedness. We are also capable of leading others according to our own pride and greed. Let's make sure we are seeking to live and lead others according to God's Word by making sure His vision is the vision we are casting for our-selves and others.

Dr. Marty Jacumin, Bay Leaf Baptist Church
Raleigh, NC

NOVEMBER 22

The Wisdom of Agur

Proverbs 30:1–10

T HE words of Agur the son of Jakeh, *his* utterance. This man declared to Ithiel—to Ithiel and Ucal:

2 Surely I *am* more stupid than *any* man,
And do not have the understanding of a man.

3 I neither learned wisdom
Nor have knowledge of the Holy One.

4 Who has ascended into heaven, or descended?
Who has gathered the wind in His fists?
Who has bound the waters in a garment?
Who has established all the ends of the earth?
What *is* His name, and what *is* His Son's name,
If you know?

5 Every word of God *is* pure;
He *is* a shield to those who put their
trust in Him.

6 Do not add to His words,
Lest He rebuke you, and you be found a liar.

7 Two *things* I request of You
(Deprive me not before I die):

8 Remove falsehood and lies far from me;
Give me neither poverty nor riches—
Feed me with the food allotted to me;

9 Lest I be full and deny *You*,
And say, "Who *is* the LORD?"
Or lest I be poor and steal,
And profane the name of my God.

10 Do not malign a servant to his master,
Lest he curse you, and you be found guilty.

DEVOTIONAL

L et's think back for a moment. Can you remember going to vacation Bible school as a child? I can remember the games we played and the best peanut butter crackers in the world! I can also remember a song I was taught. The song said, "The B-I-B-L-E, yes, that's the book for me. I stand alone on the Word of God, the B-I-B-L-E." What a simple yet profound song.

We should allow the Word of God to guide every area of our lives. We should stand not only on its promises but also on its principles. Solomon speaks to this in verse 5 when he writes, "Every word of God is pure." It is pure and perfect, and it will guide us to the place God would have us be. He goes on to say that this will protect us if we follow it. God does not give us His Word to hurt us but to protect us, because He knows what each of us needs in our lives.

In verse 6, He goes on to say that we must not add to God's Word. We see a similar warning in Revelation 22:19. God's Word is perfect, and it will perfectly guide our lives if we allow it to. Let's never be one to say, "I know what the Word of God says, but . . ." There is simply no way to recover from that statement in a way that honors God. Let's always say that we will live by the principles of God's Word. It is the B-I-B-L-E, and it is the book for God's children. We must stand upon the Word of God.

Dr. Marty Jacumin, Bay Leaf Baptist Church
Raleigh, NC

NOVEMBER 23

The Selfish Ways of Man

Proverbs 30:11–19

¹¹ *There is* a generation *that* curses its father,
And does not bless its mother.

¹² There is a generation *that is* pure in its own eyes,
Yet is not washed from its filthiness.

¹³ *There is* a generation—oh, how lofty are their
eyes!
And their eyelids are lifted up.

¹⁴ *There is* a generation whose teeth *are like* swords,
And whose fangs *are like* knives,
To devour the poor from off the earth,
And the needy from *among* men.

¹⁵ The leech has two daughters—
Give *and* Give!

There are three *things that* are never satisfied,
Four never say, "Enough!":

¹⁶ The grave,
The barren womb,
The earth *that* is not satisfied with water—
And the fire never says, "Enough!"

¹⁷ The eye *that* mocks *his* father,
And scorns obedience to *his* mother,
The ravens of the valley will pick it out,
And the young eagles will eat it.

¹⁸ There are three *things which* are too wonderful
for me,
Yes, four *which* I do not understand:

¹⁹ The way of an eagle in the air,
The way of a serpent on a rock,
The way of a ship in the midst of the sea,
And the way of a man with a virgin.

DEVOTIONAL

Our text for today tells us there is a generation that is sinful. It describes this generation as one that refuses to honor parents and repent of filthiness. It goes on to say this generation is terribly prideful. It also says they are greedy and seek to destroy people with their words. Let's face it, this is a terrible generation of individuals.

As you read this, what is your initial thought about this generation? Did you begin pointing to a different generation other than the one you are part of? As you read this text, do you look to the younger people and blame them for the changes that are occurring in your church? Were you quick to think of the older folks, perhaps for resisting change? It is interesting that Solomon does not reveal a specific generation here, but it is good for us that he doesn't. Every generation must deal with sin, because every generation is made up of fallen human beings. From the fall of man, every generation has dealt with pride and greed. They have struggled with honoring their parents and taming the tongue.

Let's begin by looking at our own sin before we point to anyone else. Let's examine our own lives and determine if there is sin we need to repent of. Many churches struggle with generational conflicts. These conflicts have centered around music, dress, church governance, and many other things. Perhaps this text can remind us that each generation has its problems, and we need to examine our own lives before we are too quick to point fingers at others.

Dr. Marty Jacumin, Bay Leaf Baptist Church
Raleigh, NC

NOVEMBER 24

Small in Size, Great in Behavior

Proverbs 30:20–33

20 This *is* the way of an adulterous woman:
She eats and wipes her mouth,
And says, "I have done no wickedness."

21 For three *things* the earth is perturbed,
Yes, for four it cannot bear up:

22 For a servant when he reigns,
A fool when he is filled with food,

23 A hateful *woman* when she is married,
And a maidservant who succeeds her
    mistress.

24 There are four *things which* are little on
    the earth,
But they *are* exceedingly wise:

25 The ants *are* a people not strong,
Yet they prepare their food in the summer;

26 The rock badgers are a feeble folk,
Yet they make their homes in the crags;

27 The locusts have no king,
Yet they all advance in ranks;

28 The spider skillfully grasps with its hands,
And it is in kings' palaces.

29 There are three *things which* are majestic
    in pace,
Yes, four *which* are stately in walk:

30 A lion, *which is* mighty among beasts
And does not turn away from any;

31 A greyhound,
A male goat also,
And a king *whose* troops *are* with him.

32 If you have been foolish in exalting yourself,
Or if you have devised evil, *put your* hand on
    your mouth.

33 For *as* the churning of milk produces butter,
And wringing the nose produces blood,
So the forcing of wrath produces strife.

DEVOTIONAL

How do you feel about the lost? Let's ask a deeper question. How do you feel about the militantly lost, such as ardent atheists or radical Muslims? As believers, we must be careful not to turn our mission field into the enemy. Our text today tells us there are things that perturb us. This word means "to make anxious." One of the examples given is when the servant becomes the ruler. A poor person who feels they have been mistreated or ignored suddenly comes to power or receives wealth and becomes overbearing and cruel. They can also fail to have compassion on the people they once associated with.

Now, back to our question about the lost. Believers must be quick to remember that we were lost and helpless to do anything about it apart from the grace of God. The Bible says that we were enemies of God. We must remember this when we look at the lost. Let's not look to them with anger or contempt, but with a broken heart, knowing we were once in their place. Let our broken hearts move us to share Jesus with them and show the love, mercy, and grace of God that has been shown to us. We were poor, but we are now rich in Christ Jesus.

Dr. Marty Jacumin, Bay Leaf Baptist Church
Raleigh, NC

NOVEMBER 25

Am I allowing others to take God's Word and hold me accountable to my words and actions? Am I coachable?

_____

_____

_____

_____

_____

_____

_____

_____

_____

_____

Are there any areas in my life that I have not surrendered to the authority of Jesus? Am I seeking to cast a vision that does not match God's desire for my life?

_____

_____

_____

_____

_____

_____

_____

_____

_____

NOVEMBER 26

The Words of King Lemuel's Mother

Proverbs 31:1–9

THE words of King Lemuel, the utterance which his mother taught him:

2 What, my son?
And what, son of my womb?
And what, son of my vows?

3 Do not give your strength to women,
Nor your ways to that which destroys kings.

4 *It is* not for kings, O Lemuel,
It is not for kings to drink wine,
Nor for princes intoxicating drink;

5 Lest they drink and forget the law,
And pervert the justice of all the afflicted.

6 Give strong drink to him who is perishing,
And wine to those who are bitter of heart.

7 Let him drink and forget his poverty,
And remember his misery no more.

8 Open your mouth for the speechless,
In the cause of all *who are* appointed to die.

9 Open your mouth, judge righteously,
And plead the cause of the poor and needy.

DEVOTIONAL

The book of Proverbs begins with the wise words of a father and ends with the wise words of a mother. First and last, the home is the strong defense of the nation. As the home goes, so goes the nation.

Solomon's mother warns her son of women, wine, and song, but he did not heed her words. He had seven hundred wives and three hundred concubines.

As a leader, Solomon is encouraged to stay clear of alcohol. Solomon's mother, not unlike ours, desired to raise and influence a son who would one day serve as a godly king. The repetition of the appeal speaks of the seriousness of the mother's desires. If Solomon followed the commands of his parents, his life would be characterized by holiness, sobriety, and compassion. We would be wise to listen to all of the warnings as well. It's been said that we are all just "one decision from stupid."

As a footnote, the abuse of alcohol[1] should concern all of us when we pause to realize how it can affect our discernment, cause us to lose our convictions, and even pervert our hearts.

As one person put it, "Alcohol makes your brake fluid leak."

Dr. Johnny Hunt, First Baptist Church Woodstock
Woodstock, GA

NOVEMBER 27
The Virtuous Wife

Proverbs 31:10–19

10 Who can find a virtuous wife?
For her worth *is* far above rubies.

11 The heart of her husband safely trusts her;
So he will have no lack of gain.

12 She does him good and not evil
All the days of her life.

13 She seeks wool and flax,
And willingly works with her hands.

14 She is like the merchant ships,
She brings her food from afar.

15 She also rises while it is yet night,
And provides food for her household,
And a portion for her maidservants.

16 She considers a field and buys it;
From her profits she plants a vineyard.

17 She girds herself with strength,
And strengthens her arms.

18 She perceives that her merchandise *is* good,
And her lamp does not go out by night.

19 She stretches out her hands to the distaff,
And her hand holds the spindle.

DEVOTIONAL

This passage serves as the greatest text in the Scriptures on the treasure of a good wife. Her qualities are integrity and moral strength, along with preciousness. Ruth is the only woman in the Old Testament who is called a "virtuous woman," reminding us of the uniqueness of such quality (Ruth 3:11).

Solomon would have given a king's ransom for a woman like Ruth. As we reflect on the character of the woman Solomon's mother, Bathsheba, desired for her son, we find strong words such as "trust" and "no lack of gain" (v. 11). *Trust* is one of the strongest words in a relationship, if not the strongest. Destroy trust and you will work the rest of your marriage mending it. To have "no lack of gain" means she satisfied her husband's every need. He benefits from her and what she brings to the marriage.

You can't read this passage without seeing the loyalty. It involves respect, support, and being a helper and supporter. Most married men must acknowledge that their successes in life have been closely related to the environment and efforts of their wives. My wife worked during college and seminary in order to help me reach my God-given potential, and for that I am forever grateful.

All of the mentioned attributes of this godly woman are wrapped up in a heart of compassion.

Dr. Johnny Hunt, First Baptist Church Woodstock
Woodstock, GA

NOVEMBER 28

The Virtuous Wife (continued)

Proverbs 31:20–31

20 She extends her hand to the poor,
Yes, she reaches out her hands to the needy.

21 She is not afraid of snow for her household,
For all her household *is* clothed with scarlet.

22 She makes tapestry for herself;
Her clothing *is* fine linen and purple.

23 Her husband is known in the gates,
When he sits among the elders of the land.

24 She makes linen garments and sells *them,*
And supplies sashes for the merchants.

25 Strength and honor *are* her clothing;
She shall rejoice in time to come.

26 She opens her mouth with wisdom,
And on her tongue *is* the law of kindness.

27 She watches over the ways of her household,
And does not eat the bread of idleness.

28 Her children rise up and call her blessed;
Her husband *also,* and he praises her:

29 "Many daughters have done well,
But you excel them all."

30 Charm *is* deceitful and beauty *is* passing,
But a woman *who* fears the LORD, she shall be
praised.

31 Give her of the fruit of her hands,
And let her own works praise her in the gates.

DEVOTIONAL

A virtuous wife is to be commended for her work. The Bible speaks of her commitment, her caring, her consideration, her clothing, her confidence, and her conclusion. Words that describe the virtuous wife are *unselfish, generosity in spirit, provider,* and *strength.*

Her children never go without; she is respected by her husband, and she helps her children become successful. Her inner strength allows her children to live without fear of the future. This lady does not fear but, to the contrary, rejoices at the coming of the judgment seat of Christ.

Two words come to mind when I think of this proverb lady: *kind* and *compassionate.* Her wisdom runs on the rails of diligence. All who know her have hearts of gratitude for the unconditional benefits of her touch. Her children can still be heard shouting, "None better."

You have heard the phrase "beauty is only skin deep"; however, you will never be deceived by the proverb lady, for her qualities are genuine and unfeigned. She is the "real deal." Her wisdom is of high quality; James 3:17 calls it "pure." She reaps what she sows. If you know her, make sure that her contribution does not go unappreciated.

Dr. Johnny Hunt, First Baptist Church Woodstock
Woodstock, GA

NOVEMBER 29

The Problem of Wisdom

Ecclesiastes 1:1–11

THE words of the Preacher, the son of David, king in Jerusalem.

2 "Vanity of vanities," says the Preacher;
"Vanity of vanities, all *is* vanity."

3 What profit has a man from all his labor
In which he toils under the sun?

4 *One* generation passes away, and *another*
generation comes;
But the earth abides forever.

5 The sun also rises, and the sun goes down,
And hastens to the place where it arose.

6 The wind goes toward the south,
And turns around to the north;
The wind whirls about continually,
And comes again on its circuit.

7 All the rivers run into the sea,
Yet the sea *is* not full;
To the place from which the rivers come,
There they return again.

8 All things *are* full of labor;
Man cannot express *it*.
The eye is not satisfied with seeing,
Nor the ear filled with hearing.

9 That which has been *is* what will be,
That which *is* done is what will be done,
And *there is* nothing new under the sun.

10 Is there anything of which it may be said,
"See, this *is* new"?
It has already been in ancient times
before us.

11 *There is* no remembrance of former *things,*
Nor will there be any remembrance of *things*
that are to come
By *those* who will come after.

DEVOTIONAL

There's a theme that makes its way through the book of Ecclesiastes. From the human perspective, life seems so unbearably empty. Power, popularity, prestige, and pleasure: none can fill the God-shaped void in man's life but God Himself. When we can view life from God's perspective, life takes on meaning and purpose, causing Solomon to entreat us to eat, drink, rejoice, do good, live joyfully, fear God, and keep His commandments! Skepticism and despair melt away when life is viewed as a daily gift from God.

Solomon, the wisest man who ever lived, is contrasting a self-centered lifestyle, one of self-indulgence, with a God-centered life.

Hear the question as it shouts from the text, "Can purpose for life be found in nature, money, self-indulgence, property, position, intelligence, philosophy, or religious observance?" Solomon will quickly come to the conclusion at the end of his wealth and fame that life is empty and without purpose if it's without God.

Meaninglessness appears on every page of life. *There must be more*, one will ponder. The good news is: there is more. There's God, and we can know Him and His purpose for our journey. Futility of life can be replaced with the fullness of a Father's love.

Dr. Johnny Hunt, First Baptist Church Woodstock
Woodstock, GA

NOVEMBER 30
The Grief of Wisdom

Ecclesiastes 1:12–18

¹²I, the Preacher, was king over Israel in Jerusalem. ¹³And I set my heart to seek and search out by wisdom concerning all that is done under heaven; this burdensome task God has given to the sons of man, by which they may be exercised. ¹⁴I have seen all the works that are done under the sun; and indeed, all *is* vanity and grasping for the wind.

¹⁵ *What is* crooked cannot be made straight,
And what is lacking cannot be numbered.

¹⁶I communed with my heart, saying, "Look, I have attained greatness, and have gained more wisdom than all who were before me in Jerusalem. My heart has understood great wisdom and knowledge." ¹⁷And I set my heart to know wisdom and to know madness and folly. I perceived that this also is grasping for the wind.

¹⁸ For in much wisdom *is* much grief,
And he who increases knowledge increases sorrow.

DEVOTIONAL

Solomon, after looking around for answers in life, begins to look within. As king of Israel, he possesses all the resources necessary for experimenting with different solutions, to see what it is that makes life worth living. Solomon is interested in principles, not methods. Methods are many, principles are few; methods always change, principles never do. He had the "bucks" and the "brains"; no limitations, no reservations. Yet life seemed so meaningless.

- Life is tough (v. 13).
- Life doesn't get easier if you try to run away from it (v. 14).
- Not everything can be changed (v. 15).
- Wisdom and experience will not solve every problem (vv. 16–18).

He is about to find out that this side of eternity, there are not explanations for why some things happen. However, instead of being distraught, why not become dependent?

There's a song written by Scott Wesley Brown that says, "When answers aren't enough, there is Jesus."[1] It is a good reminder that we are to live by promises, not explanations. Many things in my life that I daily enjoy cannot be explained in my thinking.

The only way to find "real satisfaction" and relief from boredom is through a relationship with the living God.

Dr. Johnny Hunt, First Baptist Church Woodstock
Woodstock, GA

DECEMBER 1

Pleasure Is Vain

Ecclesiastes 2:1–11

I SAID in my heart, "Come now, I will test you with mirth; therefore enjoy pleasure"; but surely, this also *was* vanity. ²I said of laughter— "Madness!"; and of mirth, "What does it accomplish?" ³I searched in my heart *how* to gratify my flesh with wine, while guiding my heart with wisdom, and how to lay hold on folly, till I might see what *was* good for the sons of men to do under heaven all the days of their lives.

⁴I made my works great, I built myself houses, and planted myself vineyards. ⁵I made myself gardens and orchards, and I planted all *kinds* of fruit trees in them. ⁶I made myself water pools from which to water the growing trees of the grove. ⁷I acquired male and female servants, and had servants born in my house. Yes, I had greater possessions of herds and flocks than all who were in Jerusalem before me. ⁸I also gathered for myself silver and gold and the special treasures of kings and of the provinces. I acquired male and female singers, the delights of the sons of men, *and* musical instruments of all kinds.

⁹So I became great and excelled more than all who were before me in Jerusalem. Also my wisdom remained with me.

¹⁰ Whatever my eyes desired I did not keep from them.
I did not withhold my heart from any pleasure,
For my heart rejoiced in all my labor;
And this was my reward from all my labor.

¹¹ Then I looked on all the works that my hands had done
And on the labor in which I had toiled;
And indeed all *was* vanity and grasping for the wind.
There was no profit under the sun.

DEVOTIONAL

Ecclesiastes seems at times to be a recipe for trouble. You are invited to try something only to find that it does not provide what it promised. One could be very disillusioned very quickly. The theme could be "try it until you find something that works for you." If life is so short, let's see what will gratify the flesh while attempting to be guided in our hearts with wisdom.

A major lesson one should learn from the study of chapter 2 is what one really values. Human gratification must not attempt to triumph over the glory of God. Solomon would build, buy, or invent almost anything in order to provide himself with a spirit of happiness, only to find himself emptier than when he began. He concludes, "There was no profit under the sun" (v. 11).

Solomon has become a testament to all that one can gain the whole world and yet be no richer for it. It was as if he had attempted to grasp wind with his hand. What seemed possible, based on his wealth and wisdom, proved vain.

These words ring so true in this passage: "Take the world, but give me Jesus."²

Dr. Johnny Hunt, First Baptist Church Woodstock
Woodstock, GA

DECEMBER 2

What have you found in life that does not provide what it promises?

_____

_____

_____

_____

_____

_____

_____

_____

_____

_____

_____

Solomon found so many things to be plain vanity or empty. What did he grasp as having of lasting value?

_____

_____

_____

_____

_____

_____

_____

_____

_____

DECEMBER 3

The End of the Wise and the Fool

Ecclesiastes 2:12–16

12 Then I turned myself to consider wisdom and
madness and folly;
For what *can* the man *do* who succeeds the
king?—
Only what he has already done.
13 Then I saw that wisdom excels folly
As light excels darkness.
14 The wise man's eyes *are* in his head,
But the fool walks in darkness.
Yet I myself perceived
That the same event happens to them all.

15 So I said in my heart,
"As it happens to the fool,
It also happens to me,
And why was I then more wise?"
Then I said in my heart,
"This also *is* vanity."
16 For *there is* no more remembrance of the wise
than of the fool forever,
Since all that now *is* will be forgotten in the
days to come.
And how does a wise *man* die?
As the fool!

DEVOTIONAL

In his journal, Solomon writes of his elusive
search for meaning, purpose, significance, and
reality. After seeking all this in sex, drugs, alcohol,
and work, he then begins comparing wisdom with
foolishness. In his quest, he discovers that both
the wise and the foolish are going to end up in
death. Even the wisest of all is no better than the
fool without the source of true meaning.

Take the opportunity today to evaluate what
sources you may be turning to for peace, significance, and meaning. The world is offering a lot
of false advertisements with its claims to provide
happiness and peace. But when tried, they prove
to be less than adequate. Our culture says that you
have to attend the right school, to get the right
degree, to land the right job, to make the right sal-
ary, to live in the right house in the right neighborhood, to drive the right car, and on and on. Don't
misunderstand. Education is wonderful and is an
aspiring goal, but as Solomon so aptly notes, it
does not provide anything of eternal significance.

Solomon was an old man by the time he fig-
ured out that unless God initiates our steps and
grants us His peace, all our attempts to prosper
on our own are "vanity" or "grasping for the wind"
(Eccl. 2:17). A life lived without a God perspective
is meaningless.

Take a moment today and ask God to deliver
you from self-effort and enable you to seek Him
with all your heart above everything else.

Dr. Mike Whitson, First Baptist Church Indian Trail
Indian Trail, NC

DECEMBER 4
What Has Man for All His Labor

Ecclesiastes 2:17–26

¹⁷Therefore I hated life because the work that was done under the sun *was* distressing to me, for all *is* vanity and grasping for the wind.

¹⁸Then I hated all my labor in which I had toiled under the sun, because I must leave it to the man who will come after me. ¹⁹And who knows whether he will be wise or a fool? Yet he will rule over all my labor in which I toiled and in which I have shown myself wise under the sun. This also *is* vanity. ²⁰Therefore I turned my heart and despaired of all the labor in which I had toiled under the sun. ²¹For there is a man whose labor *is* with wisdom, knowledge, and skill; yet he must leave his heritage to a man who has not labored for it. This also *is* vanity and a great evil. ²²For what has man for all his labor, and for the striving of his heart with which he has toiled under the sun? ²³For all his days *are* sorrowful, and his work burdensome; even in the night his heart takes no rest. This also is vanity.

²⁴Nothing *is* better for a man *than* that he should eat and drink, and *that* his soul should enjoy good in his labor. This also, I saw, was from the hand of God. ²⁵For who can eat, or who can have enjoyment, more than I? ²⁶For *God* gives wisdom and knowledge and joy to a man who *is* good in His sight; but to the sinner He gives the work of gathering and collecting, that he may give to *him who is* good before God. This also *is* vanity and grasping for the wind.

DEVOTIONAL

Today, Solomon is looking back over his accomplishments: the toys and games, status, wine, women, and song. As he sums up his findings, you can hear the cynicism in his voice. Without being too judgmental, because we have all expressed the same, let's look at his conclusions. He hates life. He hates the things that his work allowed him to accumulate. His heirs are going to wind up with everything and they don't deserve it, and all of it just produces more and more stress.

We all experience this, don't we? We try not to bring our jobs home, but our minds won't shut down. We rehash the politics of work, and we obsess over a comment someone made that day, then jump out of bed and declare, "I can't sleep!" One only needs to know the fact that over 300 million prescriptions were written last year for anxiety to see the evidence of our unrest.

Solomon is saying when you live life without a God perspective, life "under the sun" (v. 17), it is going to be the pits. You see, a life that is lived without Christ and His Love and compassion is a life that has no meaning whatsoever.

Verse 24 says that we should enjoy what we do. When Christ is first in our lives, everything else falls into place. Therefore we can go to work today, smile, and say, "Glory to God, I am glad to be here. It is a wonderful day to serve the Lord." How? Because you are doing it for Him.

Dr. Mike Whitson, First Baptist Church Indian Trail
Indian Trail, NC

DECEMBER 5

Everything Has Its Time

Ecclesiastes 3:1–8

T O everything *there is* a season,
A time for every purpose under heaven:

2   A time to be born,
     And a time to die;
   A time to plant,
     And a time to pluck *what is* planted;

3   A time to kill,
     And a time to heal;
   A time to break down,
     And a time to build up;

4   A time to weep,
     And a time to laugh;
   A time to mourn,
     And a time to dance;

5   A time to cast away stones,
     And a time to gather stones;
   A time to embrace,
     And a time to refrain from embracing;

6   A time to gain,
     And a time to lose;
   A time to keep,
     And a time to throw away;

7   A time to tear,
     And a time to sew;
   A time to keep silence,
     And a time to speak;

8   A time to love,
     And a time to hate;
   A time of war,
     And a time of peace.

U p to this point in Ecclesiastes, Solomon has described what life was like "under the sun," without a God perspective. Today he changes gears and talks about life from a heavenly perspective. The passage pictures the sovereignty of God and how He has provided a time for everything to happen under heaven. Solomon is simply expressing his faith in God's mighty power.

There are at least fourteen contrasts in this section of Scripture that are described as "purposes under heaven" orchestrated by God (v. 1). Sometimes we have difficulty making sense of these different events as they arise in our lives. The reason is we often look through the natural eyes, hear through natural hearing, and process those events from a human perspective rather than by faith and a heavenly point of view.

Whatever contrast of life you are facing today, whether it is celebrating a birth or grieving a loss, remember that God is still in control. He has not abdicated the throne no matter what change has confronted you. God has promised in His Word that He will inevitably maneuver the confrontations of life to produce something good for us in our lives as we love Him and trust Him. So as the seconds of the day tick away in your life, regardless of the circumstances, stay focused on the One who has orchestrated and controls it all.

Dr. Mike Whitson, First Baptist Church Indian Trail
Indian Trail, NC

DECEMBER 6

The God-Given Task

Ecclesiastes 3:9–15

⁹What profit has the worker from that in which he labors? ¹⁰I have seen the God-given task with which the sons of men are to be occupied. ¹¹He has made everything beautiful in its time. Also He has put eternity in their hearts, except that no one can find out the work that God does from beginning to end.

¹²I know that nothing *is* better for them than to rejoice, and to do good in their lives, ¹³and also that every man should eat and drink and enjoy the good of all his labor—it *is* the gift of God.

¹⁴ I know that whatever God does,
It shall be forever.
Nothing can be added to it,
And nothing taken from it.
God does *it,* that men should fear before Him.
¹⁵ That which is has already been,
And what is to be has already been;
And God requires an account of what is past.

DEVOTIONAL

There is a place on the highway at the foot of the Blue Ridge Mountains where I used to stop my car, put it out of gear, and it would appear that the car was rolling uphill. From my perspective, though, the car should have rolled in the other direction.

I suspect that many of you are facing some very difficult issues in your life at this present moment. Maybe your children seem to be in a state of rebellion, you're jobless, or there is too much month at the end of the money. Solomon tells us in verse 11 that God is going to make "everything beautiful in its time."

An evangelist friend of mine was gravely injured in Vietnam. From all outward appearances, the injury was devastating in that he lost both of his legs. How could something beautiful come from that? But today God has used that broken body as a mighty tool of grace to carry the gospel all over the world, and tens of thousands of people have been saved under his ministry.

That yearning and aching in your heart is a gift from God that He has planted in you so that you might know Him and realize the abiding peace only He can bring as He plants eternity in your heart. His Word proclaims, "That My joy may remain in you, and that your joy may be full" (John 15:11).

Take heart today because what currently is so tragic may not be what it appears.

Dr. Mike Whitson, First Baptist Church Indian Trail
Indian Trail, NC

DECEMBER 7

Injustice Seems to Prevail

Ecclesiastes 3:16–22

¹⁶Moreover I saw under the sun:

In the place of judgment,
Wickedness *was* there;
And *in* the place of righteousness,
Iniquity *was* there.

¹⁷I said in my heart,

"God shall judge the righteous and the wicked,
For *there is* a time there for every purpose and
for every work."

¹⁸I said in my heart, "Concerning the condition of the sons of men, God tests them, that they may see that they themselves are *like* animals." ¹⁹For what happens to the sons of men also happens to animals; one thing befalls them: as one dies, so dies the other. Surely, they all have one breath; man has no advantage over animals, for all *is* vanity. ²⁰All go to one place: all are from the dust, and all return to dust. ²¹Who knows the spirit of the sons of men, which goes upward, and the spirit of the animal, which goes down to the earth? ²²So I perceived that nothing *is* better than that a man should rejoice in his own works, for that *is* his heritage. For who can bring him to see what will happen after him?

DEVOTIONAL

In reading the book of Ecclesiastes one must be careful to understand that Solomon was very cynical. Nowhere in all of Scripture is cynicism more evident than our text today.

I am certain the thought has occurred to all of us how life is unfair, especially when we see sin where righteousness should be and injustice where justice ought to stand. We look around and wonder, *Why am I suffering? I have been faithful, and others I know who are wicked are flourishing. It makes no sense.* It is easy to think like that when you look at life from an earthly perspective instead of a heavenly one. In our quiet times, we all have asked loudly, "Where are You, God?" Job felt that way in chapter 24 when he felt that God was not treating him fairly.

The enemy wants us to focus on the injustices so that we will simply seek pleasure in this life, throw away all moral parameters, and pitch all scripture that is inconvenient. To believe that we only go around once so we must grab all the gusto we can. But trust the words of Acts 17:31: "Because He has appointed a day on which He will judge the world in righteousness by the Man whom He has ordained."

Solomon concludes by encouraging us to put our disadvantages in the hands of the Lord and watch Him make them advantages for His glory and our good. Use whatever the hand of God has dealt you and impact others for His glory.

Dr. Mike Whitson, First Baptist Church Indian Trail
Indian Trail, NC

DECEMBER 8

The Uselessness of Selfish Toil

Ecclesiastes 4:1–8

T HEN I returned and considered all the oppression that is done under the sun:

And look! The tears of the oppressed,
But they have no comforter—
On the side of their oppressors *there is* power,
But they have no comforter.
2 Therefore I praised the dead who were already dead,
More than the living who are still alive.
3 Yet, better than both *is he* who has never existed,
Who has not seen the evil work that is done under the sun.

⁴Again, I saw that for all toil and every skillful work a man is envied by his neighbor. This also *is* vanity and grasping for the wind.

5 The fool folds his hands
And consumes his own flesh.
6 Better a handful *with* quietness
Than both hands full, *together with* toil and grasping for the wind.

⁷Then I returned, and I saw vanity under the sun:

8 There is one alone, without companion:
He has neither son nor brother.
Yet *there is* no end to all his labors,
Nor is his eye satisfied with riches.
But *he never asks,*

"For whom do I toil and deprive myself of good?"
This also *is* vanity and a grave misfortune.

DEVOTIONAL

S o many people today are climbing the ladders of success only to discover after their climb that the ladder was leaned up against the wrong wall. Solomon realized the tragic mistakes he made in getting to the top without God. In our dog-eat-dog world, success is sought at any price, even if it means stepping on others to get where we want to go. Servanthood runs counterculture today, but Jesus said the greatest among us will be the servant of all. How is your servant quotient? Are you a servant, or do you expect others to serve you? Are you oppressing anyone, or are you enabling others to be successful?

Solomon is also warning about the dangers of being a workaholic. Proverbs 15:16 says, "Better is a little with the fear of the LORD, than great treasure with trouble." There is nothing wrong with having money and things, but the problem comes when those things have you.

If going and struggling and meeting quotas and working the long weeks are going to bring nothing but turmoil in your marriage and home, it is time for you to change your lifestyle. Some things are more important. Ask yourself, "Why am I working? To get to the top without God? Out of a sense of envy? To impress people?" When Jesus is on the throne of your heart, you will always work for the right reason.

Dr. Mike Whitson, First Baptist Church Indian Trail
Indian Trail, NC

DECEMBER 9

In what areas of your life are you living without a God perspective?

_____

_____

_____

_____

_____

_____

_____

_____

_____

_____

What circumstances in your life today are causing you to lose your focus on God?

_____

_____

_____

_____

_____

_____

_____

_____

_____

DECEMBER 10

The Value of a Friend

Ecclesiastes 4:9–16

9 Two *are* better than one,
Because they have a good reward for their
labor.
10 For if they fall, one will lift up his companion.
But woe to him *who is* alone when he falls,
For *he has* no one to help him up.
11 Again, if two lie down together, they will keep
warm;
But how can one be warm *alone?*
12 Though one may be overpowered by another,
two can withstand him.
And a threefold cord is not quickly broken.

13 Better a poor and wise youth
Than an old and foolish king who will be
admonished no more.
14 For he comes out of prison to be king,
Although he was born poor in his kingdom.
15 I saw all the living who walk under the sun;
They were with the second youth who stands
in his place.
16 *There was* no end of all the people over whom
he was made king;
Yet those who come afterward will not rejoice
in him.
Surely this also *is* vanity and grasping for the
wind.

DEVOTIONAL

God knows two things about everyone of us: first, *everybody needs somebody;* second, *somebody is needed by everybody.* This principle is so true: "Two are better than one" (v. 9). There is an unbelievable power in partnership that goes beyond addition to multiplication. Not even the Lone Ranger faced life alone—he had Tonto! Learn three lessons today about the importance of friendship.

1. *Two are more personally profitable than one.* *The New Living Translation* puts the verse this way: "Two people can accomplish more than twice as much as one; they get a better return for their labor" (v. 9).

2. *Two are more personally protected than one.* "For if they fall, one will lift up his companion. But woe to him who is alone when he falls" (v. 10). When we fall down or are knocked down, we need someone to pick us up.

3. *Two are more personally powerful than one.* "Though one may be overpowered by another, two can withstand him" (v. 12). Marines are trained to dig foxholes big enough for two. Don't fight the wars of life alone; do it in twos.

Dr. James Merritt, Cross Pointe Church
Duluth, GA

DECEMBER 11

Fear God and Keep Your Word

Ecclesiastes 5:1–7

WALK prudently when you go to the house of God; and draw near to hear rather than to give the sacrifice of fools, for they do not know that they do evil.

2 Do not be rash with your mouth,
   And let not your heart utter anything hastily
      before God.
   For God *is* in heaven, and you on earth;
   Therefore let your words be few.
3 For a dream comes through much activity,
   And a fool's voice *is known* by *his* many words.
4 When you make a vow to God, do not delay to
      pay it;
   For *He has* no pleasure in fools.
   Pay what you have vowed—
5 Better not to vow than to vow and not pay.

⁶Do not let your mouth cause your flesh to sin, nor say before the messenger *of God* that it *was* an error. Why should God be angry at your excuse and destroy the work of your hands? ⁷For in the multitude of dreams and many words *there is* also vanity. But fear God.

DEVOTIONAL

Watch your step! Solomon was watching how people entered God's house and gave this advice: "Walk prudently when you go to the house of God" (v. 1). What he was saying was, "What you are about to do is serious business, so you had better be serious about it." Then he told us how to do serious business with God, who means business with us.

Be careful how you enter the presence of God. "Walk prudently when you go to the house of God; and draw near to hear rather than to give the sacrifice of fools, for they do not know that they do evil" (v. 1). Enter God's house with a sense of reverence.

Be cautious in offering your prayers to God. "Do not be rash with your mouth, and let not your heart utter anything hastily before God" (v. 2). Pray boldly but wisely, always wanting His will, not your own.

Be committed in keeping your promises to God. "When you make a vow to God, do not delay to pay it; for He has no pleasure in fools. Pay what you have vowed—better not to vow than to vow and not pay" (v. 4). Integrity is doing what you say you will do, especially with God! Keep your word with God and others—and always watch your step!

Dr. James Merritt, Cross Pointe Church
Duluth, GA

DECEMBER 12

The Vanity of Gain and Honor

Ecclesiastes 5:8–20

⁸If you see the oppression of the poor, and the violent perversion of justice and righteousness in a province, do not marvel at the matter; for high official watches over high official, and higher officials are over them.

⁹Moreover the profit of the land is for all; *even* the king is served from the field.

10   He who loves silver will not be satisfied with
          silver;
       Nor he who loves abundance, with increase.
       This also *is* vanity.

11   When goods increase,
       They increase who eat them;
       So what profit have the owners
       Except to see *them* with their eyes?

12   The sleep of a laboring man *is* sweet,
       Whether he eats little or much;
       But the abundance of the rich will not permit
          him to sleep.

13   There is a severe evil *which* I have seen under
          the sun:
       Riches kept for their owner to his hurt.

14   But those riches perish through misfortune;
       When he begets a son, *there is* nothing in his
          hand.

15   As he came from his mother's womb, naked
          shall he return,
       To go as he came;
       And he shall take nothing from his labor
       Which he may carry away in his hand.

16   And this also *is* a severe evil—
       Just exactly as he came, so shall he go.
       And what profit has he who has labored for
          the wind?

17   All his days he also eats in darkness,
       And *he has* much sorrow and sickness and
          anger.

¹⁸Here is what I have seen: *It is* good and fitting *for one* to eat and drink, and to enjoy the good of all his labor in which he toils under the sun all the days of his life which God gives him; for it *is* his heritage. ¹⁹As for every man to whom God has given riches and wealth, and given him power to eat of it, to receive his heritage and rejoice in his labor—this *is* the gift of God. ²⁰For he will not dwell unduly on the days of his life, because God keeps *him* busy with the joy of his heart.

DEVOTIONAL

The richest man who ever lived tells us two important things to remember about money.

1. *Money doesn't bring satisfaction.* "He who loves silver will not be satisfied with silver; nor he who loves abundance, with increase. This also is vanity" (v. 10). Loving money is like trying to quench thirst with saltwater. If you love money, your bank account will never match your desired amount.

2. *Money doesn't bring serenity.* "The sleep of a laboring man is sweet, whether he eats little or much; but the abundance of the rich will not permit him to sleep" (v. 12). The good news is that what money can't give, God can and does give daily!

Dr. James Merritt, Cross Pointe Church
Duluth, GA

DECEMBER 13

Wealth Is Not the Goal of Life

Ecclesiastes 6:1–12

THERE is an evil which I have seen under the sun, and it *is* common among men: ²A man to whom God has given riches and wealth and honor, so that he lacks nothing for himself of all he desires; yet God does not give him power to eat of it, but a foreigner consumes it. This *is* vanity, and it *is* an evil affliction.

³If a man begets a hundred *children* and lives many years, so that the days of his years are many, but his soul is not satisfied with goodness, or indeed he has no burial, I say *that* a stillborn child *is* better than he—⁴for it comes in vanity and departs in darkness, and its name is covered with darkness. ⁵Though it has not seen the sun or known *anything,* this has more rest than that man, ⁶even if he lives a thousand years twice—but has not seen goodness. Do not all go to one place?

⁷ All the labor of man *is* for his mouth,
   And yet the soul is not satisfied.
⁸ For what more has the wise *man* than the
      fool?
   What does the poor man have,
   Who knows *how* to walk before the living?
⁹ Better *is* the sight of the eyes than the wander-
      ing of desire.
   This also *is* vanity and grasping for the wind.
¹⁰ Whatever one is, he has been named already,
   For it is known that he *is* man;
   And he cannot contend with Him who is
      mightier than he.

¹¹ Since there are many things that increase
      vanity,
   How *is* man the better?

¹²For who knows what *is* good for man in life, all the days of his vain life which he passes like a shadow? Who can tell a man what will happen after him under the sun?

DEVOTIONAL

Better to have loved and lost than never to have loved at all." That may be true with love, but it is certainly not true with life. There are some things so important that never being born at all is better than living without them. Solomon warned us not to live without three things.

1. *Don't live without grace.* "There is an evil which I have seen under the sun, and it is common among men: a man to whom God has given riches and wealth and honor, so that he lacks nothing for himself of all he desires; yet God does not give him power to eat of it" (vv. 1–2). Sad indeed are the people who do not realize that all they have is by the grace of God.

2. *Don't live without goodness.* When gold becomes more important than the goodness of God, one may have much "but his soul is not satisfied with goodness" (v. 3). No one can ever be happy until they are satisfied, and that cannot be found apart from a good life.

3. *Don't live without God.* "Who can tell a man what will happen after him under the sun?" (v. 12). Those who live for today and not tomorrow, and for gold and not God, will die both poor and empty. Don't live for nothing!

Dr. James Merritt, Cross Pointe Church
Duluth, GA

DECEMBER 14
The Value of Practical Wisdom

Ecclesiastes 7:1–7

A GOOD name *is* better than precious
ointment,
And the day of death than the day of one's
birth;

2 Better to go to the house of mourning
Than to go to the house of feasting,
For that *is* the end of all men;
And the living will take *it* to heart.

3 Sorrow *is* better than laughter,
For by a sad countenance the heart is made
better.

4 The heart of the wise *is* in the house of
mourning,
But the heart of fools *is* in the house of mirth.

5 *It is* better to hear the rebuke of the wise
Than for a man to hear the song of fools.

6 For like the crackling of thorns under a pot,
So *is* the laughter of the fool.
This also is vanity.

7 Surely oppression destroys a wise *man's*
reason,
And a bribe debases the heart.

DEVOTIONAL

R emember the saying "Good, better, best—
never let it rest, until your good is better
and your better is best." One thing to notice is the
path from good to best always goes through better.
But that raises the question, "What is better than
good?" If good is not good enough, then "better"
better be better than good or better won't be the

best! In this passage, Solomon identifies three
surprising things that are "better" than good.

1. *Reputation is better than riches.* "A good
name is better than precious ointment, and the
day of death than the day of one's birth" (v. 1). How
true this is. Everything has its price, and even precious ointment can be bought for enough money.
But reputation is not for sale. A good name can't
be bought for money, marbles, or chocolate.

2. *Contemplation is better than celebration.*
"Better to go to the house of mourning than to go
to the house of feasting, for that is the end of all
men; and the living will take it to heart" (v. 2). It
is a fact of life that you learn more in the valley
than you do on the mountaintop. Death, sorrow,
and sickness teach life's greatest lessons.

3. *Frankness is better than flattery.* "It is better
to hear the rebuke of the wise than for a man to
hear the song of fools" (v. 5). Praise is nice, but it
only polishes; rebuke—constructive criticism—
is painful, but it sharpens. Praise will make you
feel better, but rebuke will help you be better.
These are tough lessons to learn and hard to swallow, but you will be "better" if you do!

Dr. James Merritt, Cross Pointe Church
Duluth, GA

DECEMBER 15

Wisdom Is Good with an Inheritance

Ecclesiastes 7:8–18

8 The end of a thing *is* better than its beginning;
The patient in spirit *is* better than the proud
in spirit.

9 Do not hasten in your spirit to be angry,
For anger rests in the bosom of fools.

10 Do not say,
"Why were the former days better than these?"
For you do not inquire wisely concerning this.

11 Wisdom *is* good with an inheritance,
And profitable to those who see the sun.

12 For wisdom *is* a defense *as* money *is* a defense,
But the excellence of knowledge *is that*
wisdom gives life to those who have it.

13 Consider the work of God;
For who can make straight what He has made
crooked?

14 In the day of prosperity be joyful,
But in the day of adversity consider:
Surely God has appointed the one as well as
the other,
So that man can find out nothing *that will*
come after him.

15 I have seen everything in my days of vanity:
There is a just *man* who perishes in his
righteousness,
And there is a wicked *man* who prolongs *life*
in his wickedness.

16 Do not be overly righteous,
Nor be overly wise:
Why should you destroy yourself?

17 Do not be overly wicked,
Nor be foolish:
Why should you die before your time?

18 *It is* good that you grasp this,
And also not remove your hand from the other;
For he who fears God will escape them all.

DEVOTIONAL

One of my favorite movies is *The Karate Kid.* There is a scene in which Mr. Miyagi gives Daniel a piece of wise advice. He says, "Focus, Daniel-son! You must focus!" How true that is as we go through life. Here are three things to focus on as you take life's journey.

1. *Focus on the finish.* "The end of a thing is better than its beginning" (v. 8). One of the seven habits of highly effective people is to "begin with the end in mind."[1] It is not how you start but how you finish that counts—that is true both in racing and in life.

2. *Focus on the facts.* "Do not say, 'Why were the former days better than these?' For you do not inquire wisely concerning this" (v. 10). The fact is we must live for today, not pine for yesterday. If you are living for God and in the center of His will, *these are the good old days.*

3. *Focus on the Father.* "Consider the work of God; for who can make straight what He has made crooked? In the day of prosperity be joyful, but in the day of adversity consider: surely God has appointed the one as well as the other" (vv. 13–14). In the good times and the bad, God is in control of all things. Keep your mind fixed on Him, and live and die knowing that you will never be forsaken and you will be protected.

Dr. James Merritt, Cross Pointe Church
Duluth, GA

December 16

What one truth have you learned this week that could be a daily guiding principle in your life?

What one area of your life do you need to exercise God's wisdom in and how would that impact your life?

DECEMBER 17

Who Can Find Wisdom?

Ecclesiastes 7:19–29

19 Wisdom strengthens the wise
More than ten rulers of the city.

20 For *there is* not a just man on earth who does good
And does not sin.

21 Also do not take to heart everything people say,
Lest you hear your servant cursing you.

22 For many times, also, your own heart has known
That even you have cursed others.

23 All this I have proved by wisdom.
I said, "I will be wise";
But it *was* far from me.

24 As for that which is far off and exceedingly deep,
Who can find it out?

25 I applied my heart to know,
To search and seek out wisdom and the reason *of things,*
To know the wickedness of folly,
Even of foolishness *and* madness.

26 And I find more bitter than death
The woman whose heart *is* snares and nets,
Whose hands *are* fetters.
He who pleases God shall escape from her,
But the sinner shall be trapped by her.

27 "Here is what I have found," says the Preacher,
"*Adding* one thing to the other to find out the reason,

28 Which my soul still seeks but I cannot find:
One man among a thousand I have found,
But a woman among all these I have not found.

29 Truly, this only I have found:
That God made man upright,
But they have sought out many schemes."

DEVOTIONAL

*"There is a way that seems right to a man,
but its end is the way of death."*

—*Proverbs 14:12*

He should have seen it coming! Solomon's unbridled quest to pack his life with pleasure led him down many wrong turns and dead ends, and here we get to benefit from the wisdom that rises to the surface as he begins to face the reality of his consequences. Denying himself nothing, Solomon sought fulfillment in everything under the sun, only to be left with the conclusion that he wasn't as wise as he thought (Eccl. 7:23).

How can we avoid the same fate? Humorist Ashleigh Brilliant once quipped, "My opinions may have changed, but not the fact that I'm right." Like Solomon, when we take pride in our own understanding, we cease to depend on God. Instead, we must die to ourselves daily, recognizing that pride never ceases its pursuit to find an open door in our hearts. Surely Solomon lamented how he strayed from his previous counsel: "Trust in the LORD with all your heart, and lean not on your own understanding; in all your ways acknowledge Him, and He shall direct your paths" (Prov. 3:5–6).

*Brad Bowen, Heritage Church
Moultrie, GA*

DECEMBER 18

Obey Authorities for God's Sake

Ecclesiastes 8:1–9

WHO *is* like a wise *man?*
And who knows the interpretation of a
thing?
A man's wisdom makes his face shine,
And the sternness of his face is changed.

²I *say,* "Keep the king's commandment for the sake of your oath to God. ³"Do not be hasty to go from his presence. Do not take your stand for an evil thing, for he does whatever pleases him."

4   Where the word of a king is, *there is* power;
And who may say to him, "What are you doing?"
5   He who keeps his command will experience
nothing harmful;
And a wise man's heart discerns both time
and judgment,
6   Because for every matter there is a time and
judgment,
Though the misery of man increases greatly.
7   For he does not know what will happen;
So who can tell him when it will occur?
8   No one has power over the spirit to retain the
spirit,
And no one has power in the day of death.
There is no release from that war,
And wickedness will not deliver those who are
given to it.

⁹All this I have seen, and applied my heart to every work that is done under the sun: *There is* a time in which one man rules over another to his own hurt.

Before I entered the fourth grade, I heard horror stories about my upcoming teacher, Mrs. Wilson. Her short temper was legendary, and one glare from her squinty eyes was enough to make a grown man—not to mention a scrawny fourth grader—shutter with fear. I made the decision on the first day of class that I would do everything I could to please Mrs. Wilson. I would pay attention to everything she said, always respond respectfully, and try hard not to waver in my commitment to excellence.

And then one day the unimaginable happened. After responding to one of her questions to the class with an innocent but ridiculous answer, she stared at me, and then . . . without warning . . . she *laughed*! The entire class was silent for a moment, and then we all erupted in laughter together. It was such a relief to know that Mrs. Wilson had a sense of humor and that she actually liked us!

Solomon acknowledges that oftentimes in life we are faced with circumstances beyond our control. It may be an oppressive government, an unruly boss, or even a scary fourth-grade teacher. In those moments, we should take comfort in God's providence, knowing that "all things work together for good to those who love God, to those who are the called according to His purpose" (Rom. 8:28). We aren't promised that all things are good; rather, that all things will *work together* for good in the end. Give thanks today for God's goodness in spite of any negative circumstances . . . and maybe even laugh!

Brad Bowen, Heritage Church
Moultrie, GA

DECEMBER 19

Death Comes to All

Ecclesiastes 8:10–17

¹⁰Then I saw the wicked buried, who had come and gone from the place of holiness, and they were forgotten in the city where they had so done. This also *is* vanity. ¹¹Because the sentence against an evil work is not executed speedily, therefore the heart of the sons of men is fully set in them to do evil. ¹²Though a sinner does evil a hundred *times,* and his *days* are prolonged, yet I surely know that it will be well with those who fear God, who fear before Him. ¹³But it will not be well with the wicked; nor will he prolong *his* days, *which are* as a shadow, because he does not fear before God.

¹⁴There is a vanity which occurs on earth, that there are just *men* to whom it happens according to the work of the wicked; again, there are wicked *men* to whom it happens according to the work of the righteous. I said that this also *is* vanity.

¹⁵So I commended enjoyment, because a man has nothing better under the sun than to eat, drink, and be merry; for this will remain with him in his labor *all* the days of his life which God gives him under the sun.

¹⁶When I applied my heart to know wisdom and to see the business that is done on earth, even though one sees no sleep day or night, ¹⁷then I saw all the work of God, that a man cannot find out the work that is done under the sun. For though a man labors to discover *it,* yet he will not find *it;* moreover, though a wise *man* attempts to know *it,* he will not be able to find *it.*

DEVOTIONAL

Does money buy happiness? Our immediate, sophisticated response might be an emphatic, "No!" But today I argue to the contrary. Of course money buys happiness. It buys really cool gadgets, fun toys, stylish fashion accessories, and plenty of other items off our happiness wish list. However, happiness is like a good meal. It is pleasurable—but only temporarily. Sooner or later (usually sooner), the hunger returns and we find ourselves craving the next promise of pleasure.

Solomon's pursuit of happiness reveals the meaninglessness of such an endeavor. In the end, I believe he began to realize that instead of happiness, we should set our hearts on *contentment.* Happiness is determined by circumstances. Contentment is not. Happiness is fleeting. Contentment—when it reaches maturity—can be everlasting. Happiness is never fully quenched. Contentment opens the door to indescribable joy and peace by finding satisfaction in God's simple but powerful, loving presence.

The apostle Paul also discovered this life-altering principle. He experienced seasons of prosperity and season of want. And yet, because he learned the secret of contentment, he was able to endure both unshaken. He was free from the pursuit of happiness and could therefore make the bold proclamation, "I can do all things through Christ who strengthens me" (Phil. 4:13).

Brad Bowen, Heritage Church
Moultrie, GA

DECEMBER 20

All Is in God's Hands

Ecclesiastes 9:1–8

FOR I considered all this in my heart, so that I could declare it all: that the righteous and the wise and their works *are* in the hand of God. People know neither love nor hatred *by* anything *they see* before them. ²All things *come* alike to all:

One event *happens* to the righteous and the wicked;
To the good, the clean, and the unclean;
To him who sacrifices and him who does not sacrifice.
As is the good, so *is* the sinner;
He who takes an oath as *he* who fears an oath.

³This *is* an evil in all that is done under the sun: that one thing *happens* to all. Truly the hearts of the sons of men are full of evil; madness *is* in their hearts while they live, and after that *they go* to the dead. ⁴But for him who is joined to all the living there is hope, for a living dog is better than a dead lion.

⁵ For the living know that they will die;
But the dead know nothing,
And they have no more reward,
For the memory of them is forgotten.
⁶ Also their love, their hatred, and their envy have now perished;
Nevermore will they have a share
In anything done under the sun.

⁷ Go, eat your bread with joy,
And drink your wine with a merry heart;
For God has already accepted your works.

⁸ Let your garments always be white,
And let your head lack no oil.

DEVOTIONAL

How much do you really know about your parents? Where were they born? What were their childhoods like? How did they fall in love? What challenges did they face and overcome?

You may fare well in recalling details of your parents' lives, but what about the lives of your grandparents? Your great-grandparents? If you are like most, it doesn't take looking back over too many generations before your recollections quickly fade.

Here's a sobering thought: in just a couple of generations, it is entirely possible that our own descendants will struggle to recall the stories of our lives. Now I know you may be thinking, *Well, that's depressing!* but I assure you my intention is not to be a downer. On the contrary, my desire is to encourage you to live with an *eternal* mind-set. Too often we allow life's insignificant worries to rob us of living each day in the fullness of Christ. Scripture compares our time on earth to a brief vapor (Jas. 4:14). Therefore, instead of focusing so much time, energy, and attention on things that will quickly fade away, let us leave a lasting legacy by setting our hearts on the things that have no expiration date.

"Whatever things are true, whatever things are noble, whatever things are just, whatever things are pure, whatever things are lovely, whatever things are of good report, if there is any virtue and if there is anything praiseworthy—meditate on these things" (Phil. 4:8). Live for eternity!

Brad Bowen, Heritage Church
Moultrie, GA

DECEMBER 21

Wisdom Superior to Folly

Ecclesiastes 9:9–18

⁹Live joyfully with the wife whom you love all the days of your vain life which He has given you under the sun, all your days of vanity; for that *is* your portion in life, and in the labor which you perform under the sun.

¹⁰Whatever your hand finds to do, do *it* with your might; for *there is* no work or device or knowledge or wisdom in the grave where you are going.

¹¹I returned and saw under the sun that—

The race *is* not to the swift,
Nor the battle to the strong,
Nor bread to the wise,
Nor riches to men of understanding,
Nor favor to men of skill;
But time and chance happen to them all.
¹² For man also does not know his time:
Like fish taken in a cruel net,
Like birds caught in a snare,
So the sons of men *are* snared in an evil
    time,
When it falls suddenly upon them.

¹³This wisdom I have also seen under the sun, and it *seemed* great to me: ¹⁴*There was* a little city with few men in it; and a great king came against it, besieged it, and built great snares around it. ¹⁵Now there was found in it a poor wise man, and he by his wisdom delivered the city. Yet no one remembered that same poor man.

¹⁶Then I said:

"Wisdom *is* better than strength.

Nevertheless the poor man's wisdom *is* despised,
And his words are not heard.
¹⁷ Words of the wise, *spoken* quietly, *should be*
    heard
Rather than the shout of a ruler of fools.
¹⁸ Wisdom *is* better than weapons of war;
But one sinner destroys much good."

DEVOTIONAL

Life is messy. Sometimes cheaters take the gold medal. Sometimes bad things happen to nice people. In a broken world, things just don't always work out the way they are supposed to. Some may question Solomon's words in today's passage. Throughout Ecclesiastes he appears to slip in and out of a depressed and defeated mind-set. While some may choose to skim over this text, I am actually incredibly grateful that God recognizes how unfair our fallen world can be.

To the single parent struggling to make ends meet: He understands.

To the child who feels neglected and abused: He is with you.

To the young person who just can't catch a break: He has not abandoned you.

Life is messy, but God has the uncanny ability to transform it all. He brings hope to the hopeless. Meditate on the following promise today, knowing that God is faithful even when life seems unfair. "You have turned for me my mourning into dancing; you have put off my sackcloth and clothed me with gladness . . . I will give thanks to You forever" (Ps. 30:11–12).

Brad Bowen, Heritage Church
Moultrie, GA

DECEMBER 22

Wisdom and Folly

Ecclesiastes 10:1–7

DEAD flies putrefy the perfumer's ointment,
And cause it to give off a foul odor;
So does a little folly to one respected for wisdom *and* honor.

2 A wise man's heart *is* at his right hand,
But a fool's heart at his left.

3 Even when a fool walks along the way,
He lacks wisdom,
And he shows everyone *that* he *is* a fool.

4 If the spirit of the ruler rises against you,
Do not leave your post;
For conciliation pacifies great offenses.

5 There is an evil I have seen under the sun,
As an error proceeding from the ruler:

6 Folly is set in great dignity,
While the rich sit in a lowly place.

7 I have seen servants on horses,
While princes walk on the ground like servants.

DEVOTIONAL

"If trouble comes when you least expect it then maybe the thing to do is to always expect it."

—*Cormac McCarthy,* The Road[1]

F olly is not a rare commodity. In fact, we are unlikely to escape an entire day without numerous encounters. Our challenge is to navigate life without taking on foolishness in any form. To help us avoid the many pitfalls of folly, Solomon provides some great tips:

1. *It only takes a little.* You may have heard the story of the child insisting that he be allowed to watch a television show because it only contained "a little" inappropriateness. The clever parent replied by offering the child a brownie, claiming it contained only "a little" of their pet's droppings mixed in. Needless to say, the child got the point. Folly works the same way in our lives. It can easily take good intentions down a destructive path, and a reputation is quickly shattered when tainted by foolish deeds. Don't be seduced by foolishness, even in small doses!

2. *Folly refuses to be contained.* In the movie *Gremlins*, Rand Peltzer is determined to find the perfect gift for his son, Billy. When he encounters the adorable Gizmo, he ignores the stern warnings of the wise shop owner. Convinced he can handle the responsibility, Rand walks out with his treasure. Chaos ensues. Folly promises to behave, but as soon as we turn our backs, the true monster of foolishness appears. Pursue godliness. Immoral shortcuts only lead to places we don't want to visit!

3. *Folly fears forgiveness.* Solomon describes some of the injustices he encountered but offers the antidote to great offenses: conciliation. Many times in life you will be faced with unjust circumstances, and it will be very tempting to respond with contempt or indignation. This usually only adds fuel to folly's fire. Solomon calls us to a wiser path: choose peace over conflict. Being quick to forgive will oftentimes extinguish folly before it ever fully ignites.

Brad Bowen, Heritage Church
Moultrie, GA

DECEMBER 23

Like Solomon, are you caught in the never-ending pursuit of happiness? Has any of your joy in Christ been robbed by a lack of contentment? How might true contentment change the way you live? Pray through these questions and jot down any thoughts God reveals to you.

_____

_____

_____

_____

_____

_____

_____

_____

_____

Jesus reconciles us with God, and we are called to actively participate in the ministry of reconciliation with others (2 Cor. 5). Forgiveness is simple, but not always easy, and foolishly we allow bitterness to take root in our hearts. Prayerfully ask God to reveal anyone you need to forgive, or if there is anyone from whom you need forgiveness.

_____

_____

_____

_____

_____

_____

_____

_____

DECEMBER 24

The Lips of Fools Bring Destruction

Ecclesiastes 10:8–15

8 He who digs a pit will fall into it,
   And whoever breaks through a wall will be
       bitten by a serpent.
9 He who quarries stones may be hurt by them,
   And he who splits wood may be endangered
       by it.
10 If the ax is dull,
   And one does not sharpen the edge,
   Then he must use more strength;
   But wisdom brings success.

11 A serpent may bite when *it is* not charmed;
   The babbler is no different.
12 The words of a wise man's mouth *are* gracious,
   But the lips of a fool shall swallow him up;
13 The words of his mouth begin with foolishness,
   And the end of his talk *is* raving madness.
14 A fool also multiplies words.
   No man knows what is to be;
   Who can tell him what will be after him?
15 The labor of fools wearies them,
   For they do not even know how to go to the
       city!

DEVOTIONAL

Sometimes God is seen as so distant that we expect Him to only lead us in mysterious, otherworldly ways. As a result, we think God is out of touch, unable to understand us and care about what we are experiencing. But the exact opposite is true. For instance, in this section of Ecclesiastes, God warns of falling into pits, being bitten by snakes when breaking through walls, and the dangers of splitting wood. These were very practical and life-saving warnings.

What is exciting for us is that God is just as concerned about the things that matter to us today as He was about the problems of those who lived thousands of years ago. Obviously, God wants us to know how to live successfully by seeking, recognizing, and receiving His wisdom. At the same time, He warns us to reject the advice that comes from the raving madness of foolish men and women who are always talking but do not know where they are going or how to get there.

This is a great challenge, especially at a time when there are so many competing voices vying for our attention and loyalty. In the end, God warns that no human knows what the future holds. It is a knowledge He has reserved for Himself. But He promises that in real, everyday, practical life He will reveal His great wisdom to those who will follow Him, and that wisdom will bring success. As a result, we can know how to live and not fall into a pit or be bitten by a snake.

David Edwards, Evangelist, Speaker, Author
Oklahoma City, OK

DECEMBER 25

Money Answers Everything?

Ecclesiastes 10:16–20

¹⁶ Woe to you, O land, when your king *is* a child,
And your princes feast in the morning!

¹⁷ Blessed *are* you, O land, when your king *is* the
son of nobles,
And your princes feast at the proper time—
For strength and not for drunkenness!

¹⁸ Because of laziness the building decays,
And through idleness of hands the house
leaks.

¹⁹A feast is made for laughter,
And wine makes merry;
But money answers everything.

²⁰ Do not curse the king, even in your thought;
Do not curse the rich, even in your bedroom;
For a bird of the air may carry your voice,
And a bird in flight may tell the matter.

DEVOTIONAL

It's Christmas. For many this is the great day of celebration honoring the birth of our Lord Jesus. Families gather, presents are opened, carols are sung, and as a result, it is a day of genuine happiness. But not for everyone.

For others, this will not be a day of joy; rather, it will be another day of disappointment. In the midst of that disappointment, and even despair, it is easy to agree with Solomon when he wrote in this chapter of Ecclesiastes, "Money answers everything" (v. 19). If only there were money, the celebration could be good! If only I could be rich … If only I could be the king … It was to those who believed that struggles could be erased with enough money and laughter that Solomon wrote, "Woe to you, O land, when your king is a child" (v. 16).

It's a childish idea to believe money answers everything. Money can provide food, shelter, and clothing, and even put packages under the tree. But money can't protect from disappointment, disillusionment, and despair. Money can't fix a broken soul or fill an empty heart. No one really knows how much money is worth until discovering how little it can buy. Whether in abundance or lack, don't complain, compare, or covet. Instead, say thank you to King Jesus.

If your land—your life—is ruled by the immaturity of a child, then things that can be purchased with enough money or experienced with enough wine and laughter can make you happy and satisfied, at least for a time. But if you want your life to be about more than the moment or the things you own, then you need another King who is not a child.

The great news of this day is that there is such a King. Though He was born a child, He grew, and in His maturity died to pay for the sins of the world and rose from the dead so each individual can know Him as their Lord and savior. This King is Jesus. He is the One who is able to bring order and meaning to your life in such a way that genuine laughter will be heard and a feast of deep satisfaction can be enjoyed!

David Edwards, Evangelist, Speaker, Author
Oklahoma City, OK

DECEMBER 26

The Value of Diligence

Ecclesiastes 11:1–6

C AST your bread upon the waters,
For you will find it after many days.

2 Give a serving to seven, and also to eight,
For you do not know what evil will be on the
earth.

3 If the clouds are full of rain,
They empty *themselves* upon the earth;
And if a tree falls to the south or the north,
In the place where the tree falls, there it shall
lie.

4 He who observes the wind will not sow,
And he who regards the clouds will not reap.

5 As you do not know what *is* the way of the
wind,
Or how the bones *grow* in the womb of her
who is with child,
So you do not know the works of God who
makes everything.

6 In the morning sow your seed,
And in the evening do not withhold your hand;
For you do not know which will prosper,
Either this or that,
Or whether both alike *will be* good.

DEVOTIONAL

G od has designed us for success, but not
automatic success. His instructions in this
section of Ecclesiastes are challenging to each
individual who wants to achieve prosperity in any
area of life. At the foundation of His challenge is
the demand for diligence.

The challenge is seen when the writer insists,
"Cast your bread upon the waters" or "give a serving to seven, and also to eight" (vv. 1–2). God is
shouting for us to start, work hard, and do it! It is
as though He is pushing us and saying, "You can
do this. It is not beyond you. It is not for some special group of people born on the right side of the
tracks, or for those from the right families with
the right money and the right education. Start!
Launch! Try!"

Then God demands, "No excuses!" As the
writer of Ecclesiastes says, "He who observes
the wind will not sow, and he who regards the
clouds will not reap" (v. 4). Don't wait for the right
moment; the right moment is now. Do what you
know to do now. Launch and adjust.

Be diligent, and sow your seed in the morning
and again in the evening. God demands, "You do
not know which will prosper, either this or that, or
whether both alike will be good" (v. 6).

Diligence is a strong refusal to quit with a decision to remain faithful until the desired result
is reached, and then to keep on so that you may
maintain what's been gained. There's no diligence
without determination, and there's no determination without the passion to keep on casting.
Determination is the mind-set, and diligence is
doing the work required.

David Edwards, Evangelist, Speaker, Author
Oklahoma City, OK

DECEMBER 27

Rejoice in Your Youth

Ecclesiastes 11:7–10

⁷ Truly the light is sweet,
  And *it is* pleasant for the eyes to behold
    the sun;
⁸ But if a man lives many years
  And rejoices in them all,
  Yet let him remember the days of darkness,
  For they will be many.
  All that is coming *is* vanity.

⁹ Rejoice, O young man, in your youth,
  And let your heart cheer you in the days of
    your youth;
  Walk in the ways of your heart,
  And in the sight of your eyes;
  But know that for all these
  God will bring you into judgment.
¹⁰ Therefore remove sorrow from your heart,
  And put away evil from your flesh,
  For childhood and youth *are* vanity.

DEVOTIONAL

It's tough being young, especially being young and committed to following Jesus as Lord. The writer of Ecclesiastes understood and speaks of both the joy and the sorrow of the heart of a young believer.

There is a moment when the heart of a young person rejoices and begins to follow Jesus. Perhaps it is in a great worship service or some remarkable concert when the Holy Spirit is powerfully present and the young heart is filled with love and devotion to Jesus. But later comes the reality of the flesh and all its temptations. Every young Christian has this experience. It can be in a special relationship when temptation is raging, or when the need to be accepted threatens to drive the young into compromise. It is at these moments the heart is filled with sorrow and a desire to break away.

When this occurs, Ecclesiastes demands you follow your cheering heart—the heart that is cheering your relationship and commitment to the Lord Jesus. The writer insists that the young must walk in the ways of the cheering heart and in the sight the cheering heart gives to your eyes. This is the way; walk in it!

It is a willful decision with two polar opposites demanding the control of your heart, and thus your life. At times the decision is easy and you can put away the evil of your flesh, but at other moments it can be the most difficult challenge of your life as a Christian. But the promise is certain: if you order sorry away, it will leave and the cheering will return, for you have won another victory and decided again to follow Jesus as Lord of all life.

The spirit is the deepest part of you. It's the engine of life, not always seen but always felt, and it cheers us on in the ways of God. It inspires confident living, directs decisions, and tells us to keep on running when we want to stop. The cheering of the spirit keeps us focused on what really matters. Don't be distracted by distractions. Keep choosing His lordship over your life.

David Edwards, Evangelist, Speaker, Author
Oklahoma City, OK

DECEMBER 28

Seek God in Early Life

Ecclesiastes 12:1–8

REMEMBER now your Creator in the days of
your youth,
Before the difficult days come,
And the years draw near when you say,
"I have no pleasure in them":
2 While the sun and the light,
The moon and the stars,
Are not darkened,
And the clouds do not return after the rain;
3 In the day when the keepers of the house
tremble,
And the strong men bow down;
When the grinders cease because they are few,
And those that look through the windows
grow dim;
4 When the doors are shut in the streets,
And the sound of grinding is low;
When one rises up at the sound of a bird,
And all the daughters of music are brought low.
5 Also they are afraid of height,
And of terrors in the way;
When the almond tree blossoms,
The grasshopper is a burden,
And desire fails.
For man goes to his eternal home,
And the mourners go about the streets.

6 *Remember your Creator* before the silver cord
is loosed,
Or the golden bowl is broken,
Or the pitcher shattered at the fountain,
Or the wheel broken at the well.

7 Then the dust will return to the earth
as it was,
And the spirit will return to God who gave it.

8 "Vanity of vanities," says the Preacher,
"All *is* vanity."

DEVOTIONAL

The key to understanding the writer of
Ecclesiastes rests in the single word *before*
and his message to embrace the world while it is
still alive with all of its possibilities. He insists that
great change will quickly come to the young that
will rob them of their joy, courage, and vitality.
Once these things are gone, only a shell of what
was will remain. The preacher calls for youth to
seek God in early life before the difficult days.

He describes the "before" days as a time when
the sun and moon and stars are bright. It is a time
for visions and dreams, and a time when nothing
is impossible. Seek God then, when every dream
of God can be your dream. "Before" is a time of
strength and power when the young do great
exploits. Seek God when all your vitality remains.

"Before" is also a time all the doors are open
with opportunity. Fair or not, as one grows older,
doors begin to shut and possibilities narrow. The
challenge is to seek God when there is unlimited
potential to complete His will and fulfill your
destiny.

David Edwards, Evangelist, Speaker, Author
Oklahoma City, OK

DECEMBER 29

The Whole Duty of Man

Ecclesiastes 12:9–14

⁹And moreover, because the Preacher was wise, he still taught the people knowledge; yes, he pondered and sought out *and* set in order many proverbs. ¹⁰The Preacher sought to find acceptable words; and *what was* written *was* upright—words of truth. ¹¹The words of the wise are like goads, and the words of scholars are like well-driven nails, given by one Shepherd. ¹²And further, my son, be admonished by these. Of making many books *there is* no end, and much study *is* wearisome to the flesh.

¹³Let us hear the conclusion of the whole matter:

Fear God and keep His commandments,
For this is man's all.

¹⁴ For God will bring every work into judgment,
Including every secret thing,
Whether good or evil.

DEVOTIONAL

The preacher of Ecclesiastes completes his instruction with this passage of Scripture. In his wisdom, he has taught the people knowledge based on what he calls "words of truth." The challenge of our day is to sift through all the competing "truth" to discover that wisdom.

Of course, "words of truth" can be difficult to find because there are so many who claim to be telling, singing, writing, texting, or tweeting truth. Others say truth is illusive and claim it is impossible to know the truth about anything. The preacher disagreed and gave three ways in which a person can recognize genuine words of truth.

He describes words of truth as goads, tools used to drive animals. The application is clear: words of truth drive individuals to please God. Is the truth you are accepting leading you to greater confidence and faith in the Lord Jesus and His great purpose for your life? If not, it is not a genuine word of truth that will produce wisdom. Then the preacher wrote that words of truth are like well-driven nails. They are governing words that teach individuals to live righteous lives. Third, and most significantly, "words of truth" are given by one Shepherd. This Shepherd is the Lord Jesus Christ who openly claimed, "I am the way, the truth, and the life. No one comes to the Father except through Me" (John 14:6).

The preacher makes one final statement. Believing that God will judge each life, he demands, "Fear God and keep His commandments" (v. 13). It is the ultimate truth. The question is simple: Is the truth upon which you are building your life the truth given by the one Shepherd? Once it is, wisdom is yours.

This is the conclusion in full scope and design. We are brought to the place of examination of the content of our faithfulness. How did you do this year? In the pursuit of godliness? Manifesting the fruit of the Spirit? Showing patience, humility, and submission? Living in reverence and loving Him? These are not questions of behavior but of the heart.

David Edwards, Evangelist, Speaker, Author
Oklahoma City, OK

DECEMBER 30

As you've gotten older, has your view of God become worse or better? Briefly describe in what ways and why.

_____

_____

_____

_____

_____

_____

_____

_____

_____

_____

What are the excuses that are undermining your diligence? What decisions need to be made to disarm those defeating ideas?

_____

_____

_____

_____

_____

_____

_____

_____

DECEMBER 31

Our Message to You

To each of our readers, I can only trust that as you have taken the time to meditate on the wisdom literature of the Word of God, it has spoken deeply into your heart. For around 25 years now, I have been in the habit of reading through Proverbs every 30 or 31 days. I have noted how God has spoken deeply time and time again to me as I have seen different truths explode from the pages of the Holy Scripture. Probably, at least twice a year, I read through the Psalms. If ever a man found himself in trouble, and yet found deliverance through the right hand of Almighty God, it was, indeed, the psalmist.

Ecclesiastes has allowed me to think deeply about what really does have lasting value in life. Too often in my own life, I have been grasping the wind. We all know that no one can hold the wind in their hands, but I am grateful for the wind that blew upon the pages of the Bible and gave it its inspiration as the inspired, inerrant, infallible Word of God that would be a guide to lead me into deeper truths, and even the mysteries of the One Who holds the whole world in His hand.

It is my prayer that you will join us in another year of Thomas Nelson devotional readings; yet, a greater desire would be that God would speak deeper and deeper with each passing day through the truth of His Word which speaks of the breadth of His heart.

Blessings on you!

Pastor Johnny

CONTRIBUTORS

Chuck Allen .... Sugar Hill Church, Duluth, GA .... Week 6

Trevor Barton .... Hawk Creek Church, London, KY .... Week 7

Brad Bowen .... Heritage Church, Moultrie, GA .... Week 51

Scott Cannon .... Pump Springs Baptist Church, Harrogate, TN .... Week 8

Dr. Michael Cloer .... Englewood Baptist Church, Rocky Mount, NC .... Week 10

Brady Cooper .... New Vision Baptist Church, Murfreesboro, TN .... Week 29

Jeff Crook .... Blackshear Place Baptist Church, Flowery Branch, GA .... Week 2

Tim DeTellis .... New Missions, Orlando, FL .... Week 39

Chris Dixon .... Liberty Baptist Church, Dublin, GA .... Week 23

Dr. Adam Dooley ..... Dauphin Way Baptist Church, Mobile, AL .... Week 44

David Edwards ..... Evangelist, Speaker, Author, Oklahoma City, OK .... Week 52

Dr. Grant Ethridge .... Liberty Baptist Church, Hampton, VA .... Week 3

Steve Flockhart ...... New Season Church, Hiram, GA .... Week 45

Dr. Ronnie Floyd ..... Cross Church, Springdale, AR .... Week 4

Brian Fossett .... Fossett Evangelistic Ministries, Dalton, GA .... Week 46

Will Goodwin .... Oak Leaf Church, Canton, GA .... Week 16

Junior Hill .... Junior Hill Ministries, Hartselle, AL .... Week 5

Peyton Hill .... Highland Baptist Church, Grove City, OH .... Week 17

Dr. Alex Himaya ..... theChurch.at, Tulsa, OK .... Week 30

Mark Hoover .... NewSpring Church, Wichita, KS .... Week 20

Dr. Johnny Hunt ...... First Baptist Church of Woodstock, Woodstock, GA .... Week 1, 15, 48

Dr. Marty Jacumin ... Bay Leaf Baptist Church, Raleigh, NC .... Week 47

Dr. Richard Mark Lee First Baptist Church, McKinney, TX .... Week 26

Charles Lowery, Ph.D. Psychologist, Dallas, TX .... Week 38

Roy Mack .... Grace Fellowship Church, Warren, OH .... Week 40

Dr. Dwayne Mercer ... First Baptist Oviedo, Oviedo, FL .... Week 9

Dr. James Merritt ..... Cross Pointe Church, Duluth, GA .... Week 50

Eddie Middleton ..... Eddie Middleton Ministries, Acworth, GA .... Week 35

Jeremy Morton ...... Cross Point Baptist Church, Perry, GA .... Week 41

Dennis Nunn .... Every Believer a Witness Ministries, Dallas, GA .... Week 11

Mike Orr .... First Baptist Church, Chipley, FL .... Week 18

ENDNOTES

WEEK 3

1. *The Vance Havner Notebook*, compiled by Dennis J. Hester, WORDsearch Corp., wordsearchbible.com.

2. Billy Graham, *Billy Graham, God's Ambassador: A Celebration of His Life and Ministry* (HarperOne, 2007), 24.

WEEK 5

1. Warren W. Wiersbe, *Be Worshipful (Ps. 1–89): Glorifying God for Who He Is* (David C. Cook: January 1, 2009), 90.

2. John Phillips, *Exploring Psalms, Volume One* (Kregel Academic & Professional: March 7, 2002).

WEEK 10

1. Erma Bombeck, *If Life Is a Bowl of Cherries, What Am I Doing in the Pits?* (Fawcett: March 12, 1985).

WEEK 13

1. T. McIver, "Ancient Tales and Space-Age Myths of Creationist Evangelism," *The Skeptical Inquirer* 10:258-276.

2. Andy Andrews, *The Traveler's Gift: Seven Decisions that Determine Personal Success* (Nashville, TN: Thomas Nelson, 2002), 155.

WEEK 23

1. A. W. Tozer and Gerald B. Smith, *Whatever Happened to Worship?* (Christian Publications, June 1985).

2. Frances Ridley Havergal, *My King and His Service* (H. Altemus, 1892).

WEEK 25

1. Stuart Wesley Keene Hine, "How Great Thou Art," 1949, 1953 Stuart Hine Trust. Administration: U.S.A. All rights by EMI CMG, except print rights administered by Hope Publishing. North, Central and South America by Manna Music. Kingsway Communications.

2. Ibid.

WEEK 26

1. Reuben Morgan and Ben Fielding, "Stand In Awe." © 2012 Hillsong Music Publishing (APRA) (adm. in the US and Canada at EMICMGPublishing.com) All rights reserved. Used by permission.

2. Matt Redman and Jonas Myrin, "10,000 Reasons (Bless the Lord)." © 2011 Shout! Publishing (APRA) (adm. in the US and Canada at EMICMGPublishing.com) All rights reserved. Used by permission.

3. Jerry Rankin, *In the Secret Place: A Pilgrimage Through the Psalms* (Nashville, TN: B&H Books, 2009).

4. Matt and Beth Redman, "Blessed Be Your Name." © 2002 Thankyou Music (PRS) (adm. worldwide at EMICMGPublishing.com) All rights reserved. Used by permission.

5. Chris Tomlin, "Forever." © 2001 worshiptogether.com Songs (ASCAP) sixsteps Music (ASCAP) (adm. at EMICMGPublishing.com) All rights reserved. Used by permission.

WEEK 30

1. Matthew Henry, *Zondervan NIV Matthew Henry Commentary* (Grand Rapids, MI: Zondervan).

WEEK 34

1. Matthew Henry, *An Exposition on the Old and New Testament*, volume 2 (R. Carter & Brothers, 1856), 77.

2. E. M. Bounds, *Purpose in Prayer* (Fleming H. Revell Company, 1920), 9.

3. Charles H. Spurgeon, Sermon 939, "The Pilgrim's Grateful Recollections," Delivered on July 3, 1870, at the Metropolitan Tabernacle, Newington.

WEEK 37

1. "Oh Be Careful Little Eyes What You See," author unknown.

WEEK 43

1. C. T. Studd (1860-1931), "Only One Life, 'Twill Soon Be Past."

WEEK 48

1. Greg Nelson and Scott Wesley Brown, "When Answers Aren't Enough," © 1986 Greg Nelson Music (BMI) Pamela Kay Music (ASCAP) (adm. at EMICMGPublishing.com) / BMG Songs (ASCAP) / Careers BMG Music (BMI) All rights reserved. Used by permission.

2. Matt Redman, "Take the World But Give Me Jesus," © 2000 Thankyou Music (PRS) (adm. worldwide at EMICMGPublishing.com excluding Europe which is adm. by Kingswaysongs) All rights reserved. Used by permission.

WEEK 50

1. Stephen R. Covey, *The 7 Habits of Highly Effective People: Powerful Lessons in Personal Change* (Free Press, 2004).

WEEK 51

1. Cormac McCarthy, *The Road* (Vintage Books, 2006).

NOTES

NOTES

NOTES

Notes